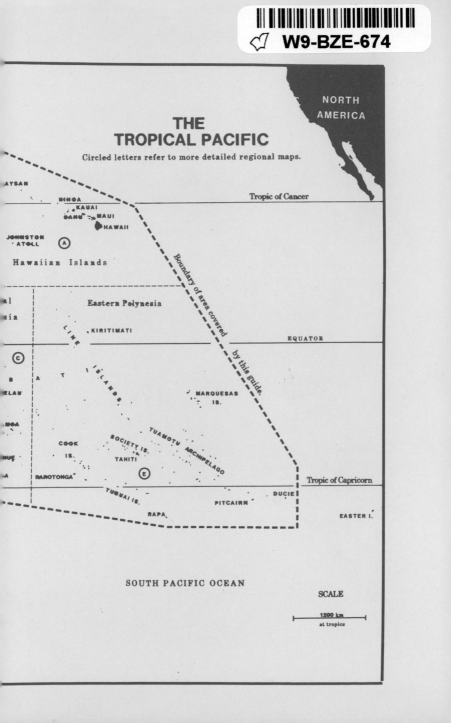

THE
TROPICAL PACIFIC

Circled letters refer to more detailed regional maps.

NORTH AMERICA

LAYSAN

Tropic of Cancer

NIHOA
KAUAI
OAHU MAUI
HAWAII

JOHNSTON ATOLL

(A)

Hawaiian Islands

Boundary of area covered by this guide.

Eastern Polynesia

LINE ISLANDS

KIRITIMATI

EQUATOR

(C)

KIRIBATI

TOKELAU

SAMOA

NIUE

RAROTONGA

MARQUESAS IS.

TUAMOTU ARCHIPELAGO

COOK IS.

SOCIETY IS.

TAHITI

(E)

Tropic of Capricorn

TUBUAI IS.

DUCIE

PITCAIRN

RAPA

EASTER I.

SOUTH PACIFIC OCEAN

SCALE

1200 km
at tropics

A FIELD GUIDE TO
THE BIRDS OF HAWAII AND THE
TROPICAL PACIFIC

SPONSORED BY THE
HAWAII AUDUBON SOCIETY

A FIELD GUIDE TO

The Birds of Hawaii and the Tropical Pacific

BY H. DOUGLAS PRATT
PHILLIP L. BRUNER AND
DELWYN G. BERRETT

ILLUSTRATED BY
H. DOUGLAS PRATT

PRINCETON UNIVERSITY PRESS

Published by Princeton University Press, 41 William Street,
Princeton, New Jersey 08540
In the United Kingdom: Princeton University Press,
Guildford, Surrey

Library of Congress Cataloging in Publication Data will be
found on the last printed page of this book

ISBN 0-691-08402-5
ISBN 0-691-02399-9 (pbk.)

This book has been composed in Linotron Baskerville

Clothbound editions of Princeton University Press books
are printed on acid-free paper, and binding materials are
chosen for strength and durability. Paperbacks, although
satisfactory for personal collections,
are not usually suitable for library rebinding

Printed in the United States of America by
Princeton University Press
Princeton, New Jersey

To Dr. Robert J. Newman

Curator Emeritus,
Louisiana State University Museum of Zoology
Teacher, Mentor, and Friend

CONTENTS

LIST OF COLOR PLATES
AND TABLES

TABLES

PREFACE

THE idea for this guide originated in discussions between Pratt and Bruner while they were graduate students under the late George H. Lowery, Jr., at Louisiana State University. Berrett, who had also studied under Lowery, later joined the effort. The authors have conducted extensive field work in all parts of the tropical Pacific. Berrett resided for many years in Hawaii and began the growing ornithological collections of Brigham Young University–Hawaii Campus with expeditions to Fiji, Samoa, and Tonga. Bruner, a nearly life-long Hawaii resident, lived for a year in French Polynesia and has worked extensively in the Society Islands, the Tuamotus, and the Marquesas. He recently made observations in the Tubuai Islands (1984) and the Marquesas (1985) that provided the most up-to-date information on these remote islands. Pratt first visited the tropical Pacific in 1974, and has returned almost annually since then for field work. The three authors together conducted a major research expedition to Micronesia in 1976, and Bruner and Pratt carried out a similar effort in Samoa and Fiji in 1977. The latter two have returned to Micronesia several times since, with independent visits to Guam, Yap, and Palau. Berrett is now at Ricks College in Rexburg, Idaho, and Bruner is Assistant Professor of Biology and Director of the Museum of Natural History at Brigham Young University–Hawaii Campus in Laie, Hawaii. Pratt resides in Baton Rouge, Louisiana, where he is a free-lance artist and Staff Research Associate of the Louisiana State University Museum of Zoology.

The production of this book has truly been a cooperative effort of the three authors, who shared about equally in the research phase and each of whom read and criticized the others' writing. Of course, there had to be some division of labor. Pratt has served as the overall editor and final arbiter of points of disagreement (which were few). He also had primary responsibility for writing the introductory sections and appendices; the facing-page notes to the color plates; many of the species accounts including all of those for Hawaiian birds, shorebirds, kingfishers, and swifts; notes on taxonomy and nomenclature; and the general accounts of families and genera.

Pratt also prepared all of the illustrations and maps. Bruner and Berrett wrote most of the remaining species accounts. Berrett and Pratt compiled the distributional checklists.

ACKNOWLEDGMENTS

The authors' field work in the Pacific has been supported by several agencies and institutions. These include Brigham Young University–Hawaii Campus, the Frank M. Chapman Memorial Fund of the American Museum of Natural History, and Louisiana State University Museum of Zoology. Since 1979 the project has been sponsored by the Hawaii Audubon Society, which subsidized Pratt's work on the color plates, provided insurance coverage of them, and assumed responsibility for getting the book published. The Society's support was crucial and the authors are grateful to the various members who have been helpful. We particularly thank Sheila Conant, Norris Henthorne, Robert L. Pyle, C. John Ralph, and Robert J. Shallenberger.

Logistical support for field work was generously provided by many people. We wish particularly to acknowledge the assistance of Robert P. Owen, John Engbring, and John Kochi at Palau; Robin Mercer and Al Hoffiens in Fiji; Edwin Kamauoha, Sr., in Western Samoa; Patoa Benioni in American Samoa; Chunio Nimwes at Truk; and Gilles Gooding, Frideane Gooding, Kisan Chancet, Rony Tumahai, Maco Tevane, and Raymond Dehors in French Polynesia. In Hawaii, a host of individuals provided lodging, field assistance, and moral support. These include Tim Burr, Tonnie L. C. Casey, Sheila Conant, Peter Donaldson, James D. Jacobi, C. J. and Carol P. Ralph, J. Michael Scott, Annarie and R. J. Shallenberger, John Sincock, Charles van Riper III, and David W. Woodside.

Many institutions have provided research assistance and access to collections. For such services we thank Alan C. Ziegler and Robert L. Pyle (Bernice P. Bishop Museum, Honolulu); Edwin C. Bryan (Pacific Scientific Information Center, Honolulu); John Farrand, Stuart Keith, Mary LeCroy, François Vuilleumier, and Robert J. Dickerman (American Museum of Natural History, New York); James L. Gulledge (Library of Natural Sounds, Cornell Laboratory of Ornithology, Ithaca); George W. Watson, Storrs L. Olson, Roger B. Clapp, Richard C. Banks, and Richard L. Zusi (National Museum of Natural History, Smithsonian Institution); Charles G. Sibley (Yale Peabody Museum); Raymond A. Paynter (Museum of Comparative Zoology, Harvard); Frank B. Gill (Philadelphia Academy of Sciences); Ned K. Johnson (Museum of Vertebrate Zoology, University of California at Berkeley); and James V. Remsen (Louisiana State University Museum of Zoology).

The personnel of the U.S. Fish and Wildlife Service in Hawaii have been of immense help in keeping us abreast of research developments and providing us with prepublication access to the results of their recent surveys in Hawaii and Micronesia. Special thanks are due John Engbring, J. Michael Scott, Stephen R. Mountainspring, and Peter Pyle.

Pratt's work on the illustrations has been greatly aided by discussions with other artists and ornithologists, some of whom graciously provided unpublished field notes and photographs of difficult species. Especially helpful were Jon Dunn, Wayne Hoffman, Joseph R. Jehl, David S. Lee, Ron Naveen, John O'Neill, Dennis Paulson, Peter Pyle, and Don Roberson.

We also wish to express our appreciation to Andrea Bruner, who translated much of the French literature and typed a major portion of the original manuscript. Judith May of Princeton University Press was instrumental in persuading us to publish with them, and has been very helpful in the final preparation of the book.

1 May 1985

H. Douglas Pratt
Phillip L. Bruner
Delwyn G. Berrett

INTRODUCTION

THE study of birds has become one of the world's most popular pastimes. Birdwatchers, or "birders" as they are commonly called today, are increasingly becoming world travelers and their infectious interest has spread to many new areas where birding has not been a tradition. This development is a welcome one, because birders have always formed the vanguard of environmental concern. Their activities inevitably lead to better appreciation and protection of the natural world. If this book makes even a small contribution to environmental awareness in the tropical Pacific, our purpose will have been met. Many Pacific island cultures held birds in high regard. For example, ancient Hawaii had a *kapu* (taboo) that protected some of the birds whose feathers were used in adornments of the *ali'i* (royalty). Such traditions have died out in many places. We hope this book will help to rekindle the ancient reverence for birdlife among Pacific island peoples. We have written the book with them, as well as the traveler, in mind. This guide is designed to allow an observer unfamiliar with birds to identify those seen. We avoid lengthy descriptions, and rely instead on illustrations and a text that emphasizes those essential characteristics ("field marks") that set one species apart from others. Our system is modeled after that originated by Roger Tory Peterson in his now-classic field guides, but we have made modifications for the island context.

This book has four interrelated parts: an introductory section devoted to birding techniques in general and special features of birding in the tropical Pacific; color plates with accompanying thumbnail notes; species accounts; and a group of appendices including regional checklists, regional maps, and a glossary.

The geographic area covered (see map) encompasses most of the islands of the tropical Pacific and the adjacent open seas. It covers all of the Hawaiian Islands, Micronesia, central Polynesia, and Fiji. Polynesia is traditionally defined as a triangular area with apices at Hawaii, Easter Island (Rapa Nui), and New Zealand. Fiji straddles the boundary between Polynesia and Melanesia and can with justification be included in either. We include Fiji because of its close political and transportational links to the nations of central Polynesia. Since New Zealand is already adequately served by bird guides (see

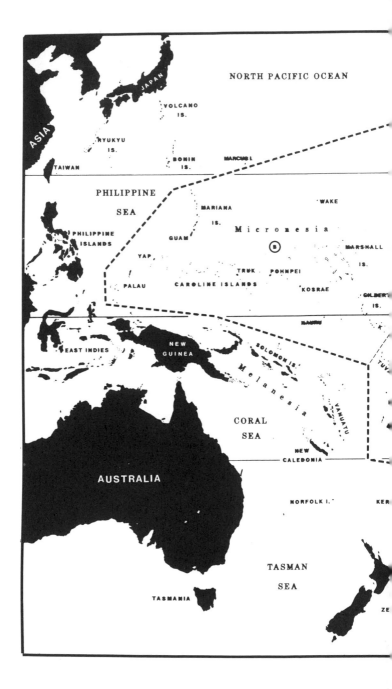

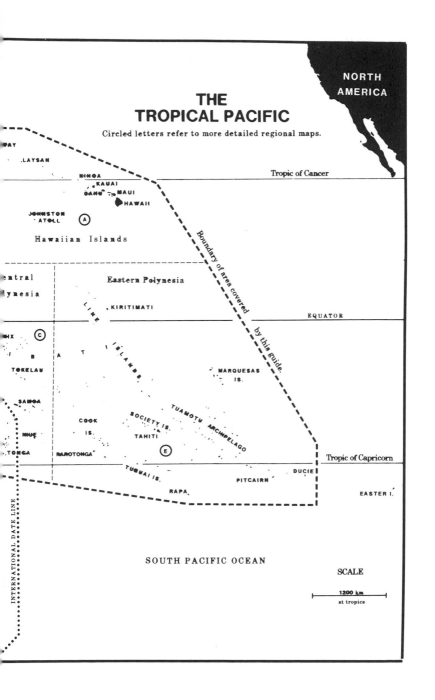

THE
TROPICAL PACIFIC

Circled letters refer to more detailed regional maps.

NORTH AMERICA

Tropic of Cancer

GAY

.LAYSAN

NIHOA
KAUAI
OAHU MAUI
HAWAII

JOHNSTON
ATOLL (A)

Hawaiian Islands

Boundary of area covered

Central
Polynesia

Eastern Polynesia

EQUATOR

KIRITIMATI

LINE

by this guide.

PHX (C)

B

A

T

ISLANDS

MARQUESAS
IS.

TOKELAU

SAMOA

TUAMOTU

COOK

SOCIETY IS.

ARCHIPELAGO

NIUE

IS.

TAHITI

TONGA

RAROTONGA

(E)

Tropic of Capricorn

TUBUAI IS.

DUCIE

PITCAIRN

EASTER I.

RAPA

INTERNATIONAL DATE LINE

SOUTH PACIFIC OCEAN

SCALE

1200 km
at tropics

Bibliography), we have not included it, nor do we cover the Chilean possession of Easter Island. Thus our area can be defined roughly as tropical Polynesia, Micronesia, and Fiji. The only subtropical islands covered are the southern Tubuai Islands and the Pitcairn group just south of the Tropic of Capricorn, and those islands of the Hawaiian chain that extend northwestward beyond the Tropic of Cancer.

All bird species that have been recorded in the above area are covered. Not all species are illustrated, however. Any species that nests on or regularly visits the islands of the tropical Pacific or regularly migrates through the surrounding oceans is shown on the color plates. The color plates also include, for comparison, a few of the rarer visitors to the area. Also shown are most of the species thought to be extinct. Extinct birds are included so that, for example, a birder on Oahu will know that the mostly dark bird he has seen is *not* an Oahu Oo, and also because we are hopeful that some of these birds may turn up again in remote, little-visited places. Bishop's Oo was found on Maui after a lapse in sightings of almost eighty years. In Fiji, the Long-legged Warbler and Fiji Petrel have also been found after long lapses (138 years in the latter case!). Thus our hope may not be in vain. Another reason for showing supposedly extinct birds is to emphasize to the observer how much has already been lost, and how great is the need to preserve what remains. Some species not included in the color plates are shown as black and white figures in the text but others are not illustrated at all. Most of these are rare migratory visitors or occasional stragglers to the tropical Pacific from Siberia, North America, Australasia, or the southern oceans. We believe that illustrating such rarities would be distracting and counterproductive, because the average birder in the tropical Pacific would encounter only a few such birds in a lifetime. Many stragglers may never be found in the region again, and some others that have not yet been recorded may be equally likely to turn up. The birder wishing to pursue rarities should have field guides to surrounding areas as well as this one. Particularly important in this regard would be any of several recent references on the birds of North America and a good book on seabirds of the world. Birders in Micronesia will want sources on the birds of eastern Asia and Australia. For birds that are not illustrated here, we have often included citations of published illustrations elsewhere. These and others are listed in the Bibliography.

ABBREVIATIONS

THE primary compass directions (N, S, E, W) and combinations thereof (NE, SW, etc.) are written as capital letters without periods (except when part of a proper name such as N. America). Lower-case directional letters, followed by periods, should be read as the adjectival form (e., eastern; nw., northwestern; etc.). Two exceptions to the foregoing are W. Samoa (Western Samoa) and NW Hawaiian Is. (Northwestern Hawaiian Islands). American Samoa is abbreviated A. Samoa. The words "island," "islands," and "archipelago" are abbreviated only when part of a proper name as "I.," "Is.," and "Arch." respectively. "Central" is abbreviated "c."

Several organizations and publications are designated by special acronyms or abbreviations as follows:

AOU	American Ornithologists' Union
BBOC	Bulletin of the British Ornithologists' Club
ICBP	International Council for Bird Preservation
NGS	National Geographic Society
L'Oiseau et RFO	L'Oiseau et la Revue Française d'Ornithologie
USFWS	Fish and Wildlife Service, U.S. Department of the Interior
WBSJ	Wild Bird Society of Japan

In the references that accompany the species accounts, as well as in the Bibliography, we have adopted the following standard abbreviations:

Am.	American	Inst.	Institution
Bd.	Board	J.	Journal
Biol.	Biology	Misc.	Miscellaneous
Bull.	Bulletin	Monogr.	Monographs
Contr.	Contributions	Mus.	Museum
Coop.	Cooperative	Nat. Hist.	Natural History
Dept.	Department		
Div.	Division	Natl.	National

Novit.	Novitates	Serv.	Service
Ornithol.	Ornithologi- cal	Soc.	Society
		Stud.	Studies
Proc.	Proceedings	Terr.	Territory
Publ.	Publications	Univ.	University
Res.	Research	Zool.	Zoology
Ser.	Series		

In the facing-page notes for the color plates, we abbreviate adult (ad.), subadult (subad.), immature (imm.), juvenile (juv.), breeding (br.), and nonbreeding (nonbr.).

A FIELD GUIDE TO
THE BIRDS OF HAWAII AND THE
TROPICAL PACIFIC

I. HOW TO USE THIS BOOK

COLOR PLATES

The color plates and their accompanying notes are the heart of this guide. One should be familiar with them before going afield and should always consult them first when making an identification. In most cases, the illustration plus the thumbnail comment on the facing page will be sufficient to identify the bird seen. Further information when needed, as well as comments on voice, distribution, and status, will be found in the cross-referenced species accounts.

The plates are organized so that birds likely to be seen together are close together in the illustrations. Some nonpasserines (seabirds, shorebirds, freshwater birds, birds of prey, etc.) are arranged in more or less taxonomic sequence because many are widespread in the tropical Pacific. Those that are not widespread must be compared with those that are. Island land birds, however, are usually very sedentary and are often endemic (found only on one island or group). Thus, even though the Elepaio of Hawaii is closely related to the Tinian Monarch of the Marianas and the Slaty Flycatcher of Fiji, it does not appear with them in the plates but rather with other Hawaiian forest birds. We believe this arrangement will be more practical for birders than a strictly taxonomic one. The plates also include photographs of some of the plants that a birder in the tropical Pacific will need to know.

SPECIES ACCOUNTS

The species accounts are arranged in taxonomic or phylogenetic sequence. Such an arrangement groups closely related birds together, but to the beginner may appear bewilderingly arbitrary. A little work with the field guide will familiarize one with the sequence. Our phylogenetic order follows that adopted in 1983 by the American Ornithologists' Union for its checklist of North American birds. Taxa that do not appear in that list are inserted where appropriate. The only exception to the AOU classification of higher categories is our treatment of the Australo-Papuan insect-eaters (Pachycephalidae), which we regard as not closely related to the Muscicapidae.

The species accounts follow a standard format with subheadings for the various kinds of information. Subheadings are sometimes combined, and for very rare or little-known birds only a single paragraph is given. A typical account will have the following subheadings:

APPEARANCE: The two numbers in parentheses are the total length of the bird in inches and centimeters. These are provided to give an idea of a bird's relative size, but such measurements are inherently imprecise and do not take into account the range of individual variation. Use them with care. After the size we give important descriptive information for distinguishing the species in question. These descriptions are written as supplements to the illustrations, which should always be consulted first.

HABITS: Here we give information about habitat, feeding behavior, diet, displays, or even nesting behavior where such is useful for identification.

VOICE: Bird vocalizations are very difficult to transcribe in words. One man's *chuck* is another man's *tchick*. We hope our pioneering effort to describe voices of Pacific island birds will be useful. Only a few of them have been previously described, often inadequately. We have often borrowed particularly apt vocal descriptions from others. If published, we cite the source; otherwise we credit the individual.

IDENTIFICATION: This section tells how to distinguish the bird in question from similar species with which it might be confused. For those species that are distinctive and unmistakable, this subheading is omitted.

OCCURRENCE: This term covers status (see Terminology, below), distribution (both geographic and elevational), and such information as whether the species is endemic, the origin and dates of introduction of exotics, and other pertinent historical facts. Geographic distribution is given by island group (printed in all capitals) with island details given in parentheses unless the bird is found on only a single island in a group, in which case the single island name is in all capitals and the group in parentheses. The larger Caroline Islands (Palau, Yap, Truk, Pohnpei, Kosrae) are usually considered separate entities. Thus a distribution might read "HAWAIIAN IS. (Midway, Laysan), SAIPAN (Mariana Is.), and YAP." This bird would be found in the Hawaiian Islands only on the two named islands, on Saipan only in the Marianas, and on Yap. Portions of a bird's range outside the area covered by this guide are always written in lower case.

REFERENCES: Where such are available, we cite books and articles published through mid-1985 that provide further information that may be useful to the birder. These references do not include regional faunal works, and are not repeated in the Bibliography. We have been highly selective in these listings, which are not intended to be exhaustive. We apologize to those authors whose works we have either overlooked or underappreciated.

OTHER NAMES: We list only names that have appeared in recent major publications. Old names long in disuse and most native-language names, except the widely used Hawaiian ones, are not listed. We include all alternative names given in three of the most recent worldwide bird checklists (Clements 1981; Howard and Moore 1980; Walters 1980).

NOTE: This section is used for miscellaneous data or comments not appropriate for other headings. In particular, we have used this section to discuss our taxonomy where it differs from that in other publications.

SCIENTIFIC NAMES

Birds, as well as other organisms, have two kinds of names: the scientific name based on classical Greek and Latin, and the vernacular or common names in various modern languages. Scientific names have two parts. A "surname" called the genus (plural genera) appears first and is always capitalized. A second word, never capitalized, is called the species epithet. The species name should never be used alone; it has meaning only when attached to a generic name. On the other hand, the species name is much more stable through time than the generic designation. Species can be, and often are, transferred from one genus to another as we learn more about them. Scientific names are the best means of identifying a species under discussion. They are used universally by ornithologists of all nationalities.

TAXONOMY

Taxonomy, the science of classifying and naming living things, is a rather esoteric field that the average birder probably would just as soon ignore. However, a little knowledge of its principles will help greatly in understanding why birds are classified as they are. Birds belong to the Class Aves, one of seven classes of vertebrate animals (the others are mammals, reptiles, amphibians, and three groups of fishes). Classes are subdivided into orders, which in the case of birds always end in -iformes. Orders are made up of families (which end in -idae), and these may or may not have recognized subfamilies (-inae). Finally, families comprise one or more genera. All of these groupings are artificial. They express relationships but are still abstract concepts. Species, however, ideally are real entities in nature, and therefore their delineation is of some importance.

A species is defined biologically as a group of populations that actually or potentially interbreed freely. The test of whether two populations are the same species is not whether they *can* interbreed, but whether they *would* interbreed under natural conditions. Thus hybrids formed in zoos tell us nothing about species limits because they were produced in an unnatural situation. When two similar birds share the same island (that is, are sympatric) without interbreeding, they are clearly different species. But what if two slightly different populations live on different islands (are allopatric)? In those cases, ornithologists must decide whether the differences are great enough to prevent interbreeding if the two should become sympatric. If the researcher thinks the differences are insufficient to prevent interbreeding, the two populations are considered the same species (i.e. conspecific), and are referred to as subspecies or races. Subspecies are indicated in the scientific name by addition of a third word after the species epithet. The first subspecies to be named (the "nominate") usually repeats the species epithet. Thus the Tahiti Kingfisher (*Halcyon venerata*) on Tahiti is called

Halcyon venerata venerata while the population on Moorea is *Halcyon venerata youngi*. In discussions of subspecies, the genus and species may be abbreviated as initials (as in *H. v. venerata*) if the name has been written out previously in the account.

The species status of allopatric populations is, at best, difficult to determine. Whether the populations are several distinct species or only races of a widespread species cannot often be verified. When the birds are well known biologically, a consensus can usually be reached. But when few data are available, as is the case with many Pacific island populations, controversy often arises. We have explained reasoning in those cases where our taxonomy differs from that published elsewhere. In most cases, our innovations are based on our own field experience.

ENGLISH NAMES

Of more immediate concern to the birder, but much less meaningful than the scientific names, are the English vernacular names of birds. Such names are subject to no universally accepted rules and vary widely from place to place, from book to book, or even from person to person. A few attempts have recently been made to standardize English names of birds internationally, but none has really succeeded. The best efforts have been those regional works that have viewed their area's names in a worldwide context. Particularly noteworthy are King and Dickinson's *Field Guide to the Birds of South-East Asia* (1975) and the 1983 AOU Check-list with its 1985 Supplement. The AOU Check-list now covers the Hawaiian Islands, and we have followed it in most cases for English names. In the 12 cases where we prefer a name different from that used in the AOU Check-list, we give the AOU name parenthetically in the species heading. In some of these cases (e.g. Green-backed Heron, Ring-necked Pheasant) the AOU name seems to be in conflict with the organization's own guidelines. In others, we believe the less preferable of alternatives was chosen. We hope our notes on names will influence future supplements to the AOU Check-list. We have particularly striven to suggest names that enhance international nomenclatural agreement, and therefore have often recommended names in use in Australia and New Zealand over AOU names, especially when the former are more suitable. In the case of seabirds, we hope to bring AOU names into line with those used in the several recent publications on seabirds of the world (Harrison 1983; Löfgren 1984; Tuck 1980; Tuck and Heinzel 1978).

We have avoided name innovations as much as possible. However, for most birds unique to the tropical Pacific no consensus on English names exists, and the names in use in other publications are often unsuitable for a variety of reasons. Because these names have not appeared in a great many publications, we believe that this field guide is as good a place as any to begin the renovation and standardization of English names for birds in the region. We have tried to suggest names that are memorable and informative as well as accurate. Explanations and comments are given under the Note heading in the species accounts where necessary.

OTHER PACIFIC LANGUAGES

Native residents of virtually all islands of the tropical Pacific speak one or another European language (usually English or French). Interisland travelers need not know the indigenous languages to "get along." But some brief acquaintance with the rules of pronunciation of native languages will greatly enhance the visitor's enjoyment. Even in places where the native tongue is now rarely used conversationally, as in Hawaii, native terms are ubiquitous and appear in names of birds, plants, and places. The following brief discussions are intended only to enable the English-speaking visitor to pronounce the native-language words encountered. Space does not permit a discussion of all native languages, but the following ones require some explanation.

POLYNESIAN LANGUAGES (HAWAIIAN, SAMOAN, TAHITIAN, ETC.). These languages are all closely related and have similar rules of pronunciation. Spelling is phonetic, with consonants more or less as in English and vowels as in Romance languages such as Spanish. In Hawaiian, the letter *w* is pronounced as the English *w* before *u* or *o*, as the English *v* before *i* or *e*, and either way before *a*. In Samoan, the letter *g* is pronounced as *ng* (e.g. Pago Pago sounds like Pango Pango). Otherwise, consonants are fairly straightforward except for the glottal stop('), a "letter" not found in European alphabets. It resembles the stoppage of sound in the interjection *oh-oh*, and functions as a consonant, not as a mark of punctuation. Unfortunately, English-speaking immigrants did not appreciate this point and the glottal stop has been deleted from the spelling of many words. In this book, we use it only for island names such as Niuafoʻou that have not yet been so corrupted in spelling as those in Hawaii and American Samoa. Otherwise, in the interest of international consistency we write the island names without glottal stops.

Stress in Polynesian languages falls on the next-to-last syllable and alternating preceding syllables except for five-syllable words, which are stressed on the first and fourth. Some words have irregular stress indicated by a macron (ˉ) over the stressed vowel. Thus Akiapolaau (written ʻakia-pō-lāʻau in Hawaiian) is pronounced *ah-kee-ah-PO-LA-ow*, not *ah-kee-ah-puh-LAU*. In cases where a bird name is likely to be mispronounced otherwise, we give the Hawaiian orthography in the Other Names section of the species account.

FIJIAN. Two different spelling systems are in use for Fijian. Both use Romance language phonetics for vowels. A new system follows, more or less, English pronunciation of all consonants. The older system, and the one most often seen in Fiji itself, has the following special case consonants:

b is pronounced as the *mb* in limber
c is pronounced as the *th* in this
d is pronounced as the *nd* in windy
g is pronounced as the *ng* in singer
q is pronounced as the *ng* in anger

We have chosen to use the old system. A few examples of how the two differ are: Buca (Mbutha), Gau (Ngau), Kadavu (Kandavu), Beqa (Mbengga).

I-KIRIBATI (FORMERLY GILBERTESE). The only peculiarity of the language of Kiribati that must be pointed out here is that the combination *ti* is pronounced much like the English *s*, and the *r* is rolled and not very different from the sound of English *l*. Thus neither Kiribati (Gilberts) nor Kiritimati (Christmas) sounds as different from the English words each represents as the spelling may seem to indicate.

NEW ISLAND NAMES

Many newly independent Pacific island nations have recently adopted new names for islands or island groups. Many of these are not really new, but are reversions to native language names (e.g. Banaba) or are spelling corrections based on more accurate transliterations of native names (e.g. Kosrae). Others are nativizations of colonial names (e.g. Kiritimati). The following are the new island names that appear in this book, with their older equivalents:

NEW	OLD
Banaba	Ocean Island
Enewetak	Eniwetok
Kiribati	Gilbert Islands
Kiritimati	Christmas Island
Kosrae	Kusaie
Pohnpei	Ponape
Tabueran	Fanning Island
Teraina	Washington Island
Tubuai Islands	Austral Islands
Tuvalu	Ellice Islands
Vanuatu	New Hebrides

The Republic of Palau has recently decided to retain that name (at least in English) rather than change to Belau, a more accurate spelling. The spelling of Palau's largest island has never been standardized (Babelthuap, Babeldaob, Babeldaop). We use the first spelling, but as we go to press the other, more phonetically accurate, spellings are being increasingly used, and one may be officially adopted before long.

TERMINOLOGY

TOPOGRAPHY. Figure 1 illustrates the topographical and anatomical terms used to describe birds. Most of these terms are not repeated in the Glossary.

MOLT. Birds replace their feathers periodically in what is called molt. Because the actual molt sequence is not known for many birds in the tropical Pacific, we have adopted a simple, functional terminology for that sequence, rather than one of the more technically precise systems. Our system is thus purposely imprecise. A bird's first full feathering is called "juvenile plumage," and birds in that stage are called "juveniles." We avoid the term "juvenal." The term "immature" is used for any plumage stage other than adult. Some birds, once mature, do not visibly alter their plumage except by feather wear (ornithologists call this the definitive plumage). Others go through annual cycles with a breeding (alternate, nuptial) plumage and a nonbreeding (basic, winter) one. Obviously the seasonal terms are inappropriate in the tropics. We use them occasionally, however, for birds that breed in temperate regions.

STATUS. Our terminology for status is necessarily imprecise because often no good quantitative population data are available for birds of the region. For resident birds, we use several general terms. "Abundant" and "common" are used for birds that are so numerous and conspicuous in their proper range and habitat that they would be hard for an observer to miss. Those that are "uncommon" are present in lower numbers and are seen regularly, but may be difficult to find on a given day. "Rare" birds have low populations and require special efforts for an observer to see them. "Very rare" or "nearly extinct" birds may be reported only once in several decades, even when competent observers have been searching for them. We do not consider any bird extinct that has been reliably reported since 1966. Birds are always unevenly distributed, so even a very rare one may be "locally common," as would be the case if only 50 individuals survived but all lived within one hectare.

For migrants, we use the above terms as well as others. A "casual" visitor has been found several times, but has no predictable pattern of occurrence. Such birds can be expected to turn up again, but not every year. "Regular" and "fairly regular" imply annual and nearly annual occurrence respectively. Birds may be both "rare" and "regular" if they are annually present in very low numbers.

The capitalized terms "Endangered Species" and "Threatened Species" are used only for those populations officially so designated under the U.S. Endangered Species Act. When not capitalized, such terms reflect our own judgment or that of nongovernmental agen-

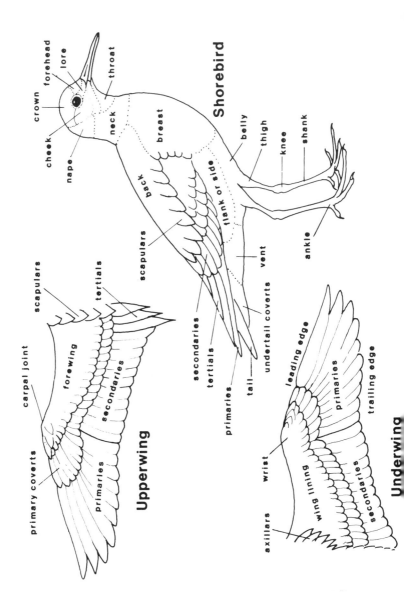

Shorebird

crown
forehead
lore
throat
cheek
nape
neck
breast
back
flank or side
belly
thigh
knee
shank
ankle
vent
undertail coverts
tail
primaries
tertials
secondaries
scapulars

Upperwing

scapulars
carpel joint
tertials
forewing
secondaries
primary coverts
primaries

Underwing

leading edge
primaries
trailing edge
wrist
wing lining
secondaries
axillars

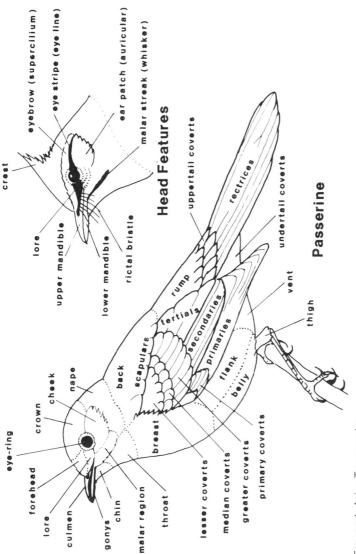

Head Features

eyebrow (supercilium)
eye stripe (eye line)
ear patch (auricular)
malar streak (whisker)
crest
lore
upper mandible
lower mandible
rictal bristle

Passerine

uppertail coverts
rectrices
undertail coverts
vent
thigh
rump
tertials
secondaries
primaries
flank
belly
scapulars
back
nape
cheek
crown
eye-ring
forehead
lore
culmen
gonys
chin
malar region
throat
breast
lesser coverts
median coverts
greater coverts
primary coverts

FIGURE 1. Avian Topography

cies such as the ICBP. That organization also uses the designation "vulnerable" for species likely to become endangered unless preventive measures are taken. It is roughly equivalent to the U.S. "Threatened" category. For further explanation of these and other terms of status, see Table 6.

II. A BIRDER'S-EYE VIEW OF THE TROPICAL PACIFIC

THE Pacific Ocean occupies over one-third of the earth's surface, an area greater than that of all the land areas combined. Within this vast expanse of water are scattered over 10,000 relatively small islands. They are concentrated in the central and southwestern parts of the ocean, with a broad band in the northern and eastern sectors entirely devoid of land. The Hawaiian Islands are the closest to North America, but are separated from that continent by about 4025 km (2500 mi.) of open ocean. Similar distances separate them from significant land masses in all directions; they are the world's most isolated archipelago. The other islands of the tropical Pacific are somewhat closer to larger land masses, but are rather isolated nevertheless.

None of the islands in the area covered by this guide is large. Hawaii and Viti Levu are the largest, and are slightly smaller than Jamaica, about twice the size of the State of Delaware, and half the size of Wales. Size drops off rapidly (see Table 1) after the three largest islands. Hawaii, for example, is larger than all the other Hawaiian islands combined. Despite the vastness of the region, the total land area of all the islands is only 46,632 sq. km (18,000 sq. mi.), over half of which is contributed by the three largest.

CONTINENTAL VS. OCEANIC ISLANDS

Islands have long been classified as either continental or oceanic, but the meaning of these terms differs among academic disciplines. Zoogeographers consider an island oceanic if it has not been attached to a continent during the history of the group of organisms being studied. Continental islands have had such connections (often called "land bridges" in the past). The distinction, from the point of view of animal dispersal, is obvious and important. All of the islands covered here are oceanic in this sense. Thus their indigenous faunas lack such continental elements as terrestrial mammals; only those groups of animals capable of over-water dispersal are represented.

TABLE 1. THE 20 LARGEST ISLANDS OF THE TROPICAL PACIFIC

Island	Location	Sq. Mi.	Sq. Km
Hawaii	Hawaiian Is.	4038	10,461
Viti Levu	Fiji	4011	10,390
Vanua Levu	Fiji	2137	5336
Maui	Hawaiian Is.	729	1889
Savaii	Samoa	703	1821
Oahu	Hawaiian Is.	607	1573
Kauai	Hawaiian Is.	553	1433
Upolu	Samoa	430	1114
Tahiti	Society Is.	402	1041
Molokai	Hawaiian Is.	259	671
Guam	Mariana Is.	209	541
Pohnpei	Caroline Is.	176	456
Taveuni	Fiji	168	435
Kadavu	Fiji	158	409
Babelthuap	Palau	143	370
Lanai	Hawaiian Is.	140	363
Nukuhiva	Marquesas Is.	127	330
Hivaoa	Marquesas Is.	120	310
Niue	Niue	102	264
Tongatapu	Tonga	100	259

Geographers and geologists use a slightly different way of distin-guishing oceanic from continental islands that is based on position relative to the earth's tectonic plates. Some plates are themselves called continental, and islands that rise from them are therefore called continental islands whether they have had an above-water connection with a continent or not. Most of the islands in the tropi-cal Pacific (as defined here) rise from the Pacific Plate, which forms the floor of the central and northern Pacific Ocean, and are thus oceanic. Fiji rises from a fragment of a plate that once was part of the Australian continental mass. It is thus continental in one sense, but oceanic in the faunistic sense. Other faunistically oceanic islands such as Tonga, Yap, Palau, and the Marianas lie along plate bound-aries.

The movement of the Pacific Plate toward the northwest helps explain why many Pacific islands lie in roughly parallel northwest-southeast arcs. Because of a tectonic shift in direction, older archipelagoes like the Line and Marshall islands have a more vertical orientation than the younger ones such as the Hawaiian and Society islands. The youngest islands tend to be at the southeastern end of each archipelago, as is the case with Hawaii and Tahiti. In Samoa, this generalization appears to be reversed, but other forces have come into play there because of the proximity of a plate boundary.

KINDS OF OCEANIC ISLANDS

Although islands can be classified on the basis of their physiography and mode of formation, it is important to understand that the forces that form them are ongoing and dynamic. Many islands are intermediate in type. From the point of view of bird distribution, islands fall into two broad categories: atolls and high islands. The latter can be further divided into three types.

ATOLLS. Atolls are rings of low sandy islets (called *motus* in Polynesia) that surround a central saltwater lagoon. Such islands form as ocean levels rise or a former island mass sinks to become a seamount. The fringing reef of the original island continues to grow if the changes in water level are gradual enough, so that the seamount wears a coral "crown." Motus of an atoll never rise more than a few feet above sea level. Examples of atolls include most of the islands of Tuvalu, Kiribati, the Marshalls, and the Tuamotus, but atolls can be found associated with most of the island groups of the Pacific.

Anything other than the island ring/lagoon stage described above must be considered one of the types of high islands. To qualify, an island need not attain great elevation, although many of them have impressive mountains, including Mauna Loa, the world's most massive mountain (see Table 2). They may be coral islands (makateas) but more often are ancient or recent volcanic islands.

MAKATEA ISLANDS. These high islands are of uplifted coral, and most were once atolls. They are characterized by rocky coralline (limestone) substrates. Many have had commercially exploitable deposits of phosphate, the result of eons of use by seabirds and the gradual drying up of the central lagoon. Examples include the namesake island of Makatea (Tuamotu Arch.), Atiu (Cook Is.),

TABLE 2. HIGHEST PEAKS OF THE TROPICAL PACIFIC

Peak	Island	Elevation Feet	Meters
Mauna Kea	Hawaii	13,796	4205
Mauna Loa	Hawaii	13,677	4169
Haleakala	Maui	10,023	3055
Hualalai	Hawaii	8271	2522
Orohena	Tahiti	7350	2241
Silisili	Savaii	6094	1858
Waialeale	Kauai	5243	1598
Kamakou	Molokai	4970	1515
Victoria	Viti Levu	4340	1323
Kaala	Oahu	4040	1233
Uluigalau	Taveuni (Fiji)	4037	1231
Tohivea	Moorea (Society Is.)	3959	1207
Pouoanuu	Hivaoa (Marquesas)	3903	1190
Kao	Kao (Tonga)	3690	1125
Fito	Upolu (Samoa)	3651	1113
Nasirilevu	Vanua Levu	3385	1032
Lanaihale	Lanai	3370	1027
Washington	Kadavu (Fiji)	2750	838
Totolom	Pohnpei	2594	791
Matafae	Tutuila (Samoa)	2303	702
Te Manga	Rarotonga	2303	702

NOTE: Except for Hawaii, only the highest peak on each island is listed.

Niue, Banaba (Kiribati), the "rock islands" of southern Palau, most of the inhabited islands of Tonga, and Nauru. Some islands are part limestone and part volcanic, as is the case with Koror (Palau) and Guam. Other islands are in the process of changing from atolls to makateas. Such islands are still low in elevation but the central lagoon may have become a freshwater lake (or lakes). The best examples of such transitional islands are Kiritimati and Swains Island (A. Samoa).

OLD VOLCANIC ISLANDS. Most of the high islands of the Pacific are of volcanic origin, and range in age from ancient, highly eroded ones (i.e. ten-million-year-old Kauai) to those with currently active volcanoes. Some of the oldest volcanic islands, such as Babelthuap (Palau) and Yap, are low and rolling, with nothing that could really be called mountains. They are classed as high islands nevertheless. Other old volcanic islands are very mountainous, with steep cliffs, huge amphitheater valleys, and deep rich soil (Figure 2). Old volcanic islands are usually heavily forested, and harbor most of the endemic birds of the region as well as most of the human population. Examples include the larger islands of Fiji, the Society Islands, the Marquesas, Pohnpei, Kosrae, and all of the main Hawaiian Islands except Hawaii itself. Occasionally, older volcanic islands experience renewed volcanic activity. Such has been the case on Maui and Savaii. Several ancient volcanic islands in the region are nearing the atoll stage. The best example of an almost-atoll is Truk (Figure 3), where the original island mass is now represented by a cluster of high islands in a reef-fringed lagoon.

FIGURE 2. Eroded Cliffs of an Ancient Volcanic Island.
Kalalau Valley, Kauai.

FIGURE 3. The Lagoon of an Almost-Atoll. Truk Lagoon looking eastward from Tol Summit.

RECENT VOLCANIC ISLANDS. Many volcanoes in the tropical Pacific are still active. Others, though dormant, still have fresh-appearing lava flows. Active volcanoes include Mauna Loa and Kilauea on Hawaii, Lofia and Niuafo'ou in Tonga, and Pagan in the Marianas. Relatively recent volcanoes that are not presently active are found on Maui (Hawaiian Is.), Savaii (W. Samoa), Kao (Tonga), and several islands in the Northern Marianas.

TROPICAL PACIFIC HABITATS

A knowledge of bird habitats is essential to successful birding anywhere, and particularly so in the tropical Pacific. The following summaries are purposely brief, but will provide an introduction to the various habitats and some of the plants typically found in each. A listing of the scientific names of all the plants mentioned here, as well as in the species accounts, is given in Table 3.

TABLE 3. SCIENTIFIC NAMES OF PLANTS MENTIONED IN THIS BOOK

Common Name	Scientific name
African tulip tree	*Spathodea campanulata*
banana poka	*Passiflora molissima*
Barringtonia	*Barringtonia asiatica*
banyan	*Ficus benghalensis*
beach heliotrope	*Messerschmidia argentea*
beach hibiscus	*Hibiscus tiliaceus*
black wattle	*Acacia decurrens*
breadfruit	*Artocarpus incisus*
candlenut	*Aleurites moluccana*
Christmasberry	*Schinus terebinthifolius*
coconut	*Cocos nucifera*
drala	*Erythrina indica*
eucalyptus	*Eucalyptus* sp.
false staghorn fern	*Dicranopteris linearis*
fig	*Ficus* sp.
haole koa	*Leucaena latisiliqua* (or *L. glauca*)
hapuu	*Cibotium* spp.
hau	*Hibiscus tiliaceus*
ieie	*Freycinetia arborea*
ironwood	*Casuarina equisetifolia*
jacaranda	*Jacaranda acutifolia*
kiawe (algoroba, mesquite)	*Prosopis pallida*
koa	*Acacia koa*
kukaenene	*Coprosma ernodioides*
kukui	*Aleurites moluccana*
lapalapa	*Cheirodendron platyphyllum*
mamane	*Sophora chrysophylla*
mango	*Mangifera indica*
monkeypod	*Samanea saman*
mountain-apple	*Eugenia malaccensis*
naio	*Myoporum sandwicense*
ohia-lehua	*Metrosideros collina*
olapa	*Cheirodendron trigynum*
oriental mangrove	*Bruguiera gymnorhiza*
pandanus	*Pandanus odoratissimus*
paperbark	*Melaleuca leucadendra*
pine	*Pinus* spp.
pukiawe	*Styphelia* spp.

TABLE 3. (cont.)

Common Name	Scientific name
red mangrove	*Rhizophora* spp.
royal poinciana	*Delonix regia*
scaevola (naupaka in Hawaii)	*Scaevola taccada*
screw-pine	*Pandanus odoratissimus*
silk oak	*Grevillea robusta*
tangan-tangan	*Leucaena latisiliqua* (or *L. glauca*)
taro	*Collocasia* spp.
uluhe	*Dicranopteris* spp.
wild plantain	*Musa fehi*
wiliwili	*Erythrina sandwicensis*

OPEN SEAS. Many birds spend most of their lives far from land and feed on organisms near the ocean surface. Some feed by diving (e.g. boobies, terns), others by dabbling the bill while swimming (e.g. phalaropes), and still others skim the waves while flying (e.g. storm-petrels, albatrosses, shearwaters, petrels). Except when they come to islands to nest, many pelagic birds are never found within sight of land. The open ocean is the most extensive habitat in the region, but its sheer vastness and the limited number of competent observers on the high seas make it the most poorly known of all.

SHELTERED WATERS. Some seabirds prefer the shallower and calmer waters near islands for feeding. Typical of such habitats are the lagoons of atolls, but most high islands also have shallow bays and lagoons protected by reefs. Fairy-terns, noddies, frigatebirds, and tropicbirds frequent such areas (although they may be seen at sea as well), and some species (e.g. Little Pied Cormorant) are almost always found in shallow salt water. Other species such as herons and shorebirds (waders) are equally at home in fresh or salt water.

WETLANDS. Restricted here to freshwater habitats, wetlands are very limited on Pacific islands, and the birds that depend on them are thus highly vulnerable to environmental disturbance. Natural marshes have often been drained for agriculture and development. Waikiki was once a large marsh! Nowadays the most significant wetlands on many islands are manmade (e.g. ponds, reservoirs, sugar mill settling basins, taro fields). These habitats are essential to the survival of resident ducks, gallinules, stilts, coots, and herons as well as migratory waterfowl and shorebirds. In the Hawaiian Islands, several National Wildlife Refuges have been established for the management of freshwater habitats and their birds (Figure 4). Throughout the tropical Pacific, wetlands are fringed with tall grasses, particularly *Phragmites karka*. These "reedbeds" are the preferred habitat of some birds such as some of the reed-warblers.

BEACH STRAND AND ATOLL VEGETATION. The plants of beaches and atolls are those that disperse easily across open seas, and thus the vegetation of such areas is remarkably similar throughout the region. The plants are usually low and shrubby, but under favorable conditions fairly tall forests can develop on atolls. Plants typical of this association are scaevola, beach heliotrope, and screw-pine or

FIGURE 4. Man-Made Wetland Habitat. Taro fields of Hanalei National Wildlife Refuge, Kauai.

pandanus (Plate 45). The dominant tree in many places is coconut (Figure 5), which is probably an aboriginal introduction in the tropical Pacific rather than a native plant. Green coconuts are the only source of drinking water on some atolls. The "Australian pine" or ironwood, also probably introduced by ancient man, is important as well as a forest tree on atolls and sandy beaches.

LITTORAL FOREST. Lowland forests behind the beach strand are found on many high islands and atolls. Their composition varies with conditions, and such forests often are thickets of a single species. Thicket-forming native trees include pandanus, beach hibiscus or hau, and Barringtonia.

MANGROVE FOREST. Mangroves grow in dense stands in muddy, reef-protected tidal areas often called "mangrove swamps." Most mangrove species have aerial or prop roots and seedlings that de-

FIGURE 5. Typical Polynesian Coral Sand Beach Lined with Coconut Palms. Savaii, Western Samoa.

FIGURE 6. Man-Made Grassland. Parker Ranch, Hawaii.

velop while attached to the parent plant. These are adaptations to periodic saltwater inundation. The most frequent species in Micronesia and Polynesia are the Oriental mangrove and the red mangrove group. Mangroves are not indigenous to the Hawaiian Islands, but have been introduced. A few birds, such as the Fiji population of Little (Green-backed) Heron, are virtually restricted to mangroves, and a few others (e.g. Cicadabird, Mangrove Flycatcher) reach their greatest numbers in such forests.

GRASSLANDS. Several of the larger islands of the tropical Pacific have extensive open lands, usually the result of deforestation followed by periodic burning. These areas are characterized by course grasses and ferns, particularly false staghorn or uluhe. Such grasslands are found on most high islands of the region, with the most extensive ones on the leeward sides of the Hawaiian Islands and Fiji's two largest islands, in southern Guam, and in the Marquesas. A somewhat different kind of grassland is maintained by grazing, usually in wetter areas. Extensive pastures may be found in Fiji, the Hawaiian Islands (Figure 6), and on Tinian (Marianas). Grasslands are not rich in birdlife, but a few native species (e.g. Short-eared Owl on Pohnpei) are virtually restricted to them. Many introduced birds, such as gallinaceous birds, skylarks, and meadowlarks, favor grasslands. Wetter grasslands, particularly those with a heavy admixture of ferns, are favored habitat for several species of rails including Banded Rail, Guam Rail, White-browed Crake, and Spotless Crake.

SAVANNAHS. Savannahs are grasslands with scattered trees. Like grasslands and fernlands, they are maintained on Pacific islands by periodic fires and other man-caused phenomena. The most common type in Micronesia and Polynesia is pandanus savannah. In Hawaii, a very dry type is found which has mainly exotic grasses and kiawe (algoroba) trees. In its overall aspect, this artificial habitat closely resembles the savannahs of Africa, which may explain why it is favored by such introduced birds as Warbling Silverbill, waxbills, and other species native to Africa.

AGRICULTURAL FOREST. Also called coconut/breadfruit forest after the two dominant tree species, this ancient man-made plant community is found in lowlands throughout the tropical Pacific. On some islands, it has replaced native lowland forests entirely. In addition to the two dominant trees, this association can include mango, kukui (candlenut), mountain-apple, and several species of *Ficus* (Plate 45) such as banyan. Native birds are less numerous in these woodlands than in primary forest, and many island endemics are not present at all. In the Hawaiian Islands, almost all birds in this habitat are aliens, such as White-rumped Shama, Japanese Bush-Warbler, and Melodious Laughing-thrush.

EXOTIC FORESTS AND PLANTATIONS. The most widely planted tree in the tropical Pacific is the coconut, which may cover huge areas on islands where it is the backbone of the local economy. Birds are not numerous in uniform stands of coconut, but a few, like the Long-tailed Cuckoo, are most easily found in such plantations. In Fiji, the Tubuai Islands, and Hawaii, large tracts have been planted with exotic trees in an attempt to establish timber industries. Viti Levu has extensive plantations of pine, while in Hawaii the trees are usually eucalyptus or paperbark. Native birds may frequent these forests, particularly during flowering, but many fewer species are represented than in native forests. The most significant Pacific island tree-planting operation from the point of view of birds was the seeding of *Leucaena latisiliqua* (Plate 45) on Micronesian islands devastated by the hostilities of World War II. This weedy tree from the American tropics (called tangan-tangan in the Marianas, haole koa in Hawaii) is now ubiquitous on Guam, Saipan, Tinian, Peleliu (Palau), and other islands. It is also common in the lowlands of the Hawaiian Islands. Wherever it grows, *Leucaena* forms dense, almost impenetrable thickets. Surprisingly, many native birds in Micronesia have adapted well to this foreign tree, and even endemics like the Tinian Monarch and Golden White-eye thrive in it. Other exotic trees that seem to be attractive to Pacific island birds include the already-mentioned kiawe, African tulip tree, silk oak, black wattle, royal poinciana, and several species of *Albizzia*.

LOWLAND DRY FOREST. This habitat may have been the richest bird and plant community in the Hawaiian Islands, but this forest and its birds are almost entirely extinct and are known to us only from fossil remains. The ancient Hawaiians cleared most of this forest for agriculture, and with it went the birds (Olson and James 1982). A few remnants of this association can be found on Hawaii (such as near Puu Waa Waa), but the native wilwili, naio, and ohia are mingled with exotic silk oak and jacaranda. About the only native forest birds still to be seen here are Common Amakihi and Hawaiian Hawk, but many exotic species seem to prefer this mixed native/exotic forest. Typically, the lowland dry forests of Hawaii today are kiawe thickets.

URBAN HABITATS. The larger cities of the tropical Pacific, such as Honolulu (Hawaii), Suva and Nadi (Fiji), Agana (Guam), Apia (W. Samoa), and Papeete (Tahiti), provide a totally artificial environment that is the preferred habitat of several introduced bird species. A few of these (e.g. House Sparrow, Eurasian Tree Sparrow, Rock Dove) are truly urban birds. Others are also found in the countryside, but are most easily seen in city parks or on suburban lawns. These include the various exotic mynas, bulbuls, doves, and finches. Surprisingly, a few native birds are also attracted to such places. Examples include Lesser Golden-Plover (throughout), Many-colored Fruit-Dove (Fiji, Samoa), Red-headed Parrotfinch (Fiji), Golden

White-eye (Saipan), and even the Common Fairy-Tern, which nests in ironwood and banyan trees in downtown Honolulu!

PRIMARY RAIN FORESTS AND CLOUD FORESTS. The original undisturbed forests of Pacific islands are the most important native landbird habitat of the region. Many endemic species are restricted to it, and are now endangered on islands where the original forests have been destroyed. On some islands, such as Rarotonga, only tiny remnants of primary forest remain, with none in the lowlands. Other islands, such as Pohnpei and Vanua Levu, have fared better and still have much of their rain forest. Even the Hawaiian Islands, severely altered by mankind over the centuries, retain extensive wilderness tracts of native forest although these remain threatened. Most of the primary rain forest and cloud forest remaining on Pacific islands is montane, but originally it probably extended into the lowlands now occupied by agricultural and other alien second growth.

Island rain forests are characterized by a large number of endemic plant species as compared to indigenous lowland floras. Few native forest trees are widespread, and each island or group has species peculiar to it. A few generalizations can be made, however. In Micronesia and Polynesia, the forests include many species of strangler figs and other *Ficus*, which provide food for the many frugivorous pigeons and doves. Also present are native palms and many nectar-producing trees favored by honeyeaters. Also characteristic are tree ferns and climbing vines such as various species of *Freycinetia*, a relative of pandanus (Plate 45).

The Hawaiian Islands are so large and so isolated that several distinct native forest types can be defined. The dominant tree in some areas, but present virtually in every forest association in the islands is ohia-lehua (ohia for short, Plate 44). This tree's spectacular brushlike red flowers are the most important source of nectar for the native honeycreepers and honeyeaters. Wet ohia forests are characterized by heavy growth of mosses and epiphytes (but not bromeliads), climbing vines such as ieie, and an understory of hapuu (tree fern). In the wettest areas, such as the Alakai Plateau on Kauai, windward East Maui, and the region northeast of Hawaii Volcanoes National Park on Hawaii, this association may be true cloud forest, with virtually perpetual mist and rain. These forests are particularly important to the endangered Ou, native thrushes, Poo-uli, and others.

In some of the drier montane areas of the Hawaiian Islands, koa (Plate 44) becomes the dominant tree, though ohia is still important. Many of the endangered forest birds in the islands today reach their greatest numbers in the koa/ohia forests. Examples include Akepa, Akiapolaau, and Hawaii Creeper. Koa forests form a belt above the wet ohia forests on windward Hawaii, and are also characteristic of the Kokee area on Kauai. Preservation of the remaining koa/ohia tracts is probably essential to the survival of many native birds. Nevertheless, logging and subsequent grazing are rapidly converting this ecosystem into pasture.

MAMANE/NAIO FOREST. Another Hawaiian plant community, this one is characteristic of dry uplands on the leeward sides of the highest mountains. The most significant tract for birds lies above the Saddle Road on the western side of Mauna Kea. It is the last stronghold of the endangered Palila, and harbors good numbers of Akiapolaau as well as a distinctive subspecies of Elepaio. The association is named for its two dominant tree species (Plate 44). It is an open, parklike forest with no canopy and a heavy growth of grasses among the trees. It is thus good habitat for alien gallinaceous birds such as Wild Turkey, Erckel's Francolin, and California Quail.

BARREN LANDS. So-called barren lands on Pacific islands may be either alpine zones or recent lava flows at any elevation. True alpine zones are found only in the highest peaks of the Hawaiian Islands (see Table 2), but many other islands have wind-swept ridges at their upper reaches that mimic alpine conditions, with rocky ground and stunted vegetation. The summits of Mauna Kea, Mauna Loa, Haleakala, and Hualalai are almost devoid of plant life. Nevertheless, they are important as nesting sites for such seabirds as White-tailed Tropicbird and the endangered Hawaiian (Dark-rumped) Petrel. Also found above tree line are Omao and Hawaiian Goose, as well as a few introduced birds such as Chukar. Elsewhere, other seabirds such as Tahiti Petrel nest on barren ridges, and cave swiftlets commonly forage in the updrafts.

Similar barren conditions are present on lava flows, which are of two types: aa, with a jagged, rough surface; and pahoehoe, a smooth ropy flow that looks like molasses poured on the ground. Despite their forbidding appearance, lava flows, like alpine zones, harbor a few bird species. Hawaiian Geese nest in such seemingly inhospitable places, and several game birds such as the Black Francolin seem at home there. Lava flows can also benefit birds indirectly by providing barriers to predators, exotic plants, and introduced herbivores. On Hawaii, lava flows have often left patches of ancient forest untouched. Such isolated forest islands are called kipukas and contain some of the least disturbed examples of native Hawaiian flora and fauna that can be found today.

ISLAND BIRDING

The islands of the tropical Pacific, with their relatively small individual lists of species, are not very rewarding to the birder in search of a long list. Still, a beginner in the region can easily become bewildered, and a few bird groups (e.g. seabirds, shorebirds) can confound even experienced birders. The first step in learning to identify birds is to study the illustrations to develop a feeling for the various kinds of birds. One cannot distinguish the Laysan from the Black-browed Albatross if one cannot tell an albatross from a booby! The overall shape of a bird and its parts (bill, tail, wings, etc.) are usually much more important initially than the pattern of coloration, yet beginners almost invariably first describe a bird in terms of color. Color may, in fact, be the least important information about a difficult bird, particularly because varying light conditions can greatly alter one's perception of color in the field. A careful observer will be thoroughly familiar with the terms for the parts of a bird (Figure 1), and will use them in making notes in the field. Of course we encourage readers to carry this book afield with them for quick reference, but there is no substitute for well-written notes, particularly to confirm identifications of hard-to-identify species. Notes should always, where possible, include descriptions of the bird's vocalizations. Some very similar-appearing species can be easily distinguished by their calls or songs.

SEABIRDS. Aside from the obvious problem of the existence of many very similar species, seabirds are a difficult group for logistical reasons. Many of them are strictly pelagic, except on the breeding grounds where, often as not, they come and go at night. Many species are not attracted to boats, even when the vessels are "chumming" (discarding edible refuse to attract birds). Often the only look one gets is distant and brief. Frequently one must settle for an identification simply of "petrel" or "shearwater." Even the experts cannot identify many of the birds seen on the open sea, and field identification techniques for seabirds are still evolving. Furthermore, most seabirds nest on uninhabited (and thus predator-free) islands which obviously are inaccessible to most birders. In the Hawaiian Islands, all offshore islets are officially designated wildlife sanctuaries and special permits are required to land on them. Elsewhere, nesting islands are remote and seldom visited. Another complication is the fact that many species do not breed in the tropical Pacific, but pass through it briefly in spring or fall migration. The paths of these migrants are not well known. Also, migrants in the tropics usually exhibit more direct flight than they do on their breeding or wintering range. Thus comments about flight behavior based on observations in temperate waters may not always apply in the tropics. Some observers have suggested that seabirds migrating through the tropics are seen most frequently during inclement weather, possibly because at other times they fly too high to be visible. We cannot confirm or deny this hypothesis, but seabird aficionados should be aware of the possibility.

Once a seabird has been allocated to one of the broad categories (booby, tern, shearwater, etc.), the observer should note such things as manner of flight, shape and color of bill and feet, and relative proportions of wings, body, and tail. Size is also important, but is difficult to determine at sea. The illustrations must be used with some understanding of the dynamics of flight. The apparent shapes of wings and tails of flying birds can change drastically under varying conditions. For example, a gadfly-petrel (Plate 5) in level, forward flight appears to have pointed wing tips and a narrow square tail. When the bird banks into the wind to change direction, however, the tail is fanned and the wing tips are forced against the air so that their outline becomes rounded rather than pointed. The plates show birds in both attitudes. The birder should realize that any still representation of a flying bird shows only a split-second of a continuous movement.

SHOREBIRDS. The problem with shorebirds (or waders, as they are called in British parlance) is less a matter of visibility than of difficulty of identification. Shorebirds on Pacific islands are relatively easy to view, and tend to concentrate in small areas such as antenna fields, garbage dumps, mudflats, and beaches. They often seem to appear magically after storms, which possibly force down high-flying migrants. The best months for shorebirds in the tropical Pacific are August-October, but they can be seen at any time of the year. Shorebirds worldwide are highly mobile, and even with so many species recorded in the region, many other as yet unreported ones will probably turn up sooner or later. Thus the observer really must know the shorebirds of the world to be sure of making accurate identifications. The serious student of these birds should have field guides to birds of North America, Eurasia, and Australia (see Bibliography) as well as this one.

NATIVE LAND BIRDS. Forest birds of tropical islands, unlike those of continents, tend to be very sedentary; they are not likely to turn up in new and unexpected places. Thus, if you think you saw an Apapane in downtown Honolulu, you should look again; it probably was a House Finch! Do not expect endemic forest birds out of habitat or on islands where they do not nest. No one has ever found, for example, an Anianiau (endemic to Kauai) on Oahu. Similarly, although Saipan and Tinian are only a few kilometers apart, the Golden White-eye has never been seen on Tinian, nor the Tinian Monarch on Saipan. Still, identifications should not be based solely on distribution. The careful birder on Oahu would make sure the little green bird in view is a Common Amakihi, and not an Anianiau. New distributional records are frequently made by amateurs.

On most tropical Pacific islands, native forest birds are still found wherever their preferred habitat remains, and in some places have even adapted well to second-growth and introduced tree species. A few such birds, such as the Great Truk White-eye and the Rarotonga Monarch, are virtually restricted to native forest, but in general, the surviving Pacific island endemics have fared surprisingly well in the face of considerable ecological change. The islands that have experienced significant declines and range contractions of native forest birds include Guam, Tahiti, Rarotonga (Cook Is.), Hivaoa (Marquesas Is.), and the main Hawaiian Islands. In most cases, the declines are obviously the result of habitat loss and competition with introduced birds such as the Common Myna. In Guam and the

Hawaiian Islands, however, other more insidious forces have come into play (see below).

For the birder wishing to see the rare Hawaiian native birds before they disappear, the task is formidable. Obviously, one must search for them only at higher elevations in remote undisturbed forests. Such an effort can require considerable physical exertion. One must also be careful that birding activities do not add to the stresses already felt by the birds. Particularly, hikers should be careful not to track alien weed seeds into wilderness areas. Birders can also be of help in conservation efforts by reporting sightings of the most critically endangered species (e.g. Bishop's Oo, Kauai Oo, Nukupuu, Ou, Kakawahie [Molokai Creeper], Oahu Creeper, Olomao, Kamao, Puaiohi [Small Kauai Thrush]) to responsible authorities such as the USFWS (offices on Kauai, Oahu, Maui, and Hawaii), the Hawaii Audubon Society (P. O. Box 22832, Honolulu, HI 96822), or the Bernice P. Bishop Museum in Honolulu.

Difficulties of finding them aside, forest birds on Pacific islands are relatively easy to identify. The region has no complexes comparable to New World *Empidonax* flycatchers or Old World *Phylloscopus* warblers. Nevertheless, some groups can be confusing, especially the "little green birds" of the Hawaiian Islands. These include not only several native honeycreepers, but also several exotics (see Table 4). Many of these little green birds differ in the form of the bill and little else. The pattern of green above, yellow-green below, with black lores is found in a total of ten native species plus the introduced Japanese White-eye! Sometimes the bill must be seen to confirm identification. Vocalizations, once learned, are a great help, but must be learned for each island separately because of varying local "dialects." For the effort, however, a careful observer may be rewarded with a sighting of a rare bird or even a "rediscovery" of a supposedly extinct one.

INTRODUCED BIRDS. Many species of birds have been artificially transported to tropical Pacific islands from other parts of the world. Most islands have only a few introduced birds, but in the Hawaiian Islands, Tahiti, Guam, and a few other places most of the land birds seen by the casual observer are alien. Birders often tend to denigrate these foreign elements of the avifauna, but the exotics can be excellent subjects for studies of bird behavior and distribution. In

TABLE 4. DISTRIBUTION AND STATUS OF LITTLE GREEN BIRDS IN HAWAII

Species	Kauai	Oahu	Molokai	Lanai	Maui	Hawaii
Common Amakihi		U	R	X	C	C
Kauai Amakihi	C					
Greater Amakihi						X
Anianiau	C					
Akialoa	X?	X		X		X
Akekee (Kauai Akepa)	C					
Akepa (female)		R			R	U
Oahu Creeper		R				
Maui Creeper				X	C	
Hawaii Creeper						U
Nukupuu	R	X			R	R
Akiapolaau						U
Japanese White-eye	C	C	C	C	C	C
Japanese Bush-Warbler	R	C	U		R	
Red-billed Leiothrix	R	U	R		C	C

SYMBOLS: C - Common to abundant.
U - Uncommon or localized to rare, but observable in suitable habitat or location.
R - Rare, nearly extinct; fewer than one sighting per year.
X - Extinct.

Hawaii, where the lowland avifauna is an amalgam of species from all over the world, an excellent opportunity exists to learn how species become established on islands, and how local faunas adjust to newcomers. The situation is still changing constantly, following a wave of new introductions in the 1960s. Birders should not overlook the exotics, even though they may seem less glamorous than the now often rare native birds.

When is an alien considered "established"? In North America, birders usually consider a period of ten years' successful breeding in the wild to be adequate to consider an introduced bird part of the avifauna. Most of the exotics in this book were introduced over 20 years ago. Nevertheless, some of them may not be permanently established (see Appendix A). Introduced birds tend to follow a pattern of initial success in a restricted area, a period of quiescence with some spread, and then either a spectacular population boom with an accompanying spread to new islands or habitats, or disappearance. The quiescent period may be quite lengthy, and the final outcome is totally unpredictable. Many of the exotics covered here are in their quiescent period. They have been present for a long time in a small area, and appear to be maintaining a stable population. The Japanese Bush-Warbler was in such a period for about 30 years on Oahu, but then underwent a spectacular increase in the late 1960s and 1970s and spread to several other islands. In contrast, the Varied Tit was seemingly established in Hawaii until about 1960, but has not been seen there for at least 25 years. Some species may "boom" and then "bust." The Red-billed Leiothrix became abundant on all the main Hawaiian Islands in the 1940s and 1950s (it was believed to be the most abundant bird on Oahu in the 1950s), but it has now all but disappeared from Kauai and Oahu and is declining elsewhere. It may be on the way out. These observations show that one decade may be too short a time to test a species' adaptability to a new environment. Nevertheless, a birder on Oahu in the 1950s would have been justified in considering the Varied Tit a part of the avifauna at that time. To help birders judge for themselves whether a bird is established or not, we give dates of introduction and population trends (where known) for all introduced species.

CONSERVATION

As mentioned in the previous section, Pacific island birds have fared surprisingly well until recently. Except in the Hawaiian Islands, few species have become extinct in historic times (see Table 5). Now, however, many species and subspecies (Table 6) are in imminent or possible danger of extinction, and on most islands few measures have been taken to aid in the recovery of declining birds. In areas under the aegis of the United States (Hawaii, Guam, Commonwealth of the Northern Marianas, American Samoa, and various scattered uninhabited islands of the central Pacific) birds are protected under the provisions of the Migratory Bird Treaty Act and the Endangered Species Act. Species not federally protected are covered by local statutes in the State of Hawaii, Guam, and the Northern Marianas. Birds are also given general legal protection in

TABLE 5. EXTINCT BIRD SPECIES OF THE TROPICAL PACIFIC

English Name	Scientific Name	Range
Wake Rail	*Rallus wakensis*	Wake I.
Kosrae Crake	*Porzana monasa*	Kosrae
Hawaiian Rail	*Porzana sandwichensis*	Hawaii
Laysan Rail	*Porzana palmeri*	Laysan (Hawaiian Is.)
Samoan Woodhen	*Gallinula pacifica*	Savaii (W. Samoa)
Tahitian Sandpiper	*Prosobonia leucoptera*	Tahiti (Society Is.)
Black-fronted Parakeet	*Cyanoramphus zealandicus*	Tahiti (Society Is.)
Raiatea Parakeet	*Cyanoramphus ulietanus*	Raiatea (Society Is.)
Amaui	*Myadestes oahensis*	Oahu (Hawaiian Is.)
Pohnpei Mountain Starling*	*Aplonis pelzelni*	Pohnpei
Kosrae Mountain Starling	*Aplonis corvina*	Kosrae
Oahu Oo	*Moho apicalis*	Oahu (Hawaiian Is.)
Hawaii Oo	*Moho nobilis*	Hawaii
Kioea	*Chaetoptila angustipluma*	Hawaii
Lesser Koa-Finch	*Rhodacanthis flaviceps*	Hawaii
Greater Koa-Finch	*Rhodacanthis palmeri*	Hawaii
Kona Grosbeak	*Chloridops kona*	Hawaii
Greater Amakihi	*Hemignathus sagittirostris*	Hawaii
Akialoa*	*Hemignathus obscurus*	Hawaiian Is.
Kakawahie (Molokai Creeper)*	*Paroreomyza flammea*	Molokai (Hawaiian Is.)
Ula-ai-hawane	*Ciridops anna*	Hawaii
Hawaii Mamo	*Drepanis pacifica*	Hawaii
Black Mamo	*Drepanis funerea*	Molokai (Hawaiian Is.)

* Not previously listed as extinct, but not reliably reported for 20 years despite careful searches by competent observers.

the Republic of Palau, Wallis and Futuna, and French Polynesia. In practical terms, bird protection laws in the tropical Pacific often exist mainly on paper.

Traditional societies of the tropical Pacific often had a fairly well developed sense of conservation, enforced through the power of traditional chiefs and kings. With the advent of modern technology and the waning of the power of local rulers, practices such as limits on the taking of certain avian resources (e.g. feathers in Hawaii, megapode and seabird eggs in several places) are no longer observed. Hunting on islands where firearms are permitted is now virtually uncontrolled, and probably is the major factor in the declines of

Symbols Used in Table 6

USFWS Terminology

E – Endangered Species in immediate danger of extinction.

T – Threatened Species likely to become an Endangered Species within the fore-seeable future throughout all or a significant portion of its range.

(E) – Candidate or Proposed Endangered Species. Those in various stages of the legal process to be listed as Endangered Species as of 1 January 1985.

ICBP Terminology

E – Endangered. Taxa in danger of extinction and whose survival is unlikely if the causal factors continue operating.

V – Vulnerable. Taxa believed likely to move into the endangered category in the near future if the causal factors continue operating.

R – Rare. Taxa with small world populations that are not at present endangered or vulnerable, but are at risk.

I – Indeterminate. Taxa that are suspected of belonging to one of the first three categories but for which insufficient information is currently available.

Other Symbols

F – Formerly listed species now believed out of danger.

x – Probably extinct, but still included in the lists.

* – Proposed for declassification as of October 1985. Now believed safe.

Table 6. Endangered and Threatened Breeding Birds of the Tropical Pacific

English Name[1]	Scientific Name[2]	Status USFWS	Status ICBP
Hawaiian (Dark-rumped) Petrel	*Pterodrama phaeopygia sandwichensis*	E	E
Newell's (Townsend's) Shearwater	*Puffinus (auricularis) newelli*	T	V
Hawaiian Goose	*Nesochen sandvicensis*	E	V
Mariana Mallard	*Anas "oustaleti"*	Ex	Rx
Hawaiian Duck	*Anas wyvilliana*	E	V
Laysan Duck	*Anas laysanensis*	E	R
Hawaiian Hawk	*Buteo solitarius*	E	R
Peregrine Falcon[3]	*Falco peregrinus*	E	V
Micronesian Megapode	*Megapodius laperouse*	E	R

TABLE 6. (cont.)

English Name[1]	Scientific Name[2]	Status USFWS	ICBP
Guam Rail	*Rallus owstoni*	E	V
Bar-winged Rail	*Rallus poecilopterus*		E
Mariana Moorhen	*Gallinula chloropus guami*	E	E
Hawaiian Moorhen	*Gallinula chloropus sandvicensis*	E	E
Hawaiian Coot	*Fulica alai*	E	R
Hawaiian Black-necked Stilt	*Himantopus mexicanus knudseni*	E	R
Tuamotu Sandpiper	*Prosobonia cancellatus*		V
Palau Nicobar Pigeon	*Caloenas nicobarica pelewensis*	(E)	E
Guam White-throated Ground-Dove	*Gallicolumba xanthonura* (in part)	(E)	
Polynesian Ground-Dove	*Gallicolumba erythroptera*		I
Marquesas Ground-Dove	*Gallicolumba rubescens*		I
Tooth-billed Pigeon	*Didunculus strigirostris*		V
Guam Mariana Fruit-Dove	*Ptilinopus roseicapilla* (in part)	(E)	V
Rapa Fruit-Dove	*Ptilinopus huttoni*		R
Radak Micronesian Pigeon	*Ducula oceanica ratakensis*	(E)	I
Truk Micronesian Pigeon	*Ducula oceanica teraokai*	(E)	E
Polynesian Pigeon	*Ducula aurorae*		V
Nukuhiva Pigeon	*Ducula galeata*		V
Blue Lorikeet	*Vini peruviana*		R
Ultramarine Lorikeet	*Vini ultramarina*		R
Pohnpei Short-eared Owl	*Asio flammeus ponapensis*	(E)	R
Mariana Island (Gray) Swiftlet	*Aerodramus vanikorensis bartschi*	E	
Guam Micronesian Kingfisher	*Halcyon cinnamomina cinnamomina*	E	
Hawaiian Crow	*Corvus hawaiiensis*	E	E
Mariana Crow	*Corvus kubaryi*	E	E
Tinian Monarch	*Monarcha takatsukasae*	E*	F
Truk Monarch	*Metabolus rugensis*	(E)	R

TABLE 6. (cont.)

English Name[1]	Scientific Name[2]	Status USFWS	ICBP
Tahiti Monarch	*Pomarea nigra*	E	E
Rarotonga Monarch	*•Pomarea dimidiata*		V
Eiao Iphis Monarch	*Pomarea iphis fluxa*		I
Hivaoa Marquesas Monarch	*Pomarea mendozae mendozae*		E
Uapou Marquesas Monarch	*Pomarea mendozae mira*		R
Nukuhiva Marquesas Monarch	*Pomarea mendozae nukuhivae*		Ex
Guam Flycatcher	*Myiagra freycineti*	E	
Guam Rufous Fantail	*Rhipidura rufifrons uraniae*	(E)	
Nightingale Reed-Warbler	*Acrocephalus luscinia*	E[4]	
Nihoa Millerbird	*Acrocephalus familiaris kingi*	E	E
Moorea Tahiti Reed-Warbler	*Acrocephalus caffra longirostris*		E
Eiao Marquesas Reed-Warbler	*Acrocephalus mendanae aquilonis*		E
Hatutu Marquesas Reed-Warbler	*Acrocephalus mendanae postremus*		R
Long-legged Warbler	*Trichocichla rufa*		E
Kamao	*Myadestes (= Phaeornis) myadestinus*	E	E
Olomao	*Myadestes (= Phaeornis) lanaiensis rutha*	E	E
Puaiohi	*Myadestes (= Phaeornis) palmeri*	E	E
Palau White-breasted Woodswallow	*Artamus leucorhynchus pelewensis*	(E)	R
Pohnpei Mountain Starling	*Aplonis pelzelni*	Ex	Vx
Guam Micronesian Starling	*Aplonis opaca guami* (in part)	(E)	
Guam Micronesian Honeyeater	*Myzomela rubratra (= cardinalis) saffordi* (in part)	(E)	

TABLE 6. (*cont.*)

English Name[1]	Scientific Name[2]	Status USFWS	ICBP
Kauai Oo	*Moho braccatus*	E	E
Guam Bridled White-eye	*Zosterops conspicillatus* [*] *conspicillatus*	E	
Rota Bridled White-eye	*Zosterops conspicillatus rotensis*		I
Great Truk White-eye	*Rukia ruki*	(E)	E
Long-billed White-eye	*Rukia longirostris*	E	R
Laysan Finch	*Telespyza cantans*	E	
Nihoa Finch	*Telespyza ultima*	E	
Ou	*Psittirostra psittacea*	E	E
Palila	*Loxioides bailleui*	E	E
Maui Parrotbill	*Pseudonestor xanthophrys*	E	V
Kauai Akialoa	*Hemignathus obscurus procerus*	Ex	Ex
Nukupuu	*Hemignathus lucidus*	E	E
Akiapolaau	*Hemignathus munroi*	E	E
Akikiki (Kauai Creeper)	*Oreomystis bairdi*		R
Hawaii Creeper	*Oreomystis mana*	E	
Kakawahie (Molokai Creeper)	*Paroreomyza flammea*	Ex	Ex

many pigeons, fruit-doves, ducks, and other large edible species. Only in the Hawaiian Islands, Guam, and the Northern Marianas are hunting laws effectively enforced. But bird protection laws, even when enforced, can do little to help species threatened by ecological disasters.

Recent forest-bird surveys by USFWS in Hawaii have confirmed that endemic birds there are restricted in range by the presence of disease-bearing mosquitoes, among other inimical factors. Mosquitoes were introduced to the islands (supposedly by a spiteful ship captain) in the 1820s. The subsequent rapid and mysterious declines of forest birds are now believed to have been caused by mosquito-borne diseases, which were a new factor in the Hawaiian environment. The avifauna thus experienced a fate similar to that of the indigenous human population, which was decimated by such European diseases as measles. The native birds of Oahu had mostly

TABLE 6. (cont.)

English Name[1]	Scientific Name[2]	Status USFWS	ICBP
Oahu Creeper	*Paroreomyza maculata*	E	E
Hawaii Akepa	*Loxops coccineus coccineus*	E	V
Maui Akepa	*Loxops coccineus ochraceus*	E	E
Akohekohe (Crested Honeycreeper)	*Palmeria dolei*	E	V
Poo-uli	*Melamprosops phaeosoma*	E	R
Palau Blue-faced Parrotfinch	*Erythrura trichroa pelewensis*		I
Pink-billed Parrotfinch	*Erythrura kleinschmidti*		R

[1] English names in this table may differ from those used elsewhere in this book, especially where only one or two subspecies or populations of a species are imperiled.

[2] Trinomials are given for individually listed subspecies.

[3] This species is so listed worldwide, but the status of the endemic Fiji subspecies has not been specifically determined.

[4] Whether this designation is intended to include the populations here classified as *Acrocephalus syrinx* is unclear. The range given by the USFWS (1984) is Mariana Is. only.

disappeared by the 1860s. On Kauai, Molokai, Maui, and Hawaii a major population crash of forest birds occurred in the 1890s and early 1900s. It was sudden, catastrophic, and mysterious to observers at the time. The birds of previously uninhabited Lanai survived this disaster, only to disappear in a short span of time after the establishment of Lanai City in the early 1920s. The surviving native birds withdrew to areas above 600 m (2000 ft.) elevation, at that time the upper limit of distribution of the mosquitoes, which were of a tropical strain. These highland refuges represented a severe contraction of available habitat and were only marginally suitable for many species. Species that were nomadic or dependent on lower-elevation forests were the most strongly affected. Many of today's most critically endangered birds would probably be more numerous if their preferred lowland habitats were not mosquito-infested. Ominously, the limit of mosquitoes may be creeping upward, and only a few native birds show any evidence of adaptation to disease. Within the last decade, the rare species that had survived so well in Kauai's Alakai Swamp have undergone a renewed sudden decline; mosquitoes are now in the Alakai.

Today, other ecological threats to Hawaiian native birds are equally significant. Logging and grazing are rapidly reducing and fragmenting available highland habitat, particularly in the important koa forest belt. Native forests are progressively being degraded by feral mammals, particularly pigs and sheep, whose destructive habits open up pristine areas to invasion by alien plants and increase the frequency of pools of standing water where mosquitoes breed. The future for native Hawaiian forest birds, despite recent research and conservation efforts, is not bright. A few may even become extinct as this book goes to press.

On Guam, a different, but possibly even more severe, avian disaster has recently taken place. Most of the island's birds had survived innumerable threats including mosquitoes; introduced birds, mammals, and reptiles; war activities; and extensive habitat alteration, and were still numerous throughout the island in the late 1960s. Then the native birds began to disappear from seemingly suitable habitat, first in the southern part of the island. By 1976, the southern two-thirds of Guam had lost virtually its entire avifauna. The apparent die-off of native birds continued northward, and as of 1985 several small species (Guam Flycatcher, Rufous Fantail, and Bridled White-eye) were nearing extinction on Guam and the larger species have declined to critically low levels. The last stronghold for forest birds has been a narrow strip below the island's northern cliffs. Extinction seems inevitable for the Guam Flycatcher, as well as the endemic subspecies of white-eye and fantail. Captive breeding programs now under way may save the Guam Rail and the local race of Micronesian Kingfisher, but the bird community of this largest Micronesian island has been irreversibly altered. The reasons for this sudden and unexpected disaster are currently under investigation. Many observers believe that the circumstances implicate disease as a causative agent, but as yet no data have emerged to confirm or refute that idea. If diseases are involved, they are unlikely to be the same as those that decimated Hawaiian birds, because Guam birds have presumably been exposed to those pathogens and their vectors for a long time. Many researchers now think that the introduced brown tree snake (*Boiga irregularis*), a bird predator, is responsible for the Guam disaster. But this hypothesis does not, in our opinion, adequately explain the rapidity or thoroughness of the bird declines, nor the ominous events on Rota, Guam's snake-free neighbor to the north. That island has lost the Island (Gray) Swiftlet since the mid-1970s, and its endemic Bridled White-eye subspecies has withdrawn to a tiny fraction of its original range. Such were the beginnings of the Guam disaster. Whatever the inimical factor is, it is the most frightening threat to birds in the tropical Pacific today.

With the exception of Hawaii, managed reserves such as parks and wildlife refuges are virtually nonexistent in the tropical Pacific. The few that we know of are Rose Atoll National Wildlife Refuge (A. Samoa), the Seventy Islands Preserve (Palau), and several small sanctuaries on Kiritimati (Kiribati). In French Polynesia a few small islands, such as Hatutu and Eiao in the Marquesas, have been set aside as scientific preserves.

In the Hawaiian Islands parks and refuges have had a long and important history. The Hawaiian Islands National Wildlife Refuge (which includes all of the NW Hawaiian Islands from Nihoa to Pearl and Hermes Reef) was so designated by President Theodore Roosevelt in 1909 in response to public indignation over the millinery feather trade. Hawaii National Park, now subdivided into Haleakala National Park and Hawaii Volcanoes National park, was established in 1916. More recently, several National Wildlife Refuges have been established on the main islands in an effort to save endangered wetland species. The State of Hawaii also has a system of state parks, a few of which (e.g. Kokee and Waimea Canyon State Parks on Kauai) are important preserves for native forest birds. Also, all offshore islets in the main Hawaiian Islands are state wildlife sanctuaries for the protection of nesting seabirds. A few other state preserves have also been designated, including one in the Alakai Swamp on Kauai. Kaneohe Marine Corps Air Station on Oahu also has an extensive program for managing the wetlands within its boundaries for the benefit of native water birds.

Despite these seemingly extensive efforts, much remains to be done even in Hawaii, particularly with regard to native forest birds. The best remaining habitat for them remains unprotected and vulnerable. Private organizations such as the Hawaii Audubon Society and the Nature Conservancy of Hawaii have led the way in forest bird conservation. The Audubon Society has been active since the 1930s in public education and in litigation on behalf of Endangered Species such as the Palila. The Nature Conservancy has recently begun a program of acquiring significant areas of habitat (or conservation easements thereon) for forest bird preserves. Their efforts have resulted in the addition of Kipahulu Valley to Haleakala National Park and in the establishment of several privately managed preserves on Kauai, Molokai, Maui, and Hawaii.

The Hawaii Audubon Society has also taken an interest in other parts of the Pacific, and in its journal *'Elepaio* publishes news and research results from the entire region. Recently, an Audubon society has been organized in the Mariana Islands, but otherwise no grassroots organization comparable to the Hawaii Audubon Society exists elsewhere in the tropical Pacific. We hope that this book will contribute to the development of more local interest in bird conservation.

III. SPECIES ACCOUNTS

ORDER GAVIIFORMES

FAMILY GAVIIDAE: Loons or Divers

Loons (divers in European literature) are large swimming birds with daggerlike beaks. They swim low in the water, with bill held up, and dive for fish. They are birds of arctic and temperate waters of the Northern Hemisphere, and only reach the tropics as rare stragglers.

ARCTIC LOON   *Gavia arctica*

This holarctic breeder has turned up twice in the tropical Pacific, both times on OAHU (Hawaiian Is.) Only birds (26;66) in winter plumage have been seen, basically gray above and white below, with crown paler than back. For full account, see N. American field guides, Flint et al. (1984), or WBSJ (1982).

ORDER PODICIPEDIFORMES

FAMILY PODICIPEDIDAE: Grebes

Grebes are mostly small diving birds almost always seen swimming. Their toes are lobed, not webbed as in ducks. They have sharp-pointed or laterally flattened bills and feed on aquatic animals and plants. In the water they look plump and tailless. They have the peculiar ability to compress their plumage (squeezing out the air) and sink slowly below the surface. They are excellent divers and may remain submerged for more than a minute. They are found worldwide, but only as rare winter visitors to the tropical Pacific.

PIED-BILLED GREBE   *Podilymbus podiceps*   Figure 7

Appearance: (13½;34) A stocky brown grebe with short, stout, chickenlike bill, yellow in winter, gray with vertical black bar in summer. Undertail coverts white. Throat becomes black in spring. Tropical visitors often molt before departing.

Habits: Found on freshwater ponds. Usually solitary and shy. Difficult to observe because it can quietly dive, remain submerged for a long time, and pop up in a different part of the pond.

Identification: Distinguished from other grebes by shorter-necked profile and stout, chickenlike bill.

Occurrence: Breeds throughout N. and S. America. Northern populations migratory. Rare visitor to the HAWAIIAN IS.

FIGURE 7. Pied-billed Grebe. Breeding plumage (*l.*) and nonbreeding plumage (*r.*).

HORNED GREBE *Podiceps auritus*

This species, called Slavonian Grebe in Europe, breeds around the Arctic and winters in the temperate Northern Hemisphere. A single individual appeared on KAUAI (Hawaiian Is.) in 1976 and remained through the following spring, when it attained full breeding dress. In winter plumage a clean-cut, dark gray and white grebe (13½;34) with clean white cheeks. Breeding plumage shows much chestnut on body, black head with yellow "horns." Eyes red. Illustrated in all N. American or Eurasian field guides.

EARED GREBE *Podiceps nigricollis*

This species, called Black-necked Grebe in Europe, breeds in Eurasia and N. America. A single individual visited OAHU (Hawaiian Is.) in 1983 and remained for several months. It acquired breeding dress before it departed. The Eared Grebe (12½;32) resembles the Horned Grebe in winter plumage, but has dark cheeks with a diffuse white spot behind the eye. Breeding birds have black head and neck, chestnut sides, and a tuft of shaggy yellow plumes on side of head. For illustrations, see N. American and Eurasian field guides.

ORDER PROCELLARIIFORMES

FAMILY DIOMEDEIDAE: Albatrosses

THE largest of seabirds, albatrosses are noted for their mastery of gliding flight. In a stiff breeze these birds can sail for hours with no perceptible movement of the wings. Some species commonly follow ships at sea for the increased food supply they provide. If it were not for this habit, these birds would seldom be seen because they rarely approach the shoreline and breed mainly on isolated, remote islands. Except for three species that breed in the North Pacific and one in the Galapagos Islands, albatrosses are restricted to the cold windy waters south of the Tropic of Capricorn and only occasionally wander to other parts of the globe. Smaller species of the southern oceans are called mollymawks in New Zealand and Australia.

WANDERING ALBATROSS   *Diomedea exulans*   FIGURE 8

Appearance: (47;121) Largest of seabirds. Immatures chocolate brown with white face mask and underwing. Gradually lightens over several years to pure white with black trailing edge to wing. Most visitors to tropical Pacific in early plumage stages. For detailed account of plumages, see Harrison (1983).

Habits: Inhabits cold oceans, but young birds occasionally wander into the tropics. Often follows ships. May glide for hours with no perceptible movement of wings.

Identification: The very similar Royal Albatross (*D. epomophora*; see Appendix A) is often indistinguishable from Wandering as an adult, but immatures very different, white with all-dark upperwing. Any very large albatross with dark feathering on the body is a Wandering. Adults of either species rarely (if ever) occur in the tropical Pacific. Juvenile giant-petrels (*Macronectes* sp.) smaller and all dark, including underwing, but may show irregular white patches at base of bill. Giant-petrels' flight much more labored than that of albatrosses.

Occurrence: Breeds on subantarctic islands. Ranges over s. seas N to about 20° S. Rare but fairly regular visitor to waters near FIJI and possibly TONGA. One very old record for the MARQUESAS.

FIGURE 8. Wandering Albatross (juvenile)

[**ROYAL ALBATROSS**   *Diomedea epomophora*   See Appendix A]

SHORT-TAILED ALBATROSS   *Diomedea albatrus*   PLATE 1

Appearance: (36;91) Largest albatross of N. Pacific. Bill and feet pink at all ages. Adult mostly white with dark brown tail and upperwing, buffy nape. White of back extends irregularly onto central part of wing above. Underwing white with complete narrow dark border. Juvenile all dark brown, gradually lightens. White appears first at base of bill and on belly, producing a collared effect below. Later, entire underparts white with white blotches appearing on upperwing near body. Subadult like adult with dark nape patch.

Habits: A bird of open seas that seldom follows ships. Occasionally visits nesting islands of other albatross species.

Identification: Laysan Albatross smaller, with solid dark mantle, white nape, and dark-tipped yellow bill. Immature Short-tailed told from Black-footed by pink bill, dark face. A few aberrant Black-footeds resemble intermediate stages of Short-tailed. They may have pale bill and legs, but lack white patches on upperwing.

Occurrence: Breeds only on Torishima (Izu Is.) near Japan. Slowly increasing, population about 250. Formerly ranged entire N. Pacific, mostly in colder seas. Rare but probably annual visitor to the NW HA- WAIIAN IS. (Midway, French Frigate Shoal, Laysan). Endangered Species.

Reference: Hasegawa, H., and A. R. DeGange. 1982. The Short-tailed Albatross, *Diomedea albatrus*, its status, distribution and natural history. *Am. Birds* 36:806-814.

Other name: Steller's Albatross.

BLACK-FOOTED ALBATROSS *Diomedea nigripes* PLATE 1

Appearance: (32;81) A dark brownish gray albatross with white at base of bill, white or buffy undertail coverts, and white band at base of tail above. Pale areas less extensive in younger birds. Bill and feet usually dark. Aberrant or very old birds occasionally almost white on head and belly.

Habits: A bird of open ocean and offshore waters. Often follows ships. On breeding grounds shyer and less aggressive than Laysan Albatross. Walks in crouched position with head held horizontally. Displays similar to those of Laysan Albatross. The two occasionally hybridize, with offspring intermediate.

Voice: Like that of Laysan Albatross but hoarser, louder, and lower pitched.

Identification: The only all-dark albatross likely to be seen in the N. Pacific. Compare Light-mantled Albatross. Aberrant Black-footed may resemble Short-tailed Albatross, but is much smaller.

Occurrence: Breeds (October-June) in the HAWAIIAN IS. (NW chain, Kaula), the MARSHALL IS. (Taongi, possibly elsewhere), JOHN- STON ATOLL, and Torishima (Izu Is.) off Japan. Wanders mostly to colder seas when not breeding. Sometimes seen from shore in the main Hawaiian Is. Common, but much less numerous than Laysan Albatross on breeding grounds.

Reference: Dunbar, W. P. 1975. Observations of Black-footed and Lay- san Albatrosses between Seattle and Guam. *'Elepaio* 36:32-35.

LAYSAN ALBATROSS *Diomedea immutabilis* PLATE 1, FIGURE 9

Appearance: (32;81) A mostly white, small albatross with back, upper- wings, and tail sooty brown, and a dark patch around eye. Feet project beyond tail in flight.

Habits: A bird of open ocean seldom seen near land except at breeding islands. Only occasionally follows ships. On land very tame, seemingly heedless of human activity. Walks with head upright. Displays include bill-clacking, bowing, foot-stomping, and pointing the bill skyward.

Voice: Displays accompanied by whinnying whistles, quacking sounds, and mooing notes. Higher pitched and less nasal than voice of Black-footed Albatross.

Identification: Adult Short-tailed Albatross larger with white back, white patches on wings, and larger pink bill. See Black-browed Albatross.

Occurrence: Most abundant albatross of N. Pacific. Formerly more widespread, now breeds only in the Ogasawara (Bonin) Is. and the HAWAIIAN IS. (NW chain, especially Laysan, Midway, Lisianski, Pearl and Hermes Reef; Kauai). Increasingly seen from shore in main Hawaiian Is. Formerly bred at WAKE, now only a visitor there. Post-breeding wanderers may reach the e. CAROLINE IS., but most move northward.

Reference: Fisher, M. L. 1970. *The albatross of Midway Island.* Carbondale and Edwardsville: Southern Illinois Univ. Press.

BLACK-BROWED ALBATROSS   *Diomedea melanophris*   FIGURE 9

Appearance: (35;89) A mostly white albatross with sooty brown mantle and tail. Underwing white, broadly bordered with black. Dark patch

FIGURE 9. Comparison of Black-browed Albatross (*l.*) and Laysan Albatross (*r.*)

before and above eye imparts a scowling look. Bill yellow. Immatures like adults but bill black, back of head and neck washed with gray, and white wing linings reduced. Feet do not project beyond tail in flight.

Habits: A bird of open ocean, sometimes in flocks. Follows ships.

Identification: Very similar to Laysan Albatross, but adult distinguished by square-cut rear edge of dark mantle (Laysan's mantle projects rearward onto upper rump), all-yellow (not dark-tipped) bill, and more clean-cut underwing pattern with broader dark borders. Immature's dark bill and dusky hindneck distinctive.

Occurrence: Breeds on subantarctic islands, ranges N to Tropic of Capricorn. Stragglers reported between the HAWAIIAN IS. and the LINE IS. (Kiribati), and from the TUAMOTU ARCH. and PITCAIRN I.

Other name: Black-browed Mollymawk.

LIGHT-MANTLED ALBATROSS *Phoebetria palpebrata*

An all-dark small (33;84) albatross of subantarctic seas. Ranges N rarely to Tropic of Capricorn. Included here on basis of one 19th-century sighting near the MARQUESAS IS. Distinguished by ashy gray back that contrasts with dark head, wings, and tail. For illustration, see Harrison (1983). Other name: Light-mantled Sooty Albatross.

FAMILY PROCELLARIIDAE: SHEARWATERS AND PETRELS

SHEARWATERS and petrels are medium-sized pelagic birds distributed throughout the oceans of the world. They are usually seen in flight so close to the surface that they often disappear momentarily behind the crest of a wave, hence the name shearwater. Typical flight exhibits brief periods of flapping and long glides. Usually seen at sea, these birds occasionally come close enough to shore to be seen from headlands or small boats. They nest mostly on remote oceanic islands, and often are nocturnal on the breeding grounds. Most species nest in burrows in the ground, and many have forsaken former nesting grounds because of the presence of introduced ground predators such as dogs, cats, rats, and mongooses. Shearwaters tend to be larger than petrels, with longer, thinner bills. Giant-petrels are as large as albatrosses, however. The gadfly-petrels are small to medium-sized pelagic birds that present a bewildering array of variation within species, compounded by the number of very similar species. They are little known and difficult to study. Observers must be careful to note the *exact* pattern of markings on the underwings, head, and mantle of any gadfly-petrel seen to even hope to identify the bird to species. Most individuals seen at sea will not be identifiable. The Range should *not* be used in the process of elimination because distributions of many gadfly-petrels are not accurately known, and many wander widely over the world's oceans. The taxonomy of gadfly-petrels has recently been reviewed by Imber (1985; see below) and we follow his classification.

Reference: Imber, M. J. 1985. Origins, phylogeny and taxonomy of the gadfly petrels *Pterodroma* spp. Ibis 127:197-229.

STREAKED SHEARWATER   *Calonectris leucomelas*   PLATE 4

Appearance: (19;48) A large slender shearwater, brown above and white below. Head white, streaked with brown (heavily on crown, finely on throat). Feathers of back lightly edged white. Underwing white. Long slender bill pale with dark tip.

Habits: A bird of the open ocean and offshore waters. Flight light and graceful for a large shearwater; glides with occasional wingbeats.

Identification: A very distinctive shearwater; no others have streaks on the head. At a distance the streaks are not discernible and the face appears white.

Occurrence: Temperate and tropical waters of w. Pacific. Nests on islands off Japan and Taiwan, migrates November-February to waters N of New Guinea and rarely to ne. Pacific. Rare migrant in w. MICRONESIA (Palau, Yap, Marianas, Truk). An unsubstantiated report for waters near the HAWAIIAN IS.

Other name: White-faced Shearwater.

PINK-FOOTED SHEARWATER   *Puffinus creatopus*   PLATE 4

Appearance: (19;48) A large shearwater, dark brown above, shading to white below. Dark/light separation uneven, with no sharp borders. Underwing white mottled with brown. Bill light yellow, tipped brown; feet flesh-colored.

Habits: Pelagic in c. Pacific. Wingbeats slower and more deliberate than those of smaller shearwaters. Does not follow ships.

Identification: Very similar to smaller light-phase Wedge-tailed Shearwater, which has darker, though sometimes pale-looking, bill. Wedge-tail has broader, more rounded wings held far forward and bowed, with cleaner-looking white wing lining.

Occurrence: Breeds on islands off Chile, migrates northward to s. Alaska. Stragglers have been found October-December at sea between the HAWAIIAN IS. and the LINE IS. (Kiribati).

FLESH-FOOTED SHEARWATER *Puffinus carneipes* PLATE 2

Appearance: (18;46) A stout, all dark brown shearwater, with dark-tipped yellow to pink bill and flesh-colored feet. From below, bases of primaries somewhat silvery. Larger than other dark shearwaters.

Habits: Pelagic in the tropics. Flight heavy with relatively slow wingbeats. Sometimes follows ships.

Voice: A sharp, high-pitched note uttered at sea.

Identification: Large size, pale bill and feet, and dark underwings distinguish Flesh-footed from other dark shearwaters. Wings longer, less bowed in flight than those of dark morph Wedge-tailed, broader than those of Sooty or Short-tailed.

Occurrence: Breeds on islands in temperate sw. Pacific, migrates to cool N. Pacific in more or less clockwise circle. Rare but regular passage migrant near the HAWAIIAN IS. (October and April), and also reported near the MARSHALL IS.

Other name: Pale-footed Shearwater.

WEDGE-TAILED SHEARWATER *Puffinus pacificus* PLATES 2,4

Appearance: (17;43) A medium-sized shearwater with long, wedge-shaped tail, flesh-colored legs, and slate-colored bill. Two morphs. Light form dark brown above, shading to grayish white below. Dark morph similar above, dark gray below, palest on throat and upper breast.

Habits: A bird of the open ocean and offshore waters. Nests in burrows on offshore islets, atolls, and barren headlands. Comes and goes at night. Flight graceful with slow, shallow flapping interspersed with long glides. Seldom follows ships.

Voice: At nest burrow, a catlike whine followed by a deep-throated breathy moan. Has an inhale-exhale quality.

Identification: Birders in the tropical Pacific should learn this ubiquitous species well so that comparison can be made with less common or less widespread species. The wedge-shaped tail, although diagnostic, is not usually apparent unless the bird banks into the wind and spreads its tail. The wings are broader and more rounded than those of other shearwaters and held further forward with more bend at the wrist. Light morphs fairly distinctive, lacking the clean-cut "tuxedo" look of most other pale-bellied shearwaters, but compare larger Pink-footed and Buller's. Dark morph generally grayer, less brown than other dark shearwaters, especially on the throat and upper breast. Underwing of dark Wedge-tail entirely dark, unlike that of Sooty or Short-tailed, which also differ in having dark legs. Flesh-footed Shearwater has pale legs, but also a pale bill, and is much darker below with longer, more pointed wings. Christmas Shearwater is smaller, darker (no contrast at all in throat), with black legs and bill. Some dark petrels have short wedge-shaped tails (e.g. Murphy's, Herald) but note shorter bills, petrel flight.

Occurrence: Abundant throughout the tropical and subtropical Pacific and Indian oceans. Breeds at scattered localities in the HAWAIIAN IS., n. MARIANA IS., c. CAROLINE IS., n. MARSHALL IS., JOHNSTON ATOLL, KIRIBATI (Phoenix Is., Line Is.), FIJI, TONGA, SAMOA, FRENCH POLYNESIA, and the PITCAIRN IS. Disperses throughout the tropical Pacific, but rare in w. Micronesia. All birds S of 10° N latitude are dark morphs, birds of Hawaii, the Marshalls, and the Marianas mostly pale morphs.

References: Byrd, G. V., D. I. Moriarty, and B. G. Brady. 1983. Breeding biology of Wedge-tailed Shearwaters at Kilauea Point, Hawaii. *Condor* 85:292-96.

Jenkins, J.A.F. 1979. Observations on the Wedge-tailed Shearwater (*Puffinus pacificus*) in the south-west Pacific. *Notornis* 26:331-48.

BULLER'S SHEARWATER   *Puffinus bulleri*   PLATE 4

Appearance: (18;46) A distinctive, large, slender, long-necked shearwater. Gray above, with contrasting dark cap, tail, and open M across mantle. Entire underparts, including underwing, pure white. Tail long, wedge-shaped. Bill long and slate-colored; feet flesh-colored.

Habits: Entirely pelagic in the tropics. Flight powerful and buoyant; often soars in calm winds. In stronger winds, flight slower and less erratic than that of larger gadfly-petrels, without the high arcs.

Identification: The pure white underwing with only a thin dark edge is distinctive among petrels and shearwaters of similar size. Pale Wedge-tailed Shearwater less clean-cut, without dark M above. Juan Fernandez and White-necked Petrel very similar in general pattern, but note short bill, different flight, darker primaries below.

Occurrence: Breeds on islands near New Zealand, migrates to temperate N. Pacific. Rare passage migrant in c. tropical Pacific recorded at sea near FIJI and the HAWAIIAN IS. (mainly April, August-November).

Other names: New Zealand Shearwater, Gray-backed Shearwater.

SOOTY SHEARWATER   *Puffinus griseus*   PLATE 2

Appearance: (18;46) A large shearwater, sooty brown above, grayish brown below. Wing linings silvery white with indistinct border. A few individuals have dark linings. Feet dark brown.

Habits: A bird of open ocean and offshore waters. Seldom seen from land. Flight fast and directional, particularly in tropical waters. Dives for food, does not follow ships. Often in huge flocks which, when they bank high above the horizon, can be seen from great distances.

Identification: Rarely, Sooty Shearwaters have dark wing linings and Short-tailed Shearwaters have pale linings. Usually all members of a flock are the same species. Thus four pale-winged birds with one dark one are probably all Sooties, but isolated individuals are probably indistinguishable at sea. Christmas Shearwater is smaller and has darker underwings than either Sooty or Short-tailed. Flesh-footed and dark Wedge-tailed have pale feet.

Occurrence: Breeds on islands off New Zealand, Australia, and S. America. Migrates N to temperate seas during nonbreeding season (April-November). Widespread and common migrant in c. Pacific W to the MARSHALL IS. Recorded near the HAWAIIAN IS., FIJI, KIRIBATI, the COOK IS., the SOCIETY IS., and the MARQUESAS, but probably occurs throughout Polynesia.

SHORT-TAILED SHEARWATER *Puffinus tenuirostris* PLATE 2

Appearance: (17;43) A medium-sized, sooty brown shearwater, darkest above. Underwing usually dark gray, but may be as pale as that of Sooty Shearwater.

Habits: Entirely pelagic in the tropics, where flight is rapid and directional. Sometimes follows ships.

Identification: Distinguished with difficulty from very similar Sooty Shearwater by darker underwing linings (not always reliable), slightly smaller size, and shorter bill. Certain identification of isolated migrants in the tropics probably impossible. Christmas Shearwater smaller with rounder wings and darker wing lining, heavier, less stiff-winged flight. Flesh-footed and dark Wedge-tail larger with pale legs.

Occurrence: Breeds off Australia, migrates April-May N through w. Pacific to arctic waters. Returns S through c. Pacific September-November. Recorded near the HAWAIIAN IS., the MARIANAS, CAROLINE IS., MARSHALL IS., KIRIBATI, FIJI, SAMOA, and TUAMOTU ARCH., but could be expected anywhere in the tropical Pacific.

Other names: Slender-billed Shearwater, Mutton Bird.

CHRISTMAS SHEARWATER *Puffinus nativitatis* PLATE 2

Appearance: (14;35) A medium-sized, chocolate brown shearwater with relatively short, rounded wings and tail.

Habits: Nests under bushes on small oceanic islands and atolls. Comes and goes at night. Very tame. Flight buoyant and graceful, with rapid wingbeats and long glides. Lacks careening arcs of transient dark Shearwaters.

Voice: Similar to that of Wedge-tailed Shearwater but with a nasal, gurgling quality. Often calls in flight.

Identification: Smallest of the all-dark shearwaters, with lower, more graceful flight than most. Totally dark wing linings diagnostic, but note also dark legs. Dark Wedge-tail grayer, less brown especially below, with noticeably longer tail. Sooty and Short-tailed Shearwaters have more pointed wings with paler linings, more careening flight.

Occurrence: Widespread in s. c. Pacific. Breeds in the HAWAIIAN IS. (NW chain, islets off Oahu and Molokai), KIRIBATI (Kiritimati, Phoenix Is.), the MARQUESAS, the TUAMOTU ARCH., the TUBUAI IS., the PITCAIRN IS. (Pitcairn, Ducie, Henderson), and Easter I. Disperses to adjacent seas. Visits MICRONESIA (n. Marianas, Kosrae, Marshall Is., Gilbert Is.), the COOK IS., and the SOCIETY IS.

NEWELL'S (TOWNSEND'S) SHEARWATER   Plate 3
Puffinus newelli

Appearance: (13;33) A small, slender shearwater, clean-cut black above and white below. Black of crown extends below eye. Wing lining white, contrasting with black flight feathers. Undertail coverts white. White of flanks extends up onto sides of rump. Bill and legs black.

Habits: A bird of the open tropical seas and offshore waters near breeding grounds. Nests in burrows under ferns on forested mountain slopes. Comes and goes at night. May be observed flying high overhead inland from the sea at dusk. At sea, flies low over the water surface with fast, stiff wingbeats interspersed with short glides. Fledglings, confused by lights on land, often come down on islands (mainly October-November) and are killed by dogs and cats or are struck by cars. Stranded birds must be launched by hand into the air, as they apparently cannot take off from level land.

Voice: A jackasslike braying near nesting colonies at night. Somewhat like voice of Wedge-tailed Shearwater.

Identification: The only black and white shearwater normally within its range. Audubon's Shearwater (as yet not recorded near Hawaii) smaller, stockier, with shorter, more rounded wings and dark undertail coverts. Little Shearwater much smaller with white extending above eye and paler underwing. Newell's distinguished from both by white extensions onto sides of rump.

Occurrence: Endemic to the HAWAIIAN IS. Breeds on Kauai, Hawaii, Molokai, possibly Oahu; formerly others. Often seen in Hawaiian waters April-October, but nearly absent the remainder of the year. Dispersal largely unknown. Has wandered to the MARIANAS. A Threatened Species.

Other name: *'a'o*.

Note: The classification of this form is controversial. It was long classed as a race of Manx Shearwater (*P. puffinus*) along with two other forms from the W coast of N. America. All Pacific forms were separated from Manx Shearwater in the 1983 AOU Check-list, with this form combined with Townsend's Shearwater (*P. auricularis*), which breeds on the Revillagigedo Is. (Mexico). Walters (1980) lists *P. newelli* as a full species with the English name Hawaiian Shearwater; other world checklists (Howard and Moore 1980; Clements 1981) overlook *newelli* altogether. The latter development demonstrates why we prefer to consider *P. newelli* a separate species until we see more reason to combine it with *P. auricularis*.

LITTLE SHEARWATER   *Puffinus assimilis*   PLATE 3

Appearance: (11;28) A very small, short-winged, short-tailed shearwater, black above and white below. White of underparts usually extends onto sides of head to above eye level. Underwing mostly white, margined and tipped with black. Undertail coverts white.

Habits: Pelagic or in offshore waters near breeding grounds. Often alights on water surface and freely dives. May dabble on surface like a storm-petrel. Flight fast and close to water with very rapid fluttering wingbeats interspersed with short glides. Follows ships.

Voice: Silent at sea. On breeding grounds a high-pitched crowing or squealing.

Identification: Distinguished from similar Audubon's and Newell's Shearwaters by distinctive face pattern, smaller size, narrower dark margins to underwing, and different flight.

Occurrence: Breeds at widely scattered localities around the world. In the S. Pacific breeds on islands in temperate waters including RAPA (Tubuai Is.). Disperses into nearby seas. Rare in tropical Pacific waters; stragglers have reached the MARQUESAS and MIDWAY (NW Hawaiian Is.).

Other names: Allied Shearwater, Dusky Shearwater.

AUDUBON'S SHEARWATER   *Puffinus lherminieri*   PLATE 3

Appearance: (12;31) A small, stocky, short-winged, long-tailed shearwater, clean-cut dark brown (looks black) above and white below. Dark upperparts extend below eye level and onto sides of breast. Wing linings white contrasting sharply with dark flight feathers. Undertail coverts brown. Legs and feet flesh-colored.

Habits: A bird of open seas and offshore waters near its breeding grounds. Usually solitary at sea, but sometimes in feeding flocks. Often alights on water; dives and swims below the surface. Flight shows rapid flutters alternating with glides. Ignores ships. Nocturnal at nesting colony; returns at dusk.

Voice: Silent at sea, but noisy around nesting colony after dark. Call a 2-syllable inhale-exhale sound *shoo-kreee*, the first part raspy, the second a screech.

Identification: Intermediate in size between two other black-and-white shearwaters. Smaller Little Shearwater has more white on side of face and in underwings. Larger Newell's has white undertail coverts, with white extending further onto sides of rump. Audubon's looks shorter-winged and longer-tailed than either. These three not normally found together.

Occurrence: Pantropical. Breeds nearly throughout the tropical Pacific except for the Hawaiian Is. Known from Vanuatu, New Caledonia, the Solomon Is., PALAU, the MARIANAS, the CAROLINE IS., KIRIBATI (Phoenix Is., Kiritimati), FIJI, SAMOA, TONGA, the SOCIETY IS., the TUAMOTU ARCH., and the MARQUESAS. Disperses to intervening seas.

Other name: Dusky-backed Shearwater.

BULWER'S PETREL *Bulweria bulwerii*   PLATE 2

Appearance: (10;25) A small, sooty brown petrel with long, wedge-shaped tail (usually looks pointed in flight). Pale buff diagonal bar across upperwing.

Habits: Flight erratic and twisting, with swooping, careening motion. Remains close to water surface. Does not usually follow ships. Nests on small oceanic islands and offshore islets. Nocturnal and noisy on breeding grounds.

Voice: Silent at sea. At nest burrow a staccato monotonous *uh-uh-uh-uh-*, etc. that sounds like a small motor running. The performance is often a duet, with each member of the pair uttering every other note.

Identification: Compared to all-dark storm-petrels, Bulwer's appears long-winged and long-tailed. It is smaller, with more erratic flight than dark shearwaters and petrels, none of which has buff bar on upperwing. See Jouanin's Petrel and Fiji Petrel.

Occurrence: Breeds on islands in the tropical Pacific and Atlantic oceans, including the HAWAIIAN IS. (offshore islets, NW Chain), JOHNSTON ATOLL, the PHOENIX IS. (Kiribati), and the MARQUESAS. Disperses to seas around breeding islands and rarely to the MARSHALL IS. and possibly the c. CAROLINE IS.

JOUANIN'S PETREL *Bulweria fallax*

Normally a resident of the nw. Indian Ocean, this species is included here on the basis of a specimen collected on LISIANSKI (NW Hawaiian Is.) in 1967. Very similar to Bulwer's Petrel, but slightly larger, with relatively larger head and bill, and without pale diagonal bar on upperwing. In flight Bulwer's Petrel remains close to the waves, but Jouanin's often towers high above. For illustrations, see Harrison (1983) or Löfgren (1984).

TAHITI PETREL *Pseudobulweria rostrata* PLATE 3

Appearance: (16;41) A medium-sized, stocky petrel with a large black bill and wedge-shaped tail. Entirely sooty brown except for sharply defined white lower breast, belly, and undertail coverts.

Habits: A solitary bird of open ocean and offshore waters near breeding grounds. May follow ships to scavenge for refuse. Flight alternates deep, relaxed wingbeats with banking arcs and glides. Does not usually bank above horizon. Breeds colonially in burrows on steep mountain slopes, comes and goes at dusk and dawn. Noisy near colonies.

Voice: A long, whistled note repeated sequentially.

Identification: Phoenix Petrel smaller, less robust, with smaller bill, white throat patch, and less distinct border between brown breast and white underparts. Intermediate-phase Kermadec and Herald Petrels may be similar, but have white markings on underwings.

Occurrence: Endemic to the tropical Pacific. Breeds in New Caledonia, the SOCIETY IS. (Tahiti, Moorea), the MARQUESAS, and possibly on RAROTONGA (Cook Is.). Abundant at sea near breeding grounds. Disperses to N and W. Stragglers reported near the HAWAIIAN and CAROLINE IS., and in KIRIBATI.

Other name: Peale's Petrel.

FIJI PETREL *Pseudobulweria macgillivrayi*

Appearance and Identification: A small, entirely dark brown petrel with a short, heavy bill and bicolored feet (pale blue tarsus, black toes and webs). Total length measurements unavailable, but somewhat larger and chunkier than Bulwer's Petrel, which has buff wing bars and a longer tail.

Habits: Poorly known. Presumably nests on high forested ridges and disperses to adjacent seas.

Occurrence: Known only from a single immature taken in 1855 and an adult captured and released in 1983 on GAU (Fiji). Apparently very rare. Possibly more widespread in prehistoric times.

Reference: Watling, D. and Ratu F. Lewanavanua. 1985. A note to record the continuing survival of the Fiji (MacGillivray's) Petrel *Pseudobulweria macgillivrayi*. *Ibis* 127:230-33.

Other name: MacGillivray's Petrel.

FIGURE 10. Juvenile Giant-Petrel (either species)

ANTARCTIC GIANT-PETREL *Macronectes giganteus* FIGURE 10

Appearance: (37;93) A huge seabird of albatross size with chunky body, long narrow wings, and huge greenish-tipped yellow bill. Two morphs: white with irregular dark spots at all ages, and dark with age-related variations. Only juveniles of the dark morph (wholly dark chocolate brown) as yet recorded in the tropical Pacific. Plumage gradually lightens, beginning at base of bill, until white-headed, white-breasted adult stage is reached.

Habits: Flight less graceful than that of albatrosses, with more flapping. Largely pelagic, but may scavenge on land. Stragglers in the tropics do not survive well; most records are of birds picked up dead or dying.

Identification: Compare Wandering Albatross (white face) and Light-mantled Albatross (pale gray mantle). Virtually identical to Hall's Giant-Petrel as juvenile except for bill color: greenish yellow in Antarctic, tan with reddish dark tip in Hall's.

Occurrence: Breeds in the Antarctic and Subantarctic. First-year individuals disperse widely, occasionally reaching the tropical Pacific at FIJI, TONGA, the SOCIETY IS., the TUBUAI IS., and the TUAMOTU ARCH. Reports of giant-petrels from MIDWAY (Hawaiian Is.) are unsubstantiated. Some of the above records may pertain to Hall's Giant-Petrel.

Reference and Other names: See following account.

HALL'S GIANT-PETREL *Macronectes halli* FIGURE 10

Appearance and Identification: (37;93) Virtually identical to Antarctic Giant-Petrel, but lacks a white morph. Bill dull tan at base with tip dull red above, dusky below. Bill color diagnostic at all ages.

Occurrence: Breeds further N than Antarctic Giant-Petrel, but disperses less often to the tropics. Has strayed at least once to the COOK IS. Many older giant-petrel records from se. Polynesia cannot be assigned to species.

Reference: Johnstone, G. W. 1974. Field characters and behaviour at sea of giant petrels in relation to their oceanic distribution. *Emu* 74:209-218.

Other names: Many seabird references and world checklists use Northern Giant-Petrel and Southern Giant-Petrel for *M. halli* and *M. giganteus* respectively. Walters (1980), however, reverses them! Obviously the directional names for giant-petrels are confusing and ambiguous as well as misleading (see Occurrence). We urge the adoption of the 1983 AOU Check-list names to avoid these problems.

NORTHERN FULMAR   *Fulmarus glacialis*   FIGURE 11

Appearance: (19;48) A medium-sized, gull-like petrel. Color varies. Light extreme resembles small gull (white with gray mantle and dark brown primaries), dark extreme all brownish gray. Intermediates occur. Both phases have stubby yellow bill and black spot in front of eye. Only dark-phase birds have been reported so far from tropical waters.

Habits: Mainly pelagic. Sometimes follows ships. In flight, stiff-winged flapping is followed by short glides. Not as graceful as other shearwaters or petrels.

Identification: Light phase distinguished from gulls by stocky form, stubby yellow bill, and lack of black wing tips. Dark-phase birds differ from dark shearwaters by the lighter color, stocky form, stubby yellow bill, and broader tail. Compare especially Flesh-footed Shearwater. Dark gadfly-petrels slimmer, longer-winged, narrower-tailed.

FIGURE 11. Northern Fulmar (dark color phase)

Occurrence: Breeds on arctic and subarctic islands around the Northern Hemisphere. Pacific birds breed on islands in the Bering Sea, the Kuriles, and the Aleutians. During winter months stragglers range southward, rarely reaching the HAWAIIAN IS.

CAPE PETREL *Daption capense*   FIGURE 12

Appearance: (16;41) A medium-sized, boldly patterned black and white petrel. Black of head faintly glossed. Upperparts checkered black and white; underparts (including most of underwing) white. Tail white, tipped black.

FIGURE 12. Cape Petrel

Habits: Bird of open ocean and offshore waters. Flies close to water, alternating between stiff-winged flapping and gliding. A scavenger that readily follows ships and enters inshore waters.

Identification: Unmistakable, but note that dark shearwaters with badly worn, molting plumage or with partial albinism can appear to have similar white wing patches and checkered pattern.

Occurrence: One of commonest petrels in the Southern Hemisphere.

Prefers cold antarctic and subantartic waters, but stragglers roam N to the Tropic of Capricorn. Has been reported rarely in waters near FIJI, the COOK IS., and once near the MARQUESAS.
Other names: Cape Pigeon, Pintado Petrel.

BLACK-WINGED PETREL *Pterodroma nigripennis* PLATE 5

Appearance: (12;31) A small petrel with bluish gray crown, nape, sides of neck, partial collar, and back. Extent of collar below variable. Black, open M across upperwings and rump. Black patch around eye. Forehead and underparts white. Tail gray with dark tip, outer feathers pale. Wing lining white with distinct diagonal bar proximal to wrist.

Habits: A bird of open seas and offshore waters near its breeding grounds. Nests in burrows, comes and goes at night. Flight rapid and bounding, with high arcs interspersed with fast, deep wingbeats. Not a ship-follower.

Voice: A loud, monotonously repeated *peet.*

Identification: Paler blue-gray above than other gadfly-petrels, with no contrast between crown and back. Individuals with pronounced collars distinctive, but compare Collared Petrel. Bonin Petrel has dark hindcrown, bold carpal patch. Cook's Petrel also has pale crown, but much whiter, almost unmarked underwing.

Occurrence: Breeds on islands of subtropical sw. Pacific and possibly RAPA (Tubuai Is.). Disperses northward into c. tropical Pacific where common April-October. Recorded from the HAWAIIAN IS., KIRIBATI, the MARSHALL IS., FIJI, the COOK IS., the SOCIETY IS., and the MARQUESAS.

Reference: Klapste, J. 1981. Notes on the Black-winged Petrel *Pterodroma nigripennis. Australian Bird Watcher* 9:35-40.

WHITE-NAPED (WHITE-NECKED) PETREL PLATE 4
Pterodroma cervicalis

Appearance: (17;43) Similar to Juan Fernandez Petrel, but has black crown separated from gray back by white collar. Tail light gray. Underwing white with thin dark leading edge, narrow diagonal bar.

Habits: At sea, like those of Juan Fernandez Petrel.

Identification: White hindneck diagnostic. Juan Fernandez Petrel has lighter crown, no white collar, darker gray tail, and less distinct or no diagonal bar on underwing. Hawaiian (Dark-rumped) Petrel uniformly dark above, with bolder underwing markings.

Occurrence: Breeds in the Kermadec Is. (New Zealand). Disperses commonly northward into w. and c. Pacific May-November. Recorded from the HAWAIIAN IS., KIRIBATI, FIJI, the COOK IS., and possibly the MARSHALL IS.

MOTTLED PETREL *Pterodroma inexpectata* PLATE 5

Appearance: (14;35) A distinctive, medium-sized, mottled gray and white petrel with open M pattern on upperwing, a striking black diagonal bar on underwing, and gray belly patch. Black markings around eye. Legs flesh-colored.

Habits: A bird of the open ocean. Flight dashing, with high arcs and glides alternating with rapid wingbeats. Flight in tropical waters often directional and rapid. Usually solitary or in pairs at sea. Does not follow ships.

Identification: Bold underwing pattern and belly patch make this species one of the more distinctive gadfly-petrels, but compare dark-phase Collared Petrel.

Occurrence: Breeds in New Zealand and nearby islands, winters in subarctic N. Pacific. A transequatorial migrant, passing rapidly through the tropics March-May and October-November. Regularly seen near the HAWAIIAN IS., and in e. KIRIBATI (Phoenix Is., Line Is.). Should be looked for in Fiji, Samoa, and Tonga.

Reference: Ainley, D. G., and B. Manolis. 1979. Occurrence and distribution of the Mottled Petrel. *W. Birds* 10:113-23.

Other names: Scaled Petrel, Peale's Petrel.

BONIN PETREL *Pterodroma hypoleuca* PLATE 5

Appearance: (12;31) A small petrel, bluish gray above and white below, with gray extending down side of neck to partial collar. A brownish M mark across wings and rump above. Hindcrown and area around eye black, forehead white. Tail all dark. Wing lining white with black diagonal bar and oval patch distal to wrist.

Habits: A bird of open seas and offshore waters near its breeding grounds. Nests in burrows on oceanic islands and atolls. Nocturnal and noisy on breeding grounds. Flight is rapid and erratic, with high arcs followed by fast, deep wingbeats. Not attracted to ships.

Voice: On breeding grounds a variety of moans, squeals, and growls, including a raucous *kuk-u-er*, a high-pitched chatter, and a low *churr*.

Identification: The similar Black-winged Petrel lacks contrasting hindcrown and distal black patch on underwing, is bluer gray above. Cook's Petrel also lacks contrasting crown, has mostly white underwing and pale outer tail feathers. Stejneger's Petrel very similar to Bonin above, but underwing as in Cook's Petrel.

Occurrence: Breeds abundantly on the Ogasawara (Bonin), Volcano, and NW HAWAIIAN IS. Disperses through n. c. Pacific, S to the MARIANA IS., the MARSHALL IS., and KIRIBATI (near Phoenix Is., Line Is.).

Reference: Grant, G. S., J. Warham, T. N. Pettit, and G. C. Whittow. 1983. Reproductive behavior and vocalizations of the Bonin Petrel. *Wilson Bull.* 96:522-39.

STEJNEGER'S PETREL   *Pterodroma longirostris*   PLATE 5

Appearance: (11½;29) A small, gray and white petrel with distinct black cap contrasting with gray back, and underwings that look all white in the field. Dark brown, indistinct M pattern on upperwings and rump. Tail all dark. Forehead and underparts white. Feather wear may reduce contrast between cap and back.
Habits: A bird of open ocean and offshore waters. Flight bounding and wheeling, with steeply banked arcs interspersed with rapid wingbeats.
Identification: Cook's Petrel, the only other petrel with entirely white underwings, lacks contrasting black cap, has more distinct M pattern on upperparts, and white outer tail feathers. Collared Petrel has less contrasting black cap, much less white on underwing, with distinct black diagonal bar across inner lining.
Occurrence: Breeds on Juan Fernandez Is. (Chile). Disperses March-September across tropical waters to temperate Pacific. Recorded at sea near the HAWAIIAN IS., the MARSHALL IS., and KIRIBATI (Phoenix Is., Line Is.).

COLLARED PETREL   *Pterodroma brevipes*   PLATE 5

Appearance: (12;31) A small, gray and white petrel with black hood and varying amounts of slate gray on belly. Black of crown shades gradually into gray of upper back. Upperparts with dark M pattern across upperwings and rump, dark tail. Forehead and throat white. Rest of underparts highly variable. Palest extreme has diffuse broken breast band of slate gray, lower underparts white. Dark extreme entirely gray from upper breast to undertail coverts. Underwing with white lining marked anteriorly with bold black border and diagonal bar, flight feathers dark. Underwing of dark morph has white replaced with pale gray.
Habits: A bird of the open seas and offshore waters near its breeding grounds. Flight erratic, with banking and rolling interspersed with flapping and gliding. Does not follow ships.
Voice: Call in flight over breeding grounds a harsh *kek-kek-kek* (Imber 1985; see Reference under Family Procellariidae introduction).
Identification: Can be distinguished from related petrels by extensive black hood forming (or partially forming) a neck collar. Black-winged Petrel may have partial collar but gray crown, nearly same color as back. Stejneger's Petrel has dark cap but underwing almost entirely

white, lacking a distinctive diagonal bar. Darkest phase Collared could be confused with much larger Mottled Petrel, which has gray smudge on belly, but lacks a black hood and collar.

Occurrence: Breeds off Australian coast to New Caledonia, Vanuatu, FIJI, and TAU (A. Samoa). Disperses into c. Pacific, with records for KIRIBATI (Phoenix Is., Line Is.), the COOK IS., and the TUA-MOTU ARCH.

Other names: Gould's Petrel.

Note: Sometimes considered conspecific with White-winged Petrel (*P. leucoptera*).

COOK'S PETREL *Pterodroma cookii*   PLATE 5

Appearance: (10½;27) A small petrel, gray above, mostly white below, with white outer tail feathers (tail looks white with dark center). Upperparts show distinct dark M pattern and eye patch with crown same color as back. Underwing looks all white in the field.

Habits: Highly pelagic. Flight rapid and erratic, with rolling or pendulum motion like that of a bat or large moth, and occasional high arcs.

Identification: Distinguished from all similar petrels by combination of mostly white underwings without noticeable diagonal bar, white outer tail feathers, no contrasting cap, and very distinct M pattern on upperwing. Stejneger's Petrel has similar underwing pattern, but has contrasting dark crown and all-dark tail. Black-winged Petrel also lacks contrasting crown, but has much broader dark trailing edge to underwing and bold black diagonal bar across wing lining.

Occurrence: Breeds in New Zealand and possibly on the Juan Fernandez Is. (Chile). Dispersal not well known. Apparently a transequatorial migrant passing through the tropics June-August. Reported near the HAWAIIAN IS. and KIRIBATI (Phoenix Is., Line Is.).

Other name: Blue-footed Petrel.

PHOENIX PETREL *Pterodroma alba*   PLATE 3

Appearance: (14;35) Very similar to Tahiti Petrel, but slimmer, with indistinct white patch on throat and less distinct border between brown breast and white belly.

Habits: A bird of open oceans and offshore waters near breeding grounds. Nests on the ground on small islands and atolls. Flight light and graceful, with banking arcs and deep, leisurely wingbeats. Does not follow ships.

Voice: At breeding colonies utters a "strange, shrill warble that ends with a low bubbling gurgling sound" (W. Donaghho in Murphy et al. 1954).

Identification: Tahiti Petrel slightly larger and stockier, with bigger bill, no white in throat. White throat patch of Phoenix Petrel highly variable, sometimes very difficult to discern in flying birds. Intermediate-phase Kermadec and Herald Petrels may suggest Phoenix Petrel, but have white markings on underwing.

Occurrence: Endemic to the tropical Pacific. Breeds in the LINE IS., the PHOENIX IS., TONGA, the MARQUESAS, the TUAMOTU ARCH., and the PITCAIRN IS. (Ducie, Oeno, Henderson, Pitcairn). Disperses to waters near breeding grounds and northward. Has been recorded from waters near the HAWAIIAN IS., SAMOA, the COOK IS. (probably), and the SOCIETY IS.

HERALD PETREL *Pterodroma heraldica* PLATES 2, 4

Appearance: (15;38) A medium-sized petrel of highly variable color. Underwing of most dark with white patch at base of primaries, from which a white line extends along secondaries. Pale morph dusky grayish brown above and white below with diffuse, light gray breast band. Crown and back grayish brown. Dark M pattern across mantle. Legs white, tipped black. Dark morph upperparts darker, obliterating M pattern, underparts dark brown, lighter on throat. Underwing may resemble that of paler birds or have much reduced white patch. Legs black. Intermediates and birds with randomly scattered white feathers often seen.

Habits: A bird of open seas and offshore waters near breeding grounds. Visits nesting colony during daylight. Nests on surface of ground. Tame and confiding on land. May be lured by imitations of call. Flight with loose, deep wingbeats, steeply banked arcs, and long glides to water surface. May follow ships.

Voice: A series of squeaky whistles, cooing or moaning notes, and a ternlike chatter at nesting colony.

Identification: Light morph of this species differs from pale Kermadec Petrel by having M pattern on upperwings and darker head. Dark phase similar to, and often indistinguishable from, dark Kermadec Petrel, but usually shows more white along base of secondaries below and always has dark legs (sometimes pale in dark Kermadec). Dark morphs with dark underwing resemble dark shearwaters, but note shorter bill, different flight.

Occurrence: Breeds in the tropical Pacific at TONGA, RAROTONGA (Cook Is.), the MARQUESAS, the TUAMOTU ARCH., the GAMBIER IS., and the PITCAIRN IS. (Henderson, Oeno, Ducie). Disperses into adjacent waters, rarely N as far as the HAWAIIAN IS.

Note: The AOU Check-list combines this species with *P. arminjoniana* of the S. Atlantic.

HAWAIIAN (DARK-RUMPED) PETREL PLATE 3

Pterodroma phaeopygia

Appearance: (17;43) A large petrel with short, wedge-shaped tail. Upperparts very dark (palest on central back) with white V at base of uppertail coverts (sometimes not visible). Forehead and underparts white. Underwing white with black margins, diagonal bar, and broad carpal patch.

Habits: A bird of open seas. Breeds in burrows in barren areas high on mountain slopes. Comes and goes from colonies at night. Flight strong, with broad, high arcs and glides, and bounding up-and-down motion.

Voice: Varied calls given in flight near nesting colony include yaps, barks, and squeals. One often-heard call is a low-pitched gurgling *goo-oooo-gouih-gouih-gooooo-o*, etc. The call inspired the Hawaiian name '*ua'u*.

Identification: Darker above than Juan Fernandez and White-naped (White-necked) petrels, without M mark across mantle. Black crown extends onto sides of neck forming partial collar, and underwing pattern has more obvious diagonal bar and carpal patch. Newell's (Townsend's) Shearwater also mainly black above and white below but has different shape and flight, black forehead, no carpal patch.

Occurrence: Breeds on the Galapagos Is. and the HAWAIIAN IS. (Maui, Lanai, Hawaii, possibly Molokai, Kauai). Largest colony in Haleakala Crater, Maui. Rare, declining; an Endangered Species. Dispersal little known. Rarely seen at sea in Hawaiian waters; more common to the SE and between the LINE IS. (Kiribati) and the MARQUESAS.

Reference: Simons, T. R. 1985. Biology and behavior of the Endangered Hawaiian Dark-rumped Petrel. *Condor* 87:229-45.

Note: This species is called Dark-rumped Petrel in most literature on Hawaiian birds and in the 1983 AOU Check-list. Current seabird guides (Harrison 1983; Löfgren 1984; Tuck and Heinzel 1978) all use Hawaiian Petrel, as do several world checklists. Because many species in this genus have dark rumps, we prefer the geographical designation.

KERMADEC PETREL *Pterodroma neglecta* PLATES 2, 4

Appearance: (15;38) A variably colored, medium-sized petrel. In all plumages underwing dark with white bases to primaries. Primary shafts and inner webs show white on upperwing (hard to see). Mantle and tail brown. Light extreme has white underparts, dusky gray breast band, and mostly white head with dark eye patch. Dark extreme sooty brown throughout with white feathers on forehead and throat. Intermediates often seen. Legs usually flesh-colored, but may be all dark.

Habits: Mainly pelagic, flight usually low to water and unhurried, with loose, deep wingbeats and long glides. In strong winds, flight more like that of other gadfly-petrels. Not a ship-follower. Makes daylight visits to breeding colonies.

Voice: On breeding grounds a long descending *ow* followed by a series of *coo*s.

Identification: Complicated by individual variation and similarity to other gadfly-petrels, but white primary shafts above diagnostic, if they can be seen. Dark phase not reliably distinguishable at sea from dark Herald Petrel, which usually has wholly dark face, paler secondary underwing coverts. Light morphs have paler head, more uniformly dark upperwing than light Herald Petrels, and show strongly contrasting dark eye patch. Solander's Petrel similar to dark-phase Kermadec but lacks white primary shafts on upperwing, usually has grayer body plumage, less white on face, and dark legs. Murphy's Petrel has all-dark wings above and below.

Occurrence: Breeds across S. Pacific from Lord Howe I., to islands off Chile, including the TUBUAI IS., the TUAMOTU ARCH., and the PITCAIRN IS. (Henderson, Oeno, Ducie). Disperses rarely N to the HAWAIIAN IS., W to the CAROLINE IS. Present year-round in c. tropical Pacific, with peak numbers November-January.

JUAN FERNANDEZ PETREL   *Pterodroma externa*   PLATE 3

Appearance: (17;43) A large petrel, dark above, white below, with wedge-shaped tail. Crown, wings, and tail dark gray (nearly black). Dark, open M pattern across mantle. Back light gray with mottling. Forehead and entire underparts including undertail coverts and underwing white. Small black bar at bend of wing from below.

Habits: A bird of open tropical seas. Flight strong, with high, wheeling arcs and glides interspersed with loose, slow wingbeats. Wings often bowed and bent at wrists. Does not normally follow ships.

Identification: White-necked Petrel has black cap set off by white collar, grayer tail, and short diagonal bar on underwing. Hawaiian (Dark-rumped) Petrel uniformly darker above, lacks M pattern on upperwings, has more dark color on side of neck, and more obvious diagonal bar, larger wrist patch on underwing. Buller's Shearwater has similar color pattern but different shape and behavior.

Occurrence: Breeds on the Juan Fernandez Is. (Chile). Disperses northward into c. Pacific where common May-November. Recorded from the HAWAIIAN IS., the MARSHALL IS., and KIRIBATI (Gilberts, Phoenix Is., Line Is.).

Note: The 1983 AOU Check-list lists this form as a subspecies of White-naped (White-necked) Petrel.

MURPHY'S PETREL   *Pterodroma ultima*   PLATE 2

Appearance: (16;41) A medium-sized, brownish gray petrel with variable amounts of white in face and throat. Top of head slightly darker than back, secondaries and coverts gray, but otherwise little contrast in all-dark upperparts. Underwing usually looks entirely dark at sea, but bases of primaries silvery. Legs flesh-colored with distal part of toes black.

Habits: A bird of open tropical seas, seen near land only at breeding grounds. Flight rapid and vigorous, with broad, wheeling arcs. Not a ship-follower.

Identification: The Great-winged Petrel (*P. macroptera*) of temperate waters is similar but larger and stockier, with dark legs. Solander's Petrel and dark and intermediate morph Kermadec and Herald Petrels also similar but slimmer, with white underwing markings. Beware dark extreme Herald Petrel, which has very little white at base of primaries.

Occurrence: Endemic to the c. tropical Pacific. Breeds in the TUBUAI IS., the TUAMOTU ARCH., and the PITCAIRN IS. (Henderson, Oeno, Ducie). Visits the SOCIETY IS. Disperses mostly to nearby seas but rarely wanders as far as the NW HAWAIIAN IS.

[**SOLANDER'S PETREL**   *Pterodroma solandri*   See Appendix A]

[**GREAT-WINGED PETREL**   *Pterodroma macroptera*   See Appendix A]

FAMILY HYDROBATIDAE: STORM-PETRELS

STORM-PETRELS are small, mostly black-and-white seabirds that breed in burrows on remote islands and disperse over the world's oceans. They are a very difficult group for the birder. Considerable experience may be needed before accurate identifications can be made, based as they must be on subtle differences in color pattern and behavior. In the tropical Pacific, storm-petrels can be grouped according to body color as follows: uniformly dark (Tristram's, dark morph Polynesian, Matsudaira's); dark above, light below (light morph Polynesian, White-bellied, Black-bellied); dark with white on rump (Band-rumped, Leach's, Wilson's); and all or partly gray (White-faced, Fork-tailed). The observer should note wing position in flight and during feeding, and the manner of flight (straight, zigzag, etc.). Unfortunately, many of the details needed to confirm identification are hard to see under field conditions.

Reference: Naveen, R. 1981-82. Storm-Petrels of the world: An introductory guide to their field identification. *Birding* 13:216-29; 14:10-15, 56-62, 140-47.

WILSON'S STORM-PETREL   *Oceanites oceanicus*   PLATE 6

Appearance: (7½;19) A small, dainty, sooty brown storm-petrel with distinct large white rump patch that encircles the tail base to underside. Indistinct pale diagonal band on upperwing. Feet black with yellow webs. Wings broad, rounded. Tail square or rounded, never forked. Feet extend beyond tail in flight.

Habits: Pelagic, with batlike or swallowlike flight. Wingbeats are shallow and rapid. When feeding, hovers over the water with feet treading the surface and wings held high above the horizontal. Follows ships and strongly attracted to chum.

Identification: Similar in color pattern to Band-rumped and Leach's Storm-Petrel, but smaller and more delicate than either, with different feeding behavior. Wilson's patters on surface much more than Leach's, which only rarely does so. Band-rumped patters, but holds wings at horizontal plane, not in high V like Wilson's. Flight of Wilson's is fluttery with less gliding than Leach's or Band-rumped. Wings of Wilson's are rounded without the sharp angle at the wrist characteristic of Leach's. Wilson's white rump is more conspicuous than in other white-rumped species because rest of upperparts are subtly darker, and white extends further onto undertail coverts. If visible, yellow webs of feet diagnostic. Also note feet projecting beyond tail in level flight.

Occurrence: Breeds in the Antarctic and Subantarctic. Migrates to the Northern Hemisphere, but rare in tropical Pacific. Recorded near the MARSHALL IS. and the PHOENIX IS. (Kiribati) but probably more widespread. Much less frequent than Band-rumped or Leach's Storm-Petrel.

Reference: Huber, L. N. 1971. Notes on the migration of the Wilson's Storm Petrel *Oceanites oceanicus* near Eniwetok Atoll, W. Pacific Ocean. *Notornis* 18:38-42.

WHITE-FACED STORM-PETREL *Pelagodroma marina*   PLATE 6

Appearance: (8;20) A distinctive storm-petrel, mostly gray above, white below, with striking head pattern. Crown and line through eye dark slate. Forehead and superciliary line white. Rump pale gray. Tail and flight feathers dark brown (looks black in field). Underwing white with dark trailing edge. Feet black with yellow webs. In flight feet extend well beyond square tail.

Habits: Pelagic. Distinctive dancing flight with body moving from side to side. Does not follow ships.

Identification: Light-phase Polynesian Storm-Petrel somewhat similar, but note gray back and white eye stripe of White-faced. Some White-faced have complete breast bands, like Polynesian, but bands are gray, not black, and much narrower. Color pattern reminiscent of non-breeding phalaropes, but note very different phalarope shape and direct, quick shorebird flight.

Occurrence: Breeds in the Atlantic and on small islands around Australia and New Zealand. Disperses across c. tropical Pacific to the Galapagos Is., but actual records few. Recorded near the LINE IS. (Kiribati), but probably passes through French Polynesia and the Cook Is. May-September.

Other name: Frigate Petrel.

WHITE-BELLIED STORM-PETREL *Fregetta grallaria* PLATE 6

Appearance: (8;20) A dark slate gray petrel with white belly and rump. Breast border concave. Feathers of back edged with white, giving a scalloped appearance, but edges may wear away. Underwing white with broad black margins. Usually no white in chin.

Habits: Pelagic. Has distinctive splashing flight: smacks the surface with the breast every few wingbeats, then uses feet to spring forward. Has erratic but direct flight, with body swinging back and forth. May accompany ships.

Voice: On the breeding grounds a high-pitched piping.

Identification: Distinguished from Black-bellied Storm-Petrel by white belly, black (rather than whitish) throat, scaled upperparts, and concave border of lower breast. Feather wear reduces usefulness of some characters, i.e. throat may look pale, upperparts may look darker. White-bellied tends to glide more, hover less than Black-bellied. Variations occur in both species that may look like the other, but no "white-bellied" Black-bellies have been recorded in the tropical Pacific. From above, both species look like Wilson's and Polynesian Storm-Petrel. The latter has narrower white rump band, forked (not square) tail, and very obvious white throat.

Occurrence: Breeds on islands of temperate s. oceans including RAPA (Tubuai Is.). Dispersal not well known, but recorded from SAMOA, the COOK IS., the SOCIETY IS., and the MARQUESAS.

BLACK-BELLIED STORM-PETREL *Fregetta tropica* PLATE 6

Appearance: (8;20) A dark slate gray petrel with white rump and underparts, the latter bisected by a broad gray central line. Underwing white with broad black margins. Throat all-dark in fresh plumage, but worn birds appear white-throated.

Habits: Very similar to White-bellied Storm-Petrel, but hovers more, glides less.

Identification: See White-bellied Storm-Petrel.

Occurrence: A circumpolar breeder on subantarctic islands. Moves northward to the tropics May-September. Has been recorded from SAMOA and the MARQUESAS, but probably occurs in low numbers all across tropical S. Pacific.

POLYNESIAN STORM-PETREL *Nesofregetta fuliginosa* PLATE 6

Appearance: (10;25) A large storm-petrel with deeply forked tail. Pale morph black above with narrow white rump patch, white below with black breast band. Underwing white with broad dark margins. Dark morph is entirely black except for paler upperwing coverts. Intermediates between dark and light phase show variable amounts of white below, streaked with black. Wings broad, rounded, with no angle at wrist. Legs relatively long, feet very large.

Habits: Pelagic. Nests in burrows on mountaintops or atolls. Erratic zig-zag flight with characteristic kick-and-glide pattern: uses feet to push off, glides 20-30 seconds on outstretched wings, then kicks off again, changing direction. Sometimes accompanies ships.

Identification: Kick-off in flight much more forceful than that of White-faced Storm-Petrel. Note also darker upperparts, dark face of Polynesian. Intermediate morphs can resemble Black-bellied, but note very different flight patterns. All-dark morph very similar to Tristram's (Sooty) Storm-Petrel, but larger, with broader wings held straight out and, again, distinctive bounding flight.

Occurrence: Endemic to the tropical Pacific. Breeds in Vanuatu, FIJI, KIRIBATI (Phoenix Is., Line Is.), SAMOA, RAPA (Tubuai Is.), the MARQUESAS, and the GAMBIER IS. Disperses to intervening island groups and N to the MARSHALL IS. Morphs unevenly distributed: dark morphs only in Samoa, all gradations in the Phoenix Is., some dark flecking below in some birds of the Line Is.; elsewhere only pale morphs.

Other names: Now that the "Samoan Storm-Petrel" and the "White-throated Storm-Petrel" are known to be color morphs of a single species, a new name, appropriate for both, is needed. This is the only storm-petrel that breeds widely in Polynesia and is the one most likely to be seen there.

FORK-TAILED STORM-PETREL *Oceanodroma furcata*

This distinctive pearly gray storm-petrel (8½;22) breeds on islands rimming the N. Pacific. Disperses to temperate seas, stragglers rarely reaching the tropics near the HAWAIIAN IS. No other all-gray storm-petrel is found in the tropical Pacific. For full account, see N. American field guides.

LEACH'S STORM-PETREL   *Oceanodroma leucorhoa*   PLATE 6

Appearance: (8;20) A sooty brown storm-petrel with white rump patch and forked tail. White rump patch divided by dark line and may show dark shaft streaks (thus appearing smudgy). Upperwing coverts form a light diagonal bar. Wings long, pointed, bent at wrists. Dark-rumped morphs not found in area of this guide.

Habits: Highly pelagic and not attracted to ships. Flight ternlike, buoyant and erratic. Bounds and leaps from side to side, rising, falling, changing speed and direction. Rarely patters feet or hovers for long in one place.

Identification: Leach's forked tail often difficult to discern at sea. Best distinguished from Wilson's and Band-rumped Storm-Petrels by less clean-cut, slightly triangular rump patch divided down the center, erratic bounding flight with deep ternlike wingbeats, and pointed, angled wings.

Occurrence: Breeds on coastal islands of N. Atlantic and N. Pacific. Disperses to tropics November-March. Common throughout c. Pacific to 15° S. Recorded near the HAWAIIAN IS., the MARIANAS, the MARSHALL IS., KIRIBATI (Phoenix Is., Line Is.), and the MARQUESAS.

BAND-RUMPED STORM-PETREL   *Oceanodroma castro*   PLATE 6

Appearance: (9;23) A sooty brown storm-petrel with broad, undivided, sharply defined white rump extending slightly onto undertail coverts. Tail square or slightly forked. Secondary coverts of upperwing form faint, light brown bar.

Habits: Highly pelagic and shy, fleeing the approach of boats. Flight a steady banking zigzag, with quick wingbeats interspersed with glides on horizontal wings, rather like that of a shearwater. May hop or dance on the surface, but does not normally patter its feet. When hovering, holds wings straight out, not in a V. Apparently nests in high mountains, but nests as yet undiscovered in the Hawaiian Is. Comes and goes from nesting islands at night.

Voice: A high squeak, like the sound of rubbing a wet finger over smooth glass. Uttered in nocturnal flight over land.

Identification: In many respects intermediate between Leach's and Wilson's, and difficult to distinguish at sea. Note Band-rump's less prominent wing bars and short stubby bill. Rump band narrower than that of Wilson's (less than length of tail), more even and clean-cut than that of Leach's, without central dividing line. Legs do not project beyond tail. Wing shape more rounded than in Leach's, but with sharper wrist angle than in Wilson's. Tail not so deeply forked as in Leach's, but not as rounded as that of Wilson's. Flight lacks vertical bounding of Leach's, is less erratic and fluttery than Wilson's.

Occurrence: Breeds at scattered localities in tropical Atlantic and Pacific, including the HAWAIIAN IS. (Kauai, possibly elsewhere). Disperses to open tropical seas. Recorded from the MARSHALL IS. and the PHOENIX IS. (Kiribati).

Other names: Harcourt's Storm-Petrel, Madeiran Storm-Petrel.

TRISTRAM'S (SOOTY) STORM-PETREL PLATE 6
Oceanodroma tristrami

Appearance: (10;25) A large, grayish brown storm-petrel with long, forked tail. Secondary coverts form prominent diagonal bars on upperwings. Rump paler than upper back, but not as pale as wing bars.

Habits: Flight petrel-like, with long glides. Occasionally patters feet on surface. May alight briefly. Rarely, if ever, follows ships.

Voice: Nocturnal vocalization on breeding grounds a series of two or more dovelike *coo*s, successively shorter as the series ends: *ooo-ooo-oo-oo-u-u-u*.

Identification: Very similar to Matsudaira's Storm-Petrel and often indistinguishable. Tristram's is grayer, less brown, with paler wing bars and contrastingly pale rump. The pale rump of Tristram's is usually more easily seen in the field than are the pale primary shafts of Matsudaira's. Thus any large storm-petrel in the w. tropical Pacific that looks all dark except for pale wing bars is probably Matsudaira's. Compare Bulwer's Petrel.

Occurrence: Nests during winter months in the Volcano and Izu Is. (Japan) and the NW HAWAIIAN IS. (Pearl and Hermes Reef, Laysan, French Frigate Shoals, Necker, Nihoa). Disperses to adjacent seas and possibly northward.

Reference: Rauzon, M. J., C. S. Harrison, and S. Conant. 1985. The status of the Sooty Storm-Petrel in Hawaii. *Wilson Bull.* 97:390-92.

Note: The 1983 AOU Check-list name, Sooty Storm-Petrel, is used for *O. tristrami* in most literature on Hawaiian birds. However, the same English name is used for *O. markhami* in most recent literature on South American birds and in several world checklists. Current references on the world's seabirds (Harrison 1983; Löfgren 1984; Tuck and Heinzel 1978) use Tristram's Storm-Petrel and Markham's Storm-Petrel respectively for these two species, and we believe that unambiguous course is best.

MATSUDAIRA'S STORM-PETREL PLATE 6
Oceanodroma matsudairae

Appearance: (10;25) A large, sooty brown storm-petrel with long, forked tail. Secondary coverts of upperwings form diagonal pale bars. Rump dark, not contrasting with back. Primary shafts white at base (inconspicuous).

Habits: Pelagic. Flapping and gliding flight, slower and less erratic than that of smaller storm-petrels. Feeds at the surface with wings held high above the horizontal. Follows ships.

Identification: Distinguished from Tristram's Storm-Petrel by brownish (rather than bluish) cast, dark rump, and pale shaft streaks of primaries, the last variable and very difficult to see at any distance.

Occurrence: Breeds only on Kita Iwojima (Volcano Is., Japan). Disperses mainly into the Indian Ocean, passing through w. MICRONESIA (recorded near Palau, the Marianas, and possibly between Pohnpei and Kosrae).

Reference: Aguon, C. F., and R. E. Beck, Jr. 1983. A Matsudaira's Storm-Petrel (*Oceanodroma matsudairae*) on Guam. *'Elepaio* 44:66.

ORDER PELECANIFORMES

FAMILY PHAETHONTIDAE: TROPICBIRDS

TROPICBIRDS are graceful, long-tailed, mostly white seabirds of tropical oceans. The three species, all known from the tropical Pacific, differ mainly in the color of bill and elongated tail feathers, and in the amount of black above.

WHITE-TAILED TROPICBIRD *Phaethon lepturus* PLATE 7

Appearance: (30;76) A small, slender tropicbird with long, white, flexible tail feathers. The mostly white plumage may be tinged peach in some individuals. A race that breeds on Christmas I. (Indian Ocean) is golden peach throughout. Bill yellow. Eyebrow stripe, diagonal bar on upperwing, and outermost primaries black. Immatures lack long tail streamers and are barred on the back.

Habits: Flight buoyant and acrobatic, particularly when birds soar on updrafts against cliff faces. At sea, they plunge to catch fish and squid. More often seen inland than other tropicbirds. Nests on cliff faces and in trees. May be seen over dense rain forest or in barren volcanic craters.

Voice: A sharp rasping scream and a guttural squawk.

Identification: More graceful and slender than other tropicbirds, with long white tail streamers and yellow bill. Red-tailed Tropicbird lacks black on upperwing. Immature has broader dorsal bars than young Red-billed Tropicbird, more black in outer primaries than Red-tailed, and is slimmer than either.

Occurrence: Pantropical, except easternmost Pacific. One of the most characteristic and conspicuous birds of the tropical w. and c. Pacific, particularly around high islands with exposed cliff faces. Breeds in virtually every island group covered by this guide. The Christmas I. (Indian Ocean) form (*P. l. fulva*) has supposedly straggled to the MARIANA IS. (Saipan, Rota), but the birds seen might represent variants in the local population.

RED-BILLED TROPICBIRD   *Phaethon aethereus*   FIGURE 13

Appearance: (40;102) A large, robust tropicbird with bright red bill, barred upperparts, and long, white tail streamers. Immature has yellow or orange bill, lacks tail streamers. Eye patches of juvenile connect across nape.

Habits: Flight lighter and more buoyant than that of Red-tailed Tropicbird, but not so graceful as that of White-tailed. Sometimes follows ships.

Identification: Adult's barred back distinctive, but sometimes not easily seen at a distance. Both adult and juvenile have much more black in outer primaries than other tropicbirds, the outer wing appearing all black with white trailing edge. Juvenile's complete black collar diagnostic. Dorsal barring finer than that of juvenile White-tailed, but like that of young Red-tailed (which, however, has much less black in outer primaries, no collar on hindneck, and often a black bill).

Occurrence: Breeds in tropical Atlantic, Indian, and e. Pacific Ocean and disperses widely. Very rare in area of this guide, with many records of immature birds questionable. May breed in the MARQUESAS (needs confirmation), has wandered to the HAWAIIAN IS. (Nihoa, Kauai) and JOHNSTON ATOLL; unconfirmed reports from Micronesia (19th century).

RED-TAILED TROPICBIRD   *Phaethon rubricauda*   PLATE 7

Appearance: (37;93) A robust, pigeonlike white bird, often with a pink suffusion to the plumage during the breeding season. Long, stiff central tail feathers and bill bright red. Conspicuous black eye stripe. Wings entirely white above, but may show small black spot at base of secondaries from below. Feet black. Juveniles finely barred on back,

FIGURE 13. Red-billed Tropicbird with Juveniles of All Tropicbirds for Comparison

lack tail streamers. Bill of immature varies from black to yellow, changing to orange and finally red.

Habits: Mated pairs have a characteristic hovering display flight with a rowing wing beat. Dives with half-folded wings to capture fish and squid. Nests on ground on atolls, or on coastal cliffs and offshore islets of high islands. More pelagic than other tropicbirds, often seen far from land.

Voice: A loud raucous squawk and ternlike screeches.

Identification: Red tail streamers and all-white upperparts diagnostic of adults. The "back-pedaling" display flight will identify this species at great distance when other details cannot be seen. Juveniles similar to young Red-billed Tropicbird, but differ in having outermost primaries mostly white with narrow black marks down centers and black eye patches not connected around nape.

Occurrence: Tropical Indian and Pacific oceans. Nests in the HAWAIIAN IS. (NW Is., Niihau, Kauai, Manana off Oahu, Lanai, Kahoolawe), the MARIANAS (Maug, Pagan), KIRIBATI (Phoenix Is., Line Is.), ROSE ATOLL (A. Samoa), FIJI, TONGA, the COOK IS., the TUAMOTU ARCH., the TUBUAI IS., and the PITCAIRN IS. Nonbreeding birds can be found anywhere in the area of this guide, but are rare to the southwest.

Reference: Fleet, R. R. 1974. The Red-tailed Tropicbird on Kure Atoll. *Ornithol. Monogr.*, no. 16.

FAMILY SULIDAE: Boobies and Gannets

BOOBIES are large seabirds that plunge from the air to capture prey. They often feed in large flocks and are much respected by Pacific islanders for guiding them to schools of fish. Boobies are frequent victims of frigatebird kleptoparasitism. Boobies even feed at night, often on squid. Around most island groups, these are the most familiar large seabirds. The ground-nesting species nest only where lack of predators allows, but the tree-nesting Red-footed Booby still maintains large colonies on heavily populated islands such as Oahu, and shows little fear of man. Gannets are similar to boobies but inhabit colder seas.

Reference: Nelson, J. B. 1978. *The Sulidae: Gannets and boobies.* Cambridge: Oxford Univ. Press.

MASKED BOOBY *Sula dactylatra* PLATE 7

Appearance: (32;81) Largest of the boobies. Adults white with blackish brown flight feathers (including tertials) and tail, black face mask. Bill, legs, and feet variable, gray in w. Pacific, olive or grayish green to the east. Eyes brown first year, then yellow. Juvenile like Brown Booby adult but has mottled plumage above with pale cervical collar, dark gray bill, more white below, and different underwing pattern.

Habits: Flight strong and steady, usually 7-10 m above water. Sometimes rests on water or floating debris. Nests on ground.

Voice: On breeding grounds female gives loud, deep honking calls, males thin high whistles.

Identification: Adults distinguished from white morph Red-footed

Booby by larger size and dark tail. Perched at a distance, Masked Booby shows much more black in folded wing. Juveniles differ from Brown Booby by light edges to mantle feathers, dark bill, and always white belly.

Occurrence: Tropical and subtropical oceans. Breeds on atolls and rocky offshore islets of the HAWAIIAN IS., TINIAN (Mariana Is.), the MARSHALL IS., KIRIBATI, FIJI, SAMOA, the PITCAIRN IS., and the TUAMOTU ARCH. (a few islands). Nonbreeding visitor to the MARQUESAS, the SOCIETY IS., and the COOK IS. May be seen at sea anywhere in the tropical Pacific.

Reference: Kepler, C. B. 1969. Breeding biology of the Blue-faced Booby, *Sula dactylatra personata*, on Green Island, Kure Atoll. *Publ. Nuttall Ornithol. Club*, no. 8.

Other names: White Booby, Blue-faced Booby.

BROWN BOOBY   *Sula leucogaster*   PLATE 7

Appearance: (30;76) A cleanly marked brown and white booby. Female larger than male. Bill and feet vary from green to yellow. Male's face blue, female's yellow-green. Juvenile shows pattern of adult but with white replaced by pale brown.

Habits: Often found near islands with steep rocky cliffs. Generally found closer to land than other boobies. Flight steady with interspersed glides, frequently close to the surface. Nests on ground, usually on uninhabited islands.

Voice: On breeding grounds female has harsh honking call, male a quiet hissing whistle.

Identification: Juvenile Masked Booby somewhat resembles adult Brown, but note its mottled back plumage and pale collar. Brown Booby has uniformly white underwing. In juvenile Masked, a dark bar divides the white into two bars. Juvenile Brown similar to smaller juvenile Red-footed, but the latter is uniformly brown below, not two-toned.

Occurrence: Pantropical. Visits or breeds in all island groups of the tropical Pacific.

Other names: Brown Gannet, White-bellied Booby.

RED-FOOTED BOOBY   *Sula sula*   PLATE 7

Appearance: (28;71) Smallest booby in the tropical Pacific. Juveniles all brown with gray feet and bill. Facial skin pink, bill blue, legs and feet bright red in adults. Four adult color morphs: white morph, all white with black flight feathers and peach-colored suffusion on head and neck; brown morph, all brown; white-tailed brown morph, brown with rump, belly, tail coverts, and tail white, head usually somewhat paler than in brown morph; and white-tailed, white-headed morph.

Habits: Bird of open sea, often far from land. Flight rapid, close to water, sometimes with skimming motion like shearwaters. Nests in bushes or trees on uninhabited islands or headlands of larger inhabited islands. Not as vulnerable to predators as ground-nesting seabirds.

Voice: Call a loud, deep *kruuck*.

Identification: Adults of all morphs differ from other boobies in having red feet, and all but brown morphs differ in having white tails. White morph differs from Masked Booby by narrower black rear edge to wing, not reaching the body. Shows much less black when perched. Juveniles lack the two-toned underparts of the similarly all-dark juvenile Brown Booby.

Occurrence: Pantropical. Found throughout the tropical Pacific, breeding in most island groups. White morph predominates in HAWAIIAN IS. and MICRONESIA, white-tailed brown morph more common in se. POLYNESIA.

Reference: Langham, N. P. 1984. Observations on the Red-footed Booby on Mabualau Island, Fiji. *Notornis* 31:23-29.

FAMILY PELECANIDAE: Pelicans

PELICANS are huge fish-eating birds with large bills and deep expandable throat pouches. They usually are seen in flocks. They reach the

FIGURE 14. Australian Pelican

tropical Pacific only on those rare occasions when their normal feeding areas are dry.

AUSTRALIAN PELICAN   *Pelecanus conspicillatus*   FIGURE 14
Appearance: (64;162) A huge, heavy-set, white bird with large pale pink bill and pouch, black tail, and black wings with bold white patches.
Habits: Flight slow and deep, with glides. Often soars in V formation or in long lines. Floats high on water. Feeds by aerial dives.
Occurrence: Breeds throughout Australia. During droughts disperses widely and in large numbers. Has reached PALAU and FIJI.

FAMILY PHALACROCORACIDAE:
CORMORANTS

CORMORANTS are medium-sized diving birds with long hook-tipped bills. Most species are black and white. Only one nests in the tropical Pacific. Cormorants swim low in the water with the bill held up at a 45° angle, and thus look different from ducks. They fly with neck outstretched.

PELAGIC CORMORANT   *Phalacrocorax pelagicus*

A small (26;66), all-dark cormorant, included here on the basis of a single record from LAYSAN (NW Hawaiian Is.). Breeds around N. Pacific coasts from Taiwan to California. Illustrated in WBSJ (1982), Harrison (1983), and N. American field guides.

LITTLE PIED CORMORANT   PLATE 7, FIGURE 15
Phalacrocorax melanoleucos

Appearance: (24;61) A black and white cormorant with a stubby, slightly hooked, yellow bill. Immature dark brown above.
Habits: Frequents lagoons, estuaries, and freshwater impoundments. Often sits in mangroves or on exposed objects such as buoys and pilings. Flight rapid with short glides. Does not usually fly in V or line formations as do many other cormorants. Nests in colonies.
Voice: Usually silent. A soft barking at rookery.
Identification: Longer-tailed and less hook-billed than many cormorants (see Figure 15), this species could be confused with Oriental Darter (see Appendix A).

FIGURE 15. Little Pied Cormorant in Flight

Occurrence: Found in coastal areas from Malaysia to the Solomons. Common resident of PALAU, straggler to the MARIANA IS.
Other name: Little Shag.

[FAMILY ANHINGIDAE: Darters]

[**ORIENTAL DARTER** *Anhinga melanogaster* See Appendix A]

FAMILY FREGATIDAE: Frigatebirds

FRIGATEBIRDS are large soaring birds of tropical seas. They are a familiar sight throughout the tropical Pacific, though sometimes an unwelcome one because in some places they are considered a bad omen. They are very skilled in the air, and soar for hours on updrafts with little perceptible movement of wings. The wings are long, narrow, and kinked at the wrist. The tail is very long and, though usually folded into one long point, can be opened scissorlike during aerial maneuvers. The bill is long and hooked at the tip, and is used to capture small prey at the water surface or on the beach. Frigatebirds are also notorious for their kleptoparasitic habits: they pursue and harass other seabirds, usually boobies, to force them to disgorge their catch. During the breeding season males often inflate their throat pouches, which then look like red balloons dangling from the throat. Frigatebirds nest mostly on remote predator-free islands, usually in the tops of small bushes or low vegetative ground cover. Adult frigatebirds of all species (five worldwide, two in tropical Pacific) are sexually dimorphic, and juveniles are also distinctive. The transitional stages can be rather confusing, but are fairly straightforward in the tropical Pacific species.

GREAT FRIGATEBIRD   *Fregata minor*   PLATE 1

Appearance: (37;93) Adult males black with iridescent purple/green mantle and bright red inflatable throat pouch (usually seen only near breeding grounds). Adult females black with diagonal buff bar on upperwing, white breast, and grayish throat. Immature black with white head and breast, variably tinged rusty in throat. Juvenile like that of Lesser Frigatebird, but usually with paler head.

Habits: Soars, often in flocks. Dives with great agility in pursuit of other seabirds. Comes inland to fresh water ponds to drink by swooping down and skimming bill on the surface.

Voice: Usually silent. At nest utters chuckling or gurgling noises.

Identification: See Lesser Frigatebird.

Occurrence: Widespread in tropical Pacific, Indian, and Atlantic oceans. Less common in w. Pacific than in c. and e. Pacific, but recorded throughout. Breeds from the MARSHALL IS. and FIJI N to the HAWAIIAN IS. and E throughout POLYNESIA, and at PALAU (Fanna, Helen I.).

LESSER FRIGATEBIRD   *Fregata ariel*   PLATE 1

Appearance: (30;76) Smaller than Great Frigatebird. Adult male allblack with white axillaries and flanks. Female black with white breast and black throat. Juvenile has dark chestnut or russet head and breast separated from white belly by a dark band. First the breast band disappears, then the head becomes dark. All sexes and plumages have white axillaries.

Habits: Like those of Great Frigatebird, but nests more often on the ground.

Voice: Usually silent. A deep chuckle at nest.

Identification: Adult males differ from Great Frigatebirds by white patches on sides under the wings. Adult female Lessers have black, not white, throats, but note that late subadult male Greats can display similar pattern. White axillaries of Lesser give white underparts (when present) a different shape from those of corresponding stage Great Frigatebirds, the white seeming to protrude onto the underwing. This feature less reliable for juveniles; some young Greats have white axillaries. Juvenile Lessers are darker russet on head than most tropical Pacific Great Frigatebirds, which usually show rusty only in throat and breast.

Occurrence: Pantropical, but breeding localities scattered. Less common than Great Frigatebird in the tropical Pacific generally, but locally abundant. Breeds in KIRIBATI (Phoenix Is., Line Is.), ROSE ATOLL (A. Samoa), FIJI, TONGA, the COOK IS. (Penrhyn, Suwarrow), the SOCIETY IS., the MARQUESAS, and the TUAMOTU ARCH. Disperses throughout tropical Pacific south of 15° N, but rare in Micronesia. Rare visitor to the NW HAWAIIAN IS. (Kure, French Frigate Shoals).

Reference: Sibley, F. C., and R. B. Clapp. 1967. Distribution and dispersal of central Pacific Lesser Frigatebirds, *Fregata ariel. Ibis* 109:328-37.

ORDER CICONIIFORMES

FAMILY ARDEIDAE: HERONS, EGRETS, AND BITTERNS

THESE are long-legged and long-necked birds that stalk their prey on land or more often by wading. They fly with the neck tucked back in an S-curve. The terms "heron" and "egret" have no precise meaning, but all egrets in the tropical Pacific are white, while herons are often not. Bitterns are characterized by camouflage plumage and a liking for grassy or reedy places, where they may freeze and point the bill skyward. Herons and egrets often have a distinct breeding plumage that includes decorative plumes. Colors of bill, legs, and bare facial skin may also change seasonally. Some species have a briefly held "high breeding" stage in which these colors intensify or change drastically. This family is distributed worldwide, with good representation in the tropical Pacific as residents and migratory visitors. Birders should become familiar with the more common resident species (Black-crowned Night-Heron and Cattle Egret in Hawaii, Pacific Reef-Heron elsewhere) so that less abundant species and rare visitors are more easily distinguished.

Reference: Hancock, J., and J. Kushlan. 1984. *The herons handbook.* New York: Harper & Row.

YELLOW BITTERN   *Ixobrychus sinensis*   PLATE 8

Appearance: (15;38) A small, thin, delicate-looking bittern. Adult male brown above, buff below with black crown, tail, and flight feathers. Conspicuous buff wing patches show in flight. Females and immatures duller with streaks, same wing pattern.

Habits: Shy and solitary. Flight slow and awkward. Forages in dense vegetation or at edge, often far from water. Feeds on insects and other small animals.

Voice: A harsh, scratchy *creek*, and a deep croak sometimes heard at night.

Identification: The only similar bird in Micronesia is the once-recorded Shrenck's Bittern, which is much darker above, with white spots on back, grayish wing patches, and paler flight feathers, all of which produce a less contrasting dorsal pattern.

Occurrence: Resident from India and e. Asia to New Guinea including w. MICRONESIA (Palau, Yap, Marianas, Truk). Fairly common.

Other names: Chinese Least Bittern, Chinese Little Bittern.

SCHRENCK'S BITTERN *Ixobrychus eurhythmus*

A small (16;41) thin bittern with dark chestnut upperparts. Similar to Yellow Bittern but wings less contrasting. Known in the tropical Pacific from three immature specimens taken in PALAU in 1931. Normal range SE. Asia and E. Indies. For illustration, see WBSJ (1982) or Flint et al. (1984).

BLACK BITTERN *Ixobrychus flavicollis*

A slender, long-necked, dark bittern as large (24;61) as a night-heron. Black (male) or brown (female and immature) with buffy yellow neck patches and buff streaks on breast. Known in the tropical Pacific from a single female taken on GUAM in 1900. Found from SE. Asia to Australia and Solomon Is. Illustrated in King and Dickinson (1975), WBSJ (1982), and Pizzey (1980). Sometimes placed in the genus *Dupetor*.

GREAT BLUE HERON *Ardea herodias*

A huge (46;117) gray heron with yellow bill and black occipital plumes. Flies with slow, deep wingbeats. A N. American species that has wandered a few times to the HAWAIIAN IS. (Kauai, Oahu, Maui, Hawaii). For full account and illustrations, consult N. American field guides.

GRAY HERON *Ardea cinerea*

Similar to the Great Blue Heron, this large bird is a rare winter straggler to w. MICRONESIA (Saipan, possibly Palau). Best identified by its large size, gray plumage, and black streak behind eye. For full accounts and illustrations, consult Eurasian field guides.

WHITE-FACED HERON *Ardea novaehollandiae*

A small (26;66), bluish gray heron with a white mask and brownish breast. More delicate than Pacific Reef-Heron. Included here on the basis of single records for FIJI and NIUE. Widespread in Australasia. For full account and illustration, see Australian or New Zealand field guides.

GREAT EGRET   *Casmerodius albus*

The largest (39;99) white heron to be found in the tropical Pacific, included on the basis of a few records from the HAWAIIAN IS. (Oahu, Maui). Similar to Intermediate Egret. Found virtually worldwide. Discussed fully and illustrated in many other guides.

INTERMEDIATE EGRET   *Egretta intermedia*   PLATE 8

Appearance: (28;71) A white egret with black legs and feet, yellow bill and facial skin. Bill may have brown tip. Neck long, with graceful S-curve.

Habits: Prefers freshwater and grassland habitats. Forages alone, in pairs, or occasionally in flocks. Flight slower than that of Cattle Egret.

Identification: Larger than black-billed Little Egret, but shaped more like it than like stocky Cattle Egret, which has similar color pattern. Note long graceful neck of Intermediate Egret. Great Egret, not yet recorded in Micronesia, is similar but larger, with a decided kink in its long neck, and a proportionately longer bill.

Occurrence: Africa to e. Asia and Australia. Uncommon winter visitor to w. MICRONESIA (Palau, Yap, Marianas, Truk).

Other names: Plumed Egret, Lesser Egret, Median Egret.

LITTLE EGRET   *Egretta garzetta*   PLATE 8

Appearance: (24;61) A delicate white egret with black bill and legs in all plumages. Color of lores and feet (toes) variable among several populations. Birds from e. Asia have greenish gray lores and yellow feet. Australian birds have yellow lores and black feet with yellow soles. Breeding birds have two long ribbonlike plumes on back of head.

Habits: May flock with Cattle Egrets, but more often seen as a solitary bird along shores or on tidal flats.

Identification: See Snowy Egret. Little Egrets in Micronesia during the n. winter probably come from ne. Asia; those present in the summer months may be of Australian origin. Both can be readily distinguished from Snowy Egret. Little Egrets are slimmer, more delicate than Cattle Egrets, which, like larger white herons and egrets, have yellow bills.

Occurrence: Found throughout much of the Eastern Hemisphere. An uncommon visitor to w. MICRONESIA (Palau, Yap, Saipan) throughout the year.

SNOWY EGRET   *Egretta thula*   PLATE 8

Appearance: (24;61) A trim white egret with black bill and legs, bright
yellow lores and feet (toes). Breeding adults have many plumes on back
of head and long recurved scapular plumes. Immatures and some
adults have a yellow stripe up back of otherwise dark legs.

Identification: Easily distinguished from similar-sized Cattle Egret by
black bill, black legs combination. Little Egret (which see) has often
been considered indistinguishable from Snowy, but this is not so in the
tropical Pacific. Snowy Egrets always have strongly contrasting golden
yellow lores and "golden slippers," both of which are apparent at considerable distance. Eurasian Little Egrets have pale yellow feet, but
their lores are not sharply set off from the base of the bill. Australian
ones have bright yellow lores like a Snowy's, but only the soles of the
feet are pale, and the feet look black in the field. The only Little Egrets
that could not readily be distinguished from Snowies are sedentary Indian Ocean forms.

Occurrence: N. and S. America. Rare straggler to the HAWAIIAN IS.
(Oahu, Maui, Hawaii), and ROSE ATOLL (A. Samoa).

Reference: Scott, J. M., R. Pyle, and R. Coleman. 1983. Records of small
white egrets in Hawaii and Samoa with notes on identification. *'Elepaio*
43:79-82.

PACIFIC REEF-HERON   *Egretta sacra*   PLATE 8

Appearance: (23;58) A small heron with three color phases: slate gray
with white chin, dark gray bill, and greenish yellow legs; white with yellow bill and yellowish green legs; and, rarely, white variably mottled
with slate gray. Bill relatively heavy, legs short, imparting a distinctive,
chunky profile.

Habits: Forages alone or in pairs on exposed reefs and mudflats, in taro
patches and ponds, and along freshwater streams inland. Often
perches on rocks and pilings. Nests in small groups inland in trees or
on rock ledges.

Voice: Low croaks. Usually silent.

Identification: Dark phase similar to Little Blue Heron (the two have
never been found together) but note reef-heron's short greenish legs,
hunched posture, and generally less graceful look. White phase distinguished from other white herons by characteristic posture, heavy bill,
and leg color. Other white egrets seldom seen in saltwater habitats in
the tropical Pacific.

Occurrence: From India E to New Zealand, MICRONESIA, FIJI, and
e. POLYNESIA (E to Tuamotu Arch., N to Samoa). Old records for
Hawaii are erroneous.

Other name: Pacific Reef Egret.

LITTLE BLUE HERON   *Egretta caerulea*

This small (24;61) heron of N. and S. America has wandered several times to the HAWAIIAN IS. (Oahu, Hawaii). Individuals thus stranded may remain for several years. Adults are entirely slate-blue, with dark-tipped blue bill. Immatures (all records to date have been adults) are all white, like several other tropical Pacific herons and egrets, but have greenish legs and dark-tipped pale bill. For full account and illustrations, see N. American field guides.

CATTLE EGRET   *Bubulcus ibis*   PLATE 8

Appearance: (20;51) A small white egret with yellow bill and yellow or dark legs. Has a distinctive, short-necked, hunched posture. Breeding birds have buff plumes on crown, back, and breast, and, at peak of nesting ("high breeding"), reddish orange bill and legs (soon fades). Immatures have greenish black legs and pale yellow bill.

Habits: Frequently flies and forages in flocks. Occurs in agricultural lands, including aquaculture projects as well as open fields, wetlands, and refuse dumps. Often accompanies livestock. Takes a wide variety of prey including insects, prawns, and mice.

Voice: A low-pitched and agitated *kwark*.

Identification: The only white heron in the tropical Pacific with both bill and legs yellow. Young birds with dark legs best told from Intermediate Egret and Great Egret by small size, hunched posture, flocking tendency.

Occurrence: Virtually cosmopolitan. Common migrant to w. MICRONESIA (E to Pohnpei with vagrants reaching the Marshall Is.). Introduced to the main HAWAIIAN IS., where now abundant from Kauai to Hawaii. Rare visitor to the NW HAWAIIAN IS. and JOHNSTON ATOLL, probably as strays from the main islands.

LITTLE (GREEN-BACKED) HERON   *Butorides striatus*   PLATE 8

Appearance: (18;46) A small chunky heron with glossy dark green back, black cap, and yellow legs, lores, and base of lower mandible. Rest of bill dark. Color of neck and breast varies geographically: gray in migrants to Micronesia, gray tinged with rust in Fiji and Tahiti, or chestnut in stragglers to Hawaii. Immatures are streaky brown in all forms. Has a distinctive neckless appearance when perched, but extends neck and raises shaggy crest when alarmed.

Habits: Confined to mangroves in Fiji, but found in riverside vegetation or trees bordering ponds elsewhere. Often perches in trees. Solitary and shy, with strong, direct flight usually low.

Voice: A loud squawk when alarmed. In Tahiti, may be a strident *ki-ki* (D. T. Holyoak in Thibault and Rives 1975).

Identification: Smallest heron of the region, but larger than bitterns and easily identified in all plumages by dark color and hunched posture.

Occurrence: Nearly cosmopolitan. In tropical Pacific, "Mangrove Heron" resident in FIJI and TAHITI (Society Is.). Nominate Little Heron rare visitor to w. MICRONESIA (Palau, Marianas, Truk), "Green Heron" to the HAWAIIAN IS.

Reference: Paton, P.W.C., and L. H. MacIvor. 1983. Green Heron in Hawaii. *Am. Birds* 37:232-33.

Note: The various forms of this cosmopolitan species were until recently considered separate species with an array of English names: Little Heron (Africa, Asia); Striated Heron (S. America); Green Heron (N. America); and Mangrove Heron (Australasia). The 1983 AOU Checklist introduced the name Green-backed Heron for the worldwide species, despite the guidelines that call for new names only when none of the older ones is suitable for a newly combined taxon. Wherever it is found, *B. striatus* is the smallest bird called a heron and thus the name Little Heron is suitable for it everywhere.

BLACK-CROWNED NIGHT-HERON   PLATE 8
Nycticorax nycticorax

Appearance: (25;64) A stocky, thick-necked heron with large bill. Adults have black crown, bill, and back with two or three white plumes protruding from nape, pearly gray underparts, darker gray wings, and red eyes. This plumage is reached through a three-stage sequence. Juvenile brown, darkest above, with white streaks above, brown streaks below, bill yellow below, eye yellow. By end of first year, streaking reduced, iris orange. By end of second year, pattern like adult, but expressed in shades of dusty brown rather than black and gray, iris red, bill slate gray.

Habits: Found along mountain streams as well as around lowland ponds and estuaries. Active at night but also forages during the day. May be seen singly or in large groups around ponds. Uses a stand-and-wait strategy to catch fish, frogs, or other aquatic life. Can become a nuisance around aquafarms. Flight slow, with deep wingbeats.

Voice: Deep croak or *kwock* given in flight or when startled.

Identification: Adults larger but superficially like gray form of Little (Green-backed) Heron. Note gray wings contrasting with black back. Immature Little Heron less streaked on back, more coarsely streaked below than juvenile and first-year night-herons. Immature Rufous Night-Heron has yellow (not orange or red) iris and subadult has paler back than Black-crowned. Juvenile Rufous very similar to Black-crowned and some may be indistinguishable, but others have black bills with no yellow below, and finer, darker streaks on neck.

Occurrence: Nearly cosmopolitan. Common resident in the HA-WAIIAN IS. Rare visitor to MICRONESIA (Marianas, Palau, Yap, Truk, Pohnpei).

RUFOUS NIGHT-HERON *Nycticorax caledonicus* PLATE 8

Appearance: (23;58) A robust heron with thick neck and large, heavy bill. Adults cinnamon on back and wings, cinnamon-buff below, with black crown and two or three long white nuchal plumes. Feet and legs greenish, iris yellow. Juvenile brown with heavy streaking above and below. Plumage sequence to adulthood apparently like that of Black-crowned Night-Heron.

Habits: Behavior similar to that described for Black-crowned Night-Heron. Roosts and forages in mangrove-lined estuaries. Feeds on tidal flats and even in garbage dumps.

Voice: A loud harsh croak.

Identification: Subadult and immatures similar to Black-crowned Night-Heron, but all stages have yellow eyes. Juvenile's neck streaks finer, darker than in Black-crowned, bill entirely black.

Occurrence: Resident throughout Australia, Melanesia, the Philippines, PALAU, and TRUK. Reported elsewhere in Micronesia, but records not well documented.

Other name: Nankeen Night-Heron.

JAPANESE NIGHT-HERON *Gorsachius goisagi*

A small (19½;49), short-billed night-heron known in the tropical Pacific from a single occurrence at PALAU. It is mostly dark chestnut, darker than Rufous Night-Heron. Wings show a bold black band on flight feathers. For illustration, see WBSJ (1982).

MALAYAN NIGHT-HERON *Gorsachius melanolophus*

Very similar to Japanese Night-Heron and also known in the tropical Pacific from a single old record for PALAU. Differs from Japanese Night-Heron in having a black cap and white-tipped primaries. Illustrated in King and Dickinson (1975) and WBSJ (1982). Other names: Malay Bittern, Tiger Bittern.

FAMILY THRESKIORNITHIDAE: Ibises

SOMEWHAT similar to herons but with long, downcurved bills, ibises are birds of mudflats, ponds, estuaries, and settling basins. They feed with a side-to-side motion of the bill. In flight they hold the neck straight out, not tucked in as do herons. Two species are potential visitors to the tropical Pacific. They have occurred only as rare solitary stragglers that often remain for several years. Such solitary birds appear never to attain their breeding dress. Ibises are entirely dark and much larger than curlews, with which they might be confused by the beginner.

WHITE-FACED IBIS   *Plegadis chihi*   PLATE 8

Appearance: (23;58) Nonbreeding plumage all dark, the head and neck with fine pale streaks; body dark glossy green. Facial skin and legs dark slate-gray. Breeding plumage (not yet observed in the region) uniformly glossy chestnut with a border of white feathers around the bare red facial skin. Iris brown in young juveniles, red thereafter.

Identification: Glossy Ibis (*P. falcinellus*) always has a brown iris. Very young individuals of the two species are therefore indistinguishable. An immature female taken in Fiji was probably a Glossy (see Appendix A).

Occurrence: Breeds in w. N. America. A rare straggler to the main HAWAIIAN IS.

Reference: Pratt, H. D. 1980. The White-faced Ibis in Hawaii. *'Elepaio* 41:45-46.

[**GLOSSY IBIS**   *Plegadis falcinellus*   See Appendix A]

ORDER ANSERIFORMES

FAMILY ANATIDAE: Waterfowl

THESE swimming birds with webbed feet and, usually, broad flat bills are familiar worldwide. They are favorites in zoos and parks, and many species are kept as ornamentals or as domestic stock. Several species are native to the tropical Pacific, and many others are regular or occasional visitors. Because they are so distinctive, waterfowl have several anatomical and other terms that apply only to them. These terms are included in the Glossary. Most waterfowl fall into three major groups: swans, geese, and ducks. Swans are huge, usually white, birds often seen in parks. One species has been recorded in the wild as a chance arrival in the tropical Pacific. Geese are more regularly seen, and one modern species is endemic to Hawaii. They are usually large, chunky waterfowl with thicker bills than ducks. They are primarily grazers on land, although they also swim. Ducks are by far the most numerous waterfowl on Pacific islands. At least six species breed or have bred in the islands, and many more are regular winter visitors. Male ducks are called drakes, females hens. Ducks fall into several subgroups. Whistling-ducks or tree-ducks are long-legged and long-necked. Dabbling ducks (mallards, teal, etc.) are usually seen on freshwater ponds and do not dive. Sea ducks or bay ducks (Canvasback, scaup, scoters, etc.) are found on fresh or salt water and dive for their food. Most ducks are vegetarian, but mergansers, another subgroup, catch fish in their long, narrow, serrated bills. The Ruddy Duck belongs to a group known as stiff-tails for obvious reasons. Ducks are further characterized by the presence of "eclipse plumage," a femalelike stage worn by drakes just after the nesting season. Early fall arrivals in the tropical Pacific often are in this plumage, at least partially, but full breeding dress is attained over the succeeding months.

FULVOUS WHISTLING-DUCK *Dendrocygna bicolor* FIGURE 16

Appearance: (20;51) A large buffy tan duck with long neck and legs. Upperparts dark brown, with prominent white band at base of tail.

FIGURE 16.
Fulvous Whistling-Duck

Habits: Characteristically in flocks. Inhabits freshwater habitats such as settling basins and aquaculture ponds.

Voice: A loud, 2-noted whistle or squeal.

Identification: Whistling-ducks are taller and lankier on land than other ducks. Their ibislike flight profile, with slightly dangling legs and neck, is distinctive. The white band on this species' posterior will distinguish it from all other ducks in Hawaii, but note similar markings on several goose species.

Occurrence: Breeds from s. U.S. to c. Argentina and from E. Africa to India. U.S. populations partly migratory. First appeared in small numbers on OAHU (Hawaiian Is.) in 1982, and has bred successfully at James Campbell National Wildlife Refuge. Now also reported on KAUAI. Probably illegally introduced, but possibly a natural colonization.

WANDERING WHISTLING-DUCK   *Dendrocygna arcuata*

Also called Water or Diving Whistling-Duck, this species is included here because it once either visited or resided in FIJI. It ranges from the Philippines to n. Australia, and is highly nomadic. Thus, although there have been no confirmed sightings in Fiji this century, it could occur again. It is a large long-legged and long-necked duck with dark brown back, black crown, buff head, neck, and breast, and chestnut underparts. Underwings dark. For full account, see Australian field guides or Watling (1982).

TUNDRA SWAN   *Cygnus columbianus*

A huge (52;132) all-white waterfowl, this swan was found once on MIDWAY. For full account and illustrations, see N. American field guides.

GREATER WHITE-FRONTED GOOSE   FIGURE 17
Anser albifrons

Appearance: (28;71) A large, grayish-brown goose with white patch surrounding base of pink bill. Underparts variably barred or splotched with black. Rump and undertail white. Legs and feet orange.

Voice: A high, multisyllabic *kah-kah-liuck*, distinct from call of Hawaiian Goose or Canada Goose.

Identification: Distinguished from other geese that reach Pacific islands by color pattern, especially splotched underparts visible overhead (hence nickname "speckle-belly"). Emperor Goose also has orange legs, but is bluish gray with all-white head.

Occurrence: Breeds in the Arctic, winters S to Mediterranean Sea, Caspian Sea, Japan, Mexico, and casually to the HAWAIIAN IS.

SNOW GOOSE   *Chen caerulescens*   FIGURE 17

Appearance: (28;71) A white goose with black primaries. Bill, legs, and feet pink. Face often stained rusty. The white-headed dark gray color phase ("Blue Goose") not recorded in tropical Pacific.

Occurrence: Breeds in arctic N. America and Siberia. Winters S to Japan, California, and Gulf of Mexico, casually to the HAWAIIAN IS. and once to the MARSHALL IS.

EMPEROR GOOSE   *Chen canagica*   FIGURE 17

Appearance: (26;66) A bluish gray goose with white head and hind-neck. Throat and upper breast black. Body feathers edged with black and white. Legs and feet orange, bill pink.

Identification: White head and nape distinctive among geese that visit Pacific islands, but note overall similarity to blue-phase Snow Goose. The latter lacks black throat.

Occurrence: Breeds in Alaska and Siberia. Winters S casually as far as California and the HAWAIIAN IS. (records for most islands, Midway-Hawaii).

BRANT   *Branta bernicla*   FIGURE 17

Appearance: (25;64) A small dark goose with a white patch on side of neck. Rump and undertail coverts white, tail black. Bill, legs, and feet black.

Identification: Darker-breasted than small Canada Goose and without throat patch.

Occurrence: Breeds in the Arctic. In the Pacific, winters along coasts S to Japan and California, and occasionally the HAWAIIAN IS.

Other names: Black Brant, Brent Goose.

CANADA GOOSE   *Branta canadensis*   FIGURE 17

Appearance: (25-36;64-91) A brown goose with striking black head and neck, white throat patch, and white uppertail coverts. Bill, legs, and feet black. Various subspecies vary widely in size. Both small and medium-sized forms have reached the tropical Pacific. The small Aleutian form is distinguished by a white ring at base of neck.

Voice: Small form utters a high-pitched cackling note, not very different from call of Hawaiian Goose.

Identification: Canada Geese usually seen and those to be expected in the Pacific are the smaller form. Rarely numerous enough to fly in flocks, and virtually never seen in Hawaiian Goose habitat. White throat patch diagnostic for all sizes of Canada Geese.

Occurrence: Breeds in N. America and winters S to Mexico. The "Cack-

BRANT

EMPEROR GOOSE

SNOW GOOSE

WHITE-FRONTED
GOOSE

CANADA GOOSE

large form

small form
("Cackling Goose")

FIGURE 17. Migratory Geese

ling" Goose (*B. c. minima*) is rare but regular in winter in the HA-WAIIAN IS.; the Aleutian subspecies (*B. c. leucopareia*) has been recorded on KWAJALEIN (Marshall Is.). Small stragglers of unknown subspecies have reached TARAWA (Kiribati). Larger Canada Geese (subspecies?) have reached the HAWAIIAN IS. but are much rarer than the smaller ones.

HAWAIIAN GOOSE   *Nesochen sandvicensis*   PLATE 14

Appearance: (25;64) A medium-sized, gray-brown goose. Face, cap, and hindneck black, side of neck buff with dark furrows. Upperparts heavily barred, underparts lightly barred. Bill and feet black. Feet with less webbing than those of other geese.

Habits: Inhabits rocky, sparsely vegetated, high volcanic slopes. Not usually observed near water, but will swim if a body of water such as a ranch pond is available. Flies in V formation, uttering loud calls.

Voice: A 2-syllable, high, nasal bark, *nay-nay*, similar to call of Canada Goose. Also a muted *moo* uttered when disturbed on the ground.

Identification: Within its habitat virtually unmistakable. Distinguished from Canada Goose by lack of white throat patch.

Occurrence: Endemic to the HAWAIIAN IS. (Hawaii, Maui). Formerly abundant, became nearly extinct in the wild by 1951. Captive breeding and release of pen-reared birds increased numbers dramatically, but the populations appear not to be self-sustaining. At present three populations exist, the largest (ca. 800 birds) on the southern and eastern slopes of Mauna Loa and in the "saddle" area, another (ca. 200) on the southern slopes of Hualalai, and fewer than 100 birds reintroduced on Haleakala, Maui. The long-term outlook for this Endangered Species is unclear.

Reference: Kear, J., and A. J. Berger. 1980. *The Hawaiian Goose: An experiment in conservation.* Vermillion, S.D.: Buteo Books.

Other name: This species is the State Bird of Hawaii, where it is officially called by its Hawaiian name, Nēnē.

GREEN-WINGED TEAL   *Anas crecca*   PLATE 9

Appearance: (14½; 37) A small, grayish brown duck with a green speculum. Male's head chestnut with broad green streak behind eye. Patch at side of tail buff outlined in black. Perched, N. American birds show a vertical white streak in front of wing, Eurasian birds a white horizontal stripe above wing. Female mottled brown with green speculum, faint stripe above eye. Bill and legs gray.

Habits: Inhabits freshwater ponds and marshes. Flight rapid.

Voice: Drake a penetrating 2-syllable whistle, hen a rapid high-pitched quack.

Identification: Smaller than most other ducks. Males distinctive, but females similar to other female teal and Garganey. Green-winged Teal has white undertail coverts contrasting with mottled flanks. Female Blue-winged and Cinnamon Teal have blue forewing. Garganey has stronger face pattern, blue-gray forewing.

Occurrence: Holarctic. Winters S to C. America, W. Indies, Africa, India, the Philippines, the HAWAIIAN IS. and the MARIANAS, rarely reaching PALAU, the MARSHALL IS., and the LINE IS. Hawaiian birds mostly American form (but Eurasian form reported Midway, Oahu); Micronesian visitors probably all Eurasian type.

MALLARD *Anas platyrhynchos* PLATE 9

Appearance: (23;58) A large duck. Drake grayish with green head separated from chestnut breast by white collar. Tail white; tail coverts black. Speculum bluish purple bordered with white. Bill yellow, legs orange. Hen mottled brown, bill orange with brown "saddle." "Mariana Mallards" all hen-plumaged, but some males with greenish heads, others like Gray Duck.

Habits: Frequents freshwater ponds, lakes, and marshes.

Voice: Hen has a loud *quack*. Drake gives a softer *quack* and a higher pitched call.

Identification: Drake distinguished from vaguely similar male Northern Shoveler by larger size, yellow bill, and chestnut breast (instead of chestnut belly contrasting with white breast). Hens resemble several other Pacific island species. Gadwall has white speculum. Gray Duck grayer brown, with green speculum and much bolder facial pattern. Hawaiian Duck similar but smaller and darker.

Occurrence: Breeds widely in Northern Hemisphere, winters S to Africa, India, Japan, Mexico, and occasionally the main HAWAIIAN IS. Stragglers have been reported from SARIGAN (Mariana Is.), YAP, KWAJALEIN (Marshall Is.), TARAWA (Kiribati), and the n. COOK IS. (Penrhyn, Suwarrow, Pukapuka). Most records lack confirmation. Most domestic ducks are descendants of wild Mallards. Some of these breed in a semiferal state on Kauai and Oahu. The endemic MARIANA IS. population is now believed extinct.

Note: The "Mariana Mallard" was probably a stabilized hybrid swarm, with both Mallard and Gray Duck ancestry. It was highly variable, with some individuals that looked like typical examples of one or the other parent species. Plate 9 shows a typical intermediate individual. See Yamashina, Y. 1948. Notes on the Marianas Mallard. *Pacific Science* 2:121-24.

HAWAIIAN DUCK *Anas wyvilliana* PLATE 9

Appearance: (20;51) Like small hen Mallard. Drakes darker than hens, tending to chestnut below. First-year male may have subdued Mallard pattern, with greenish head, black rump and undertail. Bill olive green in male, dull orange or gray with dark "saddle" in female. Legs orange in both sexes.

Habits: Nests and feeds along mountain streams and in ponds, taro fields, and river valleys. Very secretive and difficult to observe except in protected areas such as Hanalei National Wildlife Refuge (Kauai). Does not normally associate with wintering or domestic Mallards, but some interbreeding has occurred. Flight strong and direct.

Voice: Similar to that of Mallard. Usually silent.

Identification: Drakes distinguished from hen Mallard by smaller size, darker and more reddish brown plumage, and olive green bill. Hens best identified by size, bill color (if gray-billed), and association with other Hawaiian Ducks.

Occurrence: Endemic to the HAWAIIAN IS. (formerly all islands, now naturally only Kauai; reintroduced Oahu, Hawaii). An Endangered Species.

Other names: Koloa, *koloa maoli.*

LAYSAN DUCK *Anas laysanensis* PLATE 9

Appearance: (16;41) A small, dark reddish brown duck. Head very dark, sometimes with green gloss and marked irregularly with white. Some individuals nearly white-headed. Speculum green to purple. Legs and feet orange. Bill dull green (drake) or brownish yellow (hen), spotted above with black.

Habits: Usually seen on land, these ducks also swim in the saline lagoon and freshwater ponds. Usually terrestrial but capable of strong flight. Tame. Active at night. Feeds mostly on insects.

Voice: Whistles (drake) and quacks (hen).

Occurrence: Endemic to LAYSAN (NW Hawaiian Is.) Once near extinction, population now stable at about 500 birds. An Endangered Species.

Reference: Moulton, D. W., and M. W. Weller. 1984. Biology and conservation of the Laysan Duck (*Anas laysanensis*). *Condor* 86:105-117.

Other name: Laysan Teal.

GRAY DUCK *Anas superciliosa* PLATE 9

Appearance: (22;55) A large, dark brownish gray duck with striking facial pattern. Sides of face and throat buff, marked by two horizontal dark lines, one through the eye, the other below it. Crown dark, speculum green, underwing white. Bill gray, feet orange or yellow.

Habits: Inhabits mountain streams, meadows, freshwater ponds, marshes, and taro patches. Occasionally seen in brackish water or even on the outer reefs. Usually in small flocks of five to ten.

Voice: A loud quack, like that of Mallard.

Identification: Distinguished from migratory ducks by distinctive facial pattern and white underwings.

Occurrence: Resident from the E. Indies and Australasia to PALAU (rare), TRUK (rare), E to FIJI, SAMOA, TONGA, the COOK IS. (rare Aitutaki, Atiu, Mitiaro, Mauke, Mangaia; possibly extirpated Rarotonga), the SOCIETY IS. (Tahiti, Moorea, Maiao), and the TUBUAI IS. (Rapa, Tubuai, Raivavae). Declining in some parts of Polynesia.

Other names: Australian Black Duck, Pacific Black Duck.

NORTHERN PINTAIL   *Anas acuta*   PLATE 9

Appearance: (26;66, tail not included) A slender, long-necked, long-tailed duck. Speculum brown, trailing edge white. Male gray with brown head, white breast, very long pointed tail, and conspicuous white line up side of neck. Female mottled brown with shorter tail.

Habits: Prefers freshwater marshes, lakes, and ponds, but sometimes found in brackish waters. Often in flocks.

Voice: Usually silent. Drakes may give a double whistle, hens quack.

Identification: Adult male unmistakable. Females distinguished by slender profile, pointed tail, and white trailing border to speculum.

Occurrence: A holarctic breeder, wintering into the tropics. Common in the HAWAIIAN IS., uncommon in MICRONESIA (Palau, Marianas, Truk, Marshall Is.). Stragglers have reached the LINE IS., TONGA, the COOK IS., the SOCIETY IS., and the MARQUESAS.

GARGANEY   *Anas querquedula*   PLATE 9

Appearance: (15½;39) A small duck with pale blue-gray forewing and white-bordered green speculum. Breeding drake has mahogany brown head with bold white crescent from eye to side of nape, breast heavily scalloped (looks all brown at a distance) and sharply separated from paler underparts. Female mottled brown, with forewing tinged brownish. Face pattern distinctive with prominent white spot at base of upper mandible and two diffuse streaks on side of head. Fall male looks like a more strongly patterned female with male wing coloration.

Identification: Spring drake distinctive. Hens and fall males easily confused with females of other small ducks. Female Blue-winged and Cinnamon Teal have prominent blue forewings. Female Green-winged Teal is warmer brown overall, lacks blue-gray forewing, has more prominent speculum, and less distinct face pattern with dark streak through eye only.

Occurrence: Breeds in Eurasia, winters S to Old World tropics E to the Philippines, occasionally reaching PALAU, the MARIANAS, WAKE, and the HAWAIIAN IS.
Other name: Garganey Teal.

BLUE-WINGED TEAL   *Anas discors*   PLATE 9

Appearance: (15½;39) A small duck with prominent blue forewing. Male has black-spotted brown breast and underparts, gray head with white crescent in front of eye. Posterior dark with white flank patches. Bill blue-black, legs and feet orange. Female mottled brown with blue wing patch.
Identification: Immature male Northern Shoveler may be superficially similar to Blue-winged Teal in having blue forewing and slaty head with indistinct white crescent, but note its much larger size, spatulate bill, and chestnut belly. Blue forewing distinguishes Blue-winged Teal hen from all others except Cinnamon Teal and young male or eclipse Garganey (grayer forewing). Blue-wing's bill narrower at tip than that of Cinnamon. Face shows clear white spot at base of upper mandible.
Occurrence: Breeds in N. America, winters to S. America. Usually a casual winter visitor to the HAWAIIAN IS., has recently nested successfully on Hawaii.
Reference: Paton, P.W.C., A. Taylor, and P. R. Ashman. 1984. Blue-winged Teal nesting in Hawaii. *Condor* 86:219.

CINNAMON TEAL   *Anas cyanoptera*   PLATE 9

Appearance: (16;41) A small duck with prominent blue forewing. Drake uniformly bright reddish chestnut on head and body. Bill black. Legs and feet orange. Female very similar to, and often indistinguishable from, Blue-winged Teal hen.
Identification: Male virtually unmistakable. Female differs from other small ducks (except for Blue-winged Teal) in wing color. At a distance, Blue-winged and Cinnamon Teal hens may be indistinguishable, but if seen together Cinnamon looks a little larger, bulkier, longer-billed, and warmer in color. At close range, Cinnamon shows a slightly spatulate bill as compared to Blue-wing, the face pattern is less contrasting, and the pale spot at base of upper mandible is sullied with dark spots or streaks.
Occurrence: Breeds in N. and S. America. Winters from sw. U.S. to Ecuador, casually to the HAWAIIAN IS.
Reference: Wallace, D.J.M., and M. A. Ogilvie. 1980. Distinguishing Blue-winged and Cinnamon Teals. In *The frontiers of bird identification*, ed. J.T.R. Sharrock. London: Macmillan Journals Ltd.

NORTHERN SHOVELER   *Anas clypeata*   PLATE 9

Appearance: (19;48) A medium-sized duck with a spatulate bill, blue forewing, green speculum, and orange legs. Adult male boldly patterned with green head, white breast, chestnut belly, and black posterior. Immature and eclipse males (often seen in the tropical Pacific) look like blotchy adults, with indistinct white crescent (like that of Blue-winged Teal) on slate gray head. Hen mottled brown throughout, except for upperwing. Bill black (drake) or orange-bordered brown (hen). Has characteristic profile when swimming with breast low, tail high, and bill pointed toward the water.

Habits: Inhabits freshwater ponds and marshes, preferring shallow water. Has characteristic dabbling method of feeding. Shy, difficult to approach.

Voice: A croaking sound (drake), or a weak quack (hen).

Identification: Both sexes can be distinguished from other waterfowl by the peculiar large distally broadened bill and distinctive swimming posture. See Blue-winged Teal.

Occurrence: A holarctic breeder that winters S to the tropics. A common winter visitor in the HAWAIIAN IS., rare but regular in MICRONESIA (Marianas, Pohnpei E to Wake, Marshalls) and KIRIBATI (Gilbert Is., Line Is.), accidental in the TUAMOTU ARCH.

GADWALL   *Anas strepera*   PLATE 10

Appearance: (20;51) A slender, medium-sized duck with white speculum and pale gray-brown head. Drake has gray body, black posterior, chestnut wing coverts, and dark gray bill. Legs dull orange. Body of hen mottled brown with buffy flanks, orange bill with brown "saddle." Teraina form (see Occurrence) was all hen-plumaged.

Identification: White speculum diagnostic for both sexes.

Occurrence: Holarctic, wintering to the tropics. Rare visitor to the HAWAIIAN IS., the MARIANA IS., and the MARSHALL IS. A sedentary population (*A. s. couesi*), now extinct, once lived on TERAINA (Kiribati).

EURASIAN WIGEON   *Anas penelope*   PLATE 9

Appearance: (20;51) Drake gray with chestnut head, buff forehead and crown, pinkish breast, bold white patch on forewing, and black posterior bordered anteriorly with white. Hen dark brown, rusty or gray on head. In both sexes the bill is short, blue with black tip.

Identification: Male distinctive. Female very similar to female American Wigeon. Rusty-headed ones easily distinguished but less common gray-headed form differs mainly in having gray, not white, axillaries visible only in flight.

Occurrence: Breeds in Eurasia. Winters S to Africa, India, Japan, and occasionally the HAWAIIAN IS., PALAU, the MARIANAS, YAP, TRUK, the MARSHALL IS., and PALMYRA (Line Is.).

AMERICAN WIGEON   *Anas americana*   PLATE 9

Appearance: (19;48) A medium-sized, reddish-brown and gray duck with large white patch on forewing. Male has forehead and crown white, streak behind eye glossy green, and black posterior bordered anteriorly with white. Female brown with grayish head. Bill blue with black tip.

Habits: Frequents freshwater ponds and marshes.

Voice: Drake whistles, hen quacks.

Identification: Wigeons of both species are distinctive in flight with their bold white wing patches and black "trailing end." American Wigeon has paler underwing in both sexes. See Eurasian Wigeon.

Occurrence: Breeds in N. America, winters S to C. America, the W. Indies, and the HAWAIIAN IS. (uncommon but regular). Accidental on GUAM and PALMYRA (Line Is.).

Other name: Baldpate.

COMMON POCHARD   *Aythya ferina*

Hen-plumaged individuals of this Eurasian breeder have been seen twice in the tropical Pacific (GUAM, MIDWAY). Similar to Canvasback in plumage pattern but smaller (18;46), with different bill color (black at base and tip, gray centrally) and head shape (intermediate between Redhead and Canvasback). For illustration, see NGS (1983) or WBSJ (1982).

CANVASBACK   *Aythya valisineria*   PLATE 10

Appearance: (21;53) A medium-sized duck with a distinctive sloping forehead profile. Male looks white in the middle, dark fore and aft, with black breast and posterior and chestnut head. Bill black, feet grayish blue. Female grayish brown with dark breast, rusty-tinged head.

Habits: Frequents larger, deeper bodies of water. Frequently dives.

Identification: The peculiar profile is the Canvasback's most distinctive feature. Redhead and Common Pochard have stubbier bills and more rounded heads. Their drakes are similar to Canvasback in color, but darker-backed. Females lack head/breast/belly contrast of Canvasback hen.

Occurrence: Breeds in N. America and winters S to Mexico, rarely reaching the HAWAIIAN IS. and the MARSHALL IS.

REDHEAD *Aythya americana*   PLATE 10

Appearance: (19;48) Drake has chestnut-red head and neck, black breast and tail, gray mantle and underparts. Female reddish brown with indistinct light patch at base of bill, pale gray stripe on flight feathers. Bill blue with black tip. Feet bluish gray.

Identification: Canvasback drake has similar color pattern but is white-backed and has very different head shape. Scaup hens (both species) resemble female Redhead, but are duller brown, with dark foreneck, white wing stripe, and sharply defined white patch around base of bill. Ring-necked Duck hen rather similar also, but note different head shape, more distinct pale ring on bill.

Occurrence: Breeds in N. America and winters S to the tropics. Straggler in winter to the HAWAIIAN IS.

RING-NECKED DUCK *Aythya collaris*   PLATE 10

Appearance: (17;43) A medium-sized, black and white or dark brown duck with peaked head shape. Bill dark blue-gray with white subterminal band. Swimming drake black with gray flanks separated from black breast by vertical white line. Head glossed purple, inconspicuous dark red collar at base of neck visible at close range in good light. White belly shows in flight. Female dark brown with pale face and throat. Wing stripe gray.

Identification: Male scaup have gray rather than black backs. Tufted Duck drake has uniformly white sides, without contrasting vertical bar anteriorly. Hen scaup have more sharply defined white face patch, no pale ring on bill. Tufted Duck hen darker-headed, with much less white (if any) at base of bill, no band on bill, and short crest (not always visible).

Occurrence: Breeds in N. America and winters S to S. America and rarely the HAWAIIAN IS.

TUFTED DUCK *Aythya fuligula*   PLATE 10

Appearance: (17;43) A medium-sized, black-and-white or dark brown duck with prominent white wing stripe and loose backward-pointing crest. Adult drake mostly black with white flanks and underparts, black-tipped blue bill, purple-glossed head. First-year male has gray sides, less gloss, shorter crest. Female very dark brown with variable amounts (sometimes none) of white at base of bill, shorter crest, darker bill.

Identification: If visible, crest diagnostic for both sexes. Scaup drakes similarly patterned but with gray, not black, backs and less prominent wing stripe. Scaup hens usually have more, and more sharply defined, white in face. A few Tufted hens show conspicuous face patches, usually without sharp borders. Hen Ring-necked paler headed, with bold white ring on bill, adult drake gray-sided. First-year Tufted drake like Ring-necked, but lacks white anterior bar on sides.

Occurrence: Breeds throughout Eurasia. Winters S to Africa, China, the Philippines, and uncommonly to w. MICRONESIA (Palau, Yap, Marianas). Occasionally reaches the MARSHALL IS. and the HAWAIIAN IS.

[**WHITE-EYED DUCK**   *Aythya australis*   See Appendix A]

GREATER SCAUP   *Aythya marila*   PLATE 10

Appearance and Identification: (18;46) Very similar to slightly smaller Lesser Scaup, but with subtly different head and bill shape. Greater's head smoothly rounded, less peaked than that of Lesser. Bill broader, with larger dark nail at tip. In good light, drake Greater's head is glossed green, Lesser's purple. At a distance, size differences are noticeable in mixed flocks, as are the whiter flanks of Greater. In flight, Greater usually shows longer white wing stripe, extending onto primaries, but this feature somewhat variable. See Lesser Scaup.

Habits: Tends to be seen more often on salt water than Lesser Scaup, but the two frequently are seen together.

Occurrence: A holarctic breeder, wintering S to the Mediterranean, Japan, and the W. Indies. A casual visitor to the MARIANAS and the HAWAIIAN IS.

LESSER SCAUP   *Aythya affinis*   PLATE 10

Appearance: (16½;42) A dark, medium-sized duck with broad white wing stripe. Drake's head and breast black (head glossed with purple), back gray, flanks pale gray, underparts white, posterior black, bill and feet gray-blue. Female dark brown with distinct white face patch at base of bill.

Habits: In winter frequents freshwater ponds, lakes, and marshes or brackish bays and saltwater inlets. Flight rapid and direct. Patters feet on water during take-off.

Identification: Scaup drakes resemble both Ring-necked and Tufted drakes, but have gray, not black, backs. Hens are more difficult to distinguish, but note their sharply defined white face patch and uniformly colored bill. The two scaup species are very difficult to identify even under favorable circumstances. See Greater Scaup. Most scaup in Hawaii are Lessers.

Occurrence: Breeds in N. America and winters to S. America and the HAWAIIAN IS. (small numbers).

HARLEQUIN DUCK   *Histrionicus histrionicus*

A Northern Hemisphere duck (16½;42) that has been recorded twice in the NW HAWAIIAN IS. (Midway, Laysan). Named for its peculiar pattern of stripes and spots against dark plumage. For illustrations, see N. American or Eurasian field guides.

OLDSQUAW   *Clangula hyemalis*

A black and white sea-duck known in the tropical Pacific by a single 1958 record for MIDWAY. Called Long-tailed Duck in Eurasia. Illustrated in Eurasian and N. American field guides.

BLACK SCOTER   *Melanitta nigra*

A large (19;48) sea-duck known in the tropical Pacific from a single female photographed on MIDWAY in 1980. Female is dark brown with contrasting pale throat and cheeks. See field guides to N. America and Eurasia for full account.

SURF SCOTER   *Melanitta perspicillata*

A large (20;51) northern sea-duck that once visited OAHU. The bird was a female, dark brown with two pale spots on the side of the head. For full account and illustrations, see N. American or Eurasian field guides.

BUFFLEHEAD   *Bucephala albeola*   PLATE 10

Appearance: (13½;34) A small chunky duck with short stubby bill. Male boldly patterned in black and white, black parts of head glossed with green and purple. Female and first-winter male dusty brown, darkest on head, with white ear patch, white secondaries.

Identification: Male Hooded Merganser has similar head pattern, but has long thin bill, chestnut sides, and less white on back and wings. Winter male Ruddy Duck similar to same-sized female Bufflehead but has larger white cheek patch that extends forward to bill.

Occurrence: Breeds in N. America and winters S to Mexico and occasionally the HAWAIIAN IS. Most birds in Hawaii are females.

HOODED MERGANSER   *Lophodytes cucullatus*   PLATE 10

Appearance and Identification: (18;46) A slender duck with long narrow bill. Female and first-year male drab brown with black-and-white inner secondaries. Head exhibits rusty-tinged fanlike crest, which can be folded back. Adult drake, as yet unrecorded in Hawaii, a striking bird with white patch on side of head and rusty flanks. Bill dark (red in Red-breasted Merganser).

Occurrence: Breeds in N. America and winters S to Mexico. A rare visitor to the HAWAIIAN IS., usually in small groups of females and young males.

RED-BREASTED MERGANSER   *Mergus serrator*   PLATE 10

A very rare visitor to the HAWAIIAN IS.; only females have been recorded. A long, slim, dusty brown duck (23;58) with red bill and double-pointed shaggy crest. A holarctic breeder that winters S to the n. tropics, females further S than males. See N. American and Eurasian field guides.

RUDDY DUCK   *Oxyura jamaicensis*   PLATE 10

Appearance and Identification: (15;38) A tiny duck that frequently cocks its tail up. In winter, both sexes are dull brown, paler below, with cheeks clear white (male) or white crossed by a dark horizontal bar (female). Males molt in spring into rich cinnamon body plumage with black crown, and bill becomes bright blue. The bright plumage rarely seen in Hawaii. Compare Bufflehead, Cinnamon Teal.

Occurrence: Breeds in N. and S. America and the W. Indies. Northern birds winter S to Mexico, and occasionally the HAWAIIAN IS.

ORDER FALCONIFORMES

FAMILY ACCIPITRIDAE: EAGLES AND HAWKS

MOST birds of prey in the tropical Pacific belong to this large cosmopolitan family. Worldwide, there are several basic types of hawks and most are represented in the islands. Harriers are long-winged and long-tailed, and hunt by coursing over open country. Accipiters are long-tailed, but have relatively short, rounded wings and are more active and agile hunters. Buteos are chunky hawks with rounded wings and fan-shaped tails. All types occasionally soar on updrafts, revealing their characteristic flight silhouettes (Figure 18). Eagles and Ospreys are much larger than hawks, and are only visitors to the tropical Pacific. Among birds of prey, females are often much larger than males; we give two measurements in those cases.

FIGURE 18. Flight Silhouettes of Birds of Prey

Reference: Brown, L., and D. Amadon. 1968. *Eagles, hawks, and falcons of the world*. New York: McGraw-Hill Book Co.

OSPREY   *Pandion haliaetus*   FIGURE 19

Appearance: (22, 25;56, 64) A large raptor, dark brown above and white below. Head white with dark mark through eye. Breast may be lightly streaked. From below, wings show a black border with a prominent black spot at the wrist. Wings have a characteristic kink in flight.

Habits: Primarily a fisheater; usually seen over or near bodies of water May perch high on exposed snags or soar at great heights.

Identification: The largest bird of prey to visit the Pacific regularly Note the distinctive flight silhouette and pale underparts.

Occurrence: Cosmopolitan. Rare but regular winter visitor to the HA WAIIAN IS. with old records for PALAU and GUAM.

BRAHMINY KITE   *Haliastur indus*

A distinctive slow-flying hawk of coastal habitats from India to the Phil ippines and n. Australia. It was seen once at PALAU. Deep chestnut with white head, breast, and tail tip. Wings broad, rounded, tail fan shaped. Immature darker mottled brown, with streaks on head and breast. For full account, see Pizzey (1980), or other guides to Austra lian or s. Asian birds.

FIGURE 19. Osprey

STELLER'S SEA-EAGLE *Haliaetus pelagicus*

A huge (32;81) eagle with heavy yellow bill and wedge-shaped tail. Adult brown with white tail, thighs, and shoulders. Immature all dark with pale base to tail and white mottling on underwing. Ranges from e. Siberia to Japan. An immature was seen and photographed at KURE and later at MIDWAY in 1978, and an adult was seen in 1983 at FRENCH FRIGATE SHOALS (NW Hawaiian Is.). These are the only records for the tropical Pacific. See illustrations in WBSJ (1982), NGS (1983), or Flint et al. (1984).

NORTHERN HARRIER *Circus cyaneus*

A gray (male) or brown (female) harrier found throughout the Northern Hemisphere, this species has been reported twice on OAHU and once on MIDWAY (Hawaiian Is.). It has characteristic harrier behavior and silhouette, and prominent white rump. Also called Marsh Hawk and Hen Harrier. See illustrations in any Eurasian or N. American field guide.

SWAMP HARRIER *Circus approximans*   PLATE 11

Appearance: (23;58) A large harrier with variable plumage. Some have upperparts dark brown and underparts light rufous brown with dark streaks. Others (immatures?) uniformly dark brown below. Tail light brown with horizontal bars. Rump pale, especially in older birds. Legs and feet yellow.

Habits: Prefers open country. Usually seen soaring or hovering on wings held high in a characteristic V conformation. Feeds on a variety of animals and on carrion. Nests on the ground in swamps or marshes. May congregate in areas of food abundance.

Identification: The only hawk in Tonga and the Society Is. Immature Fiji Goshawk similarly colored, but much smaller with relatively shorter wings, no pale rump, and much more vigorous flight. Any soaring hawk in Fiji is likely to be a harrier.

Occurrence: From Australia and New Guinea to FIJI (throughout) and TONGA (Tofua, Kao). Introduced (1885) to the SOCIETY IS. (Bora Bora, Raiatea, Moorea, Tahiti, Tetiaroa). Common.

Reference: Baker-Gabb, D. J. 1979. Remarks on the taxonomy of the Australasian Harrier (*Circus approximans*). *Notornis* 26:325-29.

Other name: Australasian Harrier.

Note: Often regarded as a subspecies of the Marsh Harrier, *C. aeruginosus*.

JAPANESE SPARROWHAWK   *Accipiter gularis*   FIGURE 20

Appearance: (10, 12;25, 31) A small accipiter. Adult male blackish slate above, rufous below. Throat white with a hairline black streak down center. Breast and belly barred. Female lighter and more brownish above, heavily barred below with brown. Immature brown above, heavily streaked on breast, barred on belly. Underwings, including wing lining, and undertail barred in all plumages.

Identification: Very similar to both the Besra (*A. virgatus*) and the Eurasian Sparrowhawk (*A. nisus*), which could potentially reach Micronesia but are much less likely to do so than the Japanese Sparrowhawk. Besra has more prominant line down middle of throat, but immatures probably indistinguishable in the field. Eurasian Sparrowhawk larger, finely streaked on throat (adult) or barred (immature). Chinese Goshawk also very similar but with rusty tinge below confined to a band across breast in adult, wing linings unbarred in all plumages.

Occurrence: Breeds in n. China, Korea, and Japan. Winters S to Indochina and Indonesia. Probably a rare but regular winter visitor to w. MICRONESIA, but recorded with certainty only from Guam. Some of the small accipiters regularly seen at Palau probably belong to this species.

Other names: Lesser Sparrowhawk, Asiatic Sparrowhawk.

FIGURE 20. Migratory Accipiters

CHINESE GOSHAWK   *Accipiter soloensis*   FIGURE 20

Appearance: (12, 14;31, 35) A medium-sized hawk with steel blue upperparts. Adult underparts, including underwing, pale with rufous-tinged breast and wing lining. Primaries tipped black, tail barred. Immature streaked below, with flight feathers barred beneath.

Identification: Wing linings of this species unbarred in all plumages, a distinctive feature among small e. Asian accipiters (see Japanese Sparrowhawk). Rufous tinge below confined to breast, not extending onto flanks as in Japanese Sparrowhawk. Immatures very similar to Japanese Sparrowhawk, but have unbarred wing linings (Figure 20).

Occurrence: Breeds in China and Korea and winters S to the E. Indies. Probably rare but regular in w. MICRONESIA, where recorded from the MARIANA IS. (Guam, Rota), YAP, and PALAU.

Other names: Gray Frog Hawk, Chinese Sparrowhawk.

FIJI GOSHAWK   *Accipiter rufitorques*   PLATE 11

Appearance: (12, 16;31, 41) Adult pale bluish gray above, brownish pink below and around neck. Immature brown above, brown-streaked buff below, thighs rufous. Legs yellow.

Habits: Found in many habitats from dense rain forest to urban parks. Uses low, twisting flight below treetops to capture prey, but usually has more sedate flap-and-glide flight. Occasionally soars. Feeds on insects, lizards, and birds. Often mobbed by smaller birds.

Voice: Rapidly repeated, high-pitched notes, *ki . . . ki . . . ki . . .* or *weit-weit-weit-weit* (Watling 1982).

Identification: The only accipiter in Fiji (see family discussion). Immatures much smaller than Swamp Harrier and lack light rump patch.

Occurrence: Endemic to FIJI but found on large to medium-sized islands only. Common.

Reference: Clunie, F. 1981. Nesting season of the Fiji Goshawk. *Notornis* 28:136-37.

[**COMMON BUZZARD**   *Buteo buteo*   See Appendix A]

HAWAIIAN HAWK   *Buteo solitarius*   PLATE 11

Appearance: (16, 18;41, 46) A small dimorphic hawk with light and dark phases in about equal numbers. Dark-phase adult uniformly dark brown (usually appears black in the field); immature has tawny mottling on head and breast. Light-phase adult has pale underparts more or less streaked with brown on the breast. Light-phase immature clear golden buff on head and breast with a dark streak through the eye. Both immatures have blue-green cere and feet rather than the golden yellow of adults. Both phases have gray tails faintly barred with brown. Males smaller than females.

Habits: Solitary or in pairs, usually seen soaring on updrafts over forest or agricultural lands. Feeds on a variety of small animals including birds, rodents, and insects. Highly adaptable, found in most available habitats except the very driest. Pugnacious in defense of nest.

Voice: A harsh scream, *eeeee-oh*. Also an extended series of piercing *keeee-up* notes uttered at intervals of about 1 second, building in intensity and rising in pitch.

Identification: Compare Hawaiian Crow (pointed wings, pointed bill, no barring in wing and tail) and Short-eared Owl (facial disks, blunt-headed silhouette). See flight silhouette (Figure 18).

Occurrence: Endemic to the island of HAWAII, but has wandered to Maui and Oahu. Fairly common throughout in proper habitats, from

sea level to tree line. Recent USFWS surveys indicate that this species' status as an Endangered Species should be reassessed.
Other Name: '*io*.

GOLDEN EAGLE   *Aquila chrysaetos*
This widespread eagle of the Northern Hemisphere has only found its way once to the tropical Pacific, but that individual lived for 17 years on KAUAI (Hawaiian Is.) and was seen repeatedly by many observers. It presumably fed on goats and pigs. It died during a diving attack on a helicopter in 1984. Golden Eagles are huge (35;89) and all dark, with golden hindneck. Immatures have white patches in wing and tail. Discussed fully in N. American and Eurasian field guides.

FAMILY FALCONIDAE: Falcons

FALCONS are small to medium-sized birds of prey with characteristically pointed, back-swept wings and long, tapering tails. They feed by aerial dives. The family is represented worldwide, but only one species is resident in the tropical Pacific.

EURASIAN KESTREL   *Falco tinnunculus*
This palearctic species is included here on the basis of a single 1984 female specimen taken on SAIPAN (Mariana Is.). It is a small (12;31) falcon with dark-barred rusty upperparts, including the tail in females. Males have dark-tipped gray tails and gray heads. Illustrated in Eurasian field guides and NGS (1983).

[**AMERICAN KESTREL**   *Falco sparverius*   See Appendix A]

[**NORTHERN HOBBY**   *Falco subbuteo*   See Appendix A]

[**ORIENTAL HOBBY**   *Falco severus*   See Appendix A]

PEREGRINE FALCON   *Falco peregrinus*   PLATE 11, FIGURE 21
Appearance: (16, 20;41, 51) A medium-sized falcon, dark above, light below with longitudinal streaks. Immatures brown above with pale blue feet and cere. Adults slate gray (migrants) or nearly black (Fiji residents) on back with yellow cere and feet. Continental birds show dark cheeks separated from nape by pale vertical line, but Fiji birds have

side of head all dark (Figure 21). Females larger than males, with rusty tinge to breast.

Habits: Nests on cliffs, especially near the coast. Found in virtually any nearby habitat. A powerful hunter that captures prey on the wing. Feeds mostly on birds, but in parts of Fiji takes flying foxes (fruit bats).

Voice: A high-pitched *keen-keen-keen*-etc. A harder, more staccato version uttered at nest intruders.

FIGURE 21. Geographic Variation in Peregrine Falcons. Migratory e. Asian form (*l.*) and resident Fiji form (*r.*).

Identification: The only falcon recorded in Hawaii and Polynesia. Continental birds can be distinguished from Fiji residents by different face pattern, paler back.

Occurrence: Nearly cosmopolitan. Uncommon resident (*F. p. nesiotes*) in FIJI (Viti Levu, Vanua Levu, Taveuni, Wakaya, Ovalau). Wanderers from Asia or N. America occasionally reach w. MICRONESIA (Palau, Yap, Guam) and the HAWAIIAN IS., and have even come aboard ships far at sea. A bird seen on SAVAII (W. Samoa) was of unknown origin. Considered an Endangered Species worldwide, but the status of the Fiji population has not been recently assessed.

Reference: Clunie, F. 1972. A contribution to the natural history of the Fiji Peregrine. *Notornis* 19:302-322.

ORDER GALLIFORMES

FAMILY MEGAPODIIDAE: Megapodes

MEGAPODES are ground-dwelling birds with large legs and feet. They are dark-colored and vaguely rail-like or chickenlike. Despite their terrestrial habits, most species fly well and can cross water gaps between islands with ease. The family is well represented on islands of the Indo-Australian region. The two tropical Pacific species have peculiar discontinuous distributions. Megapodes use natural heat from a variety of sources to incubate their eggs in communal nest mounds. Adults usually remain in the vicinity of the mounds and tend them regularly, but the young are independent at hatching.

MICRONESIAN MEGAPODE   *Megapodius laperouse*   PLATE 14

Appearance: (15;38) A dark, brownish black, chickenlike bird with a short, pale gray crest. Red skin shows through feathers at base of yellow bill. Posture rather like that of a guinea fowl.

Habits: Terrestrial; usually forages in pairs. Members of a pair maintain contact by their sharp calls. Deceptively strong fliers. Eggs laid in huge communal mounds of sand or rock, usually on or near beaches. Heat from decaying vegetation in the mound incubates the eggs, and the young are independent at hatching. Megapodes are heard more often than seen, except on uninhabited islands, where they may be rather tame.

Voice: Call a single loud *keek!* The more complex "song" is usually a duet: one bird begins *keek-keek-keek-* . . . , gradually building in speed and pitch to a loud *keek-keeer-kew* (Palau) or *keek-keeer-keet* (Marianas); the other answers with a rapid, chuckling cackle rising in pitch and slowing near the end.

Identification: Care must be taken not to confuse megapodes with feral chickens. The megapode is smaller, has a very short tail, different posture, and always looks black in the field. At Palau the terrestrial Nicobar Pigeon may cause confusion, but is distinguished by a neck ruff and short white tail.

Occurrence: Endemic to Micronesia, restricted to PALAU (all islands) and the MARIANAS (Saipan and islands to the north, Agiguan, possibly Tinian; extirpated on Rota and Guam). Common on uninhabited islands, uncommon on Peleliu and Angaur (Palau), rare on inhabited islands. An Endangered Species.

Reference: Pratt, H. D., and P. L. Bruner. 1978. Micronesian Megapode rediscovered on Saipan. *'Elepaio* 39:57-59.
Other names: Mariana Scrub Fowl, Marianas Scrub Hen, Micronesian Incubator Bird.

NIUAFO'OU MEGAPODE *Megapodius pritchardii* PLATE 14

Appearance: (15;38) A plain, dark gray-brown, chickenlike bird with bright yellow legs and short crest.
Habits: Feeds on the ground, usually on steep forested slopes. Flies only when disturbed or pursued. Breeds year-round, laying eggs communally in tunnels in volcanic ash near steam vents. Apparently takes advantage of volcanic heat to incubate eggs.
Identification: Could be confused with feral chickens, which are larger with prominent tails. Purple Swamphen immatures show bold white undertail coverts. Banded Rail has longer bill, heavily barred plumage.
Occurrence: Endemic to NIUAFO'OU (Tonga). Found throughout the island. Maintains a healthy population despite illegal egg-gathering by island residents. Introduced to TAFAHI (Tonga) in 1968, status there unknown.
Reference: Weir, D. G. 1973. Status and habits of *Megapodius pritchardii*. *Wilson Bull.* 85:79-82.
Other names: Malau, Polynesian Scrub Hen, Niuafo'ou Incubator Bird, Pritchard's Scrub Fowl.

FAMILY PHASIANIDAE: GALLINACEOUS BIRDS

THIS family includes most of the birds that could be described as "chickenlike" (francolins, partridges, quail, pheasants, grouse, turkeys, guineafowl, and, of course, chickens). They are mainly terrestrial birds with strong feet, and feed by scratching food from the ground. Two species (chicken and turkey) are ubiquitous in domestication and are known to everyone. Other species are popular as ornamental or game birds, and for these reasons have been introduced into the tropical Pacific. None is native to the region. Feral chickens have been present since the arrival of the first humans in the islands, but other species joined the avifauna in historic times. Introductions of many species have been attempted, but most have failed to establish breeding populations. Still, gallinaceous birds are now a conspicuous part of the avifauna of the Hawaiian Islands, and a few game birds have become established elsewhere. They do not appear to compete directly with native birds, but may serve as reservoir hosts for disease.

References: Lewin, V. 1971. Exotic game birds of the Puu Waa Waa Ranch, Hawaii. *J. Wildlife Management* 35:141-55.

Schwartz, C. W., and E. R. Schwartz. 1949. *A reconnaissance of the game birds in Hawaii*. Hilo: Bd. Agriculture and Forestry, Terr. Hawaii.

BLACK FRANCOLIN   *Francolinus francolinus*   PLATE 12

Appearance: (14;35) Smallest francolin in Hawaii. Males appear black, marked with pale streaks, bars, and spots. Teardrop-shaped white cheek patch and chestnut collar conspicuous. Females buffy tan, with chestnut nape patch and pale buffy white throat. Legs red-orange in both sexes.

Habits: Found in dry grassland habitats or in open pasturelands. Entirely terrestrial except that males occasionally perch in trees to call. Usually secretive and difficult to observe, but calling males often choose high, exposed perches. Very difficult to flush; prefers to run when pursued.

Voice: A loud, far-carrying series of mechanical-sounding notes, the first a metallic *clink* followed by a series that sounds like a code message being delivered on an electrical buzzer like those heard at athletic events: *clink, kick-KIH-dick, kick-kih-DICK!* No other natural sound in Hawaii resembles it.

Identification: Males unmistakable both visually and acoustically. Females could be confused with Gray Francolin, but lack orange in throat and have orange legs, chestnut nape, and entire tail tip black.

Occurrence: Native to c. and s. Asia. Introduced (1959) to the HAWAIIAN IS. and established on Molokai, Maui, Lanai, and Hawaii. Most common in drier parts of nw. Hawaii. Also established in s. GUAM from an introduction in 1961.

GRAY FRANCOLIN   *Francolinus pondicerianus*   PLATE 12

Appearance: (13;33) A rather nondescript, sandy-colored, chickenlike bird. Entire plumage barred with roughly parallel dark lines. Throat and forehead orange-buff. Legs dull brown. Sexes similar.

Habits: Usually encountered in small groups foraging on the ground in dry habitats, particularly roadsides near kiawe thickets. Often attracted to irrigated places such as lawns and golf courses. Rarely perches in trees.

Voice: A loud, rollicking cackle composed of squeaky whistled notes: *KEE-ka-ko-KEE-ka-ko-KEE-ka-ko*. The sound carries great distances in open country.

Identification: Lack of any bold or distinctive markings distinguishes Gray Francolin from other game birds except female Black Francolin.

In flight, Gray Francolin's black-tipped chestnut lateral tail feathers contrast with paler central feathers. Also note dull-colored legs of this species.

Occurrence: Native to India. Introduced to the HAWAIIAN IS. (1959) and established on all main islands. Common to abundant in lowlands of Maui, Lanai, Molokai, and Hawaii; local and seldom seen on Oahu and Kauai. Introductions on Guam failed.

ERCKEL'S FRANCOLIN   *Francolinus erckelii*   PLATE 12

Appearance: (16;41) Large and chickenlike, with distinctive chestnut crown and bold longitudinal chestnut streaks on a gray breast. Sexes similar.

Habits: A ground-dwelling bird of grasslands and open forests. The francolin most likely to be seen in rainy areas.

Voice: A loud cackle given by males begins as a series of low *chuck* notes, accelerates gradually to a climactic roosterlike crow followed by a winding-down series of low chuckling notes: *chuck-chuck-chuck-chuck-chuck-chuck-KRA-A-A-AH! chuckaluck-chuckaluck-chuckaluck-chuckaluck.*

Identification: Chestnut crown, longitudinal streaks, and large size distinguish Erckel's Francolin from all other game birds in Hawaii.

Occurrence: Native to E. Africa. Introduced (1957) to the HAWAIIAN IS. and established on the six largest islands. Especially common on the leeward slope of Mauna Kea and on Lanai. Tends to range higher than other francolins.

CHUKAR   *Alectoris chukar*   PLATE 12

Appearance: (14;35) A large pale partridge with red bill and legs. Face and throat white with a prominent black border. Flanks boldly barred black and white.

Habits: Inhabits some of the most severe and seemingly inhospitable habitats such as the barren upper slopes of Haleakala, Maui. Usually seen running on the ground among rocks. The birds sometimes pause to survey their surroundings from atop a rocky mound.

Voice: A series of loud *chuck*s sometimes followed by a repeated 3-syllable cackle.

Identification: Larger and paler than quails, chunkier and shorter-legged than francolins. Black-bordered face and barred flanks distinguish Chukar from Gray Francolin. The very similar Rock Partridge (*A. graeca*) was introduced to Hawaii in 1959 but is not believed to be established. It is only distinguishable by its greater amount of black at base of bill and narrower bars on flanks than Chukar. Also introduced was the Barbary Partridge (*A. barbara*), which bred for a short time on

Puu Waa Waa Ranch in South Kohala, Hawaii, but which has not been reported recently. It is like Chukar in body plumage, but throat gray, not white, and bordered by chestnut rather than black.

Occurrence: Native to c. Eurasia. Introduced to the HAWAIIAN IS. (1923 and subsequently) and established on all main islands except Oahu. Most abundant on upper slopes of Mauna Kea, Hawaii, and Haleakala, Maui.

[**COMMON QUAIL** *Coturnix coturnix*   See Appendix A]

JAPANESE QUAIL *Coturnix japonica*   PLATE 12

Appearance: (7½;19) A small, sandy-colored, stub-tailed quail. Male's throat either black or rusty, female's white.

Habits: Prefers grassy fields or pastures with short (ca. 40 cm) ground cover. Can be difficult to flush, and is always hard to see. Most often located by its voice.

Voice: A sneezy *chicky-wher*.

Identification: The smallest quail in Hawaii. Can always be distinguished by size and buffy coloration. Might be confused with Western Meadowlark, which shares same habitat on Kauai, but which has white lateral tail feathers and yellow breast.

Occurrence: Native to e. Asia. Introduced to the HAWAIIAN IS. in 1921 and believed established on all main islands except Oahu. Often seen in drier parts of Hawaii, in fallow fields along N shore of Kauai, and in pasturelands on nw. slope of Haleakala, Maui.

BROWN QUAIL *Coturnix australis*   PLATE 12

Appearance: (7½;19) A plump, buffy brown quail, mottled with dark lines and spots and white streaks. Underparts finely barred.

Habits: Found singly or in coveys in grasslands. When flushed rises abruptly, then flies low back to the ground.

Voice: Call is a whistled *ffweep* or *gop-warr* (H. J. Frith in Slater 1970) that rises in pitch at the end. Also a sharp chirp or chatter when flushed.

Identification: The only quail in Fiji. Much smaller than any other chickenlike bird except rails. The latter are not found in dry grasslands in Fiji.

Occurrence: Native to Australia. Introduced to FIJI and established in the drier w. parts of Viti Levu and on Vanua Levu (central Macuata). Uncommon.

Other name: Swamp Quail.

[**STUBBLE QUAIL**   *Coturnix pectoralis*   See Appendix A]

BLUE-BREASTED QUAIL   *Coturnix chinensis*   PLATE 12

Appearance: (4;10) A tiny dark quail. Male with blue-gray breast, rusty belly, and black throat bordered with white. Female mottled brown.

Habits: Lives in grasslands only. Shy and difficult to flush, at which time it flies only a short distance and drops back to the ground.

Voice: A triple-noted *pip-it-kan*, the last note descending (Smythies 1981).

Identification: Much smaller and shorter-billed than Guam Rail or Lesser Golden-Plover, vaguely similar birds that might be found in the same habitat.

Occurrence: Ranges from India and s. China to Australia. Introduced to GUAM from the Philippines in 1895. Uncommon in grasslands throughout the island.

Other name: King Quail.

KALIJ PHEASANT   *Lophura leucomelana*   PLATE 13

Appearance: (20,29;51,73) Distinguished by long, vertically compressed tail and backward-pointing crest. Cock deep metallic blue with white barring on rump and a patch of silvery gray lance-shaped feathers on breast. Hen of similar shape, but mottled and barred with light and dark brown.

Habits: In Hawaii occupies a variety of forest types including dense native rain forests, silk oak and eucalyptus groves, and open scrubby forests both native and exotic. Usually very shy in the forest, but often seen foraging in early morning in clearings and along roadsides.

Voice: A harsh, low-pitched crow. Foraging birds utter a quiet, somewhat piglike grunt, *guat-guat*, interspersed with a high-pitched squeal.

Identification: Not likely to be confused with any other species except green form of Common (Ring-necked) Pheasant. Note high-arched tail of Kalij.

Occurrence: Native to the Himalayas. Introduced in 1962 at Puu Waa Waa on HAWAII, and now spreading explosively throughout the island in suitable habitat.

Reference: Lewin, V. and G. Lewin 1984. The Kalij Pheasant, a newly established game bird on the island of Hawaii. *Wilson Bull.* 96:634-46.

RED JUNGLEFOWL   *Gallus gallus*   PLATE 13

Appearance: (17,30;43,76) Like a small, slim version of the familiar domestic chicken, but less variable. Cock larger than hen.

Habits: Truly wild chickens are very shy, more often heard than seen.

On most islands they inhabit remote undisturbed forests. If domestic stock is kept nearby, they will interbreed with them. Where protected (as at Kokee, Kauai), Red Junglefowl may become rather tame.

Voice: Indistinguishable from that of barnyard fowl.

Identification: The problem here is not one of recognition, but of determining whether the bird seen is wild or domestic stock, since the latter is often free-ranging. We consider only those seen some distance from human habitation to be true Red Junglefowl, except at Kokee, Kauai, where wild birds have been tamed by food handouts and no domestic stock is kept.

Occurrence: Native to SE. Asia. Brought as domestic stock by ancient Micronesian and Polynesian peoples to virtually every inhabited island in the Pacific, domestic chickens spread into forests and established feral populations. Now these populations are declining drastically. Extirpated from Guam and the Hawaiian Is. (except Kauai; and reintroduced to Waimea Falls Park, Oahu).

Reference: Ball, S. C. 1933 (repr. 1971). Jungle Fowls from Pacific islands. *Bull. Bernice P. Bishop Mus.* 108.

COMMON (RING-NECKED) PHEASANT   PLATE 13
Phasianus colchicus

Appearance: (33;84) A rather large, chickenlike bird with long, pointed, brown- and tan-barred tail. Hen smaller than cock, dull buff with darker mottling above, plain below. Cocks of two color types formerly regarded as separate species. "Ring-necked" pheasants have green head, coppery-colored breast, and prominent white neck ring. "Green" pheasants lack neck ring, have glossy blue-green neck, breast, and upper belly. Intermediates occur.

Habits: Highly adaptable, found in all habitat types except dense rain forests, alpine zones, and very dry places. Very tame in Hawaii, often seen walking across open pasturelands. "Green Pheasants" found in wetter habitats than "Ring-necks," but the two hybridize freely where they come into contact.

Voice: A metallic scraping *craack-kuk* given by the cock, sometimes followed by a loud wing flutter.

Identification: Distinguished from francolins by long pointed tail. Both sexes lack the high-arched tail of the Kalij Pheasant. Hens of the two color forms probably indistinguishable in the field, but "Green" form grayer, less buffy.

Occurrence: Native to Eurasia but introduced almost worldwide. Established on all main HAWAIIAN IS. since late 19th century. Green form largely confined to windward slopes of Mauna Kea and Mauna Loa at higher elevations. Introductions on Guam failed. Also reported in French Polynesia, but status and distribution there unknown.

Note: When the 1983 AOU Check-list listed *P. versicolor* as a subspecies of *P. colchicus*, it should have proposed a new name for the combined species, because the "Green Pheasant," as well as many other forms, lacks a neck ring. AOU guidelines call for new names in such cases. We suggest Common Pheasant because this species is the world's most common and widespread pheasant.

COMMON PEAFOWL   *Pavo cristatus*   PLATE 13

Appearance: (40,100;102,254) The peacock needs no description. Peahen is a grayish brown bird of turkey size with white patch on lower breast, metallic blue-green feathers on upper neck, and a crest like the cock's.

Habits: Very shy in the wild, usually keeping to dense forests.

Voice: A loud trumpetlike call: *kee-yaah, kee-yaah.* At a distance sounds like a human crying "Help!"

Identification: Size and blue-green colors distinguish the peacock from all other birds in Hawaii. Glimpsed at a distance, a molting bird with a short train might resemble Wild Turkey, but note peacock's strongly contrasting rusty-buff primaries.

Occurrence: Native to India and SE. Asia. Introduced in 1860 to the HAWAIIAN IS. Has never done particularly well in the wild in Hawaii but persists in scattered localities on Hawaii (Hualalai above Puu Waa Waa), Oahu (N end of Waianae Range), Niihau, and the w. slope of Haleakala, Maui.

Other name: Indian Peafowl.

[PRAIRIE CHICKEN   *Tympanuchus* sp.?   See Appendix A]

WILD TURKEY   *Meleagris gallopavo*   PLATE 13

Appearance: (37,46;93,117) The heaviest game bird in Hawaii, with bronzy dark brown plumage and broad, fan-shaped tail. Males larger than females. Wild birds slimmer than the barnyard variety, but otherwise similar.

Habits: Moves about in small parties, keeping to the cover of forests except when foraging in edges or openings. Sometimes seen along highways in early morning. Found in native koa/ohia and mamane/naio forests as well as exotic forests of silk oak and eucalyptus. Favors forests with open, grassy understory.

Voice: A gobble like that of the domestic bird.

Identification: Size alone separates Wild Turkey from all other similar birds except Common Peafowl.

Occurrence: Native to N. America. Birds from domestic stock introduced (1788) to the HAWAIIAN IS. are established on Niihau, Lanai, Maui, and Hawaii. Common and easily seen on the latter (Puu Waa Waa, Hualalai, Mauna Kea).

Reference: Sakai, H. F., and J. M. Scott. 1984. Turkey sighting on Keauhou Ranch, Volcano, Hawaii. *'Elepaio* 45:19.

GAMBEL'S QUAIL   *Callipepla gambelii*   PLATE 12

Appearance and Identification: (11;28) Very similar to California Quail, but male has redder crown and flanks, no dark feather edges on belly, and underparts buffy white marked by a broad central black bar. Female like plain-bellied California hen.

Habits: Prefers drier habitats than California Quail, but otherwise similar in behavior.

Voice: Resembles that of California Quail.

Occurrence: Native to w. N. America. Introduced (1928 and later) to the HAWAIIAN IS. and established on Lanai, Kahoolawe, and possibly Hawaii (no recent reports).

CALIFORNIA QUAIL   *Callipepla californica*   PLATE 12

Appearance: (10;25) A small dark quail with a black plume on the head. Brown on back, gray on head and breast, the belly white, prominently scaled with black and with a diffuse chestnut patch in the center. Male has black face bordered by white. Female duller and without facial markings.

Habits: Usually found in flocks (coveys). Keeps to the ground, only occasionally perching in low trees. When flushed, a covey scatters in all directions with a loud burst of noise from the wings. Most common in grassland that borders wooded tracts.

Voice: Calls in covey are dry clicking sounds. Song of male is 3-noted with accent on the second syllable: *whi-klee-tew*. Rather plaintive.

Identification: Prominent head plume distinguishes this from other quails except Gambel's. The latter lacks scaling on the belly, has bold black bar across center instead.

Occurrence: Native to w. N. America. Introduced before 1855 to the HAWAIIAN IS. (established Kauai, Maui, Lanai, and Hawaii). Common only on Hawaii in three areas: North Kona, Mauna Kea, and Hawaii Volcanoes National Park.

[HELMETED GUINEAFOWL   *Numida meleagris*   See Appendix A]

ORDER GRUIFORMES

FAMILY RALLIDAE: Rails, Moorhens, Gallinules, and Coots

THIS family includes several kinds of rather chickenlike birds. Most are found in wet or aquatic habitats, and the gallinules and coots are duck-like swimmers. Although more likely to be seen walking than flying, some rails have good powers of flight; they have colonized some of the world's most remote islands. Once established on an island, however, rails tend to become flightless or nearly so and thus highly vulnerable to introduced ground predators (rats, mongooses, etc.). As a result, many Pacific island rails are endangered or extinct. Some (not included here) are known only as fossils, apparently exterminated by prehistoric man.

Reference: Ripley, S. D. 1977, *Rails of the world*. Boston: David R. Godine.

BANDED RAIL   *Rallus philippensis*   PLATE 15

Appearance: (12;31) A large, strong-billed rail with a prominent reddish brown crown, nape, and stripe through eye. Eyebrow, throat, and upper breast gray, belly and flanks barred black and white. Some individuals show a buff band on the breast.

Habits: Commonly seen along roadsides or in wet grassy fields or marshes. Runs well; rarely flies. Not shy, often seen in the open, particularly after rain. Pairs frequently call back and forth while foraging.

Voice: A sharp, harsh *skeek*, given night or day.

Identification: The much smaller, secretive White-browed Crake is found on some of the same islands. Note its yellow bill, face pattern, and lack of barring.

Occurrence: Resident from the Philippines and E. Indies to New Zealand, PALAU, and c. POLYNESIA. Found on virtually all predator-free islands of Fiji, Wallis and Futuna, Samoa, Tonga, and Niue. Common most places, but probably extirpated on Viti Levu and Vanua Levu (Fiji) because of the presence of mongooses.

Other names: Banded Land Rail, Buff-banded Rail. Sometimes placed in *Gallirallus*.

GUAM RAIL   *Rallus owstoni*   PLATE 15

Appearance: (11;28) A large dark rail similar to Banded Rail but uniformly gray-brown above. No barring on the back.

Habits: A flightless rail of forest and secondary grassland and fern thickets. Sometimes seen along highways. Most active at dawn and dusk.

Voice: Loud screeches, *keee-yu, keee-yu, keee-yu,* or a series of short notes, *kip-kip-kip* etc.

Occurrence: Endemic to GUAM. Has drastically declined recently to critically low numbers. An Endangered Species.

Reference: Jenkins, J. M. 1979. Natural history of the Guam Rail. *Condor* 81:404-408.

Other name: Sometimes placed in *Gallirallus.*

WAKE RAIL   *Rallus wakensis*   PLATE 15

Appearance: (10;25) A small pale version of Banded Rail.

Habits: Flightless.

Identification: Some observers have mistakenly identified larger shorebirds such as Lesser Golden-Plover as rails. Note bill and postural differences.

Occurrence: Endemic to WAKE, but not seen since World War II and presumed extinct.

Other names: Wake Island Rail. Sometimes placed in *Gallirallus.*

BAR-WINGED RAIL   *Rallus poecilopterus*   PLATE 15

Appearance: (13;33) A large, plainly marked rail, dark gray below, brown above, about the size of a small domestic chicken. Bill, legs, and feet yellow.

Habits: Flightless. Inhabits remote forested areas, old overgrown plantations, and possibly lowland swamps.

Identification: May be confused with young domestic or feral chickens. Easily distinguished from other rails by larger size, darker unmarked color.

Occurrence: Solomon Is. and FIJI (Viti Levu, Oualau). Unrecorded in Fiji since 1880s, but rediscovered (see Holyoak 1979) in 1973 N of Waisa near Vunidawa (Viti Levu).

Other names: Barredwing Rail, Fiji Rail. Sometimes placed in *Nesoclopeus.*

[**TAHITI RAIL**   *Rallus pacificus*   See Appendix A]

BANDED CRAKE   *Rallina eurizonoides*   PLATE 15

Appearance: (10;25) A medium-sized rail with bright chestnut head, neck, and breast, olive-brown back and wings, and underparts barred black and white. Juvenile olive-brown.

Habits: Very secretive and mainly nocturnal. Found in thickets or dense grassy areas. Often perches in low trees or bushes. Found in a variety of forest types, often near villages, but heard more often than seen.

Voice: A monotonous nasal *ow-ow-ow*-etc. usually heard at dawn, dusk, or at night. May call in flight.

Identification: See Red-legged Crake.

Occurrence: SE. Asia and the Philippines to PALAU. Uncommon. Formerly considered a vagrant but now known to breed at Palau. Possibly some birds seen are migrant visitors.

Other name: Slaty-legged Crake.

RED-LEGGED CRAKE   *Rallina fasciata*

This apparently rare vagrant to PALAU from SE. Asia and the Philippines is very similar to the Banded Crake but has broader black and white bars below, prominent buff bars on the wings (wings unmarked in Banded), and red legs. Habits and voice little known. Other name: Malay Banded Crake. For illustration, see Simpson and Day (1984).

WHITE-BROWED CRAKE   *Porzana cinerea*   PLATE 15

Appearance: (7;18) A small, long-legged, grayish rail with a prominent dark line through the eye set off by bold white lines above and below. No barring. Eyes red, legs dull yellow.

Habits: Shy and secretive, often in pairs. Difficult to flush but responds to playback of its call. Prefers wet marshy areas with grass or reeds, and taro patches, where it may perch on the broad leaves. Pairs call back and forth in duet fashion.

Voice: A plaintive two-syllable *squeak-it* while foraging and a rollicking laughing chorus given by two or more birds.

Identification: Slimmer and longer-legged than other crakes. Also note pale color, distinctive face pattern, and lack of barring.

Occurrence: E. Indies and the Philippines E to MICRONESIA (Palau, Yap, Truk, Pohnpei; formerly Guam), FIJI, and SAMOA (Savaii, Upolu). Vagrant to BIKINI (Marshall Is.).

Other names: White-browed Rail, Ashy Crake. Sometimes placed in *Poliolimnas*.

SPOTLESS CRAKE   *Porzana tabuensis*   PLATE 15

Appearance: (6;15) A very small sooty rail with red legs and feet. Browner above, grayer below.

Habits: Found in many habitats including coastal marshes, fern-covered hillsides, and secondary forests. Swims well. May forage in intertidal zone. Sometimes feeds on seabird eggs. Elusive and shy; active at dawn and dusk.

Voice: A variety of calls including purring notes, sharp crackling scolds, mechanical sounds, and a deep honking. Calls night or day.

Occurrence: The Philippines and Australia E through virtually every island group in c. and se. POLYNESIA. Found on most high islands and some atolls. Gaps in distributional records may reflect only the secretive nature of the bird or the presence of ground predators. Known from Fiji, Tonga, Samoa, Niue, the Society Is., the Marquesas, the Tuamotu Arch., Tubuai Is., Oeno, and Ducie.

Other names: Sooty Rail, Sooty Crake.

HENDERSON ISLAND CRAKE   *Porzana atra*   PLATE 15

Appearance: (7;18) A small glossy black rail with heavy red legs.

Habits: Flightless, but a fast runner. Bold and curious. Mostly in forests of island interior, where it feeds chickenlike in leaf litter.

Voice: A clattering call and a sharp *clackety-clack*. Calling begins at dawn, before other birds.

Occurrence: Endemic to HENDERSON I. (Pitcairn Is.). Common.

Other name: Henderson Island Rail.

KOSRAE CRAKE   *Porzana monasa*   PLATE 15

This tiny (7;18) black rail has not been seen since first discovered on KOSRAE (Caroline Is.) in 1827. It inhabited taro patches and dark forests. Nothing more is known of it, and recent searches have failed to find it. Presumed extinct. Other names: Kittlitz's Rail, Ponape Crake (presumably erroneous).

HAWAIIAN RAIL   *Porzana sandwichensis*   PLATE 15

Appearance: (5;13) A tiny, dark rusty brown crake. Juveniles streaked on back. Legs red.

Habits: Said to have inhabited grassy uplands adjacent to forests or forest clearings.

Occurrence: Endemic to the main HAWAIIAN IS. (in historic times Hawaii, possibly Molokai). Last seen 1884. Extinct.

Other names: Sandwich Rail, *moho*. Sometimes placed in *Porzanula*.

LAYSAN RAIL   *Porzana palmeri*   PLATE 15

Appearance: (6;15) A tiny rail. Back sandy, streaked with black, underparts gray. Eyes red.

Habits: Flightless, fearless, and inquisitive. Fed on insects and seabird eggs.

Voice: Frequently called in chorus at night. Voice had a pinging, rattling, and warbling quality.

Occurrence: Endemic to LAYSAN (NW Hawaiian Is.). Introduced successfully to MIDWAY, unsuccessfully to PEARL AND HERMES REEF. Extinct. Last recorded at Midway (Eastern I.) in 1944. Succumbed to rats inadvertently introduced as a result of war activities.
Reference: Baldwin, P. H. 1947. The life history of the Laysan Rail. *Condor* 49:14-21.
Other name: Sometimes placed in *Porzanula*.

COMMON MOORHEN *Gallinula chloropus* PLATE 14

Appearance: (13;33) A ducklike dark gray waterbird with a chickenlike red bill and broad red shield on the forehead. Bill tip yellow. Lateral undertail coverts white, flanks marked with white dashes. Legs yellow with red "garters" above the ankle. Immature olive-brown with dull-colored legs and bill. Feet unwebbed.
Habits: A secretive denizen of freshwater habitats, where it may climb about in the vegetation, walk on the shore, or swim in open water. Feeds on mollusks and plants. Particularly fond of taro patches.
Voice: Croaks and creaks similar to calls of coots but higher pitched.
Identification: Differs from ducks in having pointed bill, from coots in red color of bill and line of white on flanks.
Occurrence: Cosmopolitan. In the tropical Pacific, resident in PALAU (Angaur; formerly Peleliu), the MARIANAS. (Saipan, Tinian; formerly Guam), and the HAWAIIAN IS. (Kauai, Oahu, Molokai; formerly Maui, Hawaii). Populations in the Marianas (*G. c. guami*) and the Hawaiian Is. (*G. c. sandvicensis*) are Endangered Species.
Reference: Byrd, G. V., and C. F. Zeillemaker. 1981. Ecology of nesting Hawaiian Common Gallinules at Hanalei, Hawaii. *W. Birds* 12:105-116.
Other names: Common Gallinule, Hawaiian Gallinule, 'alae 'ula.

SAMOAN WOODHEN
Gallinula pacifica FIGURE 22

Appearance: (estimated 10;25) A small black gallinule with yellow bill and frontal shield.
Habits: Reportedly shy and restricted to primary forest. May have dug or lived in burrows.
Identification: Anyone wishing to search for this supposedly extinct bird should be thoroughly familiar with the appearance in poor light of young chickens and juvenile Purple Swamphens. The latter lack the bright colors of the adults and can look all black.
Occurrence: Endemic to SAVAII (W. Samoa). Not seen since 1908 and probably extinct.
Other names: Samoan Wood Rail, Samoan Gallinule.

FIGURE 22. Samoan Woodhen
(possible appearance)

BUSH-HEN   *Gallinula olivacea*

Included here on the basis of a single immature specimen found floating dead in the sea near PULO ANNA (Palau) in May 1979. The bird
was an apparent migratory overshoot from Australia. The Bush-hen is
a plain-colored gallinule, olive above, dull buff below, with a rusty tinge
toward the rear. Bill green, frontal shield orange. Illustrated in field
guides to Australia and New Guinea.

[**WATERCOCK**   *Gallicrex cinerea*   See Appendix A]

PURPLE SWAMPHEN   *Porphyrio porphyrio*   PLATE 14

Appearance: (17;43) A large purple-blue bird with long red legs, a
bright red bill and frontal shield, and striking white undertail coverts.
Some individuals show much green and brown above. Juveniles less
brightly colored.

Habits: Found in taro patches, banana plantations, and other lowland
wet places. Feeds on young taro and banana shoots. Secretive, prefers
to run rather than fly. Usually alone or in pairs. Constantly flicks tail
while walking, making the white undertail conspicuous.

Voice: Loud calls with harsh chickenlike squawks. Also a high clear
skeek.

Identification: Much larger and more colorful than Common Moorhen.

Occurrence: S. Eurasia and Africa to New Zealand. In tropical Pacific,
resident in PALAU, SAMOA (all major islands), FIJI (islands without

mongooses, Rotuma), NIUE, and TONGA (throughout). Common here and there, but uncommon to rare on most islands.
Other names: Purple Gallinule, Pukeko.

EURASIAN COOT   *Fulica atra*   PLATE 14

This species has been recorded as a rare visitor in the MARIANAS, but should be looked for elsewhere in the Pacific, particularly in Hawaii. There, this Old World coot could be distinguished from the local species with certainty only by the configuration of the proximal end of the bill. In the Eurasian Coot, a point of black feathers indents the white bill and shield in front of the eyes. The Eurasian Coot is also generally darker and lacks white undertail coverts (but note that these are often not visible in a swimming Hawaiian Coot).

AMERICAN COOT   *Fulica americana*   PLATE 14

Coots of the mainland N. American form are rare and apparently irregular visitors to the HAWAIIAN IS. during the winter months. They are very similar to the endemic Hawaiian Coots in general appearance and behavior, but have a much smaller frontal shield that is merely a small dark maroon nail or knob on the forehead. The bill has a broken dark subterminal ring. Even red-shielded Hawaiian Coots can be distinguished by the size of the shield, which extends backwards to a point above and between the eyes. See Hawaiian Coot. Reference: Pratt, H. D. N.d. Occurrence of the North American coot (*Fulica americana americana*) in the Hawaiian Islands, with a review of the taxonomy of the resident Hawaiian form. *'Elepaio*. In press.

HAWAIIAN COOT   *Fulica alai*   PLATE 14

Appearance: (15½;39) A dark slate gray, ducklike bird with a pointed white bill that extends backward to the crown. Color of the upper part (the "frontal shield") varies from bluish white to yellow to dark blood red, but is most often white. Red-shielded birds also have dark marks near the bill tip. Immatures show white throat and breast, dark bill with small frontal shield. Chicks are black with reddish orange heads. The toes are lobed, not webbed as in ducks.

Habits: Inhabits fresh and saltwater ponds, estuaries, and marshes. Feeds mostly on plants. Builds a floating nest among aquatic vegetation.

Voice: Chickenlike *keck-keck* calls and other clucks and creaks.

Identification: Distinguished from all ducks by pointed bill, different swimming posture. The rare American Coot has a much smaller frontal shield and dark marks near the bill tip. Red-shielded Hawaiian Coot distinguished by much more bulbous shield, visible above the crown from the rear. Immature Hawaiian Coots can look much like the mainland visitor, but have dingy-colored bills and white feathers in the throat and breast. See Eurasian Coot.

Occurrence: Endemic to the HAWAIIAN IS. Found throughout except Lanai, with stragglers reaching the NW Hawaiian Is. W to Kure. An Endangered Species, but population in the thousands.

Reference: Byrd, G. V., R. A. Coleman, R. J. Shallenberger, and C. S. Arume. 1985. Notes on the breeding biology of the Hawaiian race of the American Coot. *'Elepaio* 45:57-63.

Other name: *'alae ke'oke'o.*

Note: Regarded as a subspecies of the American Coot in the 1983 AOU Check-list. Our reasons for regarding the Hawaiian form as a full species are set forth in a paper now in preparation (see Reference for American Coot, above).

ORDER CHARADRIIFORMES

FAMILY CHARADRIIDAE: Plovers and Dotterels

PLOVERS are ground-dwelling birds of shorelines, airstrips, lawns, and other open places. They are generally rounder-headed and stockier than stints and sandpipers and their bills are usually heavier. Plovers do not nest in the tropical Pacific, but many species winter among the islands or visit them occasionally, and a few nonbreeding individuals may remain all year. Most are arctic breeders, but one species that visits the tropical Pacific nests in New Zealand. The Lesser Golden-Plover is one of the region's most familiar birds and many comparisons with it are made in the following accounts. Observers should be thoroughly familiar with that species before attempting to identify the rarer ones. Most plovers seen in the tropical Pacific are in nonbreeding dress, but they usually molt at least partly into breeding plumage before they leave for their nesting grounds. The names "plover" and "dotterel" have no taxonomic significance and are virtually interchangeable. The latter is used more often by Australians and New Zealanders.

GRAY (BLACK-BELLIED) PLOVER   PLATE 16, FIGURE 23
Pluvialis squatarola

Appearance: (11½;29) A large plover with a thick black bill. Usually seen in the Pacific in nonbreeding plumage with brownish gray upperparts, paler underparts with black axillary feathers. Many birds are seen molting into breeding plumage, salt-and-pepper gray above with black throat and breast. In all plumages note white rump and tail, the latter finely barred with black.

Habits: Frequents shorelines and mudflats. Usually solitary in the Pacific.

Voice: A plaintive whistle that drops in pitch in the middle: *plee-oo-eee*.

Identification: Very similar to Lesser Golden-Plover, but black axillars and white rump diagnostic (Figure 23). Gray Plover stockier than Lesser Golden, with relatively larger head and bill. In breeding plumage note that the black of the underparts extends to undertail coverts on Lesser Golden-Plover, but not on Gray.

Occurrence: Breeds in the Arctic. Winters uncommonly and irregularly in the HAWAIIAN IS. and MICRONESIA (Palau, Yap, Marianas, Truk, Marshall Is.) with an isolated record for MANUAE (Cook Is.). A few individuals may remain in the tropics throughout the year.

Note: The name Gray Plover is used for this nearly cosmopolitan species in all English-speaking areas except North America. The bird is always at least partly gray, but is only seasonally black below, and then most of the belly is white (unlike the breeding Lesser Golden-Plover which has an all-black belly).

LESSER GOLDEN-PLOVER   PLATE 16, FIGURE 23
Pluvialis dominica

Appearance: (10½;27) A large long-legged plover. Nonbreeding birds mottled buff below, darker brown mottled with gold and buff above. Breeding plumage males are brightly speckled with gold above, black below, and have a distinct white stripe across forehead, above eye, and down side of neck. Breeding females have buffy neck stripes and may be mottled below. Many intermediate birds, blotched with black below and with indistinct eye stripes, are seen on Pacific islands. General posture and demeanor erect and alert.

Habits: Prefers open short-grass fields, roadsides, sandy beaches, and mudflats. Feeding behavior includes short runs and stops with quick stabs at the ground. Many individuals establish winter foraging territories to which they return each year. All abandon territories at night and roost in flocks.

Voice: A loud, clear, whistled *tooeet* or *kleeip*, often uttered on take-off.

Identification: Size, erect posture, and longer legs distinguish this species from smaller plovers and dotterels. See Gray (Black-bellied) Plover.

FIGURE 23. Flight Comparison of Large Plovers.
Gray (Black-bellied) Plover (*l.*) and Lesser
Golden-Plover (*r.*), both in nonbreeding plumage.

Occurrence: Common to abundant nonbreeding visitor throughout the tropical Pacific. Found from sea level to 3000 m. Most abundant August-April, but a few are present all year. Breeds in the Arctic.

References: Connors, P. G. 1983. Taxonomy, distribution, and evolution of golden plovers (*Pluvialis dominica* and *Pluvialis fulva*). *Auk* 100:607-620

Johnson, O. W., P. M. Johnson, and P. L. Bruner. 1981. Wintering behavior and site-faithfulness of Golden Plover on Oahu. *'Elepaio* 41:123-30.

Note: Recent research (Connors 1983, above) has produced evidence that the golden-plovers of the Pacific (*P. d. fulva*), which breed in Siberia and w. Alaska, may be sympatric with *P. d. dominica*, which breeds in arctic N. America. We recommend the names Pacific Golden-Plover and American Golden-Plover respectively for the two if further evidence confirms their status as separate species.

MONGOLIAN PLOVER   *Charadrius mongolus*   PLATE 16

Appearance: (7½;19) Nonbreeding plumage gray-brown with white eyebrow and forehead. Underparts white with gray-brown patch at side of breast. Breeding plumage with broad rufous breast band. Legs dark gray.

Habits: Frequents mudflats, sandy beaches, airstrips, and lawns, often in flocks with other small shorebirds.

Voice: Varied, including a staccato *drit* sometimes doubled or trebled, a plaintive whistle, and a short, weak, high-pitched twitter.

Identification: Very similar to Great Sand-Plover but with smaller, thinner bill and, in breeding plumage, a broader breast band.

Occurrence: Breeds in e. Asia. Regular nonbreeding visitor throughout MICRONESIA. Straggler to FIJI and the HAWAIIAN IS. To be expected elsewhere.

Other names: Lesser Sand-Plover, Mongolian Dotterel, Mongolian Sand-Plover.

GREAT SAND-PLOVER   *Charadrius leschenaultii*   PLATE 16

Appearance: (9;23) Similar in all plumages to Mongolian Plover but larger with a longer bill. Breeding plumage has narrower, more sharply defined rufous breast band. Legs pale gray to dull tan.

Habits: Prefers wide sandy beaches and mudflats, but also seen on airstrips and lawns.

Voice: A clear smooth *tweep tweep* and a low-pitched chuckle, longer than twitter of Mongolian Plover and similar to some calls of Ruddy Turnstone.

Identification: Very difficult to distinguish from Mongolian Plover, except when the two are seen together, as they often are. Note larger overall size and relatively longer bill (nearly length of head) of Great Sand-Plover. In nonbreeding plumage shows more white at sides of tail and usually has paler legs.

Occurrence: Breeds in c. Asia. Uncommon winter migrant to MICRONESIA (Palau, Yap, Marianas, Truk, Kosrae).

Other names: Greater Sand Plover, Large Sand Dotterel, Large Sand-Plover.

DOUBLE-BANDED DOTTEREL   *Charadrius bicinctus*   PLATE 16

Appearance: (7;18) A small brown-backed plover with white forehead, eyebrow, and underparts. Nonbreeding plumage has a single brown breast band, breeding plumage has an upper black band and a lower, broader chestnut band.

Habits: Migrant visitors frequent coastal mudflats in Fiji.

Voice: Call a high-pitched sharp double *chip*.

Identification: Double bands of breeding plumage diagnostic. Immature and nonbreeding birds resemble nonbreeding Mongolian Plover but are a yellower brown with the dark ear patch not clearly demarcated from side of head.

Occurrence: Breeds in New Zealand, migrates to Australia and rarely to FIJI. Should be looked for January-July.

SNOWY PLOVER *Charadrius alexandrinus* PLATE 16

Appearance: (6;15) A small pale plover with a hunched posture. Dark patches at sides of breast rather than a breast band. Tail white at sides, with dark center that contrasts with pale back. Wings with pronounced white stripe. Breeding plumage has black markings behind eye and on forecrown, and rufous crown.

Identification: Incomplete breast band, black legs, and paler back distinguish Snowy Plover from others recorded in Micronesia.

Occurrence: Breeds in e. Asia and N. America. A rare visitor in winter to w. MICRONESIA (Palau, Saipan) probably from Asiatic population. An undocumented sight record for OAHU (Hawaiian Is.) must be considered hypothetical.

Other names: Kentish Plover, Sand Plover, Red-capped Dotterel.

COMMON RINGED PLOVER *Charadrius hiaticula* FIGURE 24

Very similar in all plumages to the Semipalmated Plover and sometimes regarded as conspecific with it. In breeding plumage, breast band

FIGURE 24. Breeding Plumage Comparison of Semipalmated Plover (*l.*) and Common Ringed Plover (*r.*). Also shown are webbing patterns of feet.

broader centrally, tapering as it ascends. White spot behind eye always large and prominent. Call a quiet fluted *tooee*. Unconfirmed sight records for PALAU, GUAM, and MIDWAY (NW Hawaiian Is.). A bird reported as this species by Child (1982a) on Nui (Tuvalu) was, on the basis of his descriptions of vocalizations, probably a Semipalmated Plover. Breeds in arctic Eurasia.

SEMIPALMATED PLOVER   PLATE 16, FIGURE 24
Charadrius semipalmatus

Appearance: (6;15) A small, boldly patterned plover with dark brown back, white forehead and underparts, with a single bold dark breast band. Bill orange with black tip, legs yellow-orange. White spot above and behind eye usually small, sometimes absent. Wing shows a bold white stripe in flight. Pattern similar in all plumages, but nonbreeding birds paler throughout. All forward toes connected by short webs.
Habits: Found on beaches and mudflats in winter.
Voice: Call a 2-note whistle; *too-lee* or *chew-eet.*
Identification: Distinguished from Snowy Plover by complete breast band, darker back, yellow legs; from Little Ringed Plover by prominent wing stripe and (breeding plumage only) lack of white bar on forecrown. Probably indistinguishable in nonbreeding plumage from Common Ringed Plover except by voice or tracks in mud. See Common Ringed Plover.
Occurrence: Breeds in arctic N. America. Uncommon winter visitor to the HAWAIIAN IS., straggler to JOHNSTON ATOLL and possibly JALUIT (Marshall Is.) and NUI (Tuvalu). The last two records insufficiently documented to rule out Common Ringed Plover.

LITTLE RINGED PLOVER *Charadrius dubius*   PLATE 16

Appearance: (6;15) Pattern like that of Semipalmated Plover but with a white band on forecrown, no yellow on bill, and no wing stripe. Immatures have black markings replaced by brown, no white on forehead and breast band often incomplete.
Habits: Likely to be found inland rather than along shorelines. Frequents mudflats and gravel streambeds.
Voice: A quiet downslurred whistle.
Identification: Lack of wing stripe distinguishes this species from all other small plovers in the tropical Pacific.
Occurrence: Breeds in e. Asia. Infrequent winter visitor to MICRONESIA (Palau, Yap, Guam).

KILLDEER *Charadrius vociferus*
This widespread N. American species is a very rare visitor to the HA-

WAIIAN IS., but stragglers may remain for several years. Slimmer and longer-tailed than other large (10½;27) plovers. Rufous rump and tail, double breast bands, and loud *kill-deee* whistle contribute to distinctiveness of this species. Illustrated in N. American field guides.

ORIENTAL PLOVER *Charadrius veredus*

A large (10;25) plover, intermediate in size between Great Sand-Plover and Lesser Golden-Plover. More plainly marked than the latter, usually with paler legs. Lacks sharply defined breast band of sand-plovers, but has a broad diffuse grayish brown band. Face, eyebrow, and throat dingy white. Similar in behavior to golden-plover and often found with it. Breeds in e. Asia and migrates to Australia and New Zealand. Birds in nonbreeding plumage are rare visitors to PALAU. For illustrations, see Australian field guides or Falla et al. (1979). Other name: Oriental Dotterel.

EURASIAN DOTTEREL *Charadrius morinellus*

An immature female of this species was found on KURE in 1964 for the only recorded occurrence in the area of this guide. The winter plumage is a dingy gray with an indistinct white band across the breast. Illustrated in Eurasian and N. American field guides.

FAMILY HAEMATOPODIDAE:
OYSTERCATCHERS

OYSTERCATCHERS are very large, stocky shorebirds boldly patterned in black and white with bright red bills. They only rarely visit the tropical Pacific.

EURASIAN OYSTERCATCHER *Haematopus ostralegus*

A single individual of this species was seen and photographed (Maben and Wiles 1981) on GUAM in 1980 and remained on the island for at least a year. Color illustrations in most Eurasian field guides.

FAMILY RECURVIROSTRIDAE: AVOCETS AND STILTS

THESE are long-legged, slender wading birds with bold black and white patterned plumage. Avocets have upturned bills, and have not been recorded as yet in the tropical Pacific. Stilts have red or pink legs and straight thin bills. One species breeds in the area of this guide; others are migrant visitors.

BLACK-WINGED STILT   *Himantopus himantopus*   FIGURE 25

Appearance: (15;38) Similar to Black-necked Stilt but female has head and neck entirely white, male with crown and hindneck dark gray not sharply separated from white areas (appears to have a smudgy border). Dark of male's hindneck not continuous with black back.

Identification: Stilt identification in the tropical Pacific is complicated by problems of geographic variation in potentially occurring forms. The Hawaiian bird is sedentary and unlikely to wander to other Pacific islands, but the N. American mainland form of Black-necked Stilt could. The Black-winged Stilt described above is the Asian form recorded at Palau. A stilt of unknown species recorded from Makin Atoll (Kiribati) could have been the N. American, Asian, or, perhaps more likely, the Australasian form. In the Australasian form, usually regarded as a subspecies of Black-winged Stilt, but sometimes considered a separate species, the Pied Stilt (*H. leucocephalus*), both sexes have a sharply defined black hindneck not separated from the black back, and an entirely white crown (Figure 25). The Pied Stilt has been recorded

FIGURE 25. Stilts

as a migrant to New Britain, and should be looked for elsewhere in the tropical Pacific.

Occurrence: Breeds in Eurasia (Black-winged form), Australia and New Zealand (Pied form). A very rare visitor to the tropical Pacific recorded at PALAU and possibly on MAKIN (Kiribati).

BLACK-NECKED STILT   PLATE 17, FIGURE 25
Himantopus mexicanus

Appearance: (14;35) A black and white bird with a long straight black bill and long pink legs. Males have black backs, females brown. Hawaiian immatures resemble females but have white patches on the cheeks (thus resembling the adult mainland form), and are lightly barred with buff on the back.

Habits: Noisy and conspicuous, especially when nesting. Forages by wading and probing in ponds, on mudflats, and in wet grassy areas. Even a very small wet area may attract stilts.

Voice: A loud sharp *kip-kip-kip*. One of the characteristic sounds of Hawaiian wetlands.

Identification: Unmistakable. The Hawaiian subspecies differs from the mainland form in having more extensive black on sides of neck and face. See Black-winged Stilt and Figure 25.

Occurrence: Resident in the Americas and all the main HAWAIIAN IS., except Lanai. Island population around 1200 at this writing (1985). Hawaiian form (*H. m. knudseni*) an Endangered Species.

Other names: Hawaiian Stilt, *'ae'o*.

FAMILY SCOLOPACIDAE: SANDPIPERS, PHALAROPES, AND RELATED BIRDS

THIS family includes a variety of types of shorebirds or waders: sandpipers, stints, tattlers, curlews, godwits, snipes, turnstones, and phalaropes. Some of these groups are described in separate paragraphs preceding the species accounts. In general, members of this family are characterized by long straight or curved bills that usually taper at the tip. Most exhibit plumage patterns with cryptic spots and bars, often with a streaked or barred breast. Most have three distinct plumage types: breeding, nonbreeding, and juvenile. The latter two are usually similar but can be distinguished. Only one member of the family (Tuamotu Sandpiper) now breeds in the tropical Pacific, but migratory visitors often acquire at least traces of the breeding plumage before they depart in the spring.

A few species (i.e. two tattlers, Sanderling, Bristle-thighed Curlew, Ruddy Turnstone) are widespread and even common in the region. The birder should be thoroughly familiar with them in all their plumages before attempting to identify the rare visitors. Many of the seemingly rare species are probably regular visitors in low numbers. The paucity of records is more a function of the distribution of observers than of birds. Almost every competent birder or ornithologist who has spent any time in the tropical Pacific has turned up new distributional records of shorebirds. These birds thus provide one of the greatest birding adventures in the region. One should not assume that a species occurs only on islands where previously recorded. Where shorebirds are concerned, any species can occur anywhere.

The largest shorebird list for any island group covered by this guide is that of Palau. Sooner or later probably every shorebird that migrates through or to eastern Asia or Australia will be found there. The Northwestern Hawaiian Islands are another excellent "trap" for rare shorebirds. The number of shorebird species recorded drops rapidly from west to east and from north to south so that Yap, the Marianas, Truk, and the main Hawaiian Islands have smaller, though still substantial, lists while central and eastern Polynesia have far fewer recorded species.

COMMON GREENSHANK   *Tringa nebularia*   PLATE 17

Appearance: (13½;34) A large wader with green or dull yellow legs, long, slightly upturned bill, and pale gray body. Breeding plumage has streaked breast. Rump patch white, wedge-shaped, extending up back.
Habits: A wary bird that feeds in mudflats or garbage dumps. Often calls when flushed, flies rapidly.
Voice: A noisy, strident, ringing *cheew*.
Identification: Larger, paler, and with grayer legs and thicker bill than similar Marsh Sandpiper. Greater Yellowlegs has differently shaped white rump patch, brighter legs.
Occurrence: Breeds in Siberia. Regular migrant to w. MICRONESIA (Palau, Yap, Marianas, Truk).

NORDMANN'S GREENSHANK   *Tringa guttifer*

An individual of this species, also called Spotted Greenshank, was seen on GUAM in fall 1983. Breeds e. Siberia, winters se. Asia. Similar to Common Greenshank in winter plumage, but with dull yellow rather than green legs. Shorter-legged and straighter-billed than Common Greenshank. Looks somewhat like a large tattler; distinguished from tattlers by white rump. Illustrated in WBSJ (1982).

GREATER YELLOWLEGS *Tringa melanoleuca* PLATE 17

Appearance and Identification: (14;35) Very similar to more frequent Lesser Yellowlegs, especially in nonbreeding plumage. Bill long (more than 1½ times length of head), often very slightly upturned, usually appearing bicolored. In breeding plumage, boldly streaked on neck and underparts (including belly) with bold vertical bars on the flanks. See Common Greenshank.

Voice: A loud, ringing 3- to 5-note whistle, louder and more forceful than call of Lesser Yellowlegs.

Occurrence: Breeds in Alaska and Canada. A rare visitor to the tropical Pacific with records for the HAWAIIAN IS. and an unsubstantiated report from WAKE. A yellowlegs, not positively identified but probably this species, has also been seen on RAROTONGA (Cook Is.).

LESSER YELLOWLEGS *Tringa flavipes* PLATE 17

Appearance: (10½;27) A gray, yellow-legged shorebird, larger than most sandpipers and stints. Bill black and straight, about the same length as the head. Rump white, not extending up center of back. Tail white, finely barred with black. Breeding plumage streaked with black on neck and breast, belly white. Bars on flanks not prominent.

Habits: Usually found on mudflats or shallow ponds. Often associated in loose flocks with smaller sandpipers.

Voice: One to three short whistles, less ringing than call of Greater Yellowlegs.

Identification: Beware yellowlegs with muddy shanks. See Greater Yellowlegs, Marsh Sandpiper, Wood Sandpiper.

Occurrence: Breeds in N. America. An uncommon but regular winter visitor to the HAWAIIAN IS. and JOHNSTON ATOLL.

Reference: Wilds, C. 1982. Separating the yellowlegs. *Birding* 14:172-78.

MARSH SANDPIPER *Tringa stagnatilis* PLATE 17

Appearance: (10;25) A small grayish brown wader, white below with a long, thin, straight black bill and long green legs. Rump patch white, extending up the back to a point between the wings.

Habits: Frequents freshwater wetlands and mudflats. Forages by probing and by waving bill back and forth in water.

Voice: A mellow whistled *keu*, sometimes repeated.

Identification: Similar to Common Greenshank in color pattern, but smaller and more delicate, with very thin bill and proportionately longer legs that project well beyond the tail in flight. Voice thinner, less ringing than greenshank's. Other shorebirds of similar size with pale

legs (Wood Sandpiper, Lesser Yellowlegs, Wilson's Phalarope) have white confined to the rump and not extending up the back in a point.
Occurrence: Breeds in Siberia. Regular winter visitor to w. MICRONESIA (Palau, Yap, Marianas, Truk).

COMMON REDSHANK   *Tringa totanus*   PLATE 17

Appearance: (11;28) A large, brownish gray wader with red legs, red base of bill, broad white trailing edge to wing, and white rump. Heavily streaked below in breeding plumage.
Habits: Frequents mudflats, marshes, and wet grassy fields.
Identification: Distinguished from similar Spotted Redshank by broad white wing stripe. Common Redshank also shorter-legged, stockier. Rump patch wedge-shaped with point toward middle of back as in Common Greenshank, rather than squared off as in both yellowlegs.
Occurrence: Breeds in Eurasia. An uncommon migrant in w. MICRONESIA (Palau, Yap).

SPOTTED REDSHANK   *Tringa erythropus*

Appearance and Identification: (12;31) Winter plumage like that of Common Redshank without white wing stripe. Slimmer, with longer legs and bill. Breeding plumage (unrecorded in tropical Pacific) black, with white spotting above. Illustrated in Eurasian field guides and NGS (1983).
Occurrence: Breeds in n. Siberia. Straggler to MICRONESIA (Guam, Truk; should be looked for elsewhere).

WOOD SANDPIPER   *Tringa glareola*   PLATE 17

Appearance: (8;20) A gray-brown sandpiper, spotted with buff above, and white below with long dull yellow or greenish yellow legs. Rump and tail white, the latter with narrow black bars.
Habits: A shy, nervous wader found in marshes and along shorelines. Often found near dead trees or brush. Flies high when flushed.
Voice: A loud rapid *jif-jif-jif*, louder and higher pitched than calls of Lesser Yellowlegs.
Identification: Similar to Marsh Sandpiper but darker, spotted above, and with shorter, thicker bill. Shorter-legged than Lesser Yellowlegs, the legs never as bright yellow. Also note chunkier, bigger-headed profile of Wood Sandpiper. Green Sandpiper (Appendix A) and Solitary Sandpiper similar but with dark underwings, the Solitary with dark rump and center of tail.
Occurrence: Breeds across Siberia. Migrant through w. MICRONESIA (fairly common Palau, Yap; less common Marianas, Truk). Stragglers to the MARSHALL IS. and NW HAWAIIAN IS. (Midway, Kure).

FIGURE 26. Willet. Breeding plumage (*l.*), nonbreeding plumage (*r.*).

[GREEN SANDPIPER *Tringa ochropus* See Appendix A]

SOLITARY SANDPIPER *Tringa solitarius*
This N. American species has been recorded once (1983) on HAWAII. It is like a diminutive (8½;22) Lesser Yellowlegs but much darker above and with dull olive legs. White eye-ring very prominent. Also compare Wood Sandpiper, which has white rump. Illustrated in N. American field guides.

WILLET *Catoptrophorus semipalmatus* FIGURE 26
Appearance: (15;38) A large (size of curlews and godwits) brownish gray sandpiper, nondescript except for bold black and white wing pattern visible in flight. Bill thick, straight, and dark. Legs bluish gray. Breeding plumage streaked and barred.
Voice: A musical *pill-will-willet*.
Identification: Should be compared with godwits. Note Willet's stout straight bill and distinctive wing pattern.
Occurrence: Breeds in N. America. Rare straggler to the HAWAIIAN IS. and JOHNSTON ATOLL.

WANDERING TATTLER PLATE 19, FIGURE 27
Heteroscelus incanus
Appearance: (11;28) A dark gray sandpiper, lighter below, with a white

superciliary stripe, long straight black bill, and dull yellow legs. In breeding plumage heavily barred beneath, with particularly bold bars on undertail coverts. Posture more horizontal or hunched than that of other sandpipers.

Habits: Frequents rocky shorelines, tidal flats, and rocky streams. May perch in trees. Usually solitary, occasionally in small flocks. Characteristically bobs tail while foraging. Hunts by running and probing. Prey include fishes and small invertebrates.

Voice: A clear trill of short whistles trailing off at the end. The Hawaiian name *'ulili* is imitative. Call usually uttered in flight.

Identification: Uniformly dark upperparts, short legs, and hunched posture distinguish tattlers from yellowlegs and other pale-legged sandpipers. See Siberian Tattler.

Occurrence: Breeds in Alaska and nw. Canada, migrates to the tropics. Widespread and common throughout the tropical Pacific, but less frequent to the W where Siberian Tattler predominates.

SIBERIAN (GRAY-TAILED) TATTLER   PLATE 19, FIGURE 27
Heteroscelus brevipes

Appearance: (10;25) Very similar to, and often indistinguishable from, Wandering Tattler. Superciliary stripes are clear unbroken white, meeting above the bill. Breeding plumage more finely barred below, with clear belly and undertail coverts. Paler throughout.

Habits: Like Wandering Tattler.

Voice: A 2-syllable whistle, *too-weet*, somewhat like the call of Pacific Golden-Plover, and a trill similar to, but less crisp than, that of Wandering Tattler.

Identification: The two tattlers are notoriously difficult to separate in the field. The 2-note call is diagnostic for Siberian, but that species can also sound somewhat like a Wandering Tattler. Seen together and in

FIGURE 27. Head Patterns of Siberian (Gray-tailed) Tattler (*l.*) and Wandering Tattler (*r.*)

good light, the paler color of the Siberian should be apparent. The eye stripe is variable in both species, but is characteristically mottled with dark gray and does not cross over the forehead in the Wandering (see Figure 27). In breeding plumage the ventral bars of the Siberian Tattler are much finer and more delicate than those of the Wandering, the belly is white, and undertail coverts are unmarked except for a few faint bars on the *sides*. In the Wandering Tattler the undertail coverts have the heaviest bars of the whole underparts. Wandering Tattlers molting from winter to summer plumage often show unbarred bellies, but the undertail coverts usually are barred as soon as any other part of the underside. The Siberian Tattler will have both belly and undertail coverts unbarred. Sight identifications of tattlers should be based on a combination of characters.

Occurrence: Breeds in Siberia, migrates to the w. tropical Pacific. Winters throughout MICRONESIA, and in FIJI and TUVALU. Probably occurs on other c. Polynesian islands but the only definite record is for AITUTAKI (Cook Is.). Stragglers reach the NW HAWAIIAN IS. (Kure, Midway).

Note: This species has been called both Siberian and Gray-tailed as well as Polynesian Tattler. The distributions of the two tattlers (see accounts) show how inappropriate the last name is. Australian and New Zealand literature uses Siberian Tattler, an accurate and informative name. The 1983 AOU Check-list name (Gray-tailed) is misleading because it implies a visual difference between the two tattlers that does not exist (both have gray tails). We prefer the Australian name.

COMMON SANDPIPER *Actitis hypoleucos* FIGURE 28

Appearance: (8;20) Plain brown above, white below with conspicuous white eyebrow, wing bar, and sides of tail. Chin and throat not clear white, with dark patches on sides of breast marked by thin streaks (hard to see). Tail extends well beyond tip of folded wing.

Habits: Distinctive irregular flight, with alternating glides and quick flaps. Wings held low during glides. When walking, bobs and teeters in a rocking motion. Usually solitary. Found on shorelines, mudflats, and gravel roadsides.

Voice: A shrill whistled *twee-wee-weet*, more muted than call of Spotted Sandpiper, but not strikingly different.

Identification: See Spotted Sandpiper.

Occurrence: Breeds across Eurasia. A common winter visitor to PALAU and YAP, less common at TRUK, POHNPEI, and the MARIANAS. Stragglers recorded in SAMOA and the PHOENIX IS. (Kiribati). Possibly Kosrae and the Hawaiian Is., but records unsubstantiated.

FIGURE 28. Comparison of Spotted Sandpiper (*l.*) and Common Sandpiper (*r.*)

SPOTTED SANDPIPER   *Actitis macularia*   FIGURE 28

Appearance and Identification: (7½;19) Very similar in appearance and habits to Common Sandpiper but differently shaped, with wings extending to mid-tail at rest. Spotted in winter is cleaner below, with unstreaked dark patches on sides of breast only. In flight, note shorter wing stripe, not extending to inner secondaries, and less white in sides of tail. Juvenile Spotteds have prominently barred wing coverts that contrast with an unmarked back, whereas Common juveniles have less obvious barring on both back and wing coverts. Breeding plumage is unmistakable with large brown spots below.

Voice: A shrill 2- or 3-toned piping: *twee-wee* or *twee-wee-wee*. More ringing than call of Common Sandpiper.

Occurrence: Breeds in N. America. Recorded as a straggler from TAKA (Marshall Is.) and JOHNSTON ATOLL. Several sight records

for the HAWAIIAN IS. were probably this species, but reports have not been sufficiently detailed to rule out Common Sandpiper.
Reference: Wallace, D.I.M. 1980. Identification of Spotted Sandpipers out of breeding plumage. In *Frontiers of bird identification*, ed. J.T.R. Sharrock. London: Macmillan Journals Ltd.

TEREK SANDPIPER *Xenus cinereus* PLATE 19

Appearance and Identification: (9;23) The only small sandpiper with a strongly upturned bill. The short yellow-orange legs give the bird a distinctive profile. In flight, wings show a broad white bar on trailing edge. Underparts plain white in all plumages. The black scapular markings of the breeding plumage (shown on Plate 19) disappear in the fall and winter.
Habits: Very active in feeding. Often bobs or teeters like Common Sandpiper. Frequents mudflats and garbage dumps.
Voice: A loud, rapid, high-pitched whinny, *too-too-too*, and a short rolling note.
Occurrence: Breeds in Siberia and migrates to Australasia. Regular migrant through PALAU, less common in the MARIANAS and YAP. Straggler to FIJI.

TUAMOTU SANDPIPER *Prosobonia cancellatus* PLATE 18

Appearance: (6½;17) A small, highly variable brown sandpiper with a white eye stripe. Bill short, black. Plumage streaky, especially below.
Habits: Very tame and curious. Feeds on insects among coral rubble and leaf litter. Prefers open areas along atoll shorelines. Nonmigratory, but may visit islands where it does not nest. Nests only on uninhabited atolls. Probably susceptible to introduced mammals.
Voice: A high-pitched piping or squeaky whistle uttered continuously when the bird forages.
Identification: The only other small sandpiper in the region is the Sanderling, which is much paler with darker legs and very different foraging behavior.
Occurrence: Endemic to the tropical Pacific. Now restricted to uninhabited or predator-free atolls in the TUAMOTU ARCH. Formerly KIRITIMATI (Line Is.). Vulnerable as more and more islands become disturbed by human activity.

TAHITIAN SANDPIPER *Prosobonia leucoptera*

Three specimens of this small sandpiper were collected by Cook's expedition in 1773 in the SOCIETY IS. (Tahiti, Moorea). Only one specimen is extant, and the species has not been observed again. It probably succumbed to introduced rats. The bird was similar in proportions to the Tuamotu Sandpiper but was unstreaked plain brown above, with a white eye stripe, rufous rump, and rufous underparts. Inhabited rocky streams and estuaries.

[**UPLAND SANDPIPER** *Bartramia longicauda* See Appendix A]

CURLEWS: Genus *Numenius*

CURLEWS are rather large shorebirds with downcurved bills. All are streaky brown, chunky waders with relatively long legs. They exhibit less seasonal and age variation than other members of this family. The Bristle-thighed Curlew is one of the tropical Pacific's more familiar shorebirds, and the Whimbrel is common in Micronesia. Others are rare visitors. In identifying curlews, note the relative length of bill, presence or absence of bold stripes on the crown, and color of the lower back and rump.

LITTLE CURLEW *Numenius minutus* FIGURE 29

Appearance and Identification: (12;31) Much smaller (body size of Lesser Golden-Plover) than other curlews and with relatively shorter and only slightly downcurved bill. Like a less strongly marked Whimbrel in pattern but buffier throughout, particularly the head stripes. Rump does not contrast with back as in Eurasian forms of Whimbrel.
Habits: In winter frequents grasslands, airstrips, and mudflats.
Voice: A harsh *chew-chew-chew* when alarmed. Not as shrill as Whimbrel's call.
Occurrence: Breeds in Siberia, winters mainly in Australia. A rare visitor to w. MICRONESIA (Palau, Guam).
Other name: Little Whimbrel.

WHIMBREL *Numenius phaeopus* PLATE 17

Appearance: (17½;45) A medium-sized curlew with bold stripes on the crown. Grayer brown than Little or Bristle-thighed Curlew. Asiatic subspecies has streaked white rump, pale underwings. The N. American form has brown back and rump, dingy underwings.
Habits: Can be found in almost any habitat frequented by shorebirds. Flight rapid, steady, and ducklike.
Voice: A clear, whistled *tee-tee-tee-tee-tee-tee-tee* (usually 7) on level pitch.
Identification: Far Eastern and Eurasian curlews larger, longer-billed, and lack crown stripes. Similar-sized Bristle-thighed Curlew has cinnamon rump, buffier tone to head and breast, different call. See Little Curlew.

FIGURE 29. Little Curlew

Occurrence: Breeds in n. latitudes and migrates to the south. Common transient and winter visitor throughout MICRONESIA, less common in FIJI, TUVALU, and SAMOA, rare in the HAWAIIAN IS.

Note: Although most Whimbrels in the tropical Pacific are the Asiatic form (*N.p. variegatus*), the American one (*N.p. hudsonicus*) has been found widely and occurs regularly in low numbers in New Zealand. The two are readily distinguishable by the color of the rump.

BRISTLE-THIGHED CURLEW *Numenius tahitiensis* PLATE 17

Appearance: (17;43) A stripe-headed curlew with pale orange-brown or light cinnamon rump and tail, the latter with a few bold dark bars. Plumage generally more buffy than that of Whimbrel, particularly on the neck and breast.

Habits: Usually seen in flocks of a few to over 100 individuals. Prefers sand bars, mudflats, and open grasslands from sea level to mountaintop. Often wary, probably because it is hunted on some islands. Flight strong and direct, without the turning and banking characteristic of plovers. Almost always calls when flushed, and can be induced to circle back to the observer by a good imitation.

Voice: A quick *curlew* or *weoo-weet*, totally unlike the call of Whimbrel.

Identification: Slightly larger than Whimbrel with orange-brown rump and tail, golden tone to neck and breast, more flesh tone at base of bill, and distinctive call. Much larger than Little Curlew.

Occurrence: Breeds in Alaska and winters among Pacific islands. Common in the NW HAWAIIAN IS., e. MICRONESIA, and se. POLY-

NESIA, less common in c. POLYNESIA and FIJI, rare in the main HAWAIIAN IS. and w. MICRONESIA (W to Yap).

FAR EASTERN CURLEW *Numenius madagascariensis*   PLATE 17

Appearance: (17;43) A large curlew with bill nearly half the length of the body. Upperparts pale buffy gray with dark brown streaks, head unstriped. Underparts buff, rump and tail tan barred with brown. Underwing heavily barred.

Voice: A high-pitched *kerlee* or *crooeee*.

Identification: Large size, unmarked head, and extremely long, strongly curved bill distinguish this from all curlews except Eurasian. Eurasian is similar but has white rump and wing linings.

Occurrence: Breeds in e. Siberia, migrates southward. A rare but possibly regular migrant in w. MICRONESIA (Palau E to Truk), and FIJI.

Other names: Eastern Curlew, Australian Curlew.

EURASIAN CURLEW *Numenius arquata*

Very similar to Far Eastern Curlew but larger (22;55), with white rump, black and white barred tail, and white underwings. Breeds further W than Far Eastern Curlew and usually winters to Africa. Wanderers have been recorded in SE. Asia, Australasia, SAIPAN (Mariana Is.), and NIUE. Illustrated in Eurasian field guides and NGS (1983).

GODWITS: Genus *Limosa*

GODWITS are large waders or shorebirds with long legs and long two-toned bills that in most species are upturned. They resemble curlews in habits and manner of flight, and frequent open grassy lawns, airstrips, fields, and mudflats. They visit the tropical Pacific during the northern winter, and are usually seen in nonbreeding plumage. Some may molt into breeding dress before they depart in the spring. All four godwit species have been recorded in the region, but two are very rare. Salient features to note in identifying godwits are pattern of rump and tail, presence and width of wing stripe, and color of wing lining. These features are more easily seen when the birds fly.

BLACK-TAILED GODWIT *Limosa limosa*   PLATE 17, FIGURE 30

Appearance: (16½;42) In winter a pearly gray godwit with straight bill. In flight (Figure 30) presents a striking pattern with broad white stripe across the base of flight feathers, white rump, uppertail coverts, and base of tail, and broad black band across tail. Underwings silvery white, the wing stripe not contrasting with the underwing coverts. Breeding

FIGURE 30. Comparison of Black-tailed Godwit (*l.*) and Hudsonian Godwit (*r.*)

plumage orange-rufous below, lightly barred with brown. Molt begins in March or April.

Voice: A harsh *weeka-weeka-weeka*. Usually silent on wintering grounds.

Identification: Told from all other godwits except Hudsonian (see below) by bold wing stripe, black tail. Willet has similar but more striking flight pattern (Figure 26), but has gray tail.

Occurrence: Breeds in n. Eurasia, winters in Eastern Hemisphere tropics and Australia. Rare visitor throughout MICRONESIA.

HUDSONIAN GODWIT *Limosa haemastica* FIGURE 30

Very similar to but slightly smaller (15½;39) than Black-tailed Godwit, and usually distinguishable with certainty only if underwing is seen. Wing stripe much narrower but slightly longer than that of Black-tailed, and appears as a narrow stripe on dark underwing, which has black wing lining and axillars. Breeding plumage rich chestnut below, heavily streaked and barred with dark brown. A N. American breeder and rare but regular visitor to New Zealand. Included here on the basis of a 1981 sighting in FIJI and a possible 1975 sighting on OAHU (details insufficient to eliminate Black-tailed). Reference: Skinner, N. J., and N. P. E. Langham. 1981. Hudsonian Godwit in Fiji. *Notornis* 28:128-29.

BAR-TAILED GODWIT   *Limosa lapponica*   PLATE 17

Appearance: (16;41) A mottled brown godwit with no wing stripe. Rump and tail barred black and white (European race, not seen in Pacific, has white rump), wing lining brown with white barring. Breeding plumage has unbarred brick red underparts, female paler than male. Molt begins in January.

Voice: A clear *kew-kew*.

Identification: Differs from Black-tailed and Hudsonian Godwit by lack of wing stripe. Sometimes difficult to distinguish from rare Marbled Godwit.

Occurrence: Breeds in Siberia and n. Alaska. A common visitor throughout MICRONESIA and FIJI, uncommon E to SAMOA, NIUE, and the HAWAIIAN IS.

MARBLED GODWIT   *Limosa fedoa*

Included here on the basis of a single 1966 record of two birds on LAYSAN (NW Hawaiian Is.). The largest (18;46) godwit, buff throughout with a checkered pattern on back, no wing stripe. Rump and tail barred brown and buff (tail of Bar-tailed looks paler). Cinnamon wing linings (white in Bar-tailed) diagnostic. In flight, legs trail further behind tail than in Bar-tailed. Illustrated in N. American field guides.

RUDDY TURNSTONE   *Arenaria interpres*   PLATE 16

Appearance: (9½;24) A plump short-legged shorebird with a short, thick, pointed bill. In overall proportions more like a plover than a sandpiper. In breeding plumage, has a distinctive black and white pattern on head and breast, and the back is rufous. Nonbreeding plumage is a smudgy gray-brown version of the same pattern without any rufous. Most turnstones seen in the tropical Pacific are in intermediate plumage stages and rather blotchy. Note highly distinctive black and white pattern of wings and tail in flight.

Habits: Often in small flocks in association with Lesser Golden-Plovers. Forages by constantly walking, turning and probing the substrate. Frequents open grassy fields, mudflats, sandbars, and rocky shorelines.

Voice: Metallic rattles and low slurred whistles.

Occurrence: Breeds along arctic coasts. Widespread and fairly common in tropical Pacific August-May. A few remain all year. Common from the HAWAIIAN IS. and MICRONESIA S to FIJI, TONGA, and SAMOA; uncommon E to the COOK IS., with only scattered records for the SOCIETY IS. and TUAMOTU ARCH.

SMALLER SANDPIPERS AND STINTS: Genus *Calidris*

THIS large grouping includes several different kinds of small shorebirds formerly placed in separate genera. They are all smaller than godwits and curlews and include the smallest members of the family. They are often very difficult to identify. Several species or species pairs are more distinctive: the knots, Pectoral and Sharp-tailed sandpipers, Dunlin and Curlew sandpipers, and Sanderling. The remainder fall into a group known in birding jargon as "peeps." They are called stints by Old World English-speakers, sandpipers by Americans. Thus for the English names we use stint for Eurasian breeders and sandpiper for those that nest in North America. To avoid confusion we refer to them collectively as stints.

GREAT KNOT   *Calidris tenuirostris*

Appearance and identification: (11½;29) A chunky sandpiper with a long bill drooped at the tip. Larger than a turnstone. Nonbreeding plumages like those of Red Knot in pattern, but darker above (making the white rump more conspicuous), and more heavily streaked on crown, neck, and breast. Breeding plumage heavily blotched with black across breast, scapulars boldly marked with rufous. Illustrated in WBSJ (1982) and NGS (1983).

Occurrence: Breeds ne. Siberia, winters S to Australia. Rare visitor in w. MICRONESIA (Palau, Truk).

RED KNOT   *Calidris canutus*   PLATE 19

Appearance: (10½;27) A chunky, short-necked sandpiper with a black bill about the same length as the head. In winter, upperparts gray, the feathers edged with white (broader in juveniles, which look scaly above). Eyebrow and underparts white or buff. Rump and uppertail coverts barred black and white, look almost white. Legs dull green. Breeding plumage, which may be retained well into fall, has bright rufous-red breast.

Identification: Resembles dowitchers in general shape and color, but has shorter bill and lacks white center of back. Curlew Sandpiper also has white rump and (breeding plumage only) chestnut underparts, but rump whiter, underparts darker, bill longer and downcurved, legs longer and darker, and shape slimmer.

Occurrence: Breeds in the high Arctic, winters to Southern Hemisphere. Found rarely in the HAWAIIAN IS., PALAU, and FIJI.

SANDERLING   *Calidris alba*   PLATE 18

Appearance: (8;20) A small stocky sandpiper, light gray above, white below, with black bill and legs and conspicuous black patch at bend of wing. Breeding plumage (rarely seen in the Pacific) rusty, streaked with black on back, head, and breast. White wing stripe conspicuous in flight in both plumages. Lacks hind toe.

Habits: Partial to sandy beaches; follows retreating waves like wind-up toy. Also found on exposed reefs, mudflats, or open ground inland. Usually in small flocks.

Voice: A sharp short whistled *weet* or *wheet-weet* may be uttered on take-off. In flight, flocks give a high-pitched rattling call.

Identification: The palest sandpiper of the region, appearing all white at a distance. Larger than stints, but smaller than most other Pacific sandpipers. Black shoulder patch distinctive. Birds coming into breeding plumage might be mistaken for Rufous-necked Stint, but are not as clearly red below and have white eyebrows.

Occurrence: Cosmopolitan. Breeds in the Arctic, winters to Southern Hemisphere. Probably found throughout the tropical Pacific, but records scattered. Fairly common in the HAWAIIAN IS. and MARSHALL IS., uncommon to rare in c. and w. MICRONESIA, uncommon from KIRIBATI S to FIJI and SAMOA, and rare, with only scattered records, in se. POLYNESIA (easternmost record for Ducie).

General Comments on Stints

STINTS are characterized by small size (all are smaller than Sanderling), streaked, blotched, or scaled upperparts, and nervous habits. Most migrate in flocks that are easily flushed and fly in tight formations. In flight, all tropical Pacific species show a wing stripe, white sides to the rump, and a dark line from the center of the back to the tip of the central tail feathers. Stints have three recognizable plumages: juvenile, nonbreeding (winter), and breeding (summer). The vast majority of stints seen in the tropical Pacific are in the nonbreeding stage. During the fall migration (usually August-September) the juvenile plumage may be seen, and breeding dress can begin to appear before the birds return to their breeding grounds in the spring. Migrant and wintering stints utter high-pitched short call notes that are identifiable to species with experience, but difficult to convey in words. Any bird in a flock that sounds different should be investigated. Only the Rufous-necked Stint is found in the tropical Pacific in large numbers. Birders in Micronesia should be thoroughly familiar with it in all its plumages before attempting to sort out the rarer species. Do not expect to identify every stint with certainty; even the experts sometimes give up (and know when to do so!). Detailed discussion of all stint species (several of which have been found only once or twice in the tropical Pacific) is beyond the scope of this guide. For those interested in this difficult group, we recommend either of two well-illustrated papers listed below.

References: Grant, P. J. 1984. Identification of stints and peeps. *British Birds* 77:293-315.

Veit, R. R., and L. Jonsson. 1984. Field identification of smaller sandpipers within the genus *Calidris. Am. Birds* 38:853-76.

SEMIPALMATED SANDPIPER   *Calidris pusilla*

This species breeds in arctic N. America and winters in S. America. One wintered in 1983 on OAHU (Hawaiian Is.). Intermediate (on average) in size between Western and Least Sandpiper, but overlaps with both. Winter birds very difficult to distinguish from Westerns, but note the thick bill that neither droops at the tip (as in Western) nor tapers to a point (as in Least). Least Sandpiper is browner, has pale legs. Compare also winter Rufous-necked Stint, which has somewhat thinner bill, but is otherwise very similar. Identifications of these four species in non-breeding plumage must be made with extreme care. Probably the only true diagnostic mark of Semipalmated is the partial webbing between all forward toes. It can be seen at close range or ascertained from tracks in soft mud. For illustrations and further discussions, see N. American field guides and previously cited references (see introduction to stints).

WESTERN SANDPIPER   *Calidris mauri*   PLATE 18

Appearance: (6½;17) A large stint with a long black bill that often appears slightly drooped at the tip. Full winter plumage plain gray above, but most fall migrants retain some chestnut on the back and look rather blotchy. Forecrown white, and head in general pale (resembling that of winter Rufous-necked Stint). Fall juvenile also blotchy chestnut and gray above without pale scapular stripes (unlike Little Stint); boldly marked rufous-and-black scapulars form a noticeable line of color over the wing; breast has buff-tinged band with pronounced streaks on the side. Breeding plumage rufous-brown above, particularly on the scapulars, with boldest streaks below of any stint, and dark rufous crown and auricular patch that contrast with white face and very wide white eyebrow.

Identification: The long drooped bill is unique among stints of the tropical Pacific, but this feature is variable and some individuals have bills very similar to those of other species. Western is grayer and lacks the yellow legs of the smaller, shorter-billed Least Sandpiper. Juvenile and winter Westerns resemble same-stage Rufous-necked Stints but have much longer bills and cleaner eyebrows, imparting a beady-eyed look. Semipalmated Sandpiper has a thick, short bill that, rather than tapering to a sharp tip, is slightly expanded distally. In winter plumage, this may be the only reliable field mark to separate it from Western Sandpiper.

Occurrence: Breeds in Alaska, winters along N. American coasts. Uncommon fall and rare spring migrant through the HAWAIIAN IS. and JOHNSTON ATOLL. Occasionally overwinters. Has strayed to New Zealand, so should be looked for elsewhere in Polynesia.

RUFOUS-NECKED STINT   *Calidris ruficollis*   PLATE 18

Appearance: (6;15) In nonbreeding plumage, a gray and white stint with short black bill and black legs. Sides of breast show only a smudge of gray. Forecrown white. Juvenile is darker and browner above with fine streaks on sides of breast. In breeding plumage head, neck, and breast variably washed with bright rufous (Plate 18 shows reddest extreme; some have only a tinge).

Habits: Highly gregarious. Migrating flocks often pause in open areas such as antenna fields and airstrips. Also on mudflats, beaches.

Identification: Breeding plumage distinctive, but beware red-tinged Sanderlings coming into breeding plumage. Long-toed Stint browner, streakier in winter, with dull yellow legs and more upright posture. Winter Rufous-necked clearer white below, especially on center of breast, than any other tropical Pacific stint. See Western Sandpiper, Little Stint.

Occurrence: Breeds in n. Siberia, n. Alaska; winters SE. Asia to Australia. A common migrant through w. MICRONESIA (Palau, Yap, Marianas, Truk), less common E to the MARSHALL IS. and FIJI. Straggler to the HAWAIIAN IS. (Kure, Hawaii).

Other names: Rufous-necked Sandpiper, Red-necked Stint.

LITTLE STINT   *Calidris minuta*

This Eurasian species is only a rare straggler to the tropical Pacific, with recent reports for SAIPAN (Mariana Is.) and KURE (NW Hawaiian Is.). Winter adult very similar to winter Rufous-necked Stint, but has thinner bill and complete faint breast band. First-winter birds have dark centers to the scapulars that give the upperparts a slightly scaly look. First-fall birds very rusty above, with feather edges forming buff lines on the scapulars that converge to form a prominent pale V on the back. Rufous-necked and Western juveniles may show similar, but less prominent, pattern, and are less rusty on sides of breast. Wing coverts gray on juvenile Rufous-necked, rusty-tinged or brown on Little Stint. For illustrations, see Eurasian field guides, NGS (1983), or previously cited references (see introduction to stints).

TEMMINCK'S STINT   *Calidris temminckii*

Two individuals of this Eurasian stint were photographed on SAIPAN (Mariana Is.) in the fall of 1983. Temminck's can be distinguished in all plumages from other small sandpipers and stints by its white rather than gray outer tail feathers. Also, note the dull yellow-brown legs (not black as in the larger but otherwise similar Baird's Sandpiper), thin pointed bill, and plain upperparts with no prominent markings. Illustrated in Eurasian field guides, NGS (1983), and previously cited references (see introduction to stints).

LONG-TOED STINT   *Calidris subminuta*   PLATE 18

Appearance: (6;15) A brown stint with dull yellow or yellow-olive legs and feet. Toes noticeably long. Bill all dark or with pale base. Breeding plumage like miniature Sharp-tailed Sandpiper: crown and back strongly marked with black and rufous, breast washed with orange and with prominent rows of spots (may look like streaks). Juvenile and non-breeding plumage very similar to that of Least Sandpiper, but with different head pattern (see below).

Voice: A low purring note or a light twittering, unlike calls of Least Sandpiper.

Identification: Distinguished from Rufous-necked Stint in all plumages by paler legs, browner color. Resembles Least Sandpiper closely in plumage, but note characteristic upright, long-necked posture. Breeding adults brighter, with more rufous above than Least, and lack "necklace" of streaks across breast. Juveniles and nonbreeding adults very difficult to distinguish, but note that pale superciliaries expand posteriorly and do not meet over bill, whereas those of Least are narrow throughout and connect over bill. Least also has darker lores. On those individuals that have it, the pale base of the bill is diagnostic for Long-toed Stint. The long toes can be seen with patience. Roberson (1980) describes the bird as "looking like it is wearing flippers as it walks."

Occurrence: Breeds ne. Siberia, winters from se Asia to Australia. Uncommon to rare migrant in w. MICRONESIA (Palau, Yap, Guam, Truk). Straggler to MIDWAY (NW Hawaiian Is.).

LEAST SANDPIPER   *Calidris minutilla*   PLATE 18

Appearance: (6;15) A small stint with an overall brown look in all plumages. Legs usually dull yellow or greenish yellow but may appear black. Bill short, black, straight, and pointed. In all plumages a diffuse dark breast band with more (breeding) or less (winter) well defined streaks. Breeding plumage brighter above with some chestnut, but not as bright as that of Long-toed Stint or Western Sandpiper. Fall juvenile rusty-tinged on upperparts and breast.

Voice: A high-pitched, drawn-out *stree-eep*.

Identification: Least Sandpipers with clearly pale legs easily told from all except Long-toed Stint. The Long-toed is brighter above in breeding plumage, with spots rather than streaks on sides of breast. See Long-toed Stint for separation of juveniles. Least Sandpipers with dark-appearing legs told from Westerns by browner color, darker breast, and shorter bill. The smaller size is useful only if the two are seen together. Breeding plumage Western much rustier above.

Occurrence: Breeds in arctic N. America, winters to S. America. An uncommon but regular winter visitor to the HAWAIIAN IS. Has strayed as far as New Zealand, so should be looked for on other Pacific islands.

BAIRD'S SANDPIPER   *Calidris bairdii*

This large stint breeds from Siberia to Greenland, winters to S. America, and has strayed at least twice to OAHU (Hawaiian Is.). It can be distinguished from all other stints recorded in the tropical Pacific by its long wings that project well beyond the tail of a perched bird. In all plumages has buffy neck and breast with fine streaks on sides. Illustrated in N. American field guides. Reference: Donaldson, P. V. 1981. A Baird's Sandpiper at Waipio Peninsula, Oahu, with comments on identification. *'Elepaio* 42:12-14.

PECTORAL SANDPIPER   *Calidris melanotos*   PLATE 18

Appearance: (18½;22) A large sandpiper but quite variable in size. Posture erect. Upperparts and breast brown-streaked buff, the color ending abruptly on lower breast, producing a bibbed effect. Belly white. Legs yellowish green, bill pale at base.

Habits: Solitary or in small flocks, often with Sharp-tailed Sandpipers. Usually in freshwater habitats such as mudflats, ponds.

Voice: A harsh *kriek*

Identification: Similar to Sharp-tailed Sandpiper but bigger-headed without strongly contrasting chestnut or rusty crown. Sharply demarcated, heavily streaked breast band diagnostic. No streaks on flanks. See Ruff.

Occurrence: Breeds on arctic coasts of Siberia and N. America, winters in S. America. Common fall migrant and rare winter resident in the HAWAIIAN IS. with scattered records for MICRONESIA (Palau, Marianas, Pohnpei, Marshall Is.), JOHNSTON ATOLL, the PHOENIX IS. (Kiribati), NIUE, SCILLY (Society Is.), and RAPA (Tubuai Is.). Probably a rare visitor throughout the tropical Pacific.

Reference: Kieser, J. A., and F. T. H. Smith. 1982. Field identification of the Pectoral Sandpiper *Calidris melanotos*. *Australian Bird Watcher* 9:137-46.

SHARP-TAILED SANDPIPER   *Calidris acuminata*   PLATE 18

Appearance: (8½;22) Size and posture of Pectoral Sandpiper, but slimmer and more reddish with a prominent chestnut cap and white eyebrow. Breast with a diffuse orange wash and a necklace of thin streaks around the throat (juvenile) or heavily spotted (breeding). Breast band not sharply separated from white belly. Rows of chevrons extend along flanks. Nonbreeding plumage duller than either of the above, without the orange tone to the breast, but usually retaining enough color in the crown to produce a noticeable contrasting cap.

Habits: Often in large flocks. Prefers open wetlands, freshwater and tidal mudflats. May flock with Pectoral Sandpipers.

Voice: Usually silent, but flocks may produce a twittering note.

Identification: Most similar to Pectoral Sandpiper, and also variable in size, but breast pattern distinctive in all plumages. Juvenile Ruff larger, lacks breast streaks and white eyebrow, has more white on sides of rump and longer legs. Buff-breasted Sandpiper also lacks prominent eyebrow, has silvery wing linings, and very different overall look (see Plate 19). Also compare much smaller Long-toed Stint.

Occurrence: Breeds in ne. Siberia, winters in the E. Indies and Australasia. Common fall and rare spring migrant in the HAWAIIAN IS. Passage migrant throughout MICRONESIA (most common in w. part) including WAKE and NAURU. Also recorded in e. KIRIBATI (Phoenix and Line Is.) and FIJI.

DUNLIN   *Calidris alpina*   PLATE 18

Appearance: (8½;22) A short-legged sandpiper with a long bill, drooped at the tip, heavy at the base. Breeding plumage has rusty back and black belly patch. Winter birds plain gray above, white below. Juveniles look like a blotchy washed-out version of breeding plumage. Flight pattern like stints.

Habits: Associates on mudflats and sandy beaches with Sanderlings and other small sandpipers.

Voice: Call note a nasal and rasping *treesp*.

Identification: See Curlew Sandpiper. In winter resembles stints but note larger size and long, drooped bill.

Occurrence: Breeds in the Arctic, winters to the tropics. Uncommon migrant to the HAWAIIAN IS. Occasionally overwinters. A scattering of records for MICRONESIA (Palau, Marianas, Pohnpei, Wake).

CURLEW SANDPIPER *Calidris ferruginea* PLATE 18

Appearance: (8½;22) Slightly larger than Dunlin, with more upright stance enhanced by longer neck and legs. Rump white, tail black in all plumages. Bill long, decurved throughout its length (not just at tip). Breeding plumage a rich chestnut above and below. Color plate shows a molting spring bird. Winter plumage much like Dunlin, plain gray above, white below. Juvenile has pinkish buff wash on the breast, scaly-looking back.

Voice: A whistled *cheerup*.

Identification: Similar to Dunlin but larger, with bill curved throughout its length and slimmer at the tip, longer legs, more upright stance, and white rump. In breeding plumage differs from Red Knot in darker chestnut color on back as well as breast, curved bill.

Occurrence: Breeds in n. Eurasia, winters to Africa and Australia. Uncommon migrant in w. MICRONESIA (Palau, Yap). One record for OAHU (Hawaiian Is.).

Reference: Kieser, J. A., and A. J. Tree. 1981. Field identification of "curve-billed" sandpipers. *Bokmakierie* 33:89-92.

BROAD-BILLED SANDPIPER *Limicola falcinellus*

A strongly marked, stintlike sandpiper. In all plumages shows a characteristic forked superciliary line. Dorsal pattern somewhat snipelike. Bill heavy and slightly drooping at the tip. More heavily streaked throughout than any other small sandpiper likely to be seen in the tropical Pacific. Breeds in n. Eurasia, winters to the Southern Hemisphere, and very rarely passes through PALAU. Illustrated in Eurasian field guides and NGS (1983).

BUFF-BREASTED SANDPIPER *Tryngites subruficollis* PLATE 19

Appearance: (8;20) A very distinctive, bright buff sandpiper with yellow legs. Posture upright, with thin-necked, small-headed look. Head lacks strong dark markings, and a broad buff eye-ring produces an endearing big-eyed facial expression. Back feathers are dark brown, edged buff, the edges especially bold in juvenile, which looks scaly. Adult has entire underparts buff, but juvenile has white belly. Wing linings silvery white.

Habits: Unlikely to be found in "typical" shorebird habitats. Prefers short-grassy habitats like lawns and golf courses.

Identification: Like a miniature juvenile Ruff, but lacks white at sides of rump and has bold buff eye-ring. Buff-breasted's bill much thinner.

Occurrence: Breeds in N. American Arctic, winters in S. America. Rare fall migrant in tropical Pacific with scattered records for the HA-

WAIIAN IS. (Kure, Midway, Kauai, Oahu), POHNPEI, the MAR-SHALL IS., JOHNSTON ATOLL, and RAPA (Tubuai Is.).
Reference: Kieser, J. A., and G. A. Kieser. 1983. Field identification of juvenile Buff-breasted Sandpiper. *Bokmakierie* 35:15-16.

RUFF   *Philomachus pugnax*   PLATE 19

Appearance: (12,10;31,25) A fairly large sandpiper with male much larger than female (called Reeve). Resembles in size and color a non-breeding Lesser Golden-Plover, but has rather different upright posture. Looks thick-necked, small-headed, with long legs and stocky body. Juveniles buffy throughout with dark brown, scaly-looking back. Adults in winter paler below, with white face. Dark eye stripe does not extend to base of bill. White patches on sides of lower back connect across rump to produce a bold white U, visible in flight. Leg color variable, but always pale. Breeding males (unrecorded in tropical Pacific) have variable brightly colored neck ruffs.

Habits: Found in mudflats, garbage dumps, and canefield settling basins. Less often along shorelines.

Identification: Distinguished from Lesser Golden-Plover by different stance, longer legs and bill. Much buffier or browner than other large sandpipers. Body bulkier than those of yellowlegs, legs not as bright. Lacks big-eyed face pattern of much smaller Buff-breasted Sandpiper. Breeding males, should any ever be seen in the region, would be unmistakable.

Occurrence: Breeds in n. Eurasia, winters to s. Eurasia and the E. Indies. Rare but regular visitor to the HAWAIIAN IS. and MICRONESIA (Palau, Marianas, Truk, Marshall Is.), with a record for JOHNSTON ATOLL.

Reference: Prater, A. J. 1982. Identification of Ruff. *Dutch Birding* 4:8-14.

SHORT-BILLED DOWITCHER   *Limnodromus griseus*
This species, which breeds across Alaska and Canada and winters in s. temperate and tropical America, is included here on the basis of a single 1964 record for MIDWAY, and an as yet unconfirmed sighting on Oahu (Hawaiian Is.) for the fall of 1984. The Midway birds (two) were in juvenile plumage, the easiest plumage in which to distinguish the two dowitchers, and one likely to be seen in fall vagrants. Juvenile Short-bills are browner, with buffy breasts, and the dorsal feathers are broadly edged with buff. The scapulars and tertials also have internal vermiculations, loops, and bars. The scapulars and tertials in juvenile Long-bills are plain gray, with narrow, scalloped, reddish margins.

The overall effect is of a much plainer back in juvenile Long-billed. Both dowitchers have black-and-white barred tails in all plumages, but the white bars of Short-bills are usually wider than the black ones: the reverse is often true in Long-bills.

Adult dowitchers in nonbreeding plumage are very difficult to distinguish visually. Both are plain gray, with gray throat and breast. In this plumage Short-bills are somewhat paler, and the breast is often lightly streaked and spotted, with an irregular border between the dark breast and pale belly, whereas Long-bills have plain gray breasts cleanly separated from the belly.

In breeding plumage, Short-billed Dowitchers have pale, spotted bellies (Long-bills are unspotted), are paler, more orange on breast and sides. The sides of the breast are more spotted, less barred than in Long-billed. The best character in any plumage is voice, a low, mellow *tu-tu-tu* in Short-billed in contrast to the shrill, sharp calls of Long-billed. The Short-billed Dowitcher is best illustrated in NGS (1983). Reference: Wilds, C., and M. Newlon. 1983. The identification of dowitchers. *Birding* 15:151-66.

LONG-BILLED DOWITCHER   *Limnodromus scolopaceus*   PLATE 19

Appearance: (11½;29) Dowitchers are large, plump, long-billed sandpipers with a prominent blaze of white up the center of the back, visible in flight. In breeding plumage the entire underparts of this species are rich chestnut, heavily barred on sides of breast and flanks with dark brown. Juveniles lack chestnut, are grayish brown without barring. Winter plumage at all ages gray above, white below, and rather plain except for a pale eyebrow.

Habits: Feeds in freshwater ponds, less often on tidal flats, with a characteristic up-and-down jabbing of the bill into the mud.

Voice: A high-pitched *keeep*, sometimes double or triple.

Identification: Dowitchers are plumper and longer-billed than other shorebirds in the region. Bill lengths of the two species overlap, so only extreme individuals are identifiable on that basis. Thus some winter-plumaged individuals cannot be identified visually. In breeding plumage note Long-bill's fully chestnut underparts and barred, not spotted, sides of breast. Juveniles distinctive. See Short-billed Dowitcher.

Occurrence: Breeds from ne. Siberia to the Yukon, winters along both coasts of N. America. A rare but regular migrant and occasional winter resident in the HAWAIIAN IS. A possible record for JOHNSTON ATOLL (could have been Short-billed).

SNIPES: Genus *Gallinago*

SNIPES are long-billed, stocky, cryptically colored brown birds of marshy or swampy habitats. They are not very active on the ground and are very difficult to see until they flush. They feed by probing in the mud. The various species are notoriously difficult to identify in the field. In hand they differ in characteristics of the lateral tail feathers. Two species are regular visitors to the tropical Pacific, and two others have been recorded occasionally.

COMMON SNIPE   *Gallinago gallinago*   PLATE 17

Appearance: (10½;27) A snipe with broad buffy streaks on back, white trailing edge to secondaries, and normally shaped lateral tail feathers.

Habits: Flight a fast and erratic zigzag. Often allows close approach and then takes off explosively, uttering its call.

Voice: A distinctive low raspy *zhrick*, somewhat like the tearing of cloth.

Identification: White trailing edge of secondaries, visible in flight, diagnostic.

Occurrence: Breeds in Northern Hemisphere and migrates southward. A rare but regular migrant to the HAWAIIAN IS. Straggler to WAKE and SAIPAN (Mariana Is.).

Note: Both the Asiatic (*G. g. gallinago*) and American (*G. g. delicata*) subspecies visit the Hawaiian Is. The former has broad buffy feather edges dorsally, the latter only narrow white edges. The two can be differentiated in the field on this basis.

PIN-TAILED SNIPE   *Gallinago stenura*

This snipe is named for its narrow pinlike outer rectrices, usually visible only in the hand. The pinlike feathers are darker than the narrow outer rectrices of Swinhoe's Snipe. The wings lack the pale trailing edge to the secondaries of Common Snipe. The voice is a nasal, raspy note like those of other snipes, but considered recognizably different by some observers (more data needed). Flight less erratic than that of Common Snipe, but not so heavy as that of Swinhoe's. At present, the latter two probably are indistinguishable in the field unless the tail feathers can be seen (which is seldom). The Pin-tailed Snipe has been collected once on KURE (NW Hawaiian Is.). Other snipes believed (but not confirmed) to be this species have been seen in the MARIANA IS. The species breeds in Siberia and migrates to s. Asia and the Philippines. Its occurrence in w. Micronesia would not be unreasonable. For illustrations, see King and Dickinson (1975), WBSJ (1982), or Simpson and Day (1984).

JAPANESE SNIPE   *Gallinago hardwickii*

Also called Latham's Snipe, this species breeds in Japan and winters mostly in e. Australia. It is rarely seen on migration and has been reported only once in the tropical Pacific, on KWAJALEIN (Marshall Is.). It is larger (11½;29) and paler than Common Snipe and lacks the pale trailing edge of the secondaries. Only the outermost tail feather is unusually narrow. Illustrated in Pizzey (1980), WBSJ (1982), and Simpson and Day (1984).

SWINHOE'S SNIPE   *Gallinago megala*

Appearance: (10½;27) Very similar to Common Snipe (see Plate 17) but with narrower pale lines on back, no white trailing edge to secondaries. Lateral tail feathers narrowed but not pinlike, with orange-rufous band below tip. Perched bird probably not distinguishable from Common Snipe. For illustrations, see King and Dickinson (1975), WBSJ (1982), or Simpson and Day (1984).

Habits: Prefers weedy swamps and grassy areas near marshes and streams. Flight heavier and less erratic than that of other snipes.

Voice: Like that of Common Snipe but higher pitched and less hoarse.

Identification: Probably indistinguishable, on basis of current knowledge, from Pin-tailed Snipe. Rarely, as just before the bird alights, the tail may be spread sufficiently for the outer feathers to be visible. If they are narrow (but not pinlike) and part rufous, the bird is probably a Swinhoe's. Differs from Common Snipe in shape of outer rectrices and in lacking a pale trailing edge on wings. More data are needed on vocal and behavioral differences among snipes.

Occurrence: Breeds in c. and e. Asia, and winters to n. Australia. Uncommon migrant and rare winter resident in w. MICRONESIA (Palau E to Truk).

Other names: Marsh Snipe, Forest Snipe.

PHALAROPES: Subfamily Phalaropodinae

PHALAROPES are the only shorebirds that habitually light on the water. They swim well and feed on the water surface, sometimes spinning in tight circles. Two species are highly pelagic in the tropical Pacific and are only occasionally found on land as sick or injured waifs.

WILSON'S PHALAROPE   *Phalaropus tricolor*   PLATE 19

Appearance: (9;23) A sandpiper-like phalarope with small head, long needlelike bill, white rump and tail, and no wing stripe. Nonbreeding birds plain gray above, white below with a gray streak behind the eye

Legs dull yellow to greenish gray. In breeding plumage (not yet seen in tropical Pacific) females have a bold stripe on sides of head and neck that is black on the face and shades to chestnut on the neck. Males show a faded version of the same pattern. Breeding plumage illustrated in Eurasian and N. American field guides.

Habits: Found on ponds and mudflats. The only phalarope likely to be seen walking and foraging on land.

Identification: In winter plumage more like some sandpipers than other phalaropes (from which distinguished by less strongly marked head, lack of wing stripe). Much clearer unmarked gray than other gray shorebirds with white rumps. Posturally most like Marsh Sandpiper, but compare also Wood Sandpiper and Lesser Yellowlegs.

Occurrence: Breeds in w.-c. N. America, winters in S. America. Occasional winter visitor to the main HAWAIIAN IS. and JOHNSTON ATOLL.

RED-NECKED PHALAROPE *Phalaropus lobatus*

This phalarope, which breeds in the high Arctic and winters in southern oceans, has been recorded as a straggler a few times in the HAWAIIAN IS. (Laysan, Kauai, Oahu). It is known to winter at sea N of New Guinea, but has not yet been found in Micronesia. In nonbreeding plumage it resembles the Red Phalarope but has a longer, thinner bill and prominent streaks above. Breeding birds show a rusty collar. For full accounts and illustrations, see any Eurasian or N. American field guide.

RED PHALAROPE *Phalaropus fulicarius*   PLATE 19

Appearance: (8½;22) In winter uniformly gray above, white below with dark gray eye stripe. White wing stripe prominent in flight. Breeding plumage with white face, black crown and forehead, and rich chestnut underparts. Male duller and paler than female. Molting birds, as shown on Plate 19, blotchy.

Habits: Strictly pelagic but sometimes found on land after storms. Flight rapid, close to the water, unlike other pelagic birds. Often swims in tight circles while feeding, with tail cocked up.

Identification: Resembles winter Sanderling, which almost never lights on water, but has darker back and phalarope face pattern. Red-necked Phalarope has streaked back, thinner bill.

Occurrence: Breeds in the Arctic, winters in e. S. Pacific. Passes through e.-c. Pacific February-April in large numbers, but rarely seen on land. Birds have been found ashore in the HAWAIIAN IS. and LINE IS. (Kiribati).

Other name: Gray Phalarope.

FAMILY GLAREOLIDAE: Pratincoles

Pratincoles are peculiar shorebirds in being primarily aerial feeders. In the air they are ternlike with graceful maneuvers as they hawk insects. On the ground, they resemble long-winged plovers, running and bobbing the head. They are found around open grassy or bare places such as airstrips and antenna fields.

ORIENTAL PRATINCOLE *Glareola maldivarum* PLATE 16

Appearance: (10;25) A buffy brown pratincole with a black necklace. In flight shows a bold pattern of white rump, black tail, and chestnut wing linings. Immature lacks black necklace. Tail forked.

Voice: A harsh 2-syllable call, rather ternlike.

Identification: The Small Pratincole (Appendix A) has been hypothetically reported from Guam and Saipan. It lacks the black necklace and has a shorter tail than the present species, but immature Oriental Pratincoles also may have indistinct markings and short tails. Small Pratincole has black wing linings, but the chestnut ones of the Oriental often look black in the field. The Small Pratincole's bold white wing stripe is its best field mark, and must be seen to confirm identification.

Occurrence: Breeds in e. and se. Asia. Uncommon migrant to w. MICRONESIA (Palau, Yap, Truk, Marshalls). Probably also the MARIANA IS. (but reported as Small Pratincole).

Other name: Indian Pratincole.

[**SMALL PRATINCOLE** *Glareola lactea* See Appendix A]

FAMILY LARIDAE: Jaegers, Gulls, and Terns

These seabirds are, for the most part, more likely to be seen from land than the tubenoses (shearwaters, petrels, etc.). They fall into three rather distinct subgroups discussed separately below.

Jaegers and Skuas: Subfamily Stercorariinae

These are predatory or kleptoparasitic seabirds with strong direct flight. They breed in polar regions and are rare in the tropics generally. They tend to be strictly pelagic away from their nesting grounds. They offer some very difficult problems in identification, since all species exhibit light, all-dark, and intermediate color phases or morphs as well as distinctive juvenile plumages. These birds will often follow ships, particularly if refuse or "chum" is being discarded.

POMARINE JAEGER   *Stercorarius pomarinus*   FIGURE 31

Appearance: (21;53) A large, heavy-bodied bird with dark brown upperparts and variable underparts ranging from brown to white. Light-phase adults show a black cap, dark breast band, and yellow patches on neck and sides of head. White patches at base of primaries conspicuous from below and above. Central tail feathers elongated and twisted. Immatures lack elongated central rectrices and are heavily mottled.

Habits: Flight slower and more graceful than that of the larger South Polar Skua. Pelagic, less frequently seen in bays or harbors. Steals fish from other birds and scavenges refuse from ships.

Identification: Long, blunt, twisted tail feathers distinguish adults from other jaegers, which are smaller and more delicate with straight, tapering tail feathers. Young birds can be told from immature gulls by white wing patches and different behavior, from other jaegers only with difficulty.

Occurrence: Breeds in the Arctic. Winters regularly in low numbers near the HAWAIIAN IS., KIRIBATI (Phoenix Is., Line Is.) and FIJI. Unconfirmed sighting near TRUK.

Other names: Pomarine Skua, Pomatorhine Skua.

PARASITIC JAEGER   *Stercorarius parasiticus*   FIGURE 31

Appearance: (19;48) Smaller and more slender than Pomarine Jaeger, but with similar color pattern. Palest morph lacks band across breast. Adult's central tail feathers twice as long as rest of tail, sharply pointed. Juveniles variable but patterned like young Pomarine, with central tail feathers that project beyond tail as short sharp points. Legs dark.

Habits: Strongly kleptoparasitic and pelagic. Flight direct, but more graceful and buoyant than that of Pomarine Jaeger. Sometimes described as falconlike. Often pursues terns.

Identification: Adult like Pomarine but lighter and slimmer with tapering central tail feathers. Differs from Long-tailed by shorter tail feathers, heavier build, more direct flight. Juveniles difficult to distinguish from Pomarine, but note pointed tail projections, lighter build. See Long-tailed Jaeger.

Occurrence: Breeds in the Arctic, migrates near continental coasts to Southern Hemisphere. Unknown in c. Pacific. Found rarely at sea near FIJI.

Other name: Arctic Skua.

POMARINE
ad.

POMARINE
imm.

PARASITIC
ad.

LONG-TAILED
ad.

FIGURE 31. Jaegers

LONG-TAILED JAEGER   *Stercorarius longicaudus*   FIGURE 3

Appearance: (22;55) The smallest and most delicate jaeger. Grayish
brown above with black cap. Back and scapulars paler than flight feathers, giving the wing a dark trailing edge. White breast, gray belly
Adult's central tail feathers very long and streaming, like those of a trop

icbird. White at base of primaries confined to shafts of outer two primaries in all plumages. Legs bluish gray. Dark morphs very rare.

Habits: Very ternlike in flight, lacking hawklike forcefulness of other jaegers. Attracted to carrion.

Identification: Adults are the most distinctive of jaegers. Note particularly the long tail streamers, manner of flight, and two-toned upperwing surface. Juveniles have blunt central tail feathers, blue-gray legs, and much less white at base of primaries than other jaegers.

Occurrence: Breeds in the high Arctic, winters in cold Southern Hemisphere waters. Migrates April-May and September-October through the tropics. Probably regular in low numbers in c. Pacific, but no confirmed sightings within 200 mi. (322 km) of land. Stragglers have reached PALAU and FIJI.

Other name: Long-tailed Skua.

SOUTH POLAR SKUA *Catharacta maccormicki* FIGURE 32

Appearance: (21;53) A chunky brown seabird with rounded wings, white base to flight feathers, fan-shaped tail, and hooked bill. Most seen in the tropics are juveniles. In all plumages the pale nape contrasts with a darker back.

FIGURE 32. South Polar Skua. (From photo by J. R. Jehl, used by permission.)

Habits: Powerful flight, deceptively fast and hawklike, with slow, easy wingbeats. Has never been observed from land in the tropical Pacific.

Identification: Large stocky body, rounded wings, and rounded tail distinguish skuas from jaegers. Great Skua (*C. skua*), unrecorded in tropical Pacific, lacks nape/back contrast.

Occurrence: Breeds in the Antarctic. Uncommon migrant at sea in the vicinity of the HAWAIIAN IS. and KIRIBATI (Phoenix Is., Line Is., possibly W to Gilbert Is.).

GULLS: Subfamily Larinae

THE seeming absence of gulls from the tropical Pacific is a surprise to many visitors from cooler climes. Gulls are scavengers of shallow waters and are abundant along polar and temperate coasts and on inland lakes and rivers. Tropical islands, which are mostly mountaintops protruding above the sea, have no coastal shelf and thus do not provide the kind of coastal resources preferred by gulls. Nevertheless, though none breeds, many gull species have been recorded as migrant or wintering visitors in the tropical Pacific. These are usually solitary wanderers that may remain on an island for many months. Since they are attracted to inland wetlands or coastal mudflats, habitats limited in these islands, they can be conspicuous even in low numbers. In some years, as many as six gull species have been recorded in Hawaii over the winter months; in other years only a few stragglers are present.

Gulls have a rather complex sequence of plumages, making them a very challenging group for the birder. One should not expect to identify every gull seen. Although identification of adults is relatively straightforward, most gulls seen in the tropics are subadults in various plumage stages. For the more frequent species, all plumages have been recorded. Our terminology for plumage stages is purposely imprecise. We use terms like "second winter" sparingly because research has shown that seasonal designations for gull plumages are virtually meaningless. Our discussions are intended only to supplement information and illustrations from other sources; detailed treatment of these rare visitors to the tropical Pacific is beyond the scope of this guide. We particularly recommend Harrison (1983) and NGS (1983) for birders interested in pursuing gulls in the tropical Pacific.

LAUGHING GULL   *Larus atricilla*   FIGURE 33

Appearance: (16½;42) A medium-sized, dark-mantled gull with black head in spring and summer. White eye-ring broken fore and aft, wing tips black. Bill dark red in summer, black in winter. Winter adult loses

first year

immatures

second year

summer adults

winter adults

FIGURE 33. Laughing Gull (*l.*) and Franklin's Gull (*r.*)

black on head except for gray smudge on nape and around eye. Immature (requires three years to reach adulthood) browner overall, with broad dark tail band that includes outermost rectrices. Body gradually lightens, and gray first begins to appear on the back. By second winter, the tail band becomes a broken row of subterminal spots. All plumages have been seen in the tropical Pacific.

Identification: See Franklin's Gull.

Occurrence: Breeds along coasts of e. N. America and the Caribbean, with dispersal to W coast from Mexico to Peru. Occasional visitor to the tropical Pacific, with many records for the HAWAIIAN IS., and others for JOHNSTON ATOLL, KIRIBATI (Phoenix Is., Line Is.) and SAMOA.

FRANKLIN'S GULL *Larus pipixcan* FIGURE 33

Appearance: (14½;37) A medium-sized, dark-mantled gull with black head and broken white eye-ring in summer. Black wing tips separated from gray of mantle by white bar (see Figure 33, middle bird on right). Winter adults have mottled dark half-hood. Bill red in summer, black in winter. Immatures tinged brown on wings, have narrow black tail band that does not extend onto outermost feathers. Matures in two years.

Identification: Very similar to Laughing Gull but slightly smaller with noticeably smaller, more delicate bill. Gray mantle bluer in Franklin's, browner in Laughing, a useful mark if birds are perched side by side. Summer Franklin's has broader eye-ring than Laughing. In winter, Franklin's retains more black on hindneck. Adults at all seasons most easily distinguished by distinctive wing-tip patterns. Immature Franklin's has much narrower tail band than first-year Laughing, with outermost feathers unbanded. Note that transitional first- to second-year Laughing Gull can show similar pattern. Tail band of second-year Laughing reduced to a row of subterminal spots, broken in the center.

Occurrence: Breeds in interior N. America, winters on w. coasts of S. America. Uncommon to rare visitor to the tropical Pacific with records for the HAWAIIAN IS., JOHNSTON ATOLL, TRUK, the MARSHALL IS., the LINE IS. (Kiribati), and the MARQUESAS.

COMMON BLACK-HEADED GULL FIGURE 34
Larus ridibundus

Appearance: (16;41) A small, gray-mantled gull with dark brown (often looks black) head in breeding plumage, black spot behind eye in winter. Bill and legs red. Wings show prominent white triangle on leading edge, black tips to primaries. Matures in two years. Immatures have

FIGURE 34. Common Black-headed Gull

yellowish legs and black-tipped yellow bills, dark tail bands, and brown bars on secondary coverts. Wing pattern distinctive (see Figure 34). Various characters may change at different rates, so some otherwise adult-appearing individuals may retain a tail band or other immature features.

Habits: In Micronesia frequents harbors and bays, where small flocks may sit on pilings or swim.

Identification: Bonaparte's Gull very similar in plumage but slightly smaller and always with black bill. Underside of primaries very dark in Common Black-headed (but with white leading edge), much paler in Bonaparte's.

Occurrence: Breeds across temperate Eurasia, winters S to the tropics. Uncommon but regular winter resident at PALAU, rare visitor to the MARIANA IS. and the HAWAIIAN IS. (Midway, Oahu).

BONAPARTE'S GULL   *Larus philadelphia*

Appearance and Identification: (13½;34) Very similar in all plumages to Common Black-headed Gull (see Figure 34) but with black bill. Head black in breeding plumage. Undersides of primaries show no black other than dark tips. Immatures have pink legs, black bills, and narrower black trailing edges to wings than in Common Black-headed. For illustrations, see N. American field guides.

Habits: Flight graceful and buoyant. Feeds over seacoasts or inland ponds.

Occurrence: Breeds in n. N. America, winters on both coasts. Occasional winter visitor throughout the HAWAIIAN IS.

[**SILVER GULL**   *Larus novaehollandiae*   See Appendix A]

[**MEW GULL**   *Larus canus*   See Appendix A]

RING-BILLED GULL   *Larus delawarensis*

Appearance: (17½;45) A medium-sized gull with a four-stage plumage sequence. Adults easily identified by their black-ringed yellow bills. Bill of juvenile all dark, lightening first at base, then at tip to reach adult pattern. Juveniles dark mottled gray-brown with bold black and white wing pattern (black tip and bar across secondaries, inner primaries white) and tail with prominent smudgy black terminal band. By first winter, back gray. Body feathering gradually lightens and tail band becomes much reduced as adult stage is reached. Adult has gray mantle, black-tipped primaries with subterminal white spots, mostly white body plumage and yellow legs (younger stages have dull pink legs). Head and nape of adult mottled brown in winter. Illustrated in N. American field guides.

Identification: Ringed bill of adult diagnostic, but immatures of other gulls can show similar coloration. Note bold pattern of wing and tail on Ring-billed immatures. California Gull juvenile has black-tipped pink bill, all-dark tail. Adult California has narrowly black-ringed bill but with red spot on lower mandible.

Occurrence: Breeds across N. America, winters on both coasts and inland. Relatively frequent visitor in low numbers to the HAWAIIAN IS., also reported from the LINE IS. (Kiribati).

CALIFORNIA GULL   *Larus californicus*

Appearance: (21;53) A medium-sized, gray-mantled gull. Black-ringed yellow bill has red spot on lower mandible. Adult patterned like Herring or Ring-billed Gull but with somewhat darker mantle, dark iris, and greenish gray or yellow-green legs. Head heavily streaked with brown in winter. Requires four years to reach adulthood. Immatures of all ages have two-toned bill with black tip, pale base. Juvenile very dark mottled brown with all-dark tail, dark legs. Plumage and legs lighten by first winter (legs usually pink at this stage). Second-winter birds have grayish legs, gray backs. For illustrations, see N. American field guides.

Identification: Larger than Ring-billed, smaller than Western or Herring Gull. Adults easily distinguished by bill color, dark iris. Immatures colored more like the larger species, lacking strong contrasts in wings and bold tail band, but have two-toned bill like Ring-billed. First-winter birds paler than Westerns, and differ from Herrings in having two dark bars on inner portion of wing, all-dark primaries and primary coverts. All immature Californias darker than comparable Glaucous or Glaucous-winged Gulls.

Occurrence: Breeds in interior w. N. America, winters on W coast. A rare winter visitor to the main HAWAIIAN IS.

HERRING GULL *Larus argentatus*

Appearance: (25;64) A large gray-mantled gull. Adults have black wing tips with white subterminal spots, yellow bill with red spot on lower mandible, pink (or rarely yellowish) legs, and yellow eyes. Nonbreeding birds have brownish-gray streaks on head and sides of breast. Matures in four years, beginning as a dark sooty brown, black-billed, dark-eyed juvenile. Plumage lightens on face and neck in first year. By second winter gray appears on back, eyes become yellow, and bill develops pale base. Gray of mantle increases in third year, body feathering looks like that of winter adult, tail shows broad dark subterminal band, and bill is yellow with black ring or spot. See N. American field guides for illustrations.

Identification: Larger than Ring-billed or California Gull, with heavier bill. Note pink legs of subadult whose bill can look like that of adult Ring-billed. Immature Ring-bills have stronger dark/light contrasts on mantle, narrower tail bands than Herring. First-year California has two dark bars on secondaries, Herring Gull only one. Herring also has pale patch on inner primaries. Note that some first-year Herrings have two-toned bill like that of California. Immature Herring Gulls have smaller bills, paler mantles than same-sized Westerns, and much darker primaries than Glaucous-winged Gulls.

Occurrence: Breeds around the Arctic, winters coastally to the n. tropics. Occasional to frequent visitor to the HAWAIIAN IS., with vagrants reported from the n. MARIANA IS. (Agrihan, Maug) and JOHNSTON ATOLL. An unconfirmed sighting at PALAU.

SLATY-BACKED GULL *Larus schistisagus*

This e. Siberian coastal species has strayed once (1965) to KURE (NW Hawaiian Is.). It is a large, dark-mantled gull similar to the Western Gull and not always distinguishable from it, but heavier-looking with larger head and bill. Also shows a "string of pearls" between the gray part of the upperwing and the black wing tip. Western Gull lacks these white spots and its gray mantle borders the black directly. Most Western Gulls seen in Hawaii have darker mantles than Slaty-backed Gull. For illustrations, see WBSJ (1982), Harrison (1983), or NGS (1983).

WESTERN GULL *Larus occidentalis*

Appearance and Identification: (25;64) A large gull with dark slate-colored mantle. Bill heavier than that of otherwise similar Herring Gull. Southern populations (those most likely to be seen in the tropics) have darker mantles, paler eyes than northern ones. Immatures (mature in four years) darker at all ages than Herring Gull, with stronger mantle/rump contrast. Winter adult lightly streaked on head and neck. Very similar to Slaty-backed Gull, but has different wing-tip pattern. Slaty-backed has paler mantle than southern Western Gulls, and lighter-mantled northern Westerns have dark eyes. Illustrated in N. American field guides.

Occurrence: W coast of N. America from British Columbia to Baja California. Rare visitor to the HAWAIIAN IS.

GLAUCOUS-WINGED GULL *Larus glaucescens*

Appearance and Identification: (26;66) A large, gray-mantled gull that resembles Herring Gull but lacks black wing tips and has dark eyes. Immatures are pearly gray-brown, lighter than Herrings of comparable age and have uniformly pale gray-brown wings. Wing tips darker than those of Glaucous Gulls. Bill all black into third year. Illustrated in N. American field guides.

Occurrence: Breeds and winters on coasts around temperate N. Pacific. Fairly frequent visitor to the NW HAWAIIAN IS., less common in main islands. Vagrant to JOHNSTON ATOLL.

GLAUCOUS GULL *Larus hyperboreus*

Appearance and Identification: (27;69) A very large gull, quite pale in all plumages. Adult is like large, nearly white Herring or Glaucous-winged Gull with pure white wing tips. First- and second-year birds variably checkered with buffy gray, have black-tipped pink bill. Subadult may show dark ring on yellow bill. Very pale, translucent primaries diagnostic in all plumages. For illustrations, see Eurasian and N. American field guides or Harrison (1983).

Occurrence: Breeds in the high Arctic, winters into temperate regions. Occasionally visits the HAWAIIAN IS.

BLACK-LEGGED KITTIWAKE   *Rissa tridactyla*

A small pelagic gull that breeds on arctic and subarctic coasts and winters in temperate Northern Hemisphere seas. Wanders rarely as far S as the NW HAWAIIAN IS. and once reached OAHU. Birds found in the tropics are usually starving and die soon; most records are of dessicated remains, and most also are of immature birds. Bill more delicate than those of larger gulls. Immature has gray mantle, black open M across wings, black tip to shallowly notched tail, and black bill. Adult cleanly marked white with gray mantle, "dipped-in-ink" wing tips, and yellow bill. For illustrations, see Eurasian and N. American field guides or Harrison (1983).

TERNS: Subfamily Sterninae

TERNS are slimmer and more graceful than gulls, with thinner, pointed bills and often with long, forked tails. They are active predators, diving into the water for food. Many species are typical of tropical seas. Nine species breed on islands of the tropical Pacific, two are regular migrants through the region, and several others are less frequent visitors or stragglers. Two species (Sooty Tern, Brown Noddy) are ubiquitous and so abundant that they provide good bases for comparisons with other species; birders should become familiar with them first. Most terns are predominantly white, but the noddies are mostly dark. Noddies also differ in having wedge-shaped tails and in feeding by surface skimming rather than diving.

[GULL-BILLED TERN   *Sterna nilotica*   See Appendix A]

CASPIAN TERN   *Sterna caspia*

A very large (21;53) white tern with heavy red bill, shallowly forked tail, black cap, legs, and feet, and dark undersurface to primaries. Cap streaked with white in nonbreeding plumage. A nearly cosmopolitan species but rare in the tropical Pacific, this tern was recorded recently as a straggler to the HAWAIIAN IS. Illustrated in many field guides. Reference: Ashman, P. R., A. L. Taylor, and S. Doyle. 1982. Records of the Caspian Tern in the Hawaiian Islands. *'Elepaio* 43:11-12.

GREAT CRESTED TERN *Sterna bergii* PLATE 20

Appearance: (18;46) A large pale tern with gray mantle, long yellow bill, short black legs, and black cap with narrow white forehead. Nonbreeding birds and immatures have more white on forehead. The younger birds are also mottled brown on the mantle and have dusky bills. All ages show short, shaggy crest.

Habits: Feeds over coastal lagoons and reefs. Solitary or in small flocks. Dives to the surface in pursuit of prey.

Voice: High-pitched loud screams, *kree kree*, and a harsh *kriek kriek*. Also has some softer calls.

Identification: The largest tern in most of the tropical Pacific, and the only resident one to show a crest. Most other large terns that could occur as vagrants have red bills.

Occurrence: Widespread in the tropical Indian and sw. Pacific oceans. In the tropical Pacific breeds from MICRONESIA E to KIRIBATI and in FIJI, TONGA, the SOCIETY IS., and the TUAMOTU ARCH. Visits intervening islands.

ELEGANT TERN *Sterna elegans*

A resident of the W coasts of the Americas, this species wandered once to JOHNSTON ATOLL. It resembles the slightly larger Great Crested Tern but has a bright orange-red bill. Illustrated in N. American field guides and Harrison (1983).

[ROSEATE TERN *Sterna dougalii* See Appendix A]

COMMON TERN *Sterna hirundo*

Appearance: (14½;37) A medium-sized, black-capped tern with long, deeply forked tail. In breeding dress, bill red with black tip (e. Pacific) or black (w. Pacific); all nonbreeding birds have black bills. Feet same color as bill. Immatures and winter adults have white forehead, and immatures also show a broad dark bar across the shoulders. Wings show an ill-defined dark wedge in the primaries above and a smudgy black trailing edge below. Underparts light gray in breeding plumage, darker in w. Pacific populations. For illustration of black-billed form see Simpson and Day (1984). Most other field guides show the red-billed form.

Habits: Often feeds inshore. Hovers and dives for small fish. Flight light and buoyant.

Identification: Compare Whiskered Tern (different flight and overall shape) and, in Hawaiian waters, Arctic Tern, which has uniformly colored upperwing with a thin black leading edge, and sharply defined black tips to primaries below. Little and Least Terns always have white forehead, but winter birds may resemble Micronesian (black-billed) Common Terns closely in color pattern.

Occurrence: Breeds in the Northern Hemisphere, winters to the Southern Hemisphere. Uncommon migrant (black-billed form, *S. h. longipennis*) through MICRONESIA and FIJI. Red-billed form (*S. h. hirundo*) rare migrant through main HAWAIIAN IS. and straggler to AITUTAKI (Cook Is.).

Reference: Clapp, R. B., R. C. Laybourne, and R. L. Pyle. 1983. Status of the Common Tern (*Sterna hirundo*) in the tropical Pacific, with a note on records of the Black-naped Tern (*Sterna sumatrana*) in Hawaii. '*Elepaio* 43:97-100.

ARCTIC TERN   *Sterna paradisaea*

This medium-sized (15½;39) black-capped tern breeds in the Arctic, winters in the Antarctic, and supposedly passes in low numbers through c. tropical Pacific around the HAWAIIAN IS. during migration. Has strayed once to ENEWETAK (Marshall Is.). Distinguished from very similar red-billed form of Common Tern by narrower, more clean-cut border to wing tips. Bill of breeding-plumage adult all red, underparts gray. Immatures and nonbreeding adults have white forehead, dark bill. Illustrated in most field guides.

BLACK-NAPED TERN   *Sterna sumatrana*   PLATE 20

Appearance: (12;31) A delicate, slender, nearly white tern with long black bill, deeply forked tail, and black line from eye to eye around nape. Mantle very pale gray, with outer web of outermost primary black. Underparts tinged pale pink in breeding season. Juvenile has dull yellow bill, brown mottling on mantle, streaked crown.

Habits: A graceful flier that skims the surface while feeding. Dives for prey. Gregarious, usually found close to land.

Voice: A short, sharp *krep krep* or *chit-chit-chit.*

Identification: At a distance looks all white, but note black line across nape. Common Fairy-Tern has broader wings, less deeply forked tail, and thicker bill. Common and Arctic Terns in all plumages have more black on head and in wings and darker mantles. Juvenile Black-naped resembles juvenile Little Tern, but is larger and slenderer, with different manner of flight.

Occurrence: Widespread and common around islands in tropical Indian and sw. Pacific oceans including MICRONESIA (but only rare visitor in Mariana Is.), TUVALU, FIJI, and TONGA. Uncommon E to TOKELAU, SAMOA, and the n. COOK IS. (Penrhyn, Manihiki, Suwarrow). Straggler to the LINE IS. (Kiribati). Old records for the Hawaiian Is. have been discredited (see reference under Common Tern).

LITTLE TERN   *Sterna albifrons*   FIGURE 35

Appearance: (9;23) A tiny white tern with gray mantle, black cap, white forehead and line above eye, and black-tipped yellow bill (breeding adult). Outer primaries black. Rump and tail white or very pale gray, sharply demarcated from mantle. Cap and forehead less well defined in nonbreeding plumage. Immatures have black shoulder bars, partial caps, and black bills. Juveniles are mottled with brown above.

Habits: Usually seen along shorelines or over coastal ponds. Hovers on rapidly beating wings, then plunges to the surface for prey. Flight rapid and graceful, with deep wingbeats. Often in small groups.

Voice: Wintering birds utter mostly alarm calls including a short *wiik* and a series of short, sharp staccato notes. The basic call, used mostly on nesting grounds, is a 3- to 5-syllable series of notes run together, with accent on the final syllable (Massey 1976, below).

Identification: The smallest tern in Micronesia, with distinctive bill color and plumage in adult. Juveniles resemble young Black-naped Tern, but are smaller and usually accompany adults. The nearly identical Least Tern has gray, noncontrasting rump and tail, and different vocalizations. See Least Tern.

Occurrence: Breeds from Europe to e. Asia and Australia. Uncommon migrant and winter resident in MICRONESIA, most frequent in the w. part but with scattered records E to Kosrae, Kwajalein (Marshall Is.) and Banaba (Kiribati). Straggler to UPOLU (W. Samoa). Some Micronesian records have been published with insufficient detail to rule out Least Tern (formerly considered conspecific) and are therefore only presumed to have been Little Terns.

Reference: Massey, B. W. 1976. Vocal differences between American Least Terns and the European Little Tern. *Auk* 93:760-73.

LEAST TERN   *Sterna antillarum*

Appearance and Identification: (9;23) Virtually identical in all plumages to Little Tern, but with rump and center of tail the same color as pale gray mantle. The gray may be very light and look white in the field, so careful scrutiny is necessary for use of this field mark. Best identified by voice.

Voice: All vocalizations distinct from those of Little Tern. Alarm calls include an upslurred *zwreep* and a staccato *kit-kit-kit*, both with notes of longer duration than homologous Little Tern calls. Basic call, seldom heard from winter birds, is shrill, with 4 syllables in groups of 2, ac-

FIGURE 35. Little Tern. Breeding plumage (*l.*), nonbreeding/immature plumage (*r*).

cented on the second and fourth, and the notes are more distinct than in comparable Little Tern call (see Reference under Little Tern). Anyone familiar with call of one or the other of these species should notice the differences.

Occurrence: Breeds in N. America, winters to C. America and the W. Indies. An occasional visitor to the main HAWAIIAN IS.

Note: This species' occurrence in Hawaii has not been confirmed by specimens or tape recordings, but birds we have seen on Oahu gave definite Least Tern vocalizations.

SPECTACLED (GRAY-BACKED) TERN PLATE 20
Sterna lunata

Appearance: (15;38) A medium-sized, dark-backed tern with long, deeply forked tail. Black cap accentuates narrow white forehead and superciliary stripe. Rest of upperparts bluish steel gray, palest on upper back. Outer tail feathers white. Underparts white or very pale gray. Juveniles (seen only near nesting colonies) have less well defined "spectacles" and are scaly-looking above. Characteristic posture somewhat bent over, with breast held low, wings and tail pointing upward at about 45° angle.

Habits: Flight light and graceful. Feeds on squid and fish captured by aerial dives. Usually pelagic or offshore.

Voice: High-pitched screeches, like a softer, less harsh version of call of Sooty Tern.

Identification: Similar to larger Sooty Tern, but note strong cap/back contrast, narrower white forehead, and longer eyebrow. Generally more graceful in flight, a useful feature when the two are flying together at a distance. Perched birds crouch lower than Sooties, and point wings higher. Almost identical to Bridled Tern, but bluer gray above. See Bridled Tern.

Occurrence: Widespread at sea in c. tropical Pacific. Breeds in the HA-WAIIAN IS. (Kure E to Kaula, Moku Manu off Oahu), the MARI-ANAS (uninhabited n. islands), WAKE, the n. MARSHALL IS., JOHNSTON ATOLL, FIJI, KIRIBATI (Phoenix Is., Line Is.), and the TUAMOTU ARCH. Visits intervening islands. Old extralimital records for PALAU and YAP may be questionable.

Note: Because most terns, including the very similar Bridled Tern, have gray backs, we prefer the name Spectacled Tern for this species rather than the AOU Check-list (1983) name. Spectacled Tern is widely used in world literature on seabirds (e.g. Löfgren 1984; Tuck and Heinzel 1978).

BRIDLED TERN   *Sterna anaethetus*   PLATE 20

Appearance and Identification: (15;38) Similar in all respects to Spectacled Tern, but darker and browner on back, with upper back not appreciably paler than wings, and more white in sides of tail. Underparts slightly darker, but this feature not very useful in the field. Juveniles less scaly-looking above than young Spectacled. Lighter above than Sooty Tern, with dark cap separated from back by pale collar.

Habits: At Palau, frequents inshore lagoon waters near nesting cliffs. Otherwise similar to Spectacled Tern.

Voice: A high clear barking near roosts, and harsher calls while feeding.

Occurrence: Widely distributed in world tropics, but absent from most of the tropical Pacific. Common to abundant resident of PALAU. Accidental at BIKAR (Marshall Is.). Published records for other places (Hawaiian Is., Samoa, Tonga, Fiji) possibly based on confusion with Spectacled (Gray-backed) Tern.

SOOTY TERN   *Sterna fuscata*   PLATE 20

Appearance: (17;43) A medium-sized, black and white, fork-tailed tern. Upperparts actually dark brown, but look all black at a distance. Forehead white, reaching back just to the eye. Juvenile dark sooty brown, with buff feather edges above and white belly. Subadult may retain dark feathering on throat and breast.

Habits: Highly gregarious while feeding and nesting. Forages by lightly splashing or hovering near the surface. Feeds at sea near nesting islands. Noisy in colonies. May call over land at night.

Voice: A harsh screeching *kree-a-reek* or *wide-awake*

Identification: The only tern in the tropical Pacific that looks entirely black above, white below. Larger and darker above than Spectacled or Bridled and posture on land more conventional. Juveniles resemble noddies somewhat, but have forked tails and white bellies.

Occurrence: Pantropical. Widely distributed and common in the tropical Pacific, including the HAWAIIAN IS., MICRONESIA, FIJI, and c. POLYNESIA, E to the TUAMOTU ARCH. Nests on predator-free islands of most island groups in the region.
Other name: Wideawake Tern.

WHISKERED TERN *Chlidonias hybrida*

This marsh tern is known in the tropical Pacific by a single (1976) record for YAP, but others may easily have been overlooked or misidentified. Size and color pattern in nonbreeding plumage very similar to that of Common Tern, with mottled black crown and nape, black auriculars and wing margins. Note shorter, less deeply forked tail and shorter dark maroon (not black) bill. Chunkier in flight than Common Tern, and less likely to feed over salt water. For illustrations, see Eurasian field guides or Harrison (1983). Reference: Clapp, R. B., and R. C. Laybourne. 1983. First record of the Whiskered Tern from the tropical Pacific. *'Elepaio* 43:69-70.

WHITE-WINGED TERN *Chlidonias leucopterus*

Appearance: (9½;24) A small tern with slightly notched tail. Winter adults are gray above, white below with white underwings. Primaries black above, head mottled black on crown and nape, with black spot on auriculars. Breeding plumage (black head and body, white rump and tail, pale pearly gray upperwings) seldom, if ever, seen in tropical Pacific. Molting birds may be blotched with black. For illustrations, see Eurasian field guides, Harrison (1983), or NGS (1983).
Habits: Hawks insects over ponds and marshes, with buoyant, dipping flight.
Identification: The short, only slightly forked tail and distinctive head pattern set this species apart from *Sterna* terns. Very similar to Black Tern, but without dark bar on side of breast; wings paler below, darker above.
Occurrence: Breeds across c. Eurasia, winters to Southern Hemisphere. Uncommon winter visitor to PALAU, vagrant to the MARIANAS (Guam, Tinian, Saipan).

BLACK TERN *Chlidonias niger*

A very rare visitor to the HAWAIIAN IS., this marsh tern breeds in c. N. America, winters to S. America. All Hawaiian records are of winter-plumaged individuals, dark gray above, white below, with black crown, nape, and auriculars. Dark bar on side of breast distinctive. Very similar to White-winged Tern but with gray wing lining, more deeply forked tail, and uniformly colored upperwing. Breeding plumage has black head and body. Molting birds are blotchy. For illustrations, see N. American field guides and especially Harrison (1983).

BROWN NODDY *Anous stolidus*   PLATES 2, 20

Appearance: (17;43) A medium-sized, dark brown tern with long, narrowly wedged-shaped tail and pale cap (often difficult to see at a distance). Juvenile may lack pale cap entirely, and immature may have only white lores and forehead. Outer primaries and tail darken distally; both darker than mantle.

Habits: More pelagic and more solitary than Black Noddy. Nests in varied locations from sandy beaches to tall forest trees far inland. Noisy on nesting grounds, especially at night. Flies low over water, somewhat like shearwaters.

Voice: A hoarse rolling growl, shorter croaks, and cackling notes.

Identification: Beginning birders should learn this species well, as it is easily confused with other dark seabirds. Note the sharp-pointed tern bill, the more pointed wing shape, and the long, notched, heavy-looking tail. Larger and browner than Black Noddy, without contrasting gray tail. See Black Noddy.

Occurrence: Found throughout the world's tropical oceans. Common throughout the HAWAIIAN IS., MICRONESIA, FIJI, and POLYNESIA.

Other names: Common Noddy, Noddy Tern.

BLACK NODDY *Anous minutus*   PLATE 20

Appearance: (15;38) Very similar to Brown Noddy but smaller, darker, and with longer, thinner bill. Tail gray, contrasting with rest of body plumage. Immatures have darker tails, less extensive sharply margined white caps.

Habits: An inshore species that often feeds in flocks over lagoons or coastal ponds. Nests on rocky sea cliffs or in trees.

Voice: A chattering *crick-crick-crick*, a sharper rattling call, and a sustained *kehrr*.

Identification: Often difficult to distinguish from Brown Noddy, especially at a distance against a bright sky. The most reliable field mark is the contrasting gray tail of Black Noddy, easily seen against dark backgrounds, as when the birds are viewed from atop cliffs. (This character is useful throughout the Pacific, but not in the S. Atlantic.) Also note longer, thinner bill of Black Noddy. Dark-tailed immatures have distinctive sharp-edged white caps. Noddies in flocks are almost always Blacks.

Occurrence: Breeds on islands in the tropical Atlantic and Pacific oceans. Resident from PALAU and FIJI E to the HAWAIIAN IS. and the TUAMOTU ARCH. Abundant in some areas.
Other names: White-capped Noddy, Hawaiian Noddy.

BLUE-GRAY NODDY *Procelsterna cerulea* PLATE 20

Appearance: (11;28) A small pearly gray tern with shallowly forked tail. Bill and feet black, the latter with yellow webs. Eye-ring black in front, white behind, imparting a big-eyed look. Two color morphs, a dark form with gray wing linings and a paler one with white underwings. Immature light-phase birds have sharply contrasting, nearly black primaries and brown tinge to mantle and tail.
Habits: Inhabits coastal and lagoon waters of atolls and less populated high islands. Dips and flutters over the surface to capture small fish. Flight light and buoyant.
Voice: Usually silent, but sometimes utters a loud squeal.
Identification: Very distinctive, but pale morph can resemble fairy-terns (particularly Lesser Fairy-Tern) at a distance. Note this species' more buoyant, but less agile, flight.
Occurrence: Widespread resident in the tropical Pacific, seldom seen far from nesting islands. Breeds in the HAWAIIAN IS. (Gardner Pinnacles E to Nihoa, Kaula), the n. MARSHALL IS. (Taongi, Bikar), KIRIBATI (Phoenix Is., Kiritimati), TUVALU, FIJI, the COOK IS., SAMOA, the SOCIETY IS., the TUAMOTU ARCH., the MARQUESAS IS., and HENDERSON I.
Reference: Rauzon, M. J., C. S. Harrison, and R. B. Clapp. 1984. Breeding biology of the Blue-gray Noddy. *J. Field Ornithol.* 55:309-321.
Other names: Gray Noddy, Blue-gray Fairy-Tern, Blue Ternlet, Necker Island Tern.

FAIRY-TERNS: Genus *Gygis*

WHETHER this genus comprises one or several species has not been determined with certainty. Three forms are known, two of which inhabit the tropical Pacific. Although the most recent study (see Reference) recognizes only one species, both we and other ornithologists to whom we have talked believe that at least two species may be involved. We recognize two tropical Pacific species mainly to encourage birders to look for both forms, and thus to aid our knowledge of their distribution and interactions. We do so realizing that the two may prove conspecific.

Fairy-terns are nearly all white, but have a ring of black feathers around the eye that imparts an endearing big-eyed look. They are popular both for their appearance and for their singular nesting habits. They build no nest, but balance a single egg in a tree limb, rock, or even a man-made structure, where incubation takes place and where the chick is fed until it is ready to fledge. Parents have the uncanny ability to capture several small fish in succession and carry them to the chick cross-wise in the bill.

We use the name fairy-tern because that is the name by which these birds are universally known in the popular press and because it provides a convenient group name for *Gygis* if more than one species is recognized. Ornithologists have for many years promoted the insipid name White Tern for *Gygis alba*, but it has never caught the public's fancy. That name does avoid confusion with *Sterna nereis*, an Australian bird also called Fairy Tern. Confusion can be avoided as well by using the hyphenated "fairy-tern" as a collective for *Gygis*, and the name Australian Fairy Tern for *S. nereis*.

Reference: Holyoak, D. T., and J. C. Thibault. 1976. La variation géographique de *Gygis alba*. *Alauda* 44:457-73.

COMMON FAIRY-TERN   *Gygis alba*   PLATE 20

Appearance: (12;31) A white tern with shallowly forked tail, black eye-ring, black shafts on the primaries, and heavy bill blue at base, black at tip. Bill shaped like elongated triangle.

Habits: Feeds at sea on fish taken by diving. Nests and roosts in trees of dense forests (where available) or in low vegetation on atolls. May become relatively tame and rear its young quite close to human activities, as at Midway and in Honolulu city parks. Flight graceful and light. Sometimes small flocks fly in formation. Often solitary.

Voice: A harsh, raspy laugh, *grrich-grrich-grrich-* at nest site.

Identification: Distinguished from other terns by nearly pure white upperparts, shallow tail fork, and big-eyed look. See Little Fairy-Tern.

Occurrence: Pantropical, breeding in the HAWAIIAN IS. (NW islands, Oahu), MICRONESIA, FIJI, and most of POLYNESIA. In the Marquesas, found only on HATUTU.

Reference: Ashmole, N. P. 1968. Breeding and molt in the White Tern (*Gygis alba*) on Christmas Island, Pacific Ocean. *Condor* 70:35-55.

Other name: White Tern.

LITTLE FAIRY-TERN   *Gygis microrhyncha*   PLATE 20

Appearance and Identification: (9;23) Very similar to Common Fairy-Tern but noticeably smaller, with more shallowly notched tail, more black around the eye, no black shafts on the primaries, and long narrow bill, shaped more like those of other terns and black throughout, with no blue or only a trace of blue at base.

Habits: Similar to those of Common Fairy-Tern, as far as known.

Occurrence: Once thought to be endemic to the MARQUESAS IS. (Eiao to Fatuhiva), now known to occur also in KIRIBATI (Phoenix Is., Line Is.) where supposed hybrids or intergrades with *G. alba* have also been found.

Other name: Marquesan Fairy-Tern.

FAMILY ALCIDAE: Auks and Puffins

ALCIDS are heavy-bodied, thick-billed seabirds that either fly with rapid wingbeats or swim. They inhabit cold Northern Hemisphere seas and only rarely wander south into the tropics. Those that do are doomed to starvation, and sometimes "wrecks" of many individuals swim or wash ashore on remote islands. For illustrations of the following species, see N. American field guides, WBSJ (1982), or Harrison (1983).

PARAKEET AUKLET *Cyclorrhynchus psittacula*
A small (10;25) chunky seabird, dark gray above, white below, with a short, thick, bright red bill. Normally found from the Bering Sea to n. Japan, but flocks have reached the NW HAWAIIAN IS., where several wrecks have occurred, the only evidence of which have been dead remains.

TUFTED PUFFIN *Fratercula cirrhata*
A large (15;38), stocky, big-headed alcid with a huge hatchet-shaped red bill. Known in the c. Pacific from the skeletal remains of a single bird found on LAYSAN (NW Hawaiian Is.). A bird of the temperate and subarctic N. Pacific.

HORNED PUFFIN *Fratercula corniculata*
A large (15;38), big-headed alcid with hatchet-shaped, red and brown (winter) bill. Black above, white below, with pale cheeks that are white in summer, gray in winter. Juveniles have smaller bills. A spectacular wreck of these birds occurred in the NW HAWAIIAN IS. in 1963, when many dead and two live puffins were found.

ORDER COLUMBIFORMES

FAMILY PTEROCLIDIDAE: Sandgrouse

SANDGROUSE are terrestrial birds of the arid regions of Africa and Eurasia. They are plump, short-legged, and pigeonlike, with long, pointed wings and rapid, strong flight. They are highly gregarious. One species has been introduced into the tropical Pacific.

CHESTNUT-BELLIED SANDGROUSE   PLATE 12
Pterocles exustus

Appearance: (12;31) A rather pigeon-shaped bird with long, acutely pointed tail. Sandy yellow above, with dark belly, prominent line across lower breast, and contrasting black primaries. Female shorter-tailed, heavily streaked and barred.

Habits: Almost always in flocks, sandgrouse gather at ponds or other watering places in their preferred dry habitats. In Hawaii, they are found in pastures and grasslands. Flocks move about most frequently in early morning and late afternoon.

Voice: A deep-throated, 2-syllable call given in flight.

Identification: Unlike any other birds in Hawaii in general shape, flying sandgrouse are pointed at both ends and have rapid wingbeats like those of pigeons or ducks.

Occurrence: Native to Africa and s. Asia. Introduced to the island of HAWAII in 1961 and apparently established in the S. Kohala District S and W of Waimea.

Reference: Paton, P.W.C., P. R. Ashman, and H. McEldowney. 1982. Chestnut-bellied Sandgrouse in Hawaii. *'Elepaio* 43:9-11.

FAMILY COLUMBIDAE: Pigeons and Doves

PIGEONS and doves comprise a highly successful, almost cosmopolitan, family. They have colonized most of the forested islands of the tropical Pacific, except for the Hawaiian chain. Several species have been widely introduced. Feral Rock Doves are present in virtually every city of the world including Honolulu, Suva, Apia, Agana, and Hilo, to name a few. The terms "pigeon" and "dove" have no taxonomic meaning and are sometimes used interchangeably. *Columba livia* is known colloquially to almost everyone as "the pigeon" yet its original English name is Rock Dove. In general, pigeons are larger than doves, but there are exceptions. Members of this family native to the tropical Pacific fall into three large groups: large fruiteating pigeons of the genera *Columba* and *Ducula*; ground-doves (*Gallicolumba*); and fruit-doves (*Ptilinopus*); plus two rather distinctive pigeons (Tooth-billed and Nicobar) placed in monotypic genera. The ground-doves and fruit-doves are discussed under their respective generic headings.

Pigeons and doves have a distinctive bill structure, usually rather soft with a fleshy area (cere) around the nostrils and an expanded distal end with a slightly hooked upper mandible. They are mostly arboreal and vegetarian. Most are strong fliers, and the wings may make clapping sounds on take-off or whistling sounds in flight. Vocalizations are deep-throated and ventriloquial, usually sounding farther away than they are.

References: Goodwin, D. 1970. *Pigeons and doves of the world*. London: British Mus. (Nat. Hist.) and Ithaca: Cornell Univ. Press.

Holyoak, D. T., and J. C. Thibault. 1978. Notes on the phylogeny, distribution and ecology of frugivorous pigeons in Polynesia. *Emu* 78:201-206.

ROCK DOVE   *Columba livia*   FIGURE 36

Appearance: (12½;32) A chunky, fan-tailed pigeon. Plumage highly variable. The wild ancestor is blue-gray with two broad black wing-bars, dark-tipped tail, and white rump. Feral descendants of domestic stock tend to revert to the ancestral plumage type, but may be all black, all white, reddish brown, or any combination thereof. A high percentage of feral pigeons in Honolulu are pure white.

Habits: Associated with urbanization worldwide. Sometimes reverts to a truly wild state and nests on sea cliffs or other natural rocky places. Partial to open areas; rarely seen in forests. Usually in flocks. The wings produce a loud clapping as the birds take flight.

Voice: A booming, gurgling *whoo-oo-oo*.

Identification: Smaller than native pigeons, and unlikely to be found in forests. White rump diagnostic if present. Because of their plumage variation, feral Rock Doves can cause the birder a lot of frustration. Whether a bird seen is truly wild or someone's free-ranging domestic stock often cannot be determined. Whether the white pigeons of Waikiki are wild birds is moot, as they depend heavily on handouts.

Occurrence: Feral pigeons are descendants of domestic birds bred from the Rock Dove of Europe. They can be expected almost anywhere in the Pacific, and have often been overlooked in the literature. Reported from HAWAII, FIJI, FRENCH POLYNESIA, SAMOA, and MICRONESIA.

FIGURE 36. Rock Dove
(wild plumage type)

WHITE-THROATED PIGEON   *Columba vitiensis*   PLATE 26

Appearance: (16;41) A large, dark pigeon with white throat and yellow-tipped red bill. Fiji birds purplish brown below, Samoan ones slate gray. Top of head purplish in Samoa, green-glossed slate in Fiji. Nape and side of neck have dark feather edgings that produce a scaly look.

Habits: A bird of the forest and edge. Seen frequently in lowland wet forest, plantations, and scrub. Feeds on a wide variety of fruits and seeds. Sometimes in small flocks. Flight swift and direct with steady wingbeats.

Voice: A double-noted bark, higher pitched than voice of Pacific Pigeon, and moaning, deep-throated *whoo-oo-ooo*.

Identification: May be confused with Pacific Pigeon if seen in silhouette. White throat most distinctive field character. Note two-toned color pattern and chestnut undertail of Pacific Pigeon.

Occurrence: Common on forested islands from the Philippines E to FIJI (*C. v. vitiensis*), and W. SAMOA (*C. v. castaneiceps*). Reports from Tutuila (A. Samoa) probably erroneous.

Other name: Metallic Wood Pigeon.

SPOTTED DOVE   *Streptopelia chinensis*   PLATE 40

Appearance: (12;31) A grayish brown dove with rosy breast and white-spotted black patch on nape (lacking in immatures). Tail broad, rounded, outer feathers black with white tips. Posture busty, with head often tucked back.

Habits: Widespread in a variety of habitats, from city streets to openings in native rain forest. Often feeds on the ground.

Voice: Variable low hoarse *coo*s, typically *coo-WHOO-coo*.

Identification: Much larger than Zebra Dove, slimmer and longer-tailed than Rock Dove. Mourning Dove similar but with sharply pointed tail. Peale's Pigeon larger with no white in tail.

Occurrence: Native to SE. Asia. Introduced in 19th century to the main HAWAIIAN IS. and in early 1920s to FIJI. Now common in both places, mostly below 1200 m elevation.

Other names: Chinese Dove, Lace-necked Dove, Malay Turtle-Dove.

PHILIPPINE TURTLE-DOVE   *Streptopelia bitorquata*   PLATE 21

Appearance: (13;33) A gray-brown dove with rosy breast, black crescent on nape, and long, white-bordered tail.

Habits: Feeds primarily on the ground in a wide variety of habitats, from forests to towns and villages.

Voice: A hoarse *cook-coo-COO-oo* and a monotonously repeated *cut-wool*.

Identification: The only other dove in the Marianas likely to be seen on the ground is the White-throated Ground-Dove. The female ground-dove is a darker orange-brown with no prominent markings, and has a chunkier build with shorter tail.

Occurrence: Native to the Philippines, whence introduced in the 1700s to the MARIANA IS. (Guam N to Saipan). Common.

ZEBRA DOVE   *Geopelia striata*   PLATE 40

Appearance: (8;20) A small, long-tailed dove, brownish gray barred with dark brown. Rufous webs of primaries show in flight. Face pale blue, belly pinkish.

Habits: A ground-dweller of drier lowland habitats. Common around human habitation, even coming to the tables of open-air restaurants in Waikiki.

Voice: One of the most characteristic sounds of the Hawaiian lowlands. A rapid series of short coos, higher pitched than calls of Spotted Dove: *coo-too-roo-coo-COO* or *coo-coo-coo-coo*. Has a halting, irregular rhythm.

Occurrence: Native from Malaya to Australia. Introduced to the HAWAIIAN IS. (Oahu 1922), now abundant on all main islands. Introduced in 1950 to TAHITI (Society Is.), where now established and spreading.

Other names: Barred Dove, Peaceful Dove.

MOURNING DOVE   *Zenaida macroura*   FIGURE 37

Appearance: (12;31) A medium-sized dove, dusty brown with pinkish tinge below, and oval black spots on upperwing coverts. Tail long, tapering to sharp point. Outer tail feathers tipped white.

Habits: In Hawaii, found only on ranch lands near release sites, partic-

FIGURE 37.
Mourning Dove

ularly around feedlots or water sources. Habitat open savannahs or scrublands.

Voice: A mournful ventriloquial *oh-oo-aw, oo-oo-oo*.

Identification: Smaller than Spotted Dove, but similar in overall shape. Note particularly the tail shape in flight, rounded for Spotted, wedge-shaped for Mourning. Tail of perched Spotted Dove can look pointed.

Occurrence: Native to N. America. Introduced in 1964 to the island of HAWAII and apparently established locally near Puu Waa Waa. Population may be slowly expanding.

NICOBAR PIGEON   *Caloenas nicobarica*   PLATE 21

Appearance: (14;35) A large, black-appearing pigeon with stubby white tail. A ruff of lance-shaped feathers around the neck gives the bird a rather vulturine aspect. The plumage shows its metallic iridescence only in good light.

Habits: Largely terrestrial, feeding on the forest floor. Startled individuals may run rather than fly. Most often seen in high flight between islands, usually in small flocks. Flight strong and ducklike.

Voice: Usually silent.

Identification: In flight the short-tailed, long-necked, broad-winged appearance is distinctive. Fruit bats are somewhat similar at a distance, but have much slower wingbeats. Micronesian Pigeon has much longer tail, paler plumage.

Occurrence: Restricted to islands from India to PALAU. The endemic Palau subspecies (*C. n. pelewensis*), found mostly on rock islands between Koror and Peleliu, is a Proposed Endangered Species.

WHITE-THROATED GROUND-DOVE   PLATE 21
Gallicolumba xanthonura

Appearance: (10;25) A robust, short-tailed dove. Male has buff-tinged white head and breast, black underparts, and iridescent purple back. Females are dull dusty brown with dull orange feather edges. Juveniles brighter rufous.

Habits: Secretive. May forage on the ground, but much less terrestrial than other ground-doves. Feeds mainly in trees on fruits, seeds, and flowers. Usually in pairs; the male is more apt to be seen in the open. Flight slow and labored with upper body held at an angle. Habitat mainly in forests, clearings along roadsides, and plantations. Characteristically flies high over forests.

Voice: A very deep moan, given at several-second intervals. Swells in the middle: *ooOOOoo*. Ventriloquial and easily missed among other sounds.

Identification: Could be mistaken for a fruit-dove if seen in silhouette, but note more robust shape, horizontal posture, and slower wingbeats. Female distinguished from other all-dark birds by dove shape and bill. Voice much lower pitched than any other dove calls.

Occurrence: Endemic to the MARIANA IS. (Guam N to Saipan) and YAP. Rare on Guam, uncommon elsewhere; the largest population in the Marianas is on Rota. The Guam population has been proposed as an Endangered Species.

CAROLINE ISLANDS GROUND-DOVE   PLATE 21
Gallicolumba kubaryi

Appearance: (11;28) Both sexes similar to male White-throated Ground-Dove, but larger, with head and breast whiter. Crown, nape, and stripe behind eye black. Feet purple-red. Juveniles dark rusty brown.

Habits: A shy solitary bird of dark montane forests. May be seen walking on the ground or on bare limbs of large trees. Occasionally found in the open near villages.

Voice: Normally silent, but sometimes utters a soft, deep, moaning *coo*.

Occurrence: Endemic to c. CAROLINE IS. (Truk, Pohnpei). Reasonably common, but often hard to see.

POLYNESIAN GROUND-DOVE   PLATE 27
Gallicolumba erythroptera

Appearance: (10;25) Male very similar to somewhat larger Caroline Islands Ground-Dove. Female brownish gray with rusty-tinged bib.

Voice: A low hoarse moan.

Occurrence: Found on a few uninhabited atolls of the TUAMOTU ARCH. (Maria, Actaeon Group; formerly Fakarava) and formerly in the SOCIETY IS. (Tahiti, Moorea), where now apparently extirpated.

Other names: White-fronted Ground-Dove, White-collared Ground-Dove, Society Islands Ground-Dove, Tuamotu Ground-Dove.

Note: This species is reported to have been introduced to KIRIBATI (Abemama, Nonouti) in 1940, suposedly from Nauru. Since ground-doves are not found on Nauru, we question the identity of the introduced birds. More likely they are *G. kubaryi* from nearby Truk or Pohnpei or *G. jobiensis* from Melanesia, both of which are very similar in color pattern to *G. erythroptera*. Their present status in Kiribati is unknown.

MARQUESAS GROUND-DOVE   *Gallicolumba rubescens*   PLATE 27

Appearance: (8;20) Males very similar to Caroline Islands and Polynesian ground-doves, but with head and breast pale gray, darkest on hindneck and crown. Females similar but with darker gray hood and bib. Both sexes have variable amounts of white in wings and tail. Plate 27 shows extremes.

Habits: Very tame. Found on ground among shrubby vegetation. Flies weakly and reluctantly.

Voice: A raspy, snarling note.

Occurrence: Endemic to two uninhabitated islands in the MARQUESAS (Fatuhuku, Hatutu). Common at least on the latter.

Other names: Gray-hooded Quail Dove, Marquesas Quail Dove.

SHY GROUND-DOVE   *Gallicolumba stairii*   PLATE 26

Appearance: (10;25) A mostly dark ground-dove, with slightly paler brown head and breast shield, the latter cream-edged below. Upperparts iridescent purple. Females may be similar or may have reddish brown head and breast, iridescent bronze upperparts. Juveniles are reddish brown with paler feather edges.

Habits: Shy and secretive. Restricted to high montane forests in Samoa, but found in the lowlands elsewhere. Usually solitary. Feeds on the ground. When disturbed often runs with tail fanned and held erect, or flushes into low trees.

Voice: A low melodious series of *oos*, or a *cooo* that rises and falls.

Occurrence: Endemic to c. POLYNESIA, but with a discontinuous and poorly documented distribution in FIJI, TONGA (Late and a few smaller islands in Vava'u; formerly, and perhaps still, a few islands in the Ha'apai and Nomuka groups), SAMOA (Savaii, Upolu, Ofu), and WALLIS AND FUTUNA (Mayr [1945] lists "Alofa" [Alofi?]; Watling

[1982] shows the bird on Wallis only). Introduced about 1940 to ABE-MAMA (Kiribati), but present status there unknown.

Other name: Friendly Ground-Dove. This ridiculous and misleading name is well entrenched in the literature, but virtually every author has felt the need to remark about its inappropriateness. Perhaps the name originated as a bad joke. We suggest the above alternative so that future authors will not have to explain that the name is a lie.

PALAU GROUND-DOVE   *Gallicolumba canifrons*   PLATE 21

Appearance: (8½;22) A small dove with gray head and breast, dark brown underparts, rufous hindneck, and metallic bronze back. Bend of wing purple. Feet and eye-ring bright pink.

Habits: Forages on the ground, walking adeptly on rough terrain. When pursued, takes to the wing suddenly, flies a short distance, and drops to the ground out of sight. Territorial, calling from the same area each morning and evening. Secretive and difficult to see.

Voice: A series of low, upwardly inflected *coo*s uttered in a monotonous series that may last 1 or 2 minutes. Also a low moan, similar to some calls of Palau Fruit-Dove and Micronesian Pigeon.

Identification: No other small dove at Palau forages on the ground. The rufous nape and upper back are conspicuous as the bird flies away.

Occurrence: Endemic to PALAU, where uncommon in the "rock islands" south of Koror, rare on Babelthuap.

TOOTH-BILLED PIGEON   *Didunculus strigirostris*   PLATE 26

Appearance: (12;31) A large robust pigeon with a short tail and rather parrotlike hooked and notched bill. "Teeth" in lower mandible. Plumage dark blackish green below and on head, chestnut above. Bill red and yellow. Females similar to males but duller. Immature has dark bill and dark edges to dorsal feathers.

Habits: A secretive bird of dense upland forest. Found on ground as well as in trees. Flight strong and agile, with loud clapping noise on take-off.

Voice: Not well known. Guttural howls and plaintive *coo*s have been described.

Identification: Peculiar bill distinctive, but hard to see at a distance. White-throated and Pacific Pigeons are slimmer, longer-tailed. Pacific Pigeon is paler, with prominent knob on bill.

Occurrence: Endemic to W. SAMOA (Savaii, Upolu). Rare and restricted to higher elevations. Listed as vulnerable by the ICBP (King 1981).

Reference: Ethecopar, R. D. 1976. Note sur *Didunculus strigirostris*. *L'Oiseau et R.F.O.* 46:427-29.

FRUIT-DOVES: Genus *Ptilinopus*

FRUIT-DOVES are small to medium-sized fan-tailed doves that feed on fruits, especially those of various species of fig (*Ficus*). Most larger islands of Micronesia, Polynesia, and Fiji have at least one species of fruit-dove, and they are among the characteristic land birds of the region. Most species in the tropical Pacific belong to what is called the *purpuratus* group. These are very colorful, mostly green doves with contrasting (usually red) caps on crown and forehead, bright patches of color on the underparts, and iridescent spots on the scapulars and wing coverts. The breast feathers are bifid (an individual feather looks like the distal end has been cut away), and this gives the breast feathering a distinctive indented texture. All members of the *purpuratus* group have hooting or cooing vocalizations that are among the most obvious environmental sounds on many islands. A second group of three species is found on the larger islands of Fiji. They differ from the *purpuratus* group in both appearance and voice, but in their general habits are like other members of the genus. Although fruit-doves are colorful, they are often very hard to see. They perch quietly for long periods, with only their often-ventriloquial calls to betray their presence. They move slowly and deliberately while feeding, and are most often seen in flight.

MANY-COLORED FRUIT DOVE   PLATE 26
Ptilinopus perousii

Appearance: (8½;22) Male very pale yellowish white, with a bold crimson band across upper back. Cap and undertail coverts also crimson. Female dark green above, with gray-green head and underparts, crimson cap, and deep crimson (Samoa) or red and yellow (Fiji, Tonga) undertail coverts. Juvenile more uniformly green, with yellowish belly and edges to dorsal feathers.

Habits: A bird of forest canopy, plantations, parks, and gardens. Often in small flocks. Very agile when feeding among branches of fruit trees. Flight swift, with rapid, short wingbeats.

Voice: A rapid series of *ooo*s that trails off toward the end; a series of stuttering notes *oo-ooo, oo-ooo*; and other variations. Not as stereotyped as vocalizations of Purple-capped Fruit-Dove.

Identification: Male unmistakable, but female often difficult to distinguish from Purple-capped Fruit-Dove. Many-colored is darker above, including hindneck and nape, with the dark green of the back extending further up the neck (Purple-capped has a more sharply contrasting pale "front half"). In flight, note the broad pale tail band of Purple-capped, lacking in Many-colored. In Samoa only, the deep crimson (not red-orange) undertail coverts are a good field mark from below.

Occurrence: Most islands of FIJI and TONGA (*P. p. mariae*), and SAMOA (*P. p. perousii*). Often common, but less abundant than Purple-capped Fruit-Dove where the two occur together.

Other name: Rainbow Dove.

PURPLE-CAPPED FRUIT-DOVE   PLATES 21, 26
Ptilinopus porphyraceus

Appearance: (9;23) A two-toned green fruit-dove with purple cap, dark patch between breast and belly, orange-yellow undertail coverts, and pale band at end of tail. Pale head, neck, breast, and upper back contrast strongly with rest of plumage. Color details vary geographically. Micronesian forms washed with yellow on head and breast and have bright yellow tail band and deep purple (almost black) belly patch. Polynesian birds pale greenish gray on head and breast, with pale gray (Fiji, Tonga) or yellowish gray (Samoa) tail band, and paler belly patch (dull red in Samoan birds). Sexes alike, but juveniles entirely bright green with yellow feather edgings.

Voice: Varies geographically, but typically a rhythmic series of hooting notes initiated by a halting combination of long and short notes: *hoo, hup-hoo, hup-hoo, hoo-hoo-hoo.*

Identification: See Many-colored Fruit Dove.

Occurrence: Widely distributed and common in the CAROLINE IS. (Truk, Pohnpei, Kosrae), WALLIS and FUTUNA, SAMOA, the outlying islands of FIJI (Rotuma, Lau Arch.), TONGA, and NIUE. Formerly EBON (Marshall Is.).

Other names: Crimson-crowned Fruit-Dove, Ponape Dove.

PALAU FRUIT-DOVE   *Ptilinopus pelewensis*   PLATE 21

Appearance: (9;23) Similar to Purple-capped Fruit-Dove but grayer on head and breast, with red-purple "darts" on breast (formed by red bases of bifid breast feathers), broad orange band separating breast and belly, orange-crimson undertail coverts, and yellowish white tail band. Juveniles green, yellower below, with yellow feather edging.

Voice: A long, drawn-out hooting, heard night and day. Begins irregularly but develops a steady rhythm that slows gradually as it trails off. Faster paced than call of Purple-capped Fruit-Dove. A ubiquitous sound at Palau. Also a quiet moan given while feeding.

Identification: Unmistakable if well seen. The moaning call is very similar to some calls of Palau Ground-Dove and Micronesian Pigeon, but softer. Song very similar in quality, but not in rhythm, to song of Palau Owl.

Occurrence: Endemic to PALAU and abundant on all major islands.

MARIANA FRUIT-DOVE   *Ptilinopus roseicapilla*   PLATE 21

Appearance: (9;23:) A very colorful fruit-dove with pearly gray head, neck, breast, and upper back. Rest of upperparts bright green. Cap, and sometimes short malar streak, rose red. Underparts variegated with purple transverse bar below breast, orange flanks, yellow belly, and pinkish orange undertail coverts. Tail band pale gray. Juvenile plumage (rarely seen) entirely green.

Habits: A secretive dove of forests. Usually keeps to the canopy, and most often seen in rapid flight overhead. Withdraws from heavily populated areas, especially if hunted.

Voice: A long series of plaintive *coo*s. Begins with 3 or 4 long, widely spaced notes followed by a rapid stuttering series that eventually slows to a rhythmic pattern: *cooo, cooo, cooo, cooo-cut-cucucucucucu-coo-coo-coo-coo-coo-coo.*

Occurrence: Endemic to the MARIANA IS. (Guam, Rota, Agiguan, Tinian, Saipan). Now very rare on Guam and confined to the limestone forest of the n. cliff line. Still common on other islands, with highest population on Rota. Proposed as an Endangered Species on Guam.

Other name: Rose-capped Dove.

COOK ISLANDS FRUIT-DOVE   PLATE 27
Ptilinopus rarotongensis

Appearance: (8;20) Similar to Purple-capped Fruit-Dove but with brighter magenta cap, band below breast olive with carmine-red or orange center, and silvery tail band.

Habits: Found in forest trees, where it feeds on fruit. Usually solitary or paired. Flight rapid, direct. Generally avoids heavily settled areas.

Voice: A series of coos: *OOOO-oooo-ooo-oo-oo-o* (Rarotonga) or *oooo-oooo-oooooo*, second syllable rising, third lower (Atiu) (C. J. Ralph, pers. comm.).

Occurrence: Endemic to the COOK IS. (Rarotonga, Atiu). On the former restricted to upland forests away from the populated lowlands, on the latter common in the interior makatea limestone region. Rarotonga population probably fewer than 100 individuals (*fide* C. J. Ralph).

Other name: Rarotonga Fruit-Dove.

HENDERSON ISLAND FRUIT-DOVE   PLATE 27
Ptilinopus insularis

Appearance: (8;20) Very similar to Purple-capped and Cook Islands fruit-doves, but with redder cap and no colorful patches below.
Habits: Found in forests throughout the island. Very tame, though sometimes hunted by Pitcairn islanders. Sometimes in flocks.
Voice: A coarse *coo*.
Occurrence: Endemic to HENDERSON IS. Common.

GRAY-GREEN FRUIT-DOVE   PLATE 27
Ptilinopus purpuratus

Appearance: (8;20) A rather plain, plump fruit-dove, pearly gray on the front half, olive green posteriorly with pale (Tahiti-Moorea) or bright (Leeward Is.) yellow underparts. Cap not strongly contrasting, very pale lavender (darker in Leewards). Tahiti and Moorea birds have green-tipped tail with narrow subterminal gray band, Leeward Is. birds have broad gray terminal band.
Habits: Found in lowland forests, plantations, and river valleys. Feeds in canopy and occasionally circles high over trees. Usually solitary. Flight strong, direct, with clapping wingbeats.
Voice: A mournful series of *oo*s, slow-paced at first, then accelerating and run together at the finish: *oo, oo, oo, oo, oo-oo-ou-u-u-u*. Less frequently a double-noted *wa-ou, wa-ou, wa-ou*.
Occurrence: Throughout the SOCIETY IS. from sea level to 1000 m. Three recognizable subspecies: *P. p. purpuratus* (Tahiti), *P. p. frater* (Moorea), and *P. p. chrysogaster* (Bora Bora, Huahine, Raiatea, Tahaa, Maupiti). Common, but shy where hunted.
Other names: Society Islands Fruit-Dove, Tahiti Fruit-Dove.

ATOLL FRUIT-DOVE   *Ptilinopus coralensis*   PLATE 27

Appearance: (8;20) Similar to Gray-green Fruit-Dove, but with slimmer build. Paler and with coppery highlights to the dorsal plumage. Cap two-toned, almost white at base of bill, darker lavender on crown. Tail narrowly tipped silvery white. Nearly lacks the fluted or indented texture of breast feathers seen in other fruit-doves.
Habits: Very distinctive. The only fruit-dove in the tropical Pacific adapted exclusively to low coral atolls. Feeds on insects and seeds, and usually forages on the ground. Flight weak. Very tame on uninhabited islets (motus). Allows close approach before flying off a short distance.
Voice: A weak series of low *oo*s, every third one longer and upslurred: *oo-oo-ouwe-oo-oo-ouwe*.

Occurrence: Widespread among islands of the TUAMOTU ARCH. Common on uninhabited islands, rare near settled areas.
Other name: Tuamotu Fruit-Dove.

MAKATEA FRUIT-DOVE *Ptilinopus chalcurus* PLATE 27

Appearance: (8;20) A mostly green fruit-dove with few bold markings. Cap purple, bill yellow, center of belly golden yellow. No tail band.
Occurrence: Endemic to MAKATEA (Tuamotu Arch.). Common. Once declining, the population is now apparently stable.

WHITE-CAPPED FRUIT-DOVE PLATE 27
Ptilinopus dupetithouarsii

Appearance: (8;20) A stocky two-toned green fruit-dove with a white cap, orange belly patch, and broad yellow terminal tail band. Females duller, juveniles with greenish gray cap.
Habits: Found in canopy of dense leafy trees in primary and secondary forests as well as plantations. Sometimes in small flocks in fruiting trees. Not especially shy, but often hard to see, as it may sit for long periods without moving or calling. Flight rapid with hissing wingbeats.
Voice: A slow repetitive series of plaintive *coo*s that accelerates near the end. Sings infrequently.
Identification: See Red-mustached Fruit-Dove.
Occurrence: Endemic to the MARQUESAS (Nukuhiva, Uapou, Uahuka, Hivaoa, Tahuata, Mohotani, Fatuhiva). Common to abundant at all elevations.
Other name: Northern Marquesan Fruit-Dove.

RED-MUSTACHED FRUIT-DOVE PLATE 27
Ptilinopus mercierii

Appearance: (7;18) A compact fruit-dove with a short, nearly square tail. Cap and mustachial streak crimson red, bordered posteriorly with yellow. Head, neck, and breast blue-gray, rest of underparts golden yellow. Olive green on upperparts, tail tipped pale yellow.
Habits: A little-known bird of forest canopy. May form flocks, particularly at water sources. Flight faster than that of White-capped Fruit-Dove. The two species may feed together.
Voice: Similar to that of White-capped Fruit-Dove but higher, sharper and less melancholy.
Identification: Differs from White-capped Fruit-Dove by red cap, two-toned gray/yellow underparts, and less obvious tail band.
Occurrence: Endemic to the MARQUESAS (Nukuhiva, Hivaoa; possibly Tahuata, Fatuhiva). Always considered much less common than

White-capped Fruit-Dove, and found at higher elevations. Not reported for many years; probably extinct. Bruner failed to find it in 1985 and found no islanders who knew the bird.

Other names: Southern Marquesan Fruit-Dove, Moustached Dove.

RAPA FRUIT-DOVE   *Ptilinopus huttoni*   PLATE 27

Appearance: (12;31) An unusually large, long-tailed, and long-billed fruit-dove. Mostly green, with paler head and upper breast. Cap, malar streak, and upper throat rose-pink. Undertail coverts darker purplish pink, bar across lower breast purple. Belly pale yellow. Juveniles duller, with pale feather edgings on wings and underparts.

Habits: A shy, secretive denizen of remote montane forests.

Voice: A repetitive series of doubled notes, the second higher: *oo-wa, oo-wa, oo-wa.*

Occurrence: Known only from RAPA (Tubuai Is.). Very rare, with population possibly under 30 individuals (1984). Listed as rare by ICBP (King 1981).

WHISTLING DOVE   *Ptilinopus layardi*   PLATE 26

Appearance: (8;20) A small, compact green dove. Males dark green with olive-yellow head and undertail coverts. Females have green heads. Loose velvety texture to plumage, especially that of males.

Habits: Feeds on large or small fruits in canopy of dense forest or lowland bush. More easily heard than seen.

Voice: A loud, clear, rising whistle followed by a quieter "falling tinkle," the first whistle easily imitated. Also a distinctive whine followed by a descending squeaky whistle (W. N. Beckon).

Identification: Darker, chunkier, and more uniformly green than female Many-colored Fruit-Dove, and without crimson cap.

Occurrence: Endemic to s. FIJI (Kadavu, Ono). Apparently common.

Reference: Beckon, W. N. 1982. A breeding record of the Whistling Dove of Kadavu, Fiji. *Notornis* 29:1-7.

Other names: Yellow-headed Dove, Velvet Dove.

GOLDEN DOVE   *Ptilinopus luteovirens*   PLATE 26

Appearance: (8;20) A small, chunky dove. Females bright green all over. Males at a distance look pale golden green (in flight, like a gold coin with wings). At closer range the peculiar velvety-textured plumage, with long overlapping feathers, can be seen.

Habits: Frequents the canopy of dense leafy trees in original forest and more open lowland bush. Very agile, even hanging upside down to reach fruits, yet slow and deliberate in movements. Females also eat insects. Flight a flapping/gliding combination somewhat like that of a small owl. Wings produce a whistle.

Voice: A ventriloquial bark, like that of a small dog. Also low growls and snoring notes. Very different from calls of Many-colored Fruit-Dove.

Identification: Unlikely to be mistaken for any other species except perhaps female Many-colored Fruit-Dove, which has a red cap.

Occurrence: Endemic to c. FIJI (Viti Levu, Ovalau, Beqa, Gau, Waya Group). Common in forested areas, but also found near population centers.

Other name: Lemon Dove.

ORANGE DOVE *Ptilinopus victor* PLATE 26

Appearance: (8;20) A small, stocky, brightly colored dove. Males brilliant fiery orange with olive green heads. Females dark green above, light green below. Juveniles similar but with yellow feather edgings.

Habits: Found alone or in small groups in the canopy of original forest and open bush. Feeds on fruits and berries, and females also eat insects. Despite bright colors, even males are hard to detect among the leaves. Movements slow and deliberate.

Voice: Males utter a sharp, knocking *tock, tock*, while foraging. The sound is not very loud, rather mechanical and unbirdlike. Both sexes also give a growling *weeer*. Neither sound resembles that of any other pigeon or dove.

Identification: Females are stockier and less contrastingly patterned than the female Many-colored Fruit-Dove, and lack the crimson cap.

Occurrence: Endemic to n. FIJI (Vanua Levu, Taveuni, Kioa, Rabi, Laucala, Qamea). Common.

Reference: Orenstein, R. I., and M. D. Bruce. 1976. Comments on the nesting and plumage of the Orange Dove *Ptilinopus victor. BBOC* 96: 2-4.

PACIFIC PIGEON *Ducula pacifica* PLATE 26

Appearance: (16;41) A large pigeon with long square tail and prominent bulge at base of upper mandible. Bill black. Head and neck light gray with pinkish cast, underparts cinnamon brown. Back, tail, and wings blackish green or blue-green above. Wing lining slate gray. Immatures duller and without bulge on bill.

Habits: Feeds on fruits of large trees in forest canopy or in dry beach-strand vegetation. In many places, tends to prefer smaller islands. More social than Micronesian Pigeon, sometimes in flocks. May fly between islands. Flight slow and deliberate. Often sits on exposed snags.

Voice: Low growling or barking notes that may rise and fall in pitch. Also a low soft *coo*.

Identification: The only pigeon in its range with a knob or bulge on the bill. Paler throughout than White-throated Pigeon. Distinguished from Peale's Pigeon by slate underwing and pale undertail coverts.

Occurrence: From the Bismarck Arch. (Papua New Guinea) E through tropical c. Pacific including FIJI (Lomaiviti Group, Lau Arch., Vatulele; absent from larger islands), TUVALU, the PHOENIX IS. (Kiribati), TOKELAU, WALLIS AND FUTUNA, SAMOA, TONGA, NIUE, and the COOK IS. (Pukapuka, Palmerston, Atiu, Mitiaro, Mauke, Rarotonga).

MICRONESIAN PIGEON   *Ducula oceanica*   PLATE 21

Appearance: (16;41) A large pigeon with head, neck, and breast gray. Rhinoceros-like "horn" on upper mandible. Underparts dark rusty. Back, wings, and tail black with green or brown iridescence. In flight looks two-toned, with pale front, dark rear. Immatures lack projection on bill.

Habits: Lives in the canopy of dense forests on high islands or in coconut plantations on atolls. Usually solitary, shy, and secretive especially where often hunted. Usually seen in flight. Flight steady with deep, heronlike wingbeats. Feeds on fruit and large fleshy seeds.

Voice: A loud hoarse bark, *grow-row-row-ow*, which accelerates and drops in pitch. Also a low moan.

Identification: The only pigeonlike bird on most islands where it is found. In Palau, compare all-dark, stub-tailed Nicobar Pigeon.

Occurrence: Endemic to Micronesia. Fairly common at PALAU, YAP, POHNPEI, and KOSRAE. Rare in TRUK and the MARSHALL IS. (Arno, Jaluit, Ailinglaplap, Wotje). Formerly KIRIBATI (Kuria, Aranuka). The Arno and Jaluit (*D. o. ratakensis*) and Truk (*D. o. teraokai*) populations are (as of May 1985) candidates for listing as Endangered Species.

PEALE'S PIGEON   *Ducula latrans*   PLATE 26

Appearance: (16;41) Similar to Pacific Pigeon but with no knob on bill. Gray head, neck, and upper back. Tail, wings, and lower back grayish brown. Underparts buff, undertail coverts pale reddish buff, wing lining chestnut.

Habits: A bird of the canopy in heavily forested areas from lowlands to 1000 m. Often sits on exposed snags. Feeds on a wide variety of fruits. Alone or occasionally in small groups. Flight slow. Flicks tail for a while after landing. Nods head when disturbed.

Voice: A deep barking *woof* that may be repeated (Watling 1982). Lower pitched than similar calls of Golden Dove or White-throated Pigeon. Also a parrotlike squawk and quieter cooing notes.

Identification: Much paler than White-throated Pigeon. Similar Pacific Pigeon has bulge at base of bill, chestnut undertail coverts, and dark gray, not chestnut, wing linings.

Occurrence: Endemic to FIJI and common on large to medium-sized islands but absent from small outlying ones. Range overlaps that of Pacific Pigeon only in Lomaiviti Group, Vatulele, and n. Lau Arch.

POLYNESIAN PIGEON   *Ducula aurorae*   PLATE 27

Appearance: (20;51) A large, long-tailed pigeon with silver-gray head, neck, and underparts. Back and tail dark iridescent green. Large black knob at base of bill. Sexes similar, juveniles duller and much darker on head and underparts.

Habits: A bird of dense forests with fruiting trees. Feeds on guava, wild figs, and plantains. Flight slow, with deep wingbeats. Shy and difficult to see when perched.

Voice: A loud, booming *rouw-rouw-rouw*.

Occurrence: TAHITI (Society Is.) and MAKATEA (Tuamotu Arch.). On the former very rare and found only in Papenoo Valley, but more common on the latter. Vulnerable (King 1981).

Other names: Society Islands Pigeon, Aurora Pigeon.

NUKUHIVA PIGEON   *Ducula galeata*   PLATE 27

Appearance: (22;55) A large, heavy-bodied, broad-winged, long-tailed pigeon with a broad, flat, white, feathered cere protruding almost to the tip of the bill. Back and tail glossy dark green. Head, neck, and underparts dark gray, undertail coverts chestnut.

Habits: Restricted to remote wooded valleys above 700 m. Feeds on large fruits such as guavas. Roosts in high trees against cliffs. Flight slow with deep, labored wingbeats. Seen alone or occasionally in small groups. Not particularly shy.

Voice: A deep, bellowing, cowlike *waah-waah*.

Occurrence: Endemic to NUKUHIVA (Marquesas Is.). Confined to narrow valleys at W end of island. Population in low hundreds. Vulnerable (King 1981).

Other name: Marquesas Pigeon.

ORDER PSITTACIFORMES

FAMILY PSITTACIDAE: Parrots, Parakeets, and Lories

THIS large, mostly tropical, family includes many birds familiar as pets. In the tropical Pacific, most native species belong to a group known as lories. They have brush-tipped tongues adapted for feeding on nectar and are usually seen around flowering trees. Their calls are high-pitched, irritating screeches. They are often kept locally as pets, although they do not learn to talk, and their modern distribution is probably at least partly the result of human transport among the islands. Lories and lorikeets are found throughout central and eastern Polynesia, but only one species is native to Micronesia and none are found in Hawaii. Except for the shining-parrots of Fiji, the other major groups of parrots are represented in the region today only by introduced species that have become pests. Some authorities divide this family into three: Loriidae for the lories; Cacatuidae for the cockatoos; and Psittacidae for the rest.

Reference: Forshaw, J. M., and W. T. Cooper. 1978. *Parrots of the world*. 2d [rev.] ed. Melbourne: Lansdowne Editions.

POHNPEI LORY   *Trichoglossus rubiginosus*   PLATE 22

Appearance: (9;23) A trimly built, dark maroon-red lory with olive-yellow tail and orange bill. Sexes similar except for eye color, yellow-orange in males, grayish white in females.

Habits: A bird of forest and plantation. Particularly fond of coconut palms, where it feeds on nectar and pollen. Also takes fruit. Noisy, inquisitive, and aggressive, often seen in pairs or small flocks of up to ten individuals. Nests in holes in coconut palms or other large trees.

Voice: Loud high-pitched chattering or hissing screeches given in flight as well as when perched. Soft crooning call given at dusk.

Occurrence: Endemic to POHNPEI. Common, especially in lowland plantations. A bird reported from Namoluk Atoll (Truk) was likely an escaped pet.

COLLARED LORY   *Phigys solitarius*   PLATE 28

Appearance: (7½;19) A small, short-tailed parrot with a patchwork pattern of red (throat, breast, upper back), green (lower back, wings, tail, nape), and deep purple (crown, belly, undertail coverts). Bill yellow.

Habits: A common bird of the lowland coastal forests, plantations, and gardens. Less frequent at higher elevations. Feeds in flowering trees, especially coconut, African tulip, and drala. Flight very swift and agile. Usually in small flocks of five to ten birds.

Voice: Shrill screeches.

Identification: Compare mostly green Red-throated Lorikeet, usually found at higher elevations.

Occurrence: Endemic to FIJI and common throughout except the s. Lau Arch.

RED-THROATED LORIKEET *Charmosyna amabilis* PLATE 28

Appearance: (7;18) A small green lory with red throat and thighs. Long, pointed tail has light yellow tip.

Habits: A canopy bird found up to 1000 m in montane rain forest. Feeds on nectar and pollen. Usually seen in small flocks of five or six. Flight rapid and straight.

Voice: Short, high-pitched squeaks (Watling 1982).

Identification: Distinguished from Collared Lory by all-green appearance and red throat.

Occurrence: Endemic to FIJI (Viti Levu, Vanua Levu, Taveuni, Ovalau). Generally uncommon, possibly extirpated on Ovalau.

BLUE-CROWNED LORIKEET *Vini australis* PLATE 28

Appearance: (7;18) A small green lorikeet with blue crown, red throat and cheeks, and red and purple belly patch. Tail wedge-shaped and greenish yellow below. Bill yellow.

Habits: Primarily frequents plantations and second-growth forests. Particularly fond of coconut and *Erythrina* trees. Forages in flocks. Flight rapid and direct.

Voice: A shrill high-pitched whistle.

Occurrence: Endemic to and widespread in c. Polynesia including the s. LAU ARCH. (Fiji), WALLIS AND FUTUNA, SAMOA (Savaii, Upolu, Manua), TONGA (throughout but extirpated Tongatapu, 'Eua, and NIUE.

KUHL'S LORIKEET *Vini kuhlii* PLATE 28

Appearance: (7;18) A small lorikeet with a green crown, purple nape and scarlet underparts.

Habits: Frequents coconut plantations and other flowering trees. Found in residential areas and forests. Usually in pairs or small groups. Flight direct and rapid.

Voice: A shrill croak or screech.

Occurrence: Endemic to RIMATARA (Tubuai Is.) and abundant there. Introduced prior to 1798 and again in 1957 to the LINE IS. (Kiribati). Common on Teraina and Tabuaeran, but introductions on Kiritimati failed.

STEPHEN'S LORIKEET   *Vini stepheni*   PLATE 29

Appearance: (7;18) A small lorikeet, green above, scarlet below, with a variable band of purple and green across breast.
Habits: Usually in pairs, flying over larger trees.
Voice: A shrill screech.
Occurrence: Endemic to HENDERSON I. Reportedly uncommon.
Other names: Henderson Island Lory, Henderson Parrot.

BLUE LORIKEET   *Vini peruviana*   PLATE 29

Appearance: (7;18) A small, dark blue lorikeet with white bib and bright orange bill and feet. Immature's bib dark grayish black flecked with white in throat, feet dark brown, bill black.
Habits: A bird of the lowlands. Prefers coconut trees but on atolls also forages in other flowering plants such as scaevola. Feeds on nectar and soft fruits. Flight rapid with quick, short wingbeats. Seen in pairs and flocks of up to ten birds. Nests in tree cavities.
Voice: A hissing, rolling, high-pitched screech, usually doubled: *schee-schee*.
Identification: Looks black except in good light. White bib of adults distinctive. The only lorikeet in its range.
Occurrence: Widespread but unevenly distributed in se. POLYNESIA including the SOCIETY IS. (formerly all, now extirpated except on Scilly and Bellingshausen), the TUAMOTU ARCH. (several atolls including Rangiroa), and AITUTAKI (Cook Is., possibly introduced). Still common on uninhabited islands and Aitutaki. The ICBP lists it as rare (King 1981).
Other name: Tahiti Lorikeet.

ULTRAMARINE LORIKEET   *Vini ultramarina*   PLATE 29

Appearance: (7;18) A small lorikeet, brightly colored in various shades of blue, darker on back, with mottled white and blue throat. Sexes similar.
Habits: Feeds in canopy of flowering trees on nectar, flowers, buds, fruit, and insects. Usually seen in pairs, less often in small flocks. Rarely rests long in one tree. Flight rapid with quick, shallow wingbeats. Found from sea level in coconut palms to the highest ridges in mountain forest.

Voice: A sharp piercing whistle transcribed as *iiiii*. Also occasionally a loud, high screech and a 2-part *to-weet* call repeated several times.

Occurrence: Endemic to the MARQUESAS (small population on Nukuhiva in mountainous valleys at nw. end of island; common on Uapou; introduced Uahuka, status uncertain). Considered rare by the ICBP (King 1981).

Reference: Decker, B. 1980. The probable introduction of the Uapou Blue Lorikeet to Uahuka, Marquesas. *'Elepaio* 41:8.

GREATER SULPHUR-CRESTED COCKATOO PLATE 22
Cacatua galerita

Appearance: (20;51) A large white parrot with broad wings, yellow crest, and pale yellow underwing and tail.

Habits: A noisy, conspicuous bird of the forest. Highly social, flocks in groups of up to twelve birds. Flies high above forest with rapid, shallow wingbeats. Roosts and loafs in high, dead trees. Wary and difficult to approach. Forages on fruits, seeds, and plant parts; especially fond of palm hearts. Where numerous causes much damage to endemic palms.

Voice: Loud harsh screech given in flight or when startled. Also gives a disyllabic whistle, the first note harsh and the second clear: *scraw-leek*.

Occurrence: Native to New Guinea and Australia. Introduced after World War II to PALAU, where found among the "rock islands" from Koror to Eil Malk. May be spreading. Population small but increasing.

ECLECTUS PARROT *Eclectus roratus* PLATE 22

Appearance: (14;35) A robust, colorful, broad-winged parrot. Males bright green with underwing coverts and sides of body red, upper mandible yellow. Female bright red with purple-blue belly and black bill. Immatures resemble adults.

Habits: A noisy, sociable, forest parrot seen in pairs or less often in small groups. Flocks with cockatoos. Feeds in canopy of large trees on fruits, leaves, buds, seeds, and palm hearts. Flight strong and direct, high above forest.

Voice: A loud screech, higher pitched but not as harsh as that of a cockatoo, and often paired: *scraw-scrawk*. Also a distinctive far-carrying bell-like *tunk-deee*. The first note is rather metallic, the second somewhat flutelike. Also other bell-like or flutelike notes.

Occurrence: Native to New Guinea and surrounding islands. Introduced after World War II to PALAU where confined to the forested "rock islands" from Koror to Eil Malk. Uncommon but conspicuous.

RED SHINING-PARROT *Prosopeia tabuensis* PLATE 28

Appearance: (18;46) A long-tailed parrot, predominantly green above and red below. Varies from island to island in depth of red color (crimson to maroon) and in extent of blue on hindneck.

Habits: A bird of forests and plantations. Feeds on fruits, seeds, berries, and insects gathered in the canopy. Solitary or paired, less often in small groups. Flight undulating with rapid flaps and glides. Perches in vertical upright posture and characteristically nods head forward and backward.

Voice: Loud harsh squawks and softer short notes. The Kadavu form is said to have higher-pitched calls.

Occurrence: Endemic to FIJI (common Vanua Levu, Kadavu, Taveuni, and several other small islands; introduced Viti Levu, uncommon). Introduced to TONGA (common 'Eua; formerly Tongatapu).

Other names: Red-breasted Musk Parrot, Shining Parakeet.

MASKED SHINING-PARROT *Prosopeia personata* PLATE 28

Appearance: (19;48) A large, slim-bodied parrot with a long, rounded tail and short, rounded wings. Upperparts and sides bright green, center of breast yellow, belly orange, face black. Sexes similar.

Habits: A timid bird of the forest from sea level to 1200 m. Forages mainly on fruit taken in the canopy but also takes cultivated crops such as bananas and grain. Usually seen in pairs or alone, but in nonbreeding season may form flocks. Flight alternates rapid wingbeats and glides in undulating fashion.

Voice: Loud, harsh screeches and shrieks.

Occurrence: Endemic to VITI LEVU (Fiji). Common in forested areas, particularly around fruiting trees.

Other names: Yellow-breasted Musk Parrot, Masked Parrot.

[PALE-HEADED ROSELLA *Platycercus adscitus* See Appendix A]

ROSE-RINGED PARAKEET *Psittacula krameri* FIGURE 38

Appearance: (16;41) A long-tailed, yellow-green parakeet with dark red bill. Males have a narrow black line from throat to below cheeks, and a narrow rose-pink collar. Females lack black markings and collar.

Habits: Prefers dry scrubland and cultivated orchards. Noisy and fearless, often seen in flocks. Feeds on fruits, seeds, and nectar and frequently becomes a serious agricultural pest.

Voice: Loud screeching *kee-ak*, *kee-ak*, given in flight and while perched.

Occurrence: An escaped cage bird, native of India and C. Africa, now

FIGURE 38. Rose-ringed Parakeet

breeding very locally in the HAWAIIAN IS. (Hanapepe Valley, Kauai; Waimanalo, Oahu; Hilo, Hawaii). Well established only on Kauai.
Reference: Paton, P.W.C., C. R. Griffin, and L. H. MacIvor. 1982. Rose-ringed Parakeets nesting in Hawaii: A potential agricultural threat. *'Elepaio* 43:37-39.

BLACK-FRONTED PARAKEET
Cyanoramphus zealandicus

PLATE 29

A long-tailed, dull greenish brown parrot with a reddish rump. Formerly lived on TAHITI (Society Is.) but is probably extinct. It has not been recorded since 1844 and was scarce even when Captain Cook visited Tahiti in 1773.

RAIATEA PARAKEET   *Cyanoramphus ulietanus*   PLATE 29

A long-tailed, dark brown parrot with olive-yellow underparts, rusty uppertail coverts, and blackish head. Known only from two specimens collected by Captain Cook's naturalists in 1773 on RAIATEA (Society Is.). Presumed extinct. Other names: Society Parakeet, Society Parrot.

ORDER CUCULIFORMES

FAMILY CUCULIDAE: Cuckoos

Cuckoos are medium-sized, passerine-like birds with downcurved bills. Their feet are zygodactyl—two toes forward, two behind. Many species are brood parasites. In plumage and postures, some cuckoos resemble small hawks, with long, pointed wings and an upright stance. Only one species breeds in the tropical Pacific, but several are regular nonbreeding visitors. The Long-tailed Cuckoo is the only land bird present on many atolls.

CHESTNUT-WINGED CUCKOO *Clamator coromandus*
This se. Asian species has strayed once to PALAU. It is a striking, large (17½;45), crested cuckoo with a very long tail. It is black above, rusty below, with chestnut wings and white nape. For illustration, see King and Dickinson (1975) or WBSJ (1982). Other name: Red-winged Crested Cuckoo.

HODGSON'S HAWK-CUCKOO *Cuculus fugax*
This small (12½;32), boldly patterned cuckoo has been recorded as a vagrant to PALAU. It breeds in e. Asia, and the northern populations are migratory. The upperparts are dark slate with a white band on the nape, the underparts mostly pale rufous, darkest on the breast. The tail is gray with dark bands. Illustrated in WBSJ (1982) and Flint et al. (1984). Other names: Horsfield's Hawk-Cuckoo, Fugitive Hawk Cuckoo.

COMMON CUCKOO *Cuculus canorus*   Figure 39
Very similar in all respects except voice to the more frequent Oriental Cuckoo, this species breeds across Eurasia, with northern populations migrating S in winter as far as Melanesia. Vagrant to PALAU. For identification, see Oriental Cuckoo. Other name: European Cuckoo.

ORIENTAL CUCKOO *Cuculus saturatus*   Plate 22, Figure 39
Appearance: (13;33) A medium-sized falconlike cuckoo, mostly plain gray. Belly white, boldly barred with dark gray. Tail long, graduated, and dark gray with narrow white bars. Bill black above, yellow below. Fleshy eye-ring yellow. Females have a rare "hepatic" phase in which the gray of the plumage is replaced by rufous and the entire bird is barred with black.

FIGURE 39. Migratory Cuckoos

Habits: A quiet, elusive bird on its wintering grounds. Swoops from tree to tree with deep wingbeats and long glides. Inhabits forest edge, savannah, and even residential areas where it hides in the foliage of large trees. Silent in winter.

Identification: The most likely cuckoo to be seen in w. Micronesia, but very difficult to distinguish from Common Cuckoo by appearance alone. Oriental Cuckoo has bolder, darker barring on slightly buffier underparts. Feathers of the carpal area on underwing (visible only in the hand) are barred in Common, plain in Oriental Cuckoo. Hepatic-phase Orientals have stronger barring on rump than Commons.

Occurrence: Breeds in e. Asia, winters to Australia. Uncommon migrant and winter resident at PALAU and YAP. Some may remain all year but do not breed.

FAN-TAILED CUCKOO   *Cacomantis pyrrhophanus*   PLATE 28

Appearance: (10;25) A small cuckoo, usually gray above, rufous below, with tail barred black and white. A less common melanistic phase is mostly sooty black, with slightly paler belly, and tail feathers only tipped with white. Immatures always more or less barred brown and white below, but underparts variably tinged with rufous or blotched with sooty.

Habits: Inhabits forests, forest edge, and open country. Usually perches low and makes short darting flights. A brood parasite often mobbed by smaller birds.

Voice: Advertising call a 2- or 3-syllable, monotonously repeated, quavering whistle: *too-tee, too-tee.* Alarm call a strident *ki-ki-ki-ki* (Watling 1982).

Occurrence: Resident from e. Australia and New Guinea to w. FIJI (absent from Lau Arch. and other e. islands). Dark color phase found only in Fiji. Fairly common.

BRUSH CUCKOO   *Cacomantis variolosus*

A small (9;23) pale cuckoo that was seen once at PALAU. Distributed from Malaysia and the Philippines to e. Australia. Southern populations migrate N during the southern winter. Adults, such as the Palau bird, are dusty brown above, buffy below, with barred outer tail feathers. For illustration, see Australian field guides.

LONG-TAILED CUCKOO   *Eudynamis taitensis*   PLATE 28

Appearance: (16;41) A large cuckoo with very long tail. Brown above and white streaked with brown below. Upperparts barred with russet. Crown streaked with russet. White lines above and below eye. Tail barred dark brown and russet.

Habits: Secretive and not easily seen. Usually frequents the forest canopy where it slinks about the larger branches. On migration and on its wintering grounds may be found in a variety of habitats. Often mobbed by smaller birds.

Voice: A harsh screech, frequently heard at night. May be rapidly repeated as an alarm call.

Identification: The combination of brown and white plumage and long tail usually distinguishes this species. The Fan-tailed Cuckoo in Fiji is much smaller and has rufous or brown-barred underparts. The immature Fiji Goshawk is vaguely similar but can be distinguished by its raptorial bill, shorter tail, rufous thighs, and lack of white lines above and below eye.

Occurrence: Breeds in New Zealand. Migrates to and winters throughout the islands of the c. and s. tropical Pacific from PALAU to the PIT-

CAIRN IS. Absent from northernmost groups (Mariana Is., Line Is., Hawaiian Is.). Most numerous in c. POLYNESIA.
Other name: Long-tailed Koel.

[**COMMON KOEL**   *Eudynamis scolopacea*   See Appendix A]

ORDER STRIGIFORMES

FAMILY TYTONIDAE: Barn-owls

BARN-OWLS are characterized by heart-shaped faces and softly patterned plumage. They differ from typical owls in several anatomical features. They feed almost entirely on rodents, which they hunt mainly by sound. Two species have been recorded in the tropical Pacific.

EASTERN GRASS-OWL   *Tyto longimembris*
This owl occurs in open grasslands from India to Australia and New Caledonia. Specimens were collected on VITI LEVU (Fiji) in the 1860s, but there have been no recent reports. It may have been overlooked. It resembles the Common Barn-Owl but is much darker above and below, with proportionately longer legs that extend beyond the tail in flight (only toes of Common Barn-Owl extend beyond tail tip). The Eastern Grass-Owl is elusive and hard to see, even where it is common. Look for it in the grasslands of w. Viti Levu, but note that Common Barn-Owls also live in grasslands. For illustrations of Eastern Grass-Owl, see Australian field guides. The name grass-owl should be modified to distinguish this species from the African Grass-Owl (*T. capensis*)

COMMON BARN-OWL   *Tyto alba*   PLATE 11
Appearance: (16;41) A very pale owl with heart-shaped facial disc. Looks almost ghostly in car headlights. Native Polynesian birds are all pure white below. In birds introduced to the Hawaiian Is., males are white, females honey-colored, below.
Habits: Mainly nocturnal, but can be active by day. Found from sea level to mountaintop in a variety of habitats. May roost and nest in buildings, but does not do so necessarily. Flight buoyant, with silent wingbeats.
Voice: A harsh, hissing scream.
Identification: The only owl on most islands. In Hawaii, the Short-eared Owl is more likely to be seen in daylight, but is also active at night and can appear very pale in reflected light. Note Short-eared's dark streaks below.

Occurrence: Cosmopolitan. Native in the tropical Pacific to FIJI, WAL-LIS AND FUTUNA, SAMOA, TONGA, and NIUE. Introduced (1958) to the HAWAIIAN IS. from N. America, now on all main islands. Earlier reports of this species in the Society Is. may be erroneous.

FAMILY STRIGIDAE: Typical Owls

Owls need little introduction. They are noted for their fixed, forward-directed eyes and nocturnal predatory habits. Their feathers are soft and fluffy, making their flight virtually silent. Two species are found in the tropical Pacific.

PALAU OWL *Pyrrhoglaux podargina* PLATE 22
Appearance: (9;23) A small reddish brown owl, indistinctly barred and spotted with white. The only owl in its range.
Habits: Found in all types of forest, especially in deep ravines, but also near villages. Roosts in dense foliage by day, becomes active at dusk. Feeds on arthropods and earthworms. Remains in pairs and family groups year-round, with small territories 100-200 m in diameter.
Voice: Territorial call of male is a long series of short notes, *whock, whock, whock,* that builds slowly in cadence to a peak, when the bird flies from its perch and utters a descending series of 2-syllable notes, *whut-whoo, whut-whoo,* in flight. The female may echo parts of this performance in a duet.
Identification: The only owl in Palau. The calls somewhat resemble notes of the Palau Fruit-Dove, which also calls at night, but with a little experience one can differentiate the two.
Occurrence: Endemic to PALAU, where abundant throughout, with territories very densely spaced.
Other name: Palau Scops Owl.

[**BROWN HAWK-OWL** *Ninox scutulata* See Appendix A]

SHORT-EARED OWL *Asio flammeus* PLATE 11
Appearance: (15;38) A mottled or streaky brown owl with yellow eyes and prominent facial ruff. The tiny "ears" are not often visible in the field.
Habits: Active both day and night. Most often seen coursing low over pastures, fields, or forests. Found in a wide variety of habitats. Feeds mostly on rodents.

Voice: A low bark and a catlike scream. Usually silent.

Identification: Flight profile unlike that of Hawaiian Hawk (see Figure 18). The owl is big-headed and short-necked. Common Barn-Owl much paler below, without streaks.

Occurrence: Widespread in the Northern Hemisphere, with some populations migratory. Resident on all the main HAWAIIAN IS. and POHNPEI (Caroline Is.). Uncommon in Hawaii, and very rare on Pohnpei where the local race (*A. f. ponapensis*) has been proposed as an Endangered Species. Migrants from Asia have turned up as vagrants in the MARIANAS (Guam, Tinian, Pagan), on KOSRAE, ENEWE-TAK (Marshall Is.), possibly YAP, and in the NW HAWAIIAN IS. (Kure, Midway).

Other name: Pueo (Hawaii only).

ORDER CAPRIMULGIFORMES

FAMILY CAPRIMULGIDAE: Nightjars

NIGHTJARS are insectivorous, cryptically colored, nocturnal birds noted mostly for their vocalizations. They perch horizontally on the ground or on branches of trees and are rarely seen by day. Some species hawk insects aerially. Only one species is found in the tropical Pacific.

JUNGLE NIGHTJAR   *Caprimulgus indicus*   PLATE 22

Appearance: (10;25) A dark nightjar with mottled plumage that resembles forest-floor leaf litter. The most obvious marks are a white throat patch, a white bar near tip of outer tail feathers (males only), and white (male) or buff (female) patches, visible in flight, in outer primaries. Eyes shine red in a flashlight beam.

Habits: An inhabitant of forest and mangrove swamps. Strictly nocturnal. Hawks insects in continuous acrobatic flight or by aerial sallies. Usually arboreal, but may perch on the ground.

Voice: A series of knocking sounds, like a small hammer striking hard wood. Pitch and cadence rise, *tawk - tock - tac-tac-tac-tac-tac*. Also a loud, harsh screech, *kreek, kree-kreek*.

Identification: In flight at dusk has long-winged, long-tailed silhouette and pale patches in primaries. Palau Owl is chunky and short-winged; fruit bats appear nearly tailless.

Occurrence: Breeds in s. and e. Asia and PALAU. Continental populations winter to Melanesia, including Palau. The visitors look just like the residents. Uncommon.

Other name: Gray Nightjar.

ORDER APODIFORMES

FAMILY APODIDAE: Swifts

Swifts are the most aerial of birds. They alight only on vertical surfaces and spend most of their lives on the wing, hawking insects. They are slender birds with long narrow wings held out stiffly in flight. Their bills are tiny, but the gape is enormous. Beginners should note the different flight silhouettes and overall manner of flight of swifts and swallows, which are superficially similar. All swifts in the tropical Pacific are dark sooty brown or black. All resident swifts belong to a group called cave swiftlets, now classified in the genus *Aerodramus* but formerly included in *Collocalia*.

Swiftlets are usually found in small to large flocks and may forage high overhead or near the ground. They nest colonially in caves or on rocky cliffs. Nest material, gathered in flight, is glued together with the bird's sticky saliva and attached to a vertical wall. Cave-nesting swiftlets have the ability to echolocate using audible clicks. These clicks are different from the twittering, squeaky chirps uttered by all species when flying in the open.

The taxonomy of swiftlets has undergone considerable change in recent years, and the case is far from settled. Authorities are ambivalent on whether some forms should be considered species or subspecies. Many are virtually identical morphologically. Fortunately for the birder, no island has more than one swiftlet.

References: Holyoak, D. T. and J.-C. Thibault. 1978. Notes on the biology and systematics of Polynesian swiftlets, *Aerodramus*. *BBOC* 98:59-65.

Medway, L. and J. D. Pye. 1977. Echolocation and the systematics of swiftlets. In *Evolutionary ecology*. Ed. B. Stonehouse and C. Perrins. Baltimore: Univ. Park Press. 225-38.

Pratt, H. D. 1986. A review of the English and scientific nomenclature of cave swiftlets (*Aerodramus*). '*Elepaio* 46:119-25.

WHITE-THROATED NEEDLETAIL *Hirundapus caudacutus*

A large (8;20), powerful, heavy-bodied, square-tailed swift marked below by a white throat and a white U on flanks and undertail coverts. Twice as large as cave swiftlets, this species migrates from Siberia to Australia and New Zealand through Melanesia, and once wandered E to VATULELE (Fiji). An unidentified large swift once seen at TRUK may have been this species. For illustrations, see Pizzey (1980), WBSJ (1982), or Simpson and Day (1984). Other names: Spine-tailed Swift, White-throated Spinetailed Swift.

ISLAND (GRAY) SWIFTLET   PLATE 23
Aerodramus vanikorensis

Appearance: (4;10) A small, rather narrow-winged swiftlet. Dark sooty gray above, grayish brown below. Palau birds show a more or less pale rump; other populations have occasional pale-rumped individuals.

Habits: Inhabits natural and man-made caves, such as abandoned World War II gun implacements in Micronesia. Most active at dawn and dusk, but can be seen any time of day. Flight light and fluttery. Frequently flies high above forested ridges, but may also forage near the ground. Sometimes accompanies small bats (*Emballonura* sp.).

Voice: High-pitched chirps in flight, different from the regular, toneless clicks used for echolocation in the darkness of caves.

Identification: Bats have broader wings, more erratic flight, but can be confusing as light fades. Barn Swallow paler below, with deeply forked tail. Migratory swifts larger with longer, narrower wings and more powerful swooping flight.

Occurrence: Found on forested islands from the E. Indies and Philippines to Melanesia and MICRONESIA (Palau, Truk, Marianas, Pohnpei, Kosrae). Abundant on most islands but Mariana population an Endangered Species. Now extirpated on Rota, nearly so on Guam. Uncommon Saipan, Agiguan, Tinian. Introduced from Guam to OAHU (Hawaiian Is.) in 1962 and apparently established in Halawa and Moanalua valleys N of Honolulu, but population very small. Old reports for Yap need substantiation.

Other names: Vanikoro Swiftlet, Edible-nest Swiftlet, Caroline Islands Swiftlet, Mossy-nest Swiftlet, Guam Cave Swiftlet, Uniform Swiftlet, Lowland Swiftlet. The name Gray Swiftlet has been used for four different species of *Aerodramus* in current literature!

TAHITI SWIFTLET   *Aerodramus leucophaeus*   PLATE 30

Appearance: (4;10) A dark blackish brown swiftlet with lighter brown underparts and a short square-tipped tail.

Habits: Flight a mixture of flutters and glides. Prefers wet, rocky, and forested valleys at high elevations. Colonies usually only a few pairs.

Identification: Pacific Swallow, which has a longer forked tail, forages along rivers and closer to tree-tops.

Occurrence: SOCIETY IS. (Tahiti, Moorea). Rare and local on both islands.

ATIU SWIFTLET   *Aerodramus sawtelli*

Appearance: (4;10) Virtually identical to Tahiti Swiftlet.

Habits: Nests colonially in caves in makatea limestone. Makes a shallow cup nest of plant parts glued with sticky saliva. Usually seen hawking insects on the wing over fernlands in the morning and evening. A few active at midday.

Voice: A shrill chirp while feeding, and loud clicks (probably for echolocation) in the darkness of caves.

Occurrence: Endemic to ATIU (Cook Is.) where population small but apparently stable.

Other names: Sawtell's Swiftlet, Cook Islands Swiftlet.

MARQUESAS SWIFTLET   *Aerodramus ocistus*

Appearance: (4;10) A dark blackish brown swiftlet with faint greenish gloss to the back. Lighter brown underparts. Pale rump patch indistinct. Tail relatively longer and more forked than that of Tahiti Swiftlet.

Habits: A bird of forest and edge, from sea level to mountaintop. Hunts low over canopy, on leeward side of ridges, or close to the ground in open areas. Flight slow, with weak fluttering wingbeats and glides. Solitary or in large flocks of 50 to 100 individuals. Nests in large colonies in overhanging cliffs or caves. Echolocates with clicks in caves. Nest constructed of moss and glued with small amounts of saliva.

Occurrence: Endemic to the MARQUESAS. Common on most islands except Hivaoa where the introduced Common Myna may be a disturbing factor.

WHITE-RUMPED SWIFTLET   *Aerodramus spodiopygius*   PLATE 30

Appearance: (4;10) Sooty black above with dusky gray underparts, conspicuous white rump patch and slightly forked tail.

Habits: Flight rapid with shallow, stiff wingbeats. Darts erratically in pursuit of insects. Forages above forest canopy and low over open areas such as streams, grasslands, and roads, particularly after rain. Most active at dawn and dusk. Nests in caves and echolocates with high-pitched twitters. Nest constructed of moss and small twigs glued with hardened saliva.

Identification: Pacific Swallow, with different shape and manner of flight, lacks the white rump patch.

Occurrence: Common from sea level to mountaintop from Australia and Melanesia E. to SAMOA, including FIJI and TONGA. Absent from islands without caves.

Other names: Gray Swiftlet, Gray-rumped Swiftlet.

FORK-TAILED SWIFT   *Apus pacificus*   FIGURE 40

A large (7;18) swift with long, deeply forked tail, white rump, and pale

FIGURE 40.
Fork-tailed Swift

throat. An e. Asian species that migrates from Siberia to Australia. Stragglers have recently been seen twice in the fall on SAIPAN (Mariana Is.; *fide* T. K. Pratt) and once on KWAJALEIN (Marshall Is.; photographed by W. L. Schipper). Should be looked for elsewhere in Micronesia.

ORDER CORACIIFORMES

FAMILY ALCEDINIDAE: KINGFISHERS

KINGFISHERS are big-headed, big-billed birds. Most can be described as follows: dark (usually blue) wings, back, and tail; underparts pale; head pale and encircled by a dark line from the base of the bill around the nape, including the auriculars; bill dark, with the basal two-thirds of lower mandible white. Variations include the extent of dark color in the crown and the degree to which the pale areas are tinted with rusty tones.

Most islands have only one kingfisher present, but occasionally (e.g. at Palau and Tahiti) two may be found together. All resident kingfishers in the tropical Pacific belong to what is called the Collared Kingfisher group. These birds are either subspecies of, or species closely related to, the Collared Kingfisher (*Halcyon chloris*).

Pacific island kingfishers for the most part are not, unlike some of their continental relatives, strongly tied to water. They are forest-dwellers that prey upon small animals of various types, from insects and worms to fishes, small birds, and mammals. They are often "mobbed" by white-eyes, fantails, or other small birds. They normally sit quietly for long periods, but may then dart out after flying insects, drop to the ground for a lizard, or dive into a stream for a small fish. Some are reputed to take baby chickens, but their predations around homes are probably greatly exaggerated. Nevertheless, they are among the few birds denied legal protection in some places (e.g. Palau). Their vocalizations are often loud and far-carrying. They nest in cavities, usually in trees but occasionally dug into banks or cliffs.

The classification of the Pacific members of the Collared Kingfisher group is at present in a state of confusion. Few authorities agree on where the lines between species should be drawn, because information about many forms is limited and inadequate. Much more must be learned about the birds' behavior, especially vocalizations and displays, before any classification will have a sound basis. Field birders can be of great assistance in gathering and reporting this kind of information. We are using a compromise taxonomy that we hope will serve the birder until more is known.

Reference: Fry, C. H. 1980. The evolutionary biology of the kingfishers (Alcedinidae). *Living Bird* 18:113-60.

COLLARED KINGFISHER *Halcyon chloris* PLATES 22, 28

Appearance: Size varies geographically, largest forms (9½;24) in Micronesia, smallest (8½;22) in Samoa. All forms have pure white, not rusty-tinged, underparts (underwing may be pale buff in Polynesian males). Micronesian forms lack rusty tones altogether, but Polynesian races may have an ochraceous margin to the dark crown. Blue crown most extensive in Palau, Tonga, and Fiji, much reduced in Samoa and on Rota (Marianas), and virtually lacking on Saipan and Tinian.

Habits: The prototypical *Halcyon*, with a wide range of habitats. Frequently perches on power lines. Noisy and conspicuous. Larger subspecies often harass smaller birds such as white-eyes, and may in turn be mobbed by them.

Voice: Varies geographically. At Palau, a ringing repeated *tchup-weee*; a more rapid *chup-eep*, *chup-eep*, etc., and an incisive *keep-keep-keep*. In the

Marianas, a loud barking *kip-kip-kip* and a slower *caw-heee, caw-heee*, etc. Samoan birds give a higher-pitched *kip-kip-kip* and a drawn-out *kreeeep* apparently similar to calls of the Chattering Kingfisher.

Identification: Usually the only kingfisher present. Occurs together with the Micronesian Kingfisher at Palau. Note the latter's rusty cap, slightly different vocalizations.

Occurrence: Widespread from the shores of the Red Sea E to Australia and the tropical Pacific. Common in PALAU (*H. c. teraokai*), the MARIANAS (*H. c. albicilla* on Saipan, Tinian; *H. c. orii* on Rota), the LAU ARCH. (Fiji; *H. c. marina*), TONGA (s. islands and Ha'apai Group; *H. c. sacra*), and A. SAMOA (*H. c. pealei* on Tutuila; *H. c. manuae* on Ofu, Olosega, Tau). Collared Kingfishers reported from Nauru were more likely migratory Sacred Kingfishers.

Other names: White-collared Kingfisher, Mangrove Kingfisher.

Note: The kingfishers of Futuna and the larger islands of Fiji are usually classified as Collared Kingfishers, but on the basis of coloration we regard them as Sacred Kingfishers (which see). The supposed Collared Kingfishers in e. Fiji, Tonga, and Samoa may well prove to be more closely allied with the Chattering Kingfisher.

MICRONESIAN KINGFISHER *Halcyon cinnamomina* PLATE 22

Appearance: (8-9½;20-24) A member of the *chloris* group with three distinct subspecies. Guam form large, with males blue above, rusty cinnamon below; females similar but with belly white. Pohnpei race slightly smaller, with juveniles like Guam males but with rusty feather edgings above; adults of both sexes white below with rusty-cinnamon crown. Palau birds smallest, with sexes alike and colored like Pohnpei adults, but with no distinct juvenile plumage. May have white crown at Palau.

Habits: Much quieter and less vocal than Collared Kingfisher. A bird of forests. Only rarely perches on power lines or along shorelines. Palau birds particularly secretive and difficult to see. Guam and Pohnpei birds more conspicuous but may call from concealment of dense shrubbery. Rarely flies high above forest. Nests in tree cavities.

Voice: Geographically variable. Guam birds have a harsh *kshh-skshh-skshh-kroo-ee, kroo-ee, kroo-ee* sometimes given in flight, and a plaintive *kiv-kiv* or *kiu-kiu-kiu* given from concealment. Pohnpei birds have a harsh *tchip-weer* or *skreer* and a loud *kewp-kewp-kewp-kewp* rather like some calls of the Collared Kingfisher. At Palau usually silent, but occasionally utters a loud rasping series that begins with a chatter: *che-che-che, che-kreek, kreek, kreek* (J. Engbring, unpubl. ms).

Identification: At Palau, the Collared Kingfisher is also present. It is larger and has a dark crown. Its calls are confusingly like those of this species, but not as harsh.

Occurrence: Micronesia, with endemic subspecies at PALAU (*H. c. pelewensis*), GUAM (*H. c. cinnamomina*), and POHNPEI (*H. c. reichenbachii*). Common at Palau and Pohnpei. Common until recently on Guam, but suddenly and drastically declined during 1970s and now an Endangered Species on that island.

SACRED KINGFISHER   *Halcyon sancta*   PLATE 28

Appearance: (9;23) A member of the *chloris* group, with bright blue upperparts, including the entire crown. Pale areas of plumage tinted with rufous or buff, darkest in the eyebrow and posterior underparts. Immatures greenish above with buff edgings to wing coverts, and paler below with fine black bars on sides of neck and breast.

Habits: Like other *Halcyon*. Found in a variety of habitats from seashores to deep forest. Often perches in the open, frequently on fences and power lines.

Voice: A rapid *ki-ki-ki-ki-*. . . , sometimes accelerating with notes run together at the climax (Watling 1982). Alarm note a hissing *schreee*, often reiterated.

Occurrence: Widely distributed and generally common in Australia, New Zealand, New Caledonia, FIJI (main islands), and FUTUNA (Wallis and Futuna). Southern populations migrate N to Melanesia and the E. Indies. "Overshoots" have reached KWAJALEIN (Marshall Is.; photographed by W. L. Schipper) and probably NAURU (originally reported as Collared Kingfishers) and w. MICRONESIA (Ulithi, Helen I.).

Note: Our inclusion of the rusty-bellied kingfishers of Fiji (*H. s. vitiensis*, *H. s. eximia*) and Futuna (*H. s. regina*) in this species rather than the Collared Kingfisher is new. These birds look almost exactly like the Sacred Kingfishers that inhabit nearby New Caledonia. Fry (1980; see kingfisher introduction) combined the Flat-billed Kingfisher of Samoa with the Sacred, primarily on the basis of plumage similarities, but inexplicably left the much more similar and geographically intervening Fiji birds in *H. chloris*. All other Collared Kingfishers in the area of this guide are white below. Where they are sympatric in Australia, Sacred Kingfishers and Collared Kingfishers differ mainly in size, color, and vocalizations and are difficult to distinguish in the field. The rusty-bellied Fiji birds sound more like Australian Sacred Kingfishers.

FLAT-BILLED KINGFISHER   *Halcyon recurvirostris*   PLATE 28

Appearance: (7;18) A small dark *Halcyon* with a strong rusty tinge to all pale areas of the plumage except the throat. No eyebrow, but rather a buff loral spot.

Habits: A bird of forests and plantations. Less conspicuous than its relatives, perches lower in trees or bushes, less in the open. Often in pairs. Primarily insectivorous.

Voice: A screeching *krr-eee, krr-eee, krr-eee*.

Occurrence: Endemic to W. SAMOA (Savaii, Upolu). Widespread and common.

Note: Fry (1980; see introduction to kingfishers) considers this form a subspecies of the Sacred Kingfisher.

CHATTERING KINGFISHER   *Halcyon tuta*   PLATE 29

Appearance: (7½;19) A *chloris*-group kingfisher very similar to Micronesian races of Collared Kingfisher, but smaller. No rusty tinge anywhere in the plumage. Cook Is. birds have very little blue in the crown, and those on Mauke also have a light buffy wash below.

Habits: Found primarily in montane stream valleys in original forest, but sometimes also in secondary forest and old plantations. Nests in tree cavities. Takes insects and lizards on the ground or by aerial sallies. Solitary or paired.

Voice: Alarm call a hissing screech. Also a series of sharp notes that accelerate to a rattling chatter (Holyoak 1981).

Identification: Differs from Tahiti Kingfisher in having a complete white collar and white-encircled crown patch. Never has streaks or a breast band below. Vocalizations distinctive.

Occurrence: Distributed spottily in the COOK IS. (*H. t. atiu* on Atiu, *H. t. mauke* on Mauke) and the SOCIETY IS. (*H. t. tuta* on Maupiti, Bora Bora, Raiatea, Huahine, Tahiti). Very rare on Tahiti and restricted to forests above 1000 m. Uncommon, found mostly in the mountains on Bora Bora. Common and more widespread on Raiatea, Atiu, and Mauke.

Other names: South Pacific Kingfisher, Leeward Island Kingfisher, Bora Bora Kingfisher, Respected Kingfisher.

Note: The white-bellied kingfishers of Fiji, Tonga, and A. Samoa, here included under *H. chloris*, may be related to, or conspecific with, *H. tuta*. They are smaller than most forms of *H. chloris*, are geographically isolated from them (but not from *H. tuta*), and resemble *H. tuta* in both plumage and vocalizations.

MANGAIA KINGFISHER   *Halcyon ruficollaris*   PLATE 29

Appearance: (7½;19) A typical *chloris*-type kingfisher, with eyebrow and collar strongly rufous-tinged. Some individuals show a band of rusty across the upper breast. Juveniles have pale edgings to the scapulars and wing coverts.

Habits: Inhabits woodland and scrub; nests in tree cavities. Feeds mainly on terrestrial animals such as insects and lizards.

Voice: A series of short and long mewing or whistled notes, "*ki-wow ki-wow ki-wow*" etc., and some softer chuckling notes (Holyoak 1980).

Occurrence: Endemic to MANGAIA (Cook Is.). Fairly common.

Other name: Cook Island Kingfisher.

Note: Sometimes considered conspecific with Chattering Kingfisher.

TUAMOTU KINGFISHER *Halcyon gambieri* PLATE 29

Appearance: (6½;17) Very similar to Mangaia Kingfisher. A *chloris*-type kingfisher with pale areas of head and hindneck strongly tinged rufous, and sometimes a buffy band across the otherwise white breast.

Habits: A bird of coconut plantations and villages

Occurrence: Endemic to two islands in the TUAMOTU ARCH. Extinct on Mangareva (*H. g. gambieri*) but still fairly common on Niau (*H. g. gertrudae*).

Other name: Mangareva Kingfisher.

Note: Sometimes regarded as a subspecies of *H. tuta*.

MARQUESAS KINGFISHER *Halcyon godeffroyi* PLATE 29

Appearance: (6½;17) A *chloris*-type kingfisher, very bright blue above, white below with a totally white crown. A buff triangle in center of back, just below the collar, is distinctive.

Habits: Shy, restricted to forests.

Voice: Call *treeet-tee-tee*, softer than that of the Tahiti Kingfisher.

Occurrence: Endemic to the MARQUESAS (Hivaoa, Tahuata, Fatu-hiva). Always considered rare, the species survives at least on Tahuata.

Note: May be a subspecies of Chattering Kingfisher.

TAHITI KINGFISHER *Halcyon venerata* PLATE 29

Appearance: (7;18) A distinctive, medium-sized kingfisher with relatively short bill. Color pattern differs somewhat from that of most members of the *chloris* group. No collar, no pale ring around crown. Two distinct subspecies. Tahiti birds greenish brown above with aquamarine highlights to superciliary and auriculars, white below, sometimes with a broad rufous breast band. Females plain brown above, with broad, dark brown breast band. On Moorea, plumage lacks green altogether, immatures are heavily streaked with brown in the throat and upper breast, and adults have fine streaks or bars on sides of breast.

Habits: A bird of the treetops that feeds by aerial sallies. Most common in low elevation forest, but also present in plantations and second growth.

Voice: A rattling *ki-ki-ki-ki-ki-* etc. (D. T. Holyoak in Thibault and Rives 1975) and a high, double-noted whistle.

Identification: Distinguished from Tahiti Reed-Warbler by very heavy bill, chunkier proportions. Chattering Kingfisher bluer above, unmarked white below, with bold white collar and ring around crown.

Occurrence: Endemic to Tahiti (*H. v. venerata*) and Moorea (*H. v. youngi*) in the SOCIETY IS. Common.

Other names: Society Islands Kingfisher, Venerated Kingfisher.

BELTED KINGFISHER   *Ceryle alcyon*   FIGURE 41

Appearance: (13;33) A large, double-crested kingfisher quite distinct from the *chloris* group. Blue-gray above, white below, with broad white collar and blue-gray breast band. Female also has a rufous second band below the gray one.

Habits: Always seen near water. Feeds by plunging head-first after fish. Birds seen in Hawaii have usually fed in coastal bays or estuaries.

Voice: A distinctive loud rattle, unlike the voice of any other bird in Hawaii.

Occurrence: Found throughout N. America. A very rare straggler to the HAWAIIAN IS. (Hawaii, Maui; about five records this century). All records from windward coasts.

FIGURE 41. Belted Kingfisher (male)

FAMILY MEROPIDAE: BEE-EATERS

BEE-EATERS are a group of insectivorous birds noted for long, thin, curved bills and brilliant plumage colors. Their flight is graceful and swallowlike. They are distributed from Europe and Africa to Australia, one species having barely strayed into the tropical Pacific.

RAINBOW BEE-EATER   *Merops ornatus*

This species breeds in Australia and migrates N to Melanesia during the austral winter. Several immatures were seen on TOBI (se. Palau) in 1979. Immatures are blue-green with a black streak through the eye, and lack the long central tail streamers of adults. Whether they are regular visitors to this remote outpost is not known. Illustrated in Simpson and Day (1984). Other name: Rainbowbird.

FAMILY CORACIIDAE: ROLLERS

THESE are large, big-headed, short-billed birds, often brightly colored. They are named for their rolling courtship flights. They are found in Eurasia, Africa, and Australasia, with one species occasionally visiting Micronesia.

DOLLARBIRD   *Eurystomus orientalis*   PLATE 22

Appearance: (12;31) A striking, large, dark blue-green bird with brownish head, lilac throat, and short, hooked, bright red bill. In flight, a "silver dollar" shows at the base of the primaries. Chunky, short-tailed, and big-headed. Profile somewhat like that of a small falcon.

Habits: Perches conspicuously on dead trees over forest canopy and hawks insects by aerial sallies. Usually returns to same perch. Flight erratic and swooping. Frequents forests and forest edge near streams and taro patches. Active at dusk or during cloudy weather.

Identification: Unmistakable if seen well, but in silhouette at dusk can look like a hawk, owl, or nightjar. Bill is hooked, but not raptorial. Jungle Nightjar has smaller head, longer tail in silhouette.

Occurrence: Breeds from India and Japan to Australia. Northern populations migrate S, Australian ones N during their respective winters. Australian birds rarely reach MICRONESIA (Palau, Yap, Pohnpei).

Reference: Engbring, J. 1983. First Ponape record of a Dollarbird, with a summary of the species' occurrence in Micronesia. '*Elepaio* 44:35-36.

Other name: Broad-billed Roller.

ORDER PASSERIFORMES

FAMILY ALAUDIDAE: Larks

LARKS are small birds of open habitats such as grasslands and deserts. They are a nearly cosmopolitan family. One species is a natural migratory visitor in the tropical Pacific, and has also been introduced to Hawaii. Larks are ground-dwellers that run rather than hop, and characteristically have unusually long claws on the hind toe. Most species engage in spectacular flight songs.

EURASIAN SKYLARK   *Alauda arvensis*   PLATE 42

Appearance: (7½;19) A streaky, brown, sparrowlike bird. Narrow white sides of dark tail and white trailing edge of secondaries visible in flight. Often shows a slight crest. Asiatic migrants more heavily streaked than residents.

Habits: Found in open areas, especially grasslands. Often seen as it flies up from roadsides. Sings while hovering or circling high in the air, often out of sight, then plunges to the ground as the song ends. On the ground has a horizontal, head-down posture.

Voice: A complex song of gurgles, whistles, and trills, often amazingly long sustained. Ventriloquial. Call a bubbly *cherrup*.

Identification: Distinguished from sparrows and House Finch by longer, thinner bill, white sides to tail, distinctive behavior. Pipits are more slender, have even thinner bills than skylark.

Occurrence: Native to Eurasia. Straggler from Siberia to NW HAWAIIAN IS. (Kure, Midway). Introduced to the main HAWAIIAN IS. in 1865 and now abundant on Hawaii, Maui, and Lanai. Less common on Molokai, Niihau, Lehua, and Oahu.

FAMILY HIRUNDINIDAE: Swallows

SWALLOWS are graceful, highly aerial birds, usually seen hawking insects. They superficially resemble swifts, but unlike them can perch in the usual fashion. Many species have forked tails. One species breeds in the tropical Pacific, and two others are migrants to the region.

BARN SWALLOW   *Hirundo rustica*   PLATE 2?

Appearance: (7;18) A small bird with moderately (immature) to deeply forked tail. Upperparts and breast band glossy dark blue, forehead and throat chestnut, underparts buffy white. Immature lacks gloss on upperparts, has pale forehead. Most wintering birds in Micronesia are immatures, a few of which molt into adult plumage before departing in the spring.

Habits: Very social, often in small flocks. Quick and graceful in flight. Hawks insects by swooping low over open ground or water. Often around man-made structures, frequently perches on power lines.

Voice: A long twittering call given in flight.

Identification: Distinguished from Island (Gray) Swiftlet by pale underparts, ability to perch. Long forked tail diagnostic for adults.

Occurrence: Breeds in temperate Northern Hemisphere, winters southward including most of MICRONESIA (common and present most of year at Palau; uncommon and irregular in the Marianas and Carolines; rare Marshall Is.). Straggler to the HAWAIIAN IS. (Kure, Midway, Hawaii).

PACIFIC SWALLOW   *Hirundo tahitica*   PLATE 30

Appearance: (5;13) A small bird with forked tail. Upperparts dark glossy blue-black, throat and forehead chestnut, breast and belly brownish gray (Fiji) or sooty (Tahiti). Immatures dull brown above, paler elsewhere.

Habits: Found primarily in lowlands near rivers, waterfalls, and cliffs. In Fiji prefers drier sides of islands and often found around man-made structures such as bridges. Occasionally at higher elevations. Builds cup-shaped nest on walls or ledges. Usually in small groups. Perches on dead trees, power lines, or other exposed sites.

Voice: A weak warbling song.

Identification: Distinguished from swiftlets by perching behavior, glossy back, forked tail, and (in Fiji) more contrasting underparts.

Occurrence: Melanesia E to FIJI and the Nomuka Group in TONGA (*H. t. subfusca*), and the SOCIETY IS. (Tahiti, Moorea; *H. t. tahitica*).

Other names: House Swallow, Welcome Swallow, Coast Swallow.

ASIAN HOUSE-MARTIN   *Delichon dasypus*   FIGURE 42

Appearance: (5;13) A small swallow with blue-black (adult) or brownish black (immature) upperparts, white underparts and rump. Tail forked.

Habits: Flies high in the air to feed. In Palau, associates with Barn Swallows.

Identification: Distinguished from White-breasted Woodswallow by thinner build and longer, narrower wings, from Barn Swallow and Island (Gray) Swiftlet by white rump and underparts. Whether the birds

FIGURE 42.
Asian House-Martin

seen at Palau are this species or the very similar Common House-Martin (*D. urbica*) has not been determined with certainty. The latter is virtually identical except that its throat and breast are clear snow-white, whereas Asian House-Martin has gray tinge to same areas. In hand, uppertail coverts of Asian are black, and those of Common are white.
Occurrence: Breeds in ne. Asia, winters to Indonesia. Rare spring migrant through PALAU.

FAMILY DICRURIDAE: Drongos

DRONGOS are medium to large, flycatcher-like birds. Most species are black with long, variably forked tails. They are found in se. Asia and Australasia, and one species has been introduced to the Mariana Is.

BLACK DRONGO *Dicrurus macrocercus*　　　　　PLATE 2?

Appearance: (11;28) A slender, long-tailed, black bird with dark red eyes. Tail has peculiar outward-curving bifurcation.
Habits: Commonly seen near towns and along roadways. Often perche in the open on wires and dead branches. Nest often unconcealed Quarrelsome and pugnacious; often harasses larger birds and frui

bats, but does not harm smaller birds. Feeds on insects and other small animals.

Voice: Noisy. Has a variety of clicking, buzzing, and rasping calls interspersed with clear whistles.

Identification: Widely forked tail diagnostic. Mariana Crow larger and heavier-billed. Micronesian Starling smaller, chunkier, with short tail and yellow eyes.

Occurrence: Iran E to Taiwan and Vietnam. Introduced in 1930s to ROTA (Mariana Is.), whence it spread to GUAM by early 1960s. Now abundant on both islands, mostly in lowlands.

FAMILY CORVIDAE: CROWS AND JAYS

CORVIDS, in general, are large passerines and include the ravens, largest of all. They are represented worldwide, but only two species are presently found in the tropical Pacific, and both are Endangered. Other species are known as fossils from the Hawaiian Is. The family is characterized by long, thick bills with the nostrils covered by a tuft of feathers. Crows are usually black, with loud, far-carrying calls.

Reference: Goodwin, D. 1976. *Crows of the world*. Ithaca: Cornell Univ. Press.

[**RED-BILLED BLUE MAGPIE**   *Urocissa erythrorhyncha*   See Appendix A]

HAWAIIAN CROW   *Corvus hawaiiensis*   PLATE 36

Appearance: (19;48) A large, dark sooty brown bird with long, thick, pointed bill. Primaries paler than body plumage. A passerine bird but as large as a hawk or owl.

Habits: Rather secretive, usually heard before it is seen. An omnivore especially fond of fruits such as those of ieie. Does not soar, but often flies high over the forest. Found in wet forests, scrub, and range lands.

Voice: Highly varied, including a weird-sounding *kee-o-reek*, a quiet *kwahk*, and other short notes. In flight, often utters a loud but musical *kraa-a-a-ik*, upslurred and somewhat modulated.

Identification: In flight, told from dark-phase Hawaiian Hawk by pointed wings, passerine build. The crow is so much larger than any other dark passerine that it causes little confusion.

Occurrence: Endemic to the island of HAWAII and an Endangered Species. Once abundant in Kona region, now on verge of extinction. The only remaining population of any size (ca. 20 birds) found on

higher slopes of Mauna Loa above Kealakekua Bay. Scattered pairs and individuals are found elsewhere. Decline believed to be primarily the result of habitat degradation, aggravated by illegal shooting.
Other name: *'alalā.*

MARIANA CROW   *Corvus kubaryi*   PLATE 23

Appearance: (15;38) A large bird, but small for a crow. Iris brown. Plumage entirely black, slightly glossy.

Habits: Rather wary (probably as a result of persecution by man) but occasionally confiding. Where common, moves about in small noisy flocks. Quiet when foraging on forest floor or perched in trees. Often calls in flight.

Voice: A loud screaming *kraa-ah* and quiet "conversational" notes.

Identification: Black Drongo and Micronesian Starling much smaller. Drongo has forked tail, starling has yellow eyes.

Occurrence: Endemic to the MARIANA IS. (Guam, Rota). Still relatively common on Rota, but a declining and Endangered Species on Guam, now confined to the northernmost cliffline forests.

[FAMILY PARIDAE: CHICKADEES AND TITS]

[**VARIED TIT**   *Parus varius*   See Appendix A]

FAMILY CRACTICIDAE: AUSTRALIAN MAGPIES, BUTCHERBIRDS, AND CURRAWONGS

LARGE, boldly patterned, black-and-white birds, cracticids are found only in the Australian region. They are noted for their unusual vocalizations. Most are aggressive scavengers and predators on small animals. One species has been introduced to Fiji in the tropical Pacific.

AUSTRALIAN MAGPIE   *Gymnorhina tibicen*   PLATE 41

Appearance: (16;41) A striking, large, black and white bird. Mostly black with white (male) or gray (female) patch on nape, white shoulders, rump, and base of tail. Tail broadly tipped black. Back varies from black to white. Bill bluish white tipped with black.

Habits: Usually seen in small groups. Prefers open savannahs near forests, open woodlands, pastures, and parks. Feeds on insects or scavenges on the ground. Aggressive and territorial, readily attacking intruders.

Voice: Noisy. Powerful song comprises gurgling flutelike notes woven into a complex melody that may include mimicry. Alarm note a harsh double bark.

Occurrence: Resident in Australia and s. New Guinea. Introduced in 1880s to TAVEUNI (Fiji), and fairly common, with wanderers occasionally seen on nearby parts of Vanua Levu. Two different subspecies, white-backed and black-backed, were introduced and population is now a subspecific amalgam.

FAMILY CAMPEPHAGIDAE: Cuckoo-shrikes

A FAMILY of mostly dull-colored birds with shrikelike hooked bills, cuckoolike shapes, and barred plumage. They are distributed from Africa E to Samoa. Three species are found in the tropical Pacific, the Polynesian Triller being one of central Polynesia's most characteristic and conspicuous birds.

CICADABIRD   *Coracina tenuirostris*   PLATES 24, 25

Appearance: (7;18) Males of all subspecies entirely slate gray, but females and immatures vary from island to island:

PALAU: Dusty brown above, buff stained irregularly with rufous below. Eye stripe black, superciliary and tail tip buff. Underparts heavily barred with dark brown. (Plate 24).

YAP: Similar to Palau birds, but much larger (10;25) and more rufous, with barring on sides of breast only. (Plate 24).

POHNPEI: Very distinct. Adult female has slate gray head and brown back, with rest of body plumage rufous-cinnamon. Wings and tail black with feathers edged rufous. No barring. Immatures rufous-cinnamon throughout, heavily barred above and below with black and pale buff. (Plate 25.)

Habits: A retiring and inconspicuous bird of the forest canopy. Forages for insects with slow, deliberate movements among leaves and branches. Sometimes near the ground at forest edge. Found in all forest types, including mangroves.

Voice: Palau birds utter a whistled inquisitive *tuweep*, sometimes louder, varied, and squeaky, forming a loose song. Pohnpei birds' voice totally different, with a weird song of catlike whistles and low churring notes, a rolling *preeer*, and a short *chip-chip-breer*. Voice of Yap birds not well known, but some calls resemble those heard on Pohnpei.

Identification: Male in silhouette could resemble Micronesian Starling, but note the latter's yellow eyes. At Palau, Morningbird has similar overall shape and dark colors, but is sooty brown, not gray. Pohnpei

Flycatcher also slaty gray, but with glossy crown (male) or reddish tinge in throat (female) and very different overall shape and behavior.

Occurrence: Australia, Melanesia, and MICRONESIA. Uncommon at PALAU (*C. t. monachum*) and POHNPEI (*C. t. insperatum*), apparently rare YAP (*C. t. nesiotis*).

Other names: Slender-billed Graybird, Long-billed Graybird.

POLYNESIAN TRILLER *Lalage maculosa* PLATE 31

Appearance: (6;15) A basically gray or gray-brown bird with pale wing patches prominent in flight. Also note dark cap and pale eyebrow. The many island subspecies vary considerably. Birds of Samoa, Tonga, and Niue are clean-cut black and white with large wing patches and virtually unbarred underparts. Fiji races more or less barred below and brown above. Rotuma birds very buffy on underparts. Plate 31 shows a range of variation.

Habits: Frequently seen in open areas such as gardens, parks, roadsides, and forest edges. Often on the ground, searching for insects and other animal prey.

Voice: Call a loud *tchick*. A loud *peach-it* or *pee-chew* and a ringing trill are given after short flights.

Identification: Polynesian Starling could cause confusion, but is much shyer and lacks the prominent white markings. Samoan Triller much plainer, with red-orange bill. Variation among the 12 named subspecies not so great as to cause confusion.

Occurrence: Widespread and common in FIJI (most islands including Rotuma), TONGA (most islands), FUTUNA (Wallis and Futuna), NIUE, and W. SAMOA (Savaii, Upolu).

Other name: Spotted Triller.

SAMOAN TRILLER *Lalage sharpei* PLATE 31

Appearance: (5;13) A drab bird, gray-brown above, paler below, with a bright red-orange bill. In flight, the pale edges of the tail are conspicuous.

Habits: A rather slow-moving bird that gleans its food from leaves of shrubs and small trees. Inconspicuous but not particularly shy. Inhabits native forests and forest edges.

Voice: A thin, squeaky, ascending or descending trill that sounds forced out with great effort. Easily overlooked in an ensemble of birdsong.

Identification: The bright red-orange bill is unique among Samoan birds. This species lacks the prominent eye stripe and wing patches of the Polynesian Triller. Somewhat resembles the Wattled Honeyeater in its movements.

Occurrence: Endemic to W. SAMOA, where found above 600 m on Savaii, but lower (at least to 200 m) on Upolu. Uncommon.

FAMILY PYCNONOTIDAE: Bulbuls

Bulbuls are medium-sized songbirds widely distributed in the Old World tropics from Africa to the Philippines. The Red-vented Bulbul has been introduced to many islands in the tropical Pacific, and a second species has become established in Hawaii. These two are noisy and conspicuous birds that can become serious agricultural pests. They feed primarily on fruit, but occasionally take insects.

RED-VENTED BULBUL   *Pycnonotus cafer*   PLATE 40

Appearance: (8½;22) A dark, crested bird with white rump and tail tip. Red undertail coverts often shaded, thus not a good field mark.

Habits: A conspicuous bird of towns and villages. Often perches on power lines, houses, fences, and other man-made structures, but also found in forest and agricultural areas. A fruiteater that can become a serious pest. Where common may form large flocks.

Voice: A variety of rather low-pitched chirps and whistled phrases: *chi-wheer, chip-burr,* or *cheeseburger.* Also an elaborate dawn song of flutelike whistles.

Identification: An annoyance for birders, poorly seen Red-vented Bulbuls can resemble many other birds. A closer look will reveal the distinctive crest, white rump, or red undertail. In Hawaii, see Red-whiskered Bulbul.

Occurrence: Native to India. Introduced and established widely in the Pacific including the HAWAIIAN IS. (Oahu; reported Hawaii, Molokai), FIJI (Viti Levu and a few smaller islands), TONGA (Nukualofa, 'Eua), SAMOA (Savaii, Upolu, Tutuila), and TAHITI (Society Is.). Probably will spread to other islands.

References: Watling, D. 1978. Observation on the naturalised distribution of the Red-vented Bulbul in the Pacific, with special reference to the Fiji Islands. *Notornis* 25:109-117.

Williams, R. N., and L. V. Giddings. 1984. Differential range expansion and population growth of bulbuls in Hawaii. *Wilson Bull.* 96:647-55.

RED-WHISKERED BULBUL   *Pycnonotus jocosus*   PLATE 40

Appearance: (7;18) A cleanly patterned bird, brown above, white below, with sharply pointed black crest. Cheek patch two-toned, red above, white below, outlined in black. Undertail coverts red, tail tipped white. Immatures lack red whiskers, have shorter brown crest.

Habits: In Hawaii, a bird of suburban gardens and lawns, or even court-yards of Waikiki hotels. Tends to range higher than Red-vented Bulbul, but the two are often found together.

Voice: Similar to, but higher pitched than that of Red-vented Bulbul. Phrases varied but always with a gurgling quality: *chee-purdle-chee-birdie-birdie* or *fee-dee-hur-dee-hur* or shorter phrases *cheap-beer, chee-ka-leet,* and *peet.* Call similar to but more piercing than House Sparrow's.

Identification: Red-vented Bulbul larger, mostly dark below, with prominent white rump, more rounded crest.

Occurrence: Native to India. Introduced ca. 1966 to OAHU (Hawaiian Is.) and well established in the Honolulu area. Can be expected anywhere on the island within a few years.

Reference: van Riper III, C., S. G. van Riper, and A. J. Berger. 1979. The Red-whiskered Bulbul in Hawaii. *Wilson Bull.* 91:323-28.

FAMILY PACHYCEPHALIDAE: Australo-Papuan Insect-eaters

THE members of this family are a diverse assemblage often included among the "Old World insect-eaters" of the family Muscicapidae. Recent biochemical studies have shown them to be closely related among themselves, but not particularly close to the superficially similar muscicapids. The group apparently originated in Australia and expanded into the tropical Pacific. Most are small, and all are primarily insectivorous, but take their prey by a variety of means. Some are "flycatchers" that hawk insects from the air, others are pickers and gleaners. The family has two subdivisions.

Reference: Boles, W. E. 1979. The relationships of the Australo-Papuan flycatchers. *Emu* 79:107-110.

Whistlers, Australian Robins, and Their Relatives: Subfamily Pachycephalinae

MEMBERS of this subfamily are characterized as heavy-set, often thick-headed birds with small rictal bristles (the "whiskers" at the base of the bill). Some members are superficially very similar to true thrushes (Turdinae) and Old World flycatchers (Muscicapinae), but the whistler

(*Pachycephala*) are distinctive in their own right. Whistlers are bright yellow, green, and black birds of the forest canopy, more easily heard than seen. They have loud, whistled songs.

SCARLET ROBIN   *Petroica multicolor*   PLATE 32

Appearance: (4;10) A tiny puffy bird. Male black on head and upperparts, with white spot on lores and white patch in wing. Breast rosy red, belly white. Female dull brown above and paler pink below, without white wing patch.

Habits: Frequents clearings and edges in primary forest. Males often sit on exposed perches. Tame and bold. Insectivorous. Territorial, usually seen alone or in pairs. Forages from understory to canopy, sometimes joins mixed flocks.

Voice: Call a quick series of 3-6 squeaky notes, usually accented on the second. Song a lively, quickly repeated *wheet-te-dududu-wheet*.

Identification: Small size, white forehead and wing patch, and rosy breast distinctive. Compare Cardinal Honeyeater and Orange-breasted Honeyeater.

Occurrence: Widely distributed from Australia and Melanesia E to FIJI (Viti Levu, Vanua Levu, Taveuni, Kadavu) and W. SAMOA (Savaii, Upolu). Fairly common in appropriate habitat.

GOLDEN WHISTLER   *Pachycephala pectoralis*   PLATE 32

Appearance: (7;18) Highly variable geographically. Females and immatures drab olive above, ochre to gray below. Males green above, yellow below, with black cap. Other features variable, with the various subspecies falling into three general types.

Type 1: Black breast band is wide, complete. Throat white. Female rusty ochre below, gray on crown.

Type 2: Breast band lacking, throat yellow. Yellow spot on lores, secondary coverts edged yellow. Female gray below, lightly barred with white, streaked with dark gray.

Type 3: Intermediate. Breast band variable, sometimes narrow but complete, sometimes broken. Throat yellow. Loral spots present on some, absent on others. Females intermediate. Intergrades with Group 2 in contact zones on Viti Levu and Vanua Levu.

Habits: Frequents upper parts of large trees from sea level to 1200 m. Often joins mixed flocks. Forages among leaves and branches, sometimes hovering. May sit inactively for long periods.

Voice: Loud whistles that form a complex song. Varies geographically. Some variations transcribed as: *whee-teer-whee-chew*; *chicky-ter-whee-chew*; *Did you eat? Did you eat?*; or *whichew-wheecher-teacher*.

Identification: Note plump shape, sluggish behavior. Males distinctive with yellow underparts. Females nondescript, but resemble few other birds. Polynesian Starling lacks olive tones above, has white in wing.

Occurrence: Widely distributed and common from Australia E to FIJI. Type 1 subspecies found in s. Lau Arch. (*P. p. lauana*), Kadavu and Beqa (*P. p. kandavensis*), and Gau (*P. p. vitiensis*). Type 2 forms inhabit w. Viti Levu (*P. p. graeffii*) and w. Vanua Levu (*P. p. aurantiiventris*). Type 3 races occur from ne. Viti Levu and Ovalau (*P. p. optata*) to the Natewa Peninsula of Vanua Levu, Kioa, and Rabi (*P. p. ambigua*), Taveuni (*P. p. torquata*), Koro (*P. p. koroana*), and Vatuvara (*P. p. bella*).

TONGAN WHISTLER   *Pachycephala jacquinoti*   PLATE 32

Appearance: (7;18) Similar to Golden Whistler, but male with entire head and throat black, nape and tail tip yellow. Female and immature pale yellow below, grayish brown above, head grayer.

Habits: Found in underbrush of dense primary forest. Occasionally in secondary growth or canopy of large trees. Insectivorous.

Voice: A clear whistled song that trails off toward the end. Females and immatures utter noisy chatters.

Occurrence: Endemic to VAVA'U (Tonga). Common and widespread.

Note: Some authors regard this form as a subspecies of Golden Whistler.

SAMOAN WHISTLER   *Pachycephala flavifrons*   PLATE 32

Appearance: (6;15) A plump, thick-headed bird, dark olive-gray above yellow below. Males exhibit three phases: forehead and throat yellow forehead yellow, throat white; and forehead and throat white. Female paler above with fainter yellow forehead.

Habits: Widely distributed from sea level to high montane forests Found at midlevel in primary and secondary forest, as well as plantations and gardens. Insectivorous. May form small flocks or move about in pairs. Gleans leaves and twigs or hawks insects aerially.

Voice: Call a short whistled *chweep*. Song a rapidly whistled jumble of notes *tweet-chew-twee-titi-chew-wheet* etc.

Occurrence: Endemic to W. SAMOA (Savaii, Upolu). Common.

MORNINGBIRD   *Colluricincla tenebrosa*   PLATE 2

Appearance: (7½;19) A very drab bird, mostly sooty brown with somewhat paler breast and underparts. Some individuals appear to have contrastingly darker head, others look more or less uniformly colored Thick-billed and big-headed in profile, with dark eyes.

Habits: Found mostly in deep primary forest. An inconspicuous skulk of the understory. Movements slow, deliberate. Omnivorous. Rather curious; may approach and follow an observer, and sometimes scolds quietly with bill held open. Most vocal before dawn, hence the name. Usually instigates the predawn chorus at Palau. Solitary or in pairs, occasionally small groups.

Voice: Song a pleasing jumbled warble of liquid chirps and whistles, broken into short segments. Scold is a series of harsh raspy notes.

Identification: Similar in general appearance to Micronesian Starling, but much duller and with dark eyes. Has more bull-headed profile and very different behavior. Compare also adult male Cicadabird.

Occurrence: Endemic to PALAU; common from Babelthuap to Peleliu.

Note: Sometimes placed in the genus *Pitohui*.

MONARCHS, AUSTRALIAN FLYCATCHERS, AND FANTAILS: Subfamily Monarchinae

MEMBERS of this subfamily, such as the fantails (*Rhipidura*), monarchs (*Monarcha, Pomarea*), broad-billed flycatchers (*Myiagra*), and the Elepaio (*Chasiempis*), are among the tropical Pacific's most familiar and characteristic birds. They tend to be plainly colored in earth tones, but a few have glossy or iridescent plumage. They differ from the previous subfamily in being slim, small-headed birds with prominent rictal bristles (undoubtedly an adaptation to catching insects on the wing). Monarchs have loud, whistled songs and chattering calls, *Myiagra* flycatchers utter series of short whistles and raspy calls, and fantails have high-pitched, tinkling vocalizations. Fantails are sometimes placed in their own subfamily, Rhipidurinae.

FIJI SHRIKEBILL   *Clytorhynchus vitiensis*   PLATE 33

Appearance: (7;18) A dark grayish brown bird with lighter gray underparts. Bill wedge-shaped, laterally compressed, and notched at the tip. Lateral tail feathers sometimes tipped white. General shape long and slender.

Habits: Found in dense forest. Forages below canopy in underbrush. Insectivorous. Very agile, moving deftly about tangled vines and bushes, occasionally hawking insects in the air. Frequently flicks and spreads tail. Joins mixed flocks.

Voice: Call a harsh *chick-chick-chick*. Song a descending, whinnying whistle, or a humanlike upslurred whistle.

Identification: Easily confused with female Black-faced Shrikebill which is brown, not gray, on breast. Buff undertail coverts of Fiji

Shrikebill contrast with brown flanks, but female Black-faced has uniform underparts. Also note much thinner bill of this species.

Occurrence: Patchily distributed in FIJI (main islands, Rotuma), TONGA (Niuatoputapu, Tafahi, possibly Tofua; formerly Tongatapu, 'Eua, Ha'apai), and A. SAMOA (Tau; formerly Ofu, Olosega).

Other name: Uniform Shrikebill.

BLACK-FACED SHRIKEBILL *Clytorhynchus nigrogularis* PLATE 33

Appearance: (8½;22) A large, gray-brown bird with long, thick, hooked bill. Male has black face and throat surrounding a bold white ear patch. Female similar to Fiji Shrikebill but larger, browner, with much thicker bill. Juvenile male has gray ear patch, white-spotted throat.

Habits: A skulker, shy and secretive. Prefers dense, mature wet forests from sea level to 1200 m. Forages for insects on ground and among dead leaves and tangled vines in trees. Usually in pairs. Male may sit in open briefly at dawn.

Voice: Apparently similar to that of Fiji Shrikebill, a descending mournful whistle.

Identification: See Fiji Shrikebill.

Occurrence: Santa Cruz Is., Rennell I., and FIJI (Viti Levu, Vanua Levu, Taveuni, Kadavu, Ovalau). Fairly common in suitable habitat.

Other name: Black-throated Shrikebill.

ELEPAIO *Chasiempis sandwichensis* PLATE 35

Appearance: (5½;14) A small active flycatcher that often perches with tail cocked up. The five named subspecies differ in plumage details, but all adults have two white wing bars, white-tipped tail feathers, and prominent white rump patch. Immatures are plain dull brown (Hawaii) or rusty brown (Oahu, Kauai) without white markings. The various forms differ as follows:

KAUAI (*C. s. sclateri*): Gray above, white below with orange wash across breast, often with a dingy smudge in center. Sexes similar.

OAHU (*C. s. gayi*): Rusty brown above, white below with throat black chin white. Sexes alike.

HAWAII: The three most boldly patterned subspecies occur here. A have black throats marked with white spots around the peripher (males) or white throats (females), rufous breasts, rufous streaks o underparts, and prominent eyebrows. The three forms vary in dorsa coloration and breast streaking from the gray-backed, sparsel streaked *C. s. bryani* to the dark brown-backed, heavily streaked *C. ridgwayi*; and in color of the eyebrow from pure white (*bryani*) to ru fous-tinged white (*C. s. sandwichensis*), to chestnut (*ridgwayi*). Female tend to have paler eyebrows than males in the same locality. Some *br ani* look almost white-headed in the field.

Habits: Feeds on insects obtained by foliage-gleaning, bark-picking, and aerial sallies below forest canopy. Bold and curious, especially immatures. Easily "squeaked up" or attracted by imitation of whistles. Found in both native and exotic forests.

Voice: Various calls include an upslurred whistled *wheet*, a sharp *keet*, and a raspy chatter. The song is a loudly whistled *e-le-PAI-o* or *chee-WHEE-o*.

Identification: Despite seemingly bewildering plumage variation, the Elepaio has such distinctive behavior and postures that it presents few identification problems. The white rump patch is diagnostic on Hawaii. On Kauai and Oahu, immature White-rumped Shama also has white rump, but is larger, has long tail with white sides (not white tip). On Oahu, compare Japanese Bush-Warbler.

Occurrence: Endemic to the HAWAIIAN IS. with distinctive subspecies on Kauai and Oahu, and three on Hawaii (*C. s. sandwichensis* in Kona and Kau, *C. s. ridgwayi* in wet forests of Hamakua to Volcano regions, and *C. s. bryani* on high leeward slopes of Mauna Kea). Common on Kauai and Hawaii at higher elevations, uncommon at low elevations and on Oahu generally.

References: Conant, S. 1977. The breeding biology of the Oahu 'Elepaio. *Wilson Bull.* 89:193-210.

Pratt, H. D. 1980. Intra-island variation in the 'Elepaio, *Chasiempis sandwichensis*, on the island of Hawaii. *Condor* 82:449-58.

SLATY FLYCATCHER *Mayrornis lessoni* PLATE 30

Appearance: (5;13) A small, slate gray bird, paler below, with white eye-ring and lores, and white-tipped black tail. Often cocks tail up.

Habits: Usually in the subcanopy of dense forest, but also seen in trees of parks and village gardens. Gleans insects from foliage or catches them in aerial sallies. Tame and inquisitive. Frequently joins mixed-species foraging flocks.

Voice: A harsh *rick-rick-rick-i-dee* and a descending squeaky whistle.

Identification: Distinctive in its plain gray plumage, but note similar tail pattern of Streaked Fantail. On Ogea Levu, compare Versicolor Flycatcher.

Occurrence: Endemic to FIJI and common throughout the main islands.

Other names: Fiji Flycatcher, Cinereous Flycatcher.

VERSICOLOR FLYCATCHER *Mayrornis versicolor* PLATE 30

Appearance and Identification: (4½;11) Very similar to Slaty Flycatcher, but slightly smaller with underparts, eye-ring, and tail tip cinnamon-buff. Paler above than female Vanikoro Flycatcher, with pale eye-ring and tail tip.

Habits: Apparently similar to those of Slaty Flycatcher. The two coexist on Ogea Levu, so some differences are to be expected. Voice unreported.

Occurrence: Endemic to OGEA LEVU (Lau Arch., Fiji). Status unknown.

YAP MONARCH *Monarcha godeffroyi* PLATE 24

Appearance: (6;15) A medium-sized, black and white flycatcher. Male white with black head, wings, and tail. Female black with white collar around neck. Immatures rufous brown, brighter on rump, throat, and undertail coverts; lighter below and grayer above. Adults have pale blue bills, immatures brownish yellow.

Habits: A conspicuous bird of the forest. Active, boisterous, and easily "squeaked up."

Voice: Varied. Calls are quick raspy notes: *chick-chick-chick-cher-dee*, *chick-cher-cher-chick*, or *chick-cher-deer-dee*, etc. Also a squeaky *weer*. Song comprises loud, clearly whistled phrases: *we're here, we're here* or *wheeo-wheereo*.

Occurrence: Endemic to YAP, where widespread and common.

TINIAN MONARCH *Monarcha takatsukasae* PLATE 23

Appearance: (6;15) A small bird, gray above, buffy tan below, with white wing bars, rump, and tail tip.

Habits: Less active than Rufous Fantail and often found with it. Forages higher in trees than the fantail. Occurs in dense tangan-tangan thickets as well as forest. Feeds by aerial sallies. Easily "squeaked up."

Voice: A low, rasping scold and an explosive *squeak-it*. The song, uttered mostly in the evening, a 2- or 3-note whistle: *tee-tee-wheeo*.

Identification: The dull plumage and white rump distinguish the monarch from the Rufous Fantail, the only species with which it could be confused.

Occurrence: Known only from Tinian and Agiguan in the MARIANA IS. On Tinian, abundant throughout wooded parts of the island. Proposed for removal from the Endangered Species list.

TRUK MONARCH *Metabolus rugensis* PLATE 25

Appearance: (8;20) A striking, large passerine with highly variable and poorly understood plumages. Immatures least variable, plain bright rufous above, buff below, with a suggestion of a buff supercilium; bill brown with yellow base of lower mandible. Molt from this plumage to others gradual and irregular; many individuals (particularly females) retain patches of immature plumage for several years. Adult males are almost pure white with glossy black face and throat and black tips to the primaries. Some are tinged buff or pale salmon below, perhaps a retention of immature coloring. Adult females are entirely dark slate gray, but few totally gray individuals are seen. Adult bill pale blue with black tip.

Habits: Usually a bird of primary forest, but occasionally visits low-elevation agricultural forest. Relatively slow-moving, but fairly tame and conspicuous.

Voice: Varied. A monotonously repeated, low, whistled *queer-ah*, with harsh undertones, and a variety of humanlike whistles slurred up or down: *wheeer* or *wheeo*.

Identification: Adults unmistakable. Immatures similar to Caroline Islands Reed-Warbler but more robust, with heavier bill, rustier dorsal color, and less well defined supercilium.

Occurrence: Endemic to TRUK. Found on all high islands and some low islets. Generally fairly common, but uncommon on Moen. Proposed as an Endangered Species.

RAROTONGA MONARCH *Pomarea dimidiata* PLATE 34

Appearance: (5½;14) Male dark slate gray above, white below. Female and immature very similar to immature Tahiti Monarch, bright rufous above, lighter rufous-buff below.

Habits: Inhabits thick undergrowth in upland native forests. Absent from secondary forest, even those of good stature. Gleans insects from leaves and twigs. Bold, noisy, and conspicuous.

Voice: Varied chattering calls and whistled songs including a raspy *rick-rick-ree-dee*, a squeaky *ter-wickee-der*, and a quickly whistled *chep-ur-weo* or *chee-chee-dur*.

Occurrence: Endemic to RAROTONGA (Cook Is.) and now very rare and restricted to upper forested gulleys. Population about 25 birds. Highly vulnerable (King 1981).

Other names: Rarotonga Flycatcher, Cook Island Flycatcher.

Note: Because the genus *Pomarea* is very closely related to, and possibly best merged with, *Monarcha*, we use the group name "monarch," rather than the more customary "flycatcher," for its members.

TAHITI MONARCH *Pomarea nigra* PLATE 34

Appearance: (6;15) Adults black with bluish gray bills and feet. Immatures dark cinnamon-brown or bright rufous above, rufous-buff below.

Habits: A sedentary bird of dense primary forest between 700 and 950 m. Highly territorial, noisy and vocal. Forages in treetops or in undergrowth, rarely seen in the open. Gleans leaves and branches for insects. Occasionally fans tail. Flight slow and direct.

Voice: Song similar to that of Tahiti Reed-Warbler but much shorter and more flutelike. Alarm call a sharp *tick-tick-tick*.

Occurrence: Endemic to the SOCIETY IS. (rare and localized on Tahiti; extinct Maupiti). An Endangered Species.

Other names: Tahiti Flycatcher, Society Islands Flycatcher.

IPHIS MONARCH   *Pomarea iphis*   PLATE 34

Appearance: (6½;17) Two different-looking subspecies: *P. i. iphis* (Uahuka) males mostly black with white mottling on the belly, females and immatures light brown above, white below; *P. i. fluxa* (Eiao) males mottled on back and lower breast as well as belly, females mottled above with white, heavily streaked on throat; immatures like females but streaked more extensively.

Habits: Forages in dense brush along coastal cliffs. Gleans insects from branches or hawks them in dark shaded areas beneath brush-covered canopy. Territorial. Flicks tail when perched.

Voice: Soft low whistles and rasping chips. Song described as *tchi-weu, tchi-weu, tchi-tchi-tchi*.

Occurrence: Endemic to the n. MARQUESAS (Uahuka, Eiao). Still common on Uahuka, much reduced but still present on Eiao.

Other names: Allied Flycatcher, Marquesan Flycatcher, Eiao Flycatcher, Huahuna Flycatcher, Uahuka Flycatcher.

MARQUESAS MONARCH   *Pomarea mendozae*   PLATE 34

Appearance: (6½;17) Adult male glossy black, immature reddish brown above, pinkish buff below with white eye-ring. Females differ among the four subspecies: *P. m. mira* (Uapou) black with white tail and much white in wings; *P. m. nukuhivae* (Nukuhiva) similar but with white back and rump; *P. m. motanensis* (Mohotani) with body and tail white, tinged pinkish buff below, head and wings (except white edgings of tertials) black; *P. m. mendozae* (Hivaoa, Tahuata) similar but tail with black subterminal spots.

Habits: Found in forested valleys at high elevations. Probably originally preferred lowland forest, now destroyed. Bold and inquisitive. Male often cocks tail up and flutters wings when agitated.

Voice: Call *sherkee-six* or *tchioui-tchioui*. Song (?) a clear *sue-eeet*.

Occurrence: Endemic to the c. MARQUESAS, where probably extirpated on Nukuhiva and Tahuata, rare on Hivaoa and Uapou, common only on Mohotani. Several forms are recognized as rare or endangered (see Table 6).

Other names: Marquesas Flycatcher, Hivaoa Flycatcher, Uapou Flycatcher, Nukuhiva Flycatcher, Mendoza Flycatcher.

FATUHIVA MONARCH   *Pomarea whitneyi*   PLATE 34

Appearance: (7½;19) Adults of both sexes black with purple gloss. Feathers of forehead stiff and plushlike, making that area appear blacker than the rest of the plumage. Immatures dull brown, paler below.

Habits: Inhabits forests and wooded thickets at all elevations, more common in drier low-elevation habitats. "Squeaks up" for close observations.

Voice: Alarm call described as *cri-ri-a-rik*, similar to the shrill meow of a cat whose tail is stepped on. Also said to give a *kik-kik-kik* call.

Occurrence: Endemic to FATUHIVA (Marquesas Is.), where common.

Other names: Large Flycatcher, Fatuhiva Flycatcher.

VANIKORO FLYCATCHER   *Myiagra vanikorensis*   PLATE 30

Appearance: (6;15) A small flycatcher. Male glossy blue-black with rufous-cinnamon breast and belly. Female dark gray above, pale buff below. Bill black.

Habits: A tame and confiding bird found in all types of forested habitat, including parks and gardens in cities and towns. Snatches insects from foliage in quick sallying flights, and often hovers to glean prey.

Voice: Calls include a buzzy *bzzuip-bzzuip* and a short *chick*. Song a series of thin whistles on a level pitch, *tsee-tsee-tsee-tsee*, or a quavering upslurred whistle.

Identification: More uniformly colored than Blue-crested Flycatcher. Also note the latter's orange bill.

Occurrence: Santa Cruz Is. and FIJI. Widespread and common.

Other names: Vanikoro Broadbill, Vanikoro Myiagra, Red-bellied Flycatcher.

Note: Elsewhere (Pratt et al. 1979) we have discussed the inadvisability of using the term "broadbill" as a group-name in the genus *Myiagra*. Although "flycatcher" is somewhat overused worldwide, and thus now has no taxonomic significance, we follow Australian practice in using it for the members of this genus.

BLUE-CRESTED FLYCATCHER   *Myiagra azureocapilla*   PLATE 30

Appearance: (6;15) Similar to Vanikoro Flycatcher, but with a striking sky blue crest. Underparts white, throat rufous (Viti Levu, Vanua Levu) or deep chestnut (Taveuni). Tail feathers tipped white except on Taveuni, where birds also larger and darker. Bill red-orange.

Habits: Found in lower strata of dense primary forest. Usually solitary, in pairs, or in small family groups that frequently join mixed-species foraging flocks. Insectivorous, with feeding technique similar to that of Vanikoro Flycatcher.

Voice: A high-pitched buzzy *zreet* and a variety of catlike squeaks. Song a high, shrill, whistled *zreeee-zreee*, usually double but sometimes in groups of 4 notes.

Identification: Distinguished in all plumages from comparable Vanikoro Flycatchers by white underparts, orange bill.

Occurrence: Endemic to FIJI, with recognizable subspecies on Viti Levu (*M. a. whitneyi*), Vanua Levu (*M. a. castaneigularis*), and Taveuni (*M. a. azureocapilla*). Fairly common in suitable habitat.

Other names: Blue-crested Broadbill, Blue-crested Myiagra, Blue-headed Flycatcher.

SAMOAN FLYCATCHER   *Myiagra albiventris*   PLATE 30

Appearance: (6;15) A medium-sized, glossy blue-black flycatcher with orange-brown throat and white breast and belly. Females and immatures gray above, with paler throat.

Habits: Found mostly in native forest and forest edge at all elevations. Solitary or in pairs. Captures insect by aerial sallies or gleans them from foliage during hovering flight. Characteristically flutters tail upon alighting.

Voice: A whistled *feeu-weet, feeu-weet*, or a low-pitched raspy *bzerr-it, bzerr-it*, the two often alternating.

Occurrence: Endemic to W. SAMOA (Savaii, Upolu). Common.

Other names: Samoan Broadbill, Samoan Myiagra, White-vented Flycatcher.

MANGROVE FLYCATCHER   *Myiagra erythrops*   PLATE 24

Appearance: (5;13) A small flycatcher, blue-gray above with underparts, forehead, and eye-ring rufous-orange. Female similar to male, but browner above and paler below.

Habits: Frequents all forest types but especially numerous in mangroves. Active and inquisitive. Feeds on insects caught by aerial sallies.

Voice: Call a quickly repeated *zhrick*. Song a series of 4 or 5 pure whistles on a level pitch or a faster series of 7-8 notes that descend the scale.

Occurrence: Endemic to PALAU and common throughout the main islands.

Other names: Micronesian Broadbill, Micronesian Myiagra, Palau Myiagra Flycatcher, Palau Broadbill.

GUAM FLYCATCHER   *Myiagra freycineti*   PLATE 23

Appearance: (5;13) A small, clean-cut flycatcher, glossy blue-black (male) or brownish gray (female) above, white below with variable amounts of buff tinge on breast.

Habits: A secretive denizen of forests and tangan-tangan thickets, more often heard than seen. Feeds mostly by aerial sallies.

Voice: Calls include a loud *ker-zwick*, rapidly repeated, a descending series of short squeaks, and buzzy rasping notes. Song a quick series of 6-8 upslurred whistles or a series of 4 slower, quavering notes.

Occurrence: Endemic to GUAM (Mariana Is.). An Endangered Species now nearing extinction. Widespread and common in n. Guam into mid-1970s. The population crashed, along with those of other Guam forest birds, in ensuing decade as result of as yet undetermined causes.

Other names: Guam Broadbill, Micronesian Broadbill, Micronesian Myiagra, Guam Myiagra Flycatcher.

OCEANIC FLYCATCHER   *Myiagra oceanica*   PLATE 25

Appearance: (6;15) A medium-sized flycatcher. Upperparts glossy blue-black (male) or dark blue-gray (female). Underparts white with rufous breast, paler in females. Immatures resemble adult females.

Habits: Found in all types of forest and forest edge, often in village gardens. Forages in low shrubbery, usually singly or in pairs. Hawks insects by aerial sallies. Erects crown feathers when agitated.

Voice: Highly varied. Calls include a low chatter; various raspy notes; a descending squeaky whinny; short *tick* notes; a 3-note *erick-erick-erick* or *zhrick-zhrick-zhrick*; and a particularly characteristic phrase, *quick-erick*, accented on the last syllable. Songs comprise series of upslurred or downslurred whistles: *pwee-pwee-pwee-pwee* or *keel-keel-keel-keel*.

Occurrence: Endemic to TRUK. Widespread and common.

Other names: Micronesian Broadbill, Micronesian Myiagra, Truk Myiagra Flycatcher.

Note: In older literature this species included all the *Myiagra* flycatchers in Micronesia. The complex now comprises four species.

POHNPEI FLYCATCHER   *Myiagra pluto*   PLATE 25

Appearance: (6;15) A medium-sized, dark slate gray (nearly black in males) flycatcher. Upperparts have bluish metallic sheen, more pronounced in males. Some individuals, mostly females, show deep chestnut throat and breast. Immatures resemble adult females.

Habits: Inhabits forest understory and open areas with scattered trees. Usually solitary or in pairs. Forages near the ground, feeding by aerial sallies. Twitches tail and raises crown feathers when disturbed.

Voice: Calls include a high, thin *szick-szick*, a harsh, shrill chatter, and a squeaky whinny. Song may be 6 upslurred whistles in series or a quavering upslurred whistle, repeated.

Identification: Posture and behavior distinctive, but compare male Cicadabird.

Occurrence: Endemic to POHNPEI. Common.

Other names: Micronesian Broadbill, Micronesian Myiagra, Ponape Myiagra Flycatcher, Ponape Broadbill.

SILKTAIL   *Lamprolia victoriae*   PLATE 30

Appearance: (5;13) A very striking, iridescent black and white bird. Entire body (except for rump and tail) velvety black with metallic blue or green spangles about the head and breast. Feathers of head and breast scalelike. Rump and central tail feathers silky white. Wings long and rounded. Tail short and rounded. Female like male but with less gloss.

Habits: An inhabitant of the understory of wet rain forest. Feeds among lower branches and on the ground in leaf litter where it flicks its tail prominently. Occasionally hovers while feeding. Usually seen in groups of two to five.

Voice: Usually silent. The song has 3 initial notes followed by 2 or 3 elaborations of the same note descending in pitch (B. D. Heather). Call a short twitter (Watling 1982).

Occurrence: Endemic to FIJI. Common on Taveuni (*L. v. victoriae*) and rare on Vanua Levu (*L. v. kleinschmidti*), where apparently restricted to the Natewa Peninsula.

Reference: Heather, B. D. 1977. The Vanua Levu Silktail (*Lamprolia victoriae kleinschmidti*): A preliminary look at its status and habits. *Notornis* 24:94-128.

Other name: Satin Flycatcher.

PALAU FANTAIL   *Rhipidura lepida*   PLATE 24

Appearance: (7;18) A slender, mostly bright rufous bird with white throat and breast crossed by a bold dark band. Tail rufous at base, pale rufous at tip, black in between. Sexes similar. Immatures have dark throat and breast.

Habits: Found in most types of forest, particularly second-growth and ravine forests, but also mature primary forest. Avoids dense mangroves. Feeds in the subcanopy and understory by gleaning insects from leaves or capturing them in quick flights. Frequently wags tail from side to side, or fans it when particularly excited. Sings infrequently, mostly in early morning.

Voice: Single call notes are loud and squeaky with a downward inflec tion: *keee-up* or *queeer*. Song is an excited jumble of chirps and squeaks like the sound of a heavy piece of furniture being rolled on wooden casters.

Occurrence: Endemic to PALAU and common from Babelthuap to Peleliu.

RUFOUS FANTAIL *Rhipidura rufifrons*   PLATE 23

Appearance: (6;15) A tiny, long-tailed, brown bird with rusty forehead and black-spotted breast. Lower back and base of tail bright rufous, tail tipped white. Immature dingy below. The several subspecies vary in amount of black in throat, intensity of rufous coloration.

Habits: Extremely active in forest undergrowth. Often seen in pairs, chasing vigorously about. Feeds by hawking insects in the air. Often holds boldly patterned tail open like a fan.

Voice: The song begins as a jumble of *peet* notes followed by a cascade of whistles, all very high pitched. Varies somewhat from island to island, but the general quality of the notes remains the same.

Identification: Tinian Monarch has white rump and wing bars. Yap Monarch lacks markings on breast.

Occurrence: Widely distributed from the MARIANA IS. and YAP to Australia. Common on Saipan, Tinian, and Agiguan (*R. r. saipanensis*) and Yap (*R. r. versicolor*), less common on Rota (*R. r. mariae*), and nearly extinct on Guam (*R. r. uraniae*) where proposed as an Endangered Species.

Other name: Rufous-fronted Fantail.

Note: The Pohnpei Fantail is usually included in this species.

POHNPEI FANTAIL *Rhipidura kubaryi*   PLATE 25

Appearance: (6;15) A small, dark gray bird with white eyebrow, malar streak, and tail tip. Belly and undertail coverts white. Breast feathers edged white, look scaly. Sexes similar.

Habits: Frequents the lower strata of forest and forest edge. Very active. Frequently fans and wags its long tail and often flutters about with drooping wings. Feeds by aerial sallies and by gleaning insects from the foliage.

Voice: A harsh scolding chatter and a high-pitched jumble of short *peet* notes without any clear pattern.

Occurrence: Endemic to POHNPEI. Common.

Note: This form was classified as a subspecies of the Rufous Fantail by Mayr and Moynihan (1946. Evolution in the *Rhipidura rufifrons* group. *American Mus. Novit.* 1144:1-11) in a study based entirely on museum specimens. Although we agree that the two are closely related, our field observations indicate that they should probably not be considered conspecific. In addition to the very striking plumage differences, the two have distinctive vocalizations and foraging behavior.

STREAKED FANTAIL   *Rhipidura spilodera*   PLATE 30

Appearance: (6;15) A small bird with long fanlike tail, often spread. Brownish gray or rusty brown above, with white eyebrow. White below with brown streaks on breast, rusty tinge on flanks. Intensity of color varies geographically.

Habits: Found in gardens and second growth, as well as in primary forest from sea level to 1200 m. Bold and inquisitive. Insectivorous, feeds by aerial hawking and gleaning foliage. Prefers scrub and dense brush, less often seen in canopy. Sometimes joins mixed-species flocks.

Voice: A whistled *who-whee-who*, a harsh chipping call, and a scolding chatter.

Occurrence: Vanuatu and Loyalty Is. (New Caledonia) E to FIJI where three endemic subspecies are found: *R. s. layardi* (Viti Levu, Ovalau), *R. s. erythronota* (Vanua Levu, Kioa), and *R. s. rufilateralis* (Taveuni). Common.

Other name: Spotted Fantail. This name, used in all previous works on Fiji birds, is unfortunate because the bird is streaked rather than spotted, and the name is also used for the Malaysian *Rhipidura perlata*, which really *is* spotted.

KADAVU FANTAIL   *Rhipidura personata*   PLATE 30

Appearance: (6;15) Similar to Streaked Fantail, but without streaks below. A single, bold, dark brown band crosses upper breast.

Habits: Insectivorous. Usually in small groups in dense underbrush especially along streams.

Voice: Similar to that of Streaked Fantail.

Occurrence: Endemic to KADAVU (Fiji). Common.

Other name: Kandavu Fantail.

SAMOAN FANTAIL   *Rhipidura nebulosa*   PLATE 3

Appearance: (5½;14) A puffy dark gray bird with long, white-tipped fanlike tail and white spot behind eye. Belly pale buff, undertail coverts white. Savaii birds have more white below and some have a white throat.

Habits: Frequents dense underbrush in forests or roadside brush a edges of fields. Insectivorous, foraging by aerial sallies and by probing among leaves and branches. Often fans tail and flutters drooped wings. Tame and easily approached or "squeaked up." Often in pairs

Voice: Song a high-pitched jumble of squeaks. Call a short *kzeek*. Also a rasping chatter.

Occurrence: Endemic to W. SAMOA (*R. n. altera* on Savaii, *R. n. nebulosa* on Upolu). Common. Found at higher elevations on Savaii, to near sea level on Upolu.

FAMILY MUSCICAPIDAE: Old World Insect-eaters

This family, as now constituted, is so large and diverse that few generalizations can be made about it, and no single vernacular name is very suitable. The above name is misleading in that "Old World" describes only the family's hypothesized point of evolutionary origin, not its present-day distribution. The group includes many subfamilies (formerly considered families) that are much easier to characterize than the group as a whole. Two of these subfamilies are well represented in the native avifauna of the tropical Pacific, a third is present as rare visitors, and another includes four species introduced to the Hawaiian Is.

Old World Warblers: Subfamily Sylviinae

The Old World warblers (as distinguished from the New World wood-warblers) are mostly small, thin-billed, drab-colored, insectivorous passerines. They are vocally adept, and include some of the tropical Pacific's finest songsters. Two genera, the bush-warblers (*Cettia*) and the reed-warblers (*Acrocephalus*), are particularly prominent in the region, and are also widespread in Eurasia and Africa. The reed-warblers have colonized some of the remotest Pacific islands, and on several such outposts are the only passerine present. They have apparently been present in the region for a long time, because they exhibit a patchy, probably relictual, distribution and have diverged quite far morphologically from their mostly smaller continental counterparts. Reed-warblers are so named because many species inhabit reeds and tall grasses. Most Pacific species do so as well, but they may also be found in forests. Reed-warblers and bush-warblers tend to be skulkers, more often heard than seen. Taped playback of their songs will lure them into view.

PALAU BUSH-WARBLER *Cettia annae*   PLATE 24

Appearance: (6;15) A drab olive and yellow bird with yellow-orange legs, pale eyebrow, and long thin bill.

Habits: A shy skulker in dense vegetation near the ground in all forest types except mangroves. Much more often heard than seen, but occasionally boldly approaches and scolds an observer. Primarily insectivorous. Sings incessantly during daylight hours.

Voice: Call or scold a dry chatter. Typical song a long whistle, reiterated at varying pitches and occasionally followed by a quick jumble of short whistles. A chorus of these variably pitched whistles produces haunting harmonies and dissonances, and is one of the characteristic environmental sounds in Palau. A second song is a lively series of melodic whistles heard most often at dawn.

Identification: Color pattern similar to that of Giant White-eye, but overall impression very different. The white-eye's legs are dark, its bill heavier, and its cheek darker with fine streaks, making more of a contrast with the pale eyebrow. Behaviorally Giant White-eye is more boisterous and inquisitive, and much more likely to be seen in the forest canopy.

Occurrence: Endemic to PALAU. Common and widespread from Babelthuap to Peleliu.

Reference: See Fiji Bush-Warbler.

JAPANESE BUSH-WARBLER   *Cettia diphone*   PLATE 42

Appearance: (5½;14) A plain, thin-billed bird, olive-gray above, paler below, with a white eyebrow. Immature yellower than adult.

Habits: Extremely difficult to see, even when nearby. In exceptional circumstances may "squeak up" into view. A denizen of dense wet-forest undergrowth or drier thickets of haole koa.

Voice: Call a dry ticking sound, somewhat like the call of the White-rumped Shama. Two different songs are given, the most frequent a haunting, flutelike, sustained, pulsating whistle followed by a quick triplet of notes. The bird's Japanese name *uguisu* is imitative (the first syllable held out, the *i* accented). The whistle may be given alone. A longer, more complex song begins with a descending cascade of whistles that blends into a series of double phrases *pe-chew, pe-chew, pe-chew*, etc., that may continue, gradually slowing cadence, for more than a minute. Singing highly seasonal, ceasing entirely from September to December.

Identification: Songs unmistakable. If the birder is lucky enough to see the singer, its drab plumage and pale eyebrow will identify it.

Occurrence: Native to Japan. Introduced in the 1930s to the HAWAIIAN IS. Abundant on Oahu, has recently spread to Molokai, Lanai, Maui, and possibly Kauai.

Reference: Berger, A. J. 1975. The Japanese Bush Warbler on Oahu. *'Elepaio* 36:19-21.

FIJI BUSH-WARBLER   *Cettia ruficapilla*   PLATE 30

Appearance: (5;13) A small, thin-billed, dark brown bird. Underparts gray. Head shows distinctive pattern of dark eye line, pale eyebrow, and rufous-chestnut crown (Viti Levu, Taveuni, Vanua Levu); or rufous crown and cheeks, no eyebrow (Kadavu). Taveuni birds larger and darker, with chestnut cheeks.

Habits: A skulker in dense shrubbery, where it gleans insects. More often heard than seen, but widespread in any habitat with heavy low vegetation.

Voice: A long, sometimes quavering whistle followed by a quick phrase: *feee-e-e-e-fiddle-dee-dee*. The long whistle varies in pitch from song to song, but the quick phrase is more or less stereotyped. The performance may be a duet, with one bird uttering the whistle and another bird answering with the second part of the song.

Identification: Contrasting rufous or chestnut cap diagnostic for all forms, but rare Long-legged Warbler also has pale eyebrow. The latter is more uniformly reddish brown, less olive above than Fiji Bush-Warbler, and much larger.

Occurrence: Endemic to FIJI, with distinct subspecies on Viti Levu (*V. r. badiceps*), Vanua Levu (*V. r. castaneoptera*), Taveuni (*V. r. funebris*), and Kadavu (*V. r. ruficapilla*). Widespread and common.

Reference: Orenstein, R. I., and H. D. Pratt. 1983. The relationships and evolution of the southwest Pacific warbler genera *Vitia* and *Psamathia* (Sylviinae). *Wilson Bull.* 95:184-98.

Other name: Fiji Warbler.

LANCEOLATED GRASSHOPPER-WARBLER
Locustella lanceolata

A small (4½;11) brownish bird with prominent streaks on back and underparts. Tail rounded, graduated. Breeds in ne. Asia, migrates to the E. Indies. Recently reported from HELEN I. (Palau) and as a straggler that came aboard a ship near Palau. For illustration, see WBSJ (1982).

[GREAT REED-WARBLER   *Acrocephalus arundinaceus*   See Appendix A]

NIGHTINGALE REED-WARBLER   PLATE 23
Acrocephalus luscinia

Appearance: (7;18) A very long-billed, yellowish bird with few prominent markings. Darker above, with yellow eyebrow. Head feathers shaggy, often erect.

Habits: More often heard than seen, this bird skulks in reed beds, thickets, and forest undergrowth. Particularly abundant in dense stands of tangan-tangan.

Voice: Call a loud *chuck*. Song is varied and complex, loud and melodic. Resembles songs of American thrashers and mockingbirds, as well as that of Melodious Laughing-thrush. Includes trills, warbles, and whistles. Song may last uninterrupted for several minutes. Often sings at night.

Identification: The long bill and drab colors distinguish this bird from all other songbirds in the Marianas.

Occurrence: Endemic to the MARIANA IS. Still widespread and common on Saipan, but of unknown status on Alamagan and extinct on Guam (*A. l. luscinia*), nearly extinct on Agiguan (*A. l. nijoi*), and probably extinct on Pagan (*A. l. yamashinae*). The status of the Saipan population as an Endangered Species is being reassessed.

CAROLINE ISLANDS REED-WARBLER   PLATE 25
Acrocephalus syrinx

Appearance: (6;15) Brown above, yellowish white below, with pale stripe over eye. Bill long, but much shorter than that of Nightingale Reed-Warbler.

Habits: Most often found in thick stands of tall grass, but also common in gardens, second-growth forest, and even in the canopy of montane rain forests. A skulker, not easily observed. Usually nests in small trees.

Voice: A complex series of warbles and trills, usually broken into short bursts with intermittent pauses. Not so long-sustained as song of Nightingale Reed-Warbler.

Identification: Note pale eyebrow. On most islands where this bird occurs, it is unlike any other. On Pohnpei, the Long-billed White-eye looks somewhat similar. Immature Truk Monarch resembles reed-warbler slightly, but is larger, with much heavier bill.

Occurrence: Widespread in the CAROLINE IS., where found on atolls as well as high islands. Common at Truk and Pohnpei, but probably extirpated from Kosrae. Found at least as far W as Woleai.

Note: Many recent authorities consider this species conspecific with the Nightingale Reed-Warbler. We believe its much shorter bill, different song, and different ecology warrant separate species status for *A. syrinx*.

NAURU REED-WARBLER   *Acrocephalus rehsei*

Appearance: (6;15) A small, drab, grayish bird with a thin straight bill.

Habits: Little known, but probably similar to those of other Micronesian reed-warblers.

Occurrence: Endemic to NAURU. Status unknown, but island residents reported it still present in remaining brushy areas on the island in 1983. May not survive unless some habitat is preserved.
Other names: Finsch's Reed Warbler, Pleasant Warbler.
Note: The relationship of this form to the other two Micronesian reed-warblers has not been adequately studied.

BOKIKOKIKO   *Acrocephalus aequinoctialis*   PLATE 34

Appearance: (6;15) A small, soft-plumaged, gray reed-warbler with white edges to the feathers. Underparts lighter. Tail tip white.
Habits: Inhabits dense brush where it gleans insects from leaves and small branches. Flight weak and fluttering. Bold and inquisitive. Nests in low trees or bushes, particularly beach heliotrope.
Voice: A descending squeaky song. Name is imitative.
Occurrence: Endemic to the LINE IS. (Kiribati). Common on Teraina, Tabueran, and Kiritimati.
Reference: Schreiber, R. W. 1979. The egg and nest of the Bokikokiko. *BBOC* 99:120-24.
Other names: Line Islands Reed-Warbler, Kokikokiko, Christmas Warbler, Polynesian Reed-Warbler, Equinoctial Warbler.

MILLERBIRD   *Acrocephalus familiaris*   PLATE 35

Appearance and Identification: (5;13) A small brown and white warbler. The only thin-billed bird on Nihoa.
Habits: A secretive denizen of brushy hillsides. Feeds on insects, including miller moths, by probing and gleaning leaves and twigs, and by aerial hawking. Highly territorial and sedentary. Flight weak and fluttering.
Voice: A thin, metallic, energetic song, mainly heard during breeding season. Sings from exposed perches.
Occurrence: NW HAWAIIAN IS. (extinct Laysan, common Nihoa). Laysan form became extinct between 1912 and 1923. Nihoa form an Endangered Species.
Other names: Hawaiian Reed-Warbler, Nihoa Warbler.
Note: The Laysan (*A. f. familiaris*) and Nihoa (*A. f. kingi*) forms are sometimes regarded as separate species.

TAHITI REED-WARBLER   *Acrocephalus caffra*   PLATE 34

Appearance: (7½;19) A large, slender reed-warbler with long tail and very long, straight bill. Two color phases, the dark one rare. Light phase olive above with pale feather edges, underparts pale yellow. Dark phase entirely dark brown.

Habits: Found in bamboo thickets and second-growth forests in river valleys and on hillsides to 1700 m. Highly territorial. Primarily insectivorous, but also takes lizards, small fish, crayfish, snails, and nectar. Forages mainly in the canopy by gleaning. Usually shy and difficult to observe.

Voice: Alarm call a harsh *chrrr*. Song a complex series of whistles, warbles, and *churr*s lasting several minutes.

Identification: Note very long, thin bill. Pale phase distinctive. Compare dark phase with Tahiti Monarch.

Occurrence: Endemic to the SOCIETY IS. (Tahiti, Moorea), Rare and local. Possibly formerly on other islands. Moorea form (*A. c. longirostris*) listed as endangered by the ICBP (King 1981).

Other name: Long-billed Reed-Warbler.

MARQUESAS REED-WARBLER

PLATE 34

Acrocephalus mendanae

Appearance: (7;18) A large reed-warbler, bright yellow below with medium-length, slightly curved bill. The eight subspecies differ only in measurements and subtle shades of color.

Habits: Highly adaptable, found in lowland plantations, dry brushy hillsides, and wet upland forests to 1200 m. Less common in dense forests. Forages in foliage and on the ground. Primarily insectivorous but also eats lizards, fruits, and nectar. Defends territories against all intruders, not just conspecifics. Easily "squeaked up." Sometimes sings at night.

Voice: A complex and variable combination of whistles, *churr*s, warbles, and rasping scolds.

Occurrence: Endemic to the MARQUESAS IS. with described subspecies for virtually all islands. Abundant on all major islands except Hivaoa, where less numerous. Populations on Eiao and Hatutu (see Table 6) are considered endangered and rare respectively by the ICBP (King 1981).

Other name: Marquesan Warbler.

Note: Many recent authors have regarded this form as a subspecies of *A. caffra*. Research by P. L. Bruner (unpublished M.S. thesis) has shown that in addition to the obvious morphological differences, the two forms have distinctive displays and different nesting behavior. They are, in our opinion, best regarded as separate species.

TUAMOTU REED-WARBLER *Acrocephalus atypha* PLATE 34

Appearance: (6;15) A slender brown reed-warbler, darker above, lighter below with a straight, medium-length bill. Sometimes shows white feathers scattered asymmetrically through wings, tail, or head.

Variable geographically, mainly in measurements and the darkness of upperparts. Some populations yellowish below. Napuka subspecies (*A. a. flavida*) bright yellow below. Makatea form (*A. a. erema*) very distinctive in being larger, with a much longer, downcurved bill, and heavily tinted throughout with cinnamon.

Habits: A bird of forested bush on atolls or raised coral islands. Primarily insectivorous, but also takes crustaceans and lizards. Forages in coconut palms, brushy scrub, and on the ground. Often hawks insects in the air. Territorial, especially during breeding season. Inquisitive and easily "squeaked up." Flight slower and weaker than that of larger reed-warblers.

Voice: Song similar to that of other Polynesian reed-warblers but shorter and not as lavish.

Occurrence: Known from 47 of the 76 atolls of the TUAMOTU ARCH. Common away from human disturbance, less numerous around villages.

COOK ISLANDS REED-WARBLER   PLATE 34
Acrocephalus kerearako

Appearance: (6½;16) A slender straight-billed bird, olive above, yellowish white below. Mitiaro subspecies indistinctly streaked below.

Habits: Inhabits various habitats from reeds to gardens and woodlands. Insectivorous. Sings from high exposed perches.

Voice: Call a harsh *chru*, often repeated. Song includes short, loud, whistled phrases and trills, with pauses between (Holyoak 1981).

Occurrence: Endemic to the COOK IS. with distinct subspecies on Mangaia (*A. k. kerearako*) and Mitiaro (*A. kerearako kaoko*). Common.

Reference: Holyoak, D. T. 1974. Undescribed land birds from the Cook Islands, Pacific Ocean. *BBOC* 94:145-50.

Note: Discovered in 1973 and first described (see Reference) as two subspecies of *A. vaughani*. That species lacks song, whereas this one is a good singer. We agree with Holyoak (1981) that this form is best regarded as a separate species. Plate 34, painted before the taxonomic change became known to Pratt, groups the two forms together.

PITCAIRN REED-WARBLER *Acrocephalus vaughani* PLATE 34

Appearance: (6½;17) A slender, straight-billed reed-warbler with three described subspecies that vary from brownish gray to dark olive above and white to yellowish below. Immatures yellower than adults. Partial albinism of wing and tail feathers and body plumage characteristic of populations on Rimatara and Henderson, less so on Pitcairn. Many Henderson and Rimatara birds nearly white.

Habits: Frequents brushy forest and villages. Forages in foliage and leaf litter. Frequents orange trees and bananas on Pitcairn. Insectivorous. Bold and inquisitive, easily "squeaked up." Territorial, always seen in pairs.

Voice: Alarm note a loud *chack-chack* or a shrill chirp. No song.

Occurrence: PITCAIRN IS. (*A. v. vaughani* on Pitcairn, *A. v. taiti* on Henderson) and RIMATARA (Tubuai Is.; *A. v. rimitarae*). Common.

Other names: Pitcairn Warbler, Henderson Warbler, Sparrow (on Pitcairn).

LONG-LEGGED WARBLER   *Trichocichla rufa*   PLATE 30

Appearance: (7½;19) A large slender warbler with long tail and legs. Mostly dark reddish brown with white throat, breast, and belly. Prominent white eyebrow stripe.

Habits: A denizen of dense rain forests above 800 m. Secretive; forages on ground beneath dense vegetation such as fern and scrub brush.

Voice: A harsh *che* (F. C. Kinsky). Song unknown.

Identification: Fiji Bush-Warbler much smaller, has gray underparts and more olive upperparts.

Occurrence: Endemic to FIJI (Viti Levu, Vanua Levu). Long believed extinct since 1800s, but reportedly seen in 1973 near Vunidawa, Viti Levu. A new subspecies (*T. r. cluniei*) was discovered in 1974 on Vanua Levu. Apparently rare and local. Listed as endangered by the ICBP (King 1981).

Reference: Kinsky, F. C. 1975. A new subspecies of the Long-legged Warbler *Trichocichla rufa* Reichenow, from Vanua Levu, Fiji. *BBOC* 95:98-101.

OLD WORLD FLYCATCHERS: Subfamily Muscicapinae

THE term "flycatcher" is applied to several only distantly related groups of passerines that are similar ecologically. Most tropical Pacific flycatchers belong to the monarchine group of the Australian region. Two rare visitors, however, are members of this mainly Afro-Eurasian subfamily.

NARCISSUS FLYCATCHER   *Ficedula narcissina*

A small (5½;14) bird that breeds in ne. Asia and has occurred at least once as a winter visitor to PALAU. Male strikingly patterned in yellow below, black above with yellow rump and eyebrow. Immature duller. Female similar to Gray-spotted Flycatcher but with mottled, not streaked, breast and no white around eye. For illustration, see WBSJ (1982).

GRAY-SPOTTED FLYCATCHER   *Muscicapa griseisticta*

This small (6;15), drab grayish brown bird breeds in e. Asia and winters
S to New Guinea. A rare winter visitor to PALAU, it is stocky with a
short, notched tail. Darker above, with white eye-ring and lores. Pale
breast boldly streaked. No other small bird recorded from Palau is
streaked below. For illustrations, see WBSJ (1982) or NGS (1983).

THRUSHES: Subfamily Turdinae

THRUSHES are a cosmopolitan group of muscicapids characterized by
bills of medium length, with a small notch near the tip of the upper
mandible, and "booted tarsi," i.e. legs encased in an unbroken sheath
with no separate scutes (scales). Many species, such as the legendary
nightingales (*Luscinia*) and the solitaires (*Myadestes*), are notable vocalists
with clear, haunting, complex, flutelike songs. Tropical Pacific thrushes
are likewise fine singers, and the Hawaiian native thrushes (discussed
separately) are actually island solitaires. In addition to the Hawaiian
thrushes, the subfamily is represented in the region by one widespread
member of the genus *Turdus*, which includes the European Blackbird
(*T. merula*) and the American Robin (*T. migratorius*), by several migratory visitors, and by one introduced species.

SIBERIAN RUBYTHROAT   *Luscinia calliope*   FIGURE 43

Appearance: (6;15) A long-legged, short-tailed thrush, brown above
and grayish white below. Sides of head conspicuously marked by pale
superciliary and malar stripe contrasting with dark lores, the markings
less prominent in females. Throat bright red in males, white in females
and immatures.

FIGURE 43.
Siberian Rubythroat
(adult male)

Habits: A secretive bird usually found skulking in low vegetation. Often cocks tail up. Usually silent in winter.

Identification: The bold superciliary line distinguishes this bird from most others in Micronesia. The Eye-browed Thrush is somewhat similar to the female, but is larger and salmon-colored on the flanks.

Occurrence: Breeds in n. Eurasia; winters in tropical Asia. A rare but fairly frequent winter visitor to PALAU.

WHITE-RUMPED SHAMA *Copsychus malabaricus*   PLATES 40, 41

Appearance: (10;25) Male glossy blue-black with rusty belly, white rump, and white outer feathers in the unusually long tail. Female similar in pattern with black replaced by gray, belly more yellowish, and tail shorter. Immature spotted on breast and gray above, with short tail.

Habits: In Hawaii, occurs mostly in the lower levels of lush heavy forest but also frequents dense haole koa thickets. Sometimes enters suburban yards, rarely penetrates very far into native rain forests. More often heard than seen. Often holds the tail up and fluffs the white rump feathers.

Voice: Call a dry *tchk!* The song is one of the most beautiful sounds of lowland forests in Hawaii. It comprises varied liquid, flutelike notes and often includes excellent imitations of other native and introduced birds. The shama and Melodious Laughing-thrush sometimes imitate each other, making identification by voice alone somewhat more difficult.

Identification: The shama's white rump and sides of tail are very conspicuous as the bird flies away through the underbrush. No other bird in Hawaii exhibits such a pattern. Immatures have less white on rump, often cock tail up and thus could be mistaken for an Elepaio. The latter is smaller and has the tail only tipped with white.

Occurrence: Native to SE. Asia. Introduced to the HAWAIIAN IS. (1931) and now common on Kauai and Oahu.

Other names: Common Shama, Shama Thrush.

[**MAGPIE-ROBIN** *Copsychus saularis*   See Appendix A]

BLUE ROCK-THRUSH *Monticola solitarius*

Appearance: (10;25) A chunky slate-blue thrush with black and buff feather edges that produce a scaly appearance. Female less blue above, with dark-scaled white underparts. Most males have chestnut underparts. Illustrated in King and Dickinson (1975) and WBSJ (1982).

Identification: Both sexes could be confused with the respective sex of

Cicadabird. Male Cicadabird never has chestnut belly, never looks scaly. Female barred, not scaly, below. Both are much smaller than rock-thrushes and are forest-dwellers. Blue Rock-Thrush perches in open, even on buildings.

Occurrence: Breeds in ne. Asia, migrates to the E. Indies. Rare winter vagrant to PALAU.

THE HAWAIIAN NATIVE THRUSHES: Genus *Myadestes*

THE native thrushes of the Hawaiian Islands are related to the solitaires of North and South America. They were long classified in a separate genus (*Phaeornis*) but are now classified with the solitaires (AOU 1985), following Pratt (see Reference below). Hawaiian thrushes or solitaires as adults are drab brown above and gray below. Immature birds are darker brown above, spotted with buff, with pale underparts scalloped with dark brown. All species share a peculiar habit of shivering the wings while perched. They are accomplished singers, and sometimes sing on the wing. The songs vary among the five species, but the call notes are similar. The four larger species are primarily fruiteaters but also take insects.

Reference: Pratt, H. D. 1982. Relationships and speciation of the Hawaiian thrushes. *The Living Bird* 19:73-90.

KAMAO   *Myadestes myadestinus*   PLATE 35

Appearance: (8;20) Resembles other Hawaiian thrushes but has faintly mottled breast, brown forehead, and shortest, broadest bill of all.

Habits: Occurs in dense montane forest. Sings from the tops of dead snags over the forest, especially in early morning and late afternoon.

Voice: Call resembles a police whistle. Also a catlike raspy note higher pitched than that of the Omao. Song a long, complex, flutelike melody of whistles, trills, and liquid warbles.

Identification: Told from the smaller Puaiohi by its dark legs and feet and short stubby bill. Female White-rumped Shama also grayish but has prominent white sides to the tail, white rump. Melodious Laughing-thrush much darker rusty brown with yellow bill, white spectacles.

Occurrence: Endemic to KAUAI (Hawaiian Is.) Has declined drastically in recent years and only a few individuals of this Endangered Species survive as of this writing, in the Alakai Swamp area (USFWS survey data). Still reported occasionally on Pihea Ridge Trail above Kalalau Valley.

Other name: Large Kauai Thrush.

AMAUI *Myadestes oahensis?*

A native thrush is known to have lived on OAHU, and to have been called by this name by the Hawaiians. The only specimens collected in historial times were lost, and the species has not been seen since the 1820s. Fossil remains, recently unearthed on Oahu, may help to clarify this bird's relationships and species status.

OLOMAO *Myadestes lanaiensis*   PLATE 35

Appearance: (7;18) Resembles Omao but whiter on belly. Buffy patch at base of primaries more prominent than in other Hawaiian thrushes.

Habits: A shy and retiring bird, keeping beneath the forest canopy except for occasional short flights. Frequently calls from concealment. Now seldom (if ever) sings.

Voice: A variety of calls including a catlike rasp. Song is a long, thrushlike, somewhat halting melody with a ventriloquial quality.

Identification: Melodious Laughing-thrush much darker, redder brown.

Occurrence: Endemic to the c. HAWAIIAN IS. of Lanai (last seen 1933), Maui (extirpated by historic times), and Molokai, where it clings precariously to existence as an Endangered Species. Only a few individuals remain scattered through the upper forests of Mt. Olokui, the Kamakou Preserve, and the Ohialele Plateau (USFWS survey data).

Other names: Molokai Thrush, Lanai Thrush.

OMAO *Myadestes obscurus*   PLATE 35

Appearance: (7;18) Grayest Hawaiian thrush below, with gray forehead. From below sides of tail often appear white because of transmitted light.

Habits: An inconspicuous bird easily missed except for its loud vocalizations. Fond of olapa fruits. Found in native ohia forests, ohia scrub on lava flows, and in the treeless alpine zone.

Voice: Many different calls, including a catlike raspy note, a froglike croak, a high-pitched trill rather like a police whistle, and a twangy ascending series of buzzy notes. The song is jerky but pleasing, composed of liquid chirps and short whistles, quite unlike any other song heard in native forests of Hawaii.

Identification: No other native bird on Hawaii resembles the Omao. I might be confused by the novice with Melodious Laughing-thrush (rusty below with yellow bill) or Northern Mockingbird (prominent white in wings and tail, drier habitats).

Occurrence: Endemic to the island of HAWAII, where still fairly common in undisturbed forests at higher elevations, such as along Stain back Highway, the Saddle Road, and in Hawaii Volcanoes National Park. A disjunct population above tree line on Mauna Loa. No longer found in Kona.

Other name: Hawaiian Thrush.

Reference: van Riper III, C., and J. M. Scott. 1979. Observations on the distribution, diet, and breeding of the Hawaiian Thrush. *Condor* 81:65-71.

PUAIOHI   *Myadestes palmeri*   PLATE 35

Appearance: (6½;17) Small and plain, with pinkish tan legs and feet. In certain lights appears almost uniformly brownish gray. Some individuals have a dark malar streak or white above the eye. Immatures also have pale legs.

Haibts: Extremely secretive, keeping to the undergrowth in dense forest, especially fern-covered streambanks. Eats insects and fruit.

Voice: Call a toneless rasping hiss, fairly loud. High-pitched and reedy song shorter and less complex than that of Kamao. Resembles some songs of Apapane. Often calls from concealment. Ventriloquial.

Identification: Kamao larger with dark legs and feet. Bill of Puaiohi much longer and thinner. Adult Puaiohi paler on face than Kamao, but juvenile darker throughout.

Occurrence: Endemic to KAUAI (Hawaiian Is.). Always rare and restricted to the Alakai Swamp but now apparently outnumbers Kamao. An Endangered Species with only a few dozen (or fewer) living individuals.

Other name: Small Kauai Thrush.

References: Ashman, P.R., P. Pyle, and J. Jeffrey. 1984. A second nest of the Small Kauai Thrush. *'Elepaio* 45:33-34.

Kepler, C. B., and A. K. Kepler, 1983. A first record of the nest and chicks of the Small Kauai Thrush. *Condor* 85:497-99.

EYE-BROWED THRUSH   *Turdus obscurus*

Appearance and Identification: (9;23) A drab gray, medium-sized songbird with a prominent white eyebrow. Males are gray-headed and olive-backed, with gray upper breast, salmon-colored lower breast and flanks, white belly and undertail coverts. Females duller throughout, the gray largely replaced by olive, with a white throat. The only bird likely to be confused with this species in Palau is the female Siberian Rubythroat. For color illustrations, see King and Dickinson (1975), WBSJ (1982), or NGS (1983).

Occurrence: Breeds ne. Asia, migrates S to the E. Indies. A rare winter visitor to PALAU.

DUSKY THRUSH   *Turdus naumanni*

A migratory species from e. Asia that has been recorded twice in the n. MARIANA IS. (Uracas, Maug). Identified by bright rufous wings and bold black and white face pattern (black crown and auriculars, white eyebrow and throat). For illustration, see NGS (1983).

[**ULIETA MYSTERY THRUSH**   *"Turdus ulietensis"*   See Appendix A]

ISLAND THRUSH   *Turdus poliocephalus*   PLATE 31

Appearance: (9;23) A medium-sized bird with golden yellow bill, legs, and eye-ring. Plumage color varies widely from island to island: all black (Samoa, Gau); black with gray or brown hood (Taveuni); black with rufous-tawny hood, juveniles tawny below with black spots (Kadavu); all brownish gray, darker above, with juveniles black-spotted below (Vanua Levu); dark brown above with gray throat and breast, chestnut flanks, and white belly, juveniles uniformly brown, spotted below (Viti Levu and nearby islands).

Habits: Restricted to dense forest, where it feeds by scratching on the ground in leaf litter. Shy and difficult to approach; calls as it flies away quickly through the undergrowth.

Voice: Call a sharp chatter. Song a complex melody of flutelike notes.

Identification: Despite wide plumage variation, causes little confusion because of distinctive habits. Note especially the bright yellow bill, which contrasts strongly with the dark plumage of most subspecies. Shrikebills and Long-legged Warbler have darker bills.

Occurrence: Widespread on islands from Taiwan and Cocos I. to Norfolk I. and C. Polynesia. Found from sea level upwards in FIJI (*T. p. layardi*, Viti Levu, Koro, Ovalau, Yasawa Is.; *T. p. vitiensis*, Vanua Levu; *T. p. tempesti*, Taveuni; *T. p. hades*, Gau; *T. p. ruficeps*, Kadavu) and SAMOA (*T. p. samoensis*, Savaii, Upolu).

BABBLERS: Subfamily Timaliinae

BABBLERS are a highly diverse group of muscicapids distributed from Africa to Australia. They are absent from cold regions and from most oceanic islands, including those of the tropical Pacific. However, four species have been introduced to the Hawaiian Islands. These include three laughing-thrushes, large jaylike birds with skulking habits and loud voices.

GREATER NECKLACED LAUGHING-THRUSH   PLATE 41
Garrulax pectoralis

Appearance: (13;33) A large, long-tailed bird with a long thin bill. Rusty brown above, white below with a black "necklace" and black-streaked ear converts. Tail feathers tipped pale buff.

Habits: Moves about in small flocks, probing the branches of large trees or skulking in the undergrowth. Found in lowland wet forests of monkeypod, hau, and kukui.

Voice: A descending series of whistles *WHEE-whi-whi-whee*.

Identification: The best field mark is the buff band at the tip of the tail visible as the bird flies away. The tail band distinguishes this species at a glance (which is all you may get!) from Melodious Laughing-thrush.

Occurrence: Native to se. Asia. Introduced, possibly as early as 1920, to KAUAI (Hawaiian Is.). Uncommon and local, apparently nomadic, along stream valleys in the lowlands. Most often seen along Huleia Stream.

Other name: Black-gorgeted Laughing-thrush.

GRAY-SIDED LAUGHING-THRUSH   PLATE 41
Garrulax caerulatus

Appearance: (11;28) A robust, mostly olive-brown bird with prominent triangular black mask, blue skin around eye, white throat and breast, and gray flanks.

Habits: A skulker in dense forest that feeds by probing the bark of trees. Said to respond to whistles. Sometimes in flocks of up to 15 birds.

Voice: A rapid low chattering, a plaintive *kew-wee*, and a short upslurred humanlike whistle.

Identification: Distinguished from Melodious Laughing-thrush by white throat and breast, black mask, and dark bill.

Occurrence: Native to China. Introduced to OAHU (Hawaiian Is.) sometime before 1947. Apparently established in n. Koolau Mts. (Poamoho Trail) but rarely seen.

Reference: Taylor, A. L., Jr., and M. L. Collins. 1979. Rediscovery and identification of the "mystery" *Garrulax* on Oahu. *'Elepaio* 39:79-81.

[WHITE-THROATED LAUGHING-THRUSH   *Garrulax albogularis*   See Appendix A]

MELODIOUS LAUGHING-THRUSH   PLATE 41
Garrulax canorus

Appearance and Identification: (10;25) A rusty brown bird with yellow bill and white "spectacles." The color, broad round wings, and fan-shaped tail produce a distinctive look that identifies this species in flight. The two other laughing-thrushes in Hawaii are larger, have pale tips to lateral tail feathers.

Habits: A skulker in dense forest, usually solitary but occasionally in flocks. Typically very difficult to see, but often flies across roads. May become tame and approachable in parks and gardens. Found in a variety of habitats, from native ohia and mamane/naio forests to thickets of introduced haole koa and Christmasberry.

Voice: Call a rolling, raspy whistle or rattle. Song very loud and highly varied, including slurred whistles and imitations of other birds. Sometimes difficult to distinguish from song of White-rumped Shama (the two imitate each other), but more insistent and less flutelike.

Occurrence: Native to China. Introduced in the early 1900s to the HAWAIIAN IS. (common on Kauai, Maui, Hawaii; uncommon to rare Oahu, Molokai).

Other names: Chinese Thrush, Hwa-mei, Hwamei Laughingthrush.

RED-BILLED LEIOTHRIX *Leiothrix lutea* PLATE 42

Appearance: (5½;14) A green and yellow bird with conspicuous red bill. Primaries edged yellow. A patch of red shows at base of primaries on folded wing. Tail peculiarly forked, with outer feathers curving outward. Immatures and adults with worn plumage less strongly marked and paler than others.

Habits: Extremely active and therefore difficult to see well as it flits about in the undergrowth. Can sometimes be "squeaked up." Often found in small (family?) groups. In virtually any habitat with leafy shrubs, but most common in native rain forests, mamane scrub, and planted groves of conifers, black wattle, and eucalyptus.

Voice: A low-pitched scolding chatter uttered at humans or other intruders. Two songs, one a series of 4-7 plaintive whistles on a level pitch, *plee-plee-plee-plee-plee.* The second a loud melodious warble difficult to transcribe; will remind N. Americans of some grosbeak songs.

Identification: Red bill and forked tail distinctive, but sometimes hard to see. None of the green Hawaiian honeycreepers has such a brightly contrasting throat and breast. Japanese White-eye smaller and not a skulker.

Occurrence: Native to s. Asia. Introduced (1920s) to the HAWAIIAN IS. Abundant on most islands by 1940s but has been declining since. Now rare on Kauai, Oahu; still common on Molokai, Maui, Hawaii.

Other names: Hill Robin, Pekin Robin, Pekin Nightingale.

FAMILY MIMIDAE: Mockingbirds and Thrashers

This New World family is represented in the tropical Pacific by a single introduced species. These are long-billed, long-tailed, thrushlike birds noted for their great powers of vocal mimicry.

NORTHERN MOCKINGBIRD *Mimus polyglottos* PLATE 41

Appearance: (10;25) A gray, long-tailed bird with prominent flashes of white in wings and tail. Sexes similar. Juveniles streaked below.

Habits: In Hawaii found mostly in dry brushy habitats. Seemingly less vocal than in continental range.

Voice: Call a loud *tchack*. Sings wide repertoire of original songs as well as imitations of both native and introduced birds. Song loud but less vigorous than that of Melodious Laughing-thrush and with fewer slurred whistles. Song of White-rumped Shama more gurgling and flutelike. All three imitate each other.

Identification: Female White-rumped Shama also gray with white in tail. Note her rusty belly, white rump. Common Myna also has white wing patches, but is much darker and chunkier than mockingbird. Native thrushes much stockier, confined to native forests.

Occurrence: Native to N. America. Introduced (1931) to the main HAWAIIAN IS. and now established on the six largest. Fairly common and widespread on Kauai, uncommon and local elsewhere. Vagrant to NW HAWAIIAN IS. (Midway, French Frigate Shoals, Necker, Nihoa).

FAMILY MOTACILLIDAE: Wagtails and Pipits

These are ground-dwelling birds of open habitats. Wagtails are named for their habit of pumping the tail up and down. Pipits are streaked, sparrowlike birds with long, thin, bills. All members of the family have unusually long hind claws and most exhibit undulating flight. They are distributed worldwide, but are only rare migrant visitors in the tropical Pacific.

YELLOW WAGTAIL *Motacilla flava* FIGURE 44

Appearance: (6½;17) A slender, long-tailed bird, lemon yellow below with olive green mantle, black cheeks, and pale eyebrow. Tail black

FIGURE 44. Wagtails

with white outer feathers. Females and winter males duller, with variable amounts of yellow. Immatures dirty white below with dusky breast band.

Habits: In winter quarters found in open savannahs and fields, often on the ground.

Voice: Call a loud *tsweep*.

Identification: Gray Wagtail very similar but note its yellowish rump, white wing bar, and longer tail. Siberian Rubythroat female resembles immature Yellow Wagtail, but has darker belly and lacks white in tail.

Occurrence: Breeds throughout Eurasia and winters S to Africa, the E Indies, and the Philippines. An uncommon migrant and winter resident in w. MICRONESIA (Palau, Yap, Rota).

GRAY WAGTAIL *Motacilla cinerea*   FIGURE 44

Appearance and Identification: (8;20) Similar to Yellow Wagtail bu larger and longer-tailed. Best distinguished by prominent white wing bar, yellow rump, and distinctive call. Breeding males have black throats.

Voice: A metallic 2- or 3-note call, very distinct from upslurred single note of Yellow Wagtail.

Occurrence: Eurasia. Winters S to Africa, s. Asia, Philippines, and New Guinea. Rare migrant to w. MICRONESIA (Palau, Guam).

[**WHITE WAGTAIL**   *Motacilla alba*   See Appendix A]

OLIVE TREE-PIPIT   *Anthus hodgsoni*

A flock of these birds, which breed in ne. Asia and migrate to se. Asia, turned up on KURE (NW Hawaiian Is.) in fall 1983. A robust pipit, with olive-gray upperparts, buff throat, white belly, and heavily streaked breast. Face pattern distinctive, with broad white line nearly encircling dark auricular patch. For illustrations, see WBSJ (1982) or NGS (1983). Other names: Indian Tree-Pipit, Olive-backed Pipit.

RED-THROATED PIPIT   *Anthus cervinus*   FIGURE 45

Appearance: (6;15) A heavily streaked pipit, both above and below. Outer tail feathers white. Legs dull pink. Brick red tone of face and throat in breeding plumage usually lost or reduced in winter.

Voice: Call in flight a clear, explosive *pseep.*

Identification: Water Pipit darker, less heavily streaked on back. Eura-

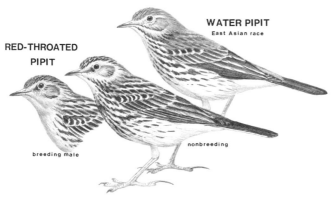

FIGURE 45. Pipits

sian Skylark superficially similar but chunkier, thicker-billed, with broader, slightly notched tail.

Occurrence: Breeds in n. Eurasia and w. Alaska, winters to Africa, s. Asia, and the Philippines. Rare fall migrant to PALAU and KURE (NW Hawaiian Is.).

WATER PIPIT *Anthus spinoletta* FIGURE 45

A dull brown pipit distributed around the Northern Hemisphere. Recorded as a fall straggler to KURE (NW Hawaiian Is.). Very similar to Red-throated Pipit, but more uniformly brown on back and with different flight call: a piercing *chee-eet*. Pacific records are for the Asiatic race *A. s. japonicus*, which is much more heavily streaked below than N. American ones, and has pinkish legs.

FAMILY ARTAMIDAE: WOODSWALLOWS

WOODSWALLOWS are graceful, long-winged, gregarious birds distributed from s. and e. Asia to Micronesia, Melanesia, and Australia. They are somewhat swallowlike, but are more robust and have heavier slightly downcurved bills. Their plumage is soft and fluffy, usually with somber colors.

WHITE-BREASTED WOODSWALLOW PLATE 31, FIGURE 46
Artamus leuocorhynchus

Appearance: (7;18) A chunky, dark sooty gray bird with white belly and rump. Bill steel blue with black tip. The two tropical Pacific subspecies differ in amount of white in throat (Figure 46).

Habits: Inhabits savannahs, pastures, and other open areas. Usually seen on telephone wires or dead branches of trees. Highly social, usually in small groups that nestle tightly on a perch. Graceful in the air. Hawks large insects on the wing or by sallying from a perch. Sometimes soars high overhead. Pugnacious, often attacking large birds and mammals.

Voice: Call notes are harsh chatters. Song a soft continuous jumble of whistles and warbles.

Identification: In Palau, compare rare Asian House-Martin, which also has white rump. Note woodswallow's heavier blue bill.

Occurrence: Resident from Malaysia and the Philippines to Australia, PALAU (mainly interior Babelthuap; wanders to Koror), and FIJI (Viti Levu, Vanua Levu, Taveuni, and nearby islands). Common in Fiji, uncommon and local at Palau, where the indigenous race *A. l. pelewensis* is proposed as an Endangered Species.

FIGURE 46. Geographic Variation in
White-breasted Woodswallows. Fiji form (*l.*)
and Palau form (*r.*)

FAMILY LANIIDAE: SHRIKES

SHRIKES are like passerine miniature hawks. They capture live prey
such as large insects, small reptiles, and even mice. They have heavy,
hooked bills, well adapted to such habits. They are distributed from Africa to Eurasia and N. America, but only a single species has ever
reached the tropical Pacific.

BROWN SHRIKE   *Lanius cristatus*

A medium-sized (8;20) shrike with brown (male) or gray (female) upperparts, white underparts and eyebrow, and a bold black mask
through the eye and auriculars. Breeds in e. Asia and winters to New
Guinea. Recorded once on TOBI (sw. Palau), but possibly a regular migrant to this remote and seldom-visited island. For illustration, see
King and Dickinson (1975) or WBSJ (1982).

FAMILY STURNIDAE: STARLINGS AND MYNAS

THIS large family was originally distributed only in Africa and Eurasia,
with one genus reaching the tropical Pacific and northeastern Australia.
Man has extended the group's range worldwide, mainly by introducing
the European Starling to the Western Hemisphere, southern Australia,
and New Zealand. Several species of mynas have also been transported

to new localities, including many tropical Pacific islands. Members of this family are clad mostly in black or brown, but many are very glossy and could be considered colorful. Mynas often show white wing patches. The group exhibits a variety of bill shapes from thin and sharp-pointed to thick and blunt. The introduced starlings and mynas in the region are gregarious and aggressive birds, sometimes implicated in declines of native species. The native starlings include at least one species now extinct, and several others of uncertain or endangered status. Some, however, are widespread and common. Two species are rare migratory visitors from eastern Asia.

POHNPEI MOUNTAIN STARLING   *Aplonis pelzelni*   PLATE 25

Appearance: (7;18) A small, dusky gray-brown (looks black at a distance) starling with no gloss to the plumage. Wings and tail browner than body. Iris brown.

Habits: Solitary or in pairs. A shy, difficult-to-see inhabitant of the forest canopy. Not necessarily confined to mountains. Easily overlooked except for distinctive vocalizations.

Voice: A very high-pitched shrill whistle, sometimes with descending inflection, sometimes bell-like. Shorter and higher than notes of Micronesian Starling. The native name *sie* is imitative (J. T. Marshall, unpubl. field notes).

Identification: Distinguished from adult Micronesian Starling by smaller size, slimmer bill, lack of gloss, and dark iris. Juvenile Micronesian Starlings on Pohnpei often look entirely dull black in the field, and have brown eyes. Note their thicker bills and association with adults of their species.

Occurrence: Endemic to POHNPEI. An Endangered Species, last reliably reported by J. T. Marshall (in litt.) in 1956. More recent sightings need corroboration. Recent surveys by the authors (1976, 1978) and USFWS personnel (1984) failed to find it. Possibly extinct.

SAMOAN STARLING   *Aplonis atrifusca*   PLATE 35

Appearance: (10;25) A large, long-billed, sooty brown bird. Head and breast darker, with purple and green gloss. Looks all black in the field. Iris brown.

Habits: Found both in forests and around villages and plantations. Often in small flocks. Can be an agricultural pest.

Voice: No well-organized song, but a variety of hoots, whistles, rasp notes, and squeaks.

Identification: Easily distinguished from Polynesian Starling by large size, dark iris, and (except in Manua Is.) more uniform color. Mao s

perficially similar, but olive posteriorly, with thinner, more decurved bill.
Occurrence: Endemic to SAMOA and common throughout.

KOSRAE MOUNTAIN STARLING *Aplonis corvina*

Appearance: (10;25) A large, long-billed, glossy black bird. Iris red.
Identification: Larger and longer-billed than Micronesian Starling, with red, not yellow, iris.
Occurrence: Endemic to KOSRAE. Discovered and last seen by ornithologists in 1828. The only specimens are in Leningrad. Extinct.

RAROTONGA STARLING *Aplonis cinerascens* PLATE 33

Appearance: (8;20) A plump, brownish gray bird with white undertail coverts.
Habits: A shy and inconspicuous inhabitant of undisturbed montane forests. Forages quietly in the canopy. Solitary or in pairs.
Voice: Variable whistles, some squeaky, others bell-like. Resembles some vocalizations of Common Myna or New Zealand Bellbird.
Identification: Distinguished from similar-sized Common Myna by gray, not brown, body plumage and lack of white wing patches.
Occurrence: Endemic to RAROTONGA (Cook Is.), where rare and thinly distributed in remaining original forest in the interior. Probably fewer than 100 individuals remain (*fide* C. J. Ralph).

POLYNESIAN STARLING *Aplonis tabuensis* PLATE 33

Appearance: (7;18) A medium-sized, stubby-billed, mainly gray-brown bird, darker above and lighter below. Crown often dark and contrasting, usually glossed green or violet. Considerable geographic variation. Secondaries variably edged white, producing a white longitudinal streak on folded wing of some forms. Underparts variably streaked with buffy white in most subspecies, but unstreaked and scaly-appearing in dark Manua Is. form. Iris yellow in most places, changing gradually to brown in w. Fiji. Darkest populations in Manua Is. and n. Tonga (Niuafo'ou, Niuatoputapu, Tafahi), lightest ones in Fiji, s. Tonga, and Wallis and Futuna. Niue birds browner than others, slightly rufous above. Plate 33 shows a range of variation.
Habits: On most islands bold and conspicuous. Found at all elevations, often near towns and villages in coconut and breadfruit trees. In Samoa, where Samoan Starling also present, shyer and more often seen in montane forests.
Voice: A dry rattling call, *tzeeip-breee*, with a buzzy quality, and a single

tchizp. Also a harsh rasp, and a complex whisper song that includes mimicry.

Occurrence: Widely distributed from the Santa Cruz Is. E throughout FIJI, WALLIS AND FUTUNA, TONGA, SAMOA, and NIUE. Common. Ten subspecies in the area of this guide as follows: *A. t. rotumae,* Rotuma (Fiji); *A. t. fortunae,* Wallis and Futuna; *A. t. brevirostris,* W. Samoa; *A. tabuensis tutuilae,* Tutuila (A. Samoa); *A. t. manuae,* Manua Is. (A. Samoa); *A. t. vitiensis,* most of Fiji; *A. t. tabuensis,* extreme se. Fiji and most of Tonga; *A. t. nesiotes,* Niuafo'ou (Tonga); *A. tabuensis tenebrosus,* Niuatoputapu and Tafahi (Tonga); and *A. t. brunnescens,* Niue.

Other name: Striped Starling.

MICRONESIAN STARLING   *Aplonis opaca*   PLATES 23, 25

Appearance: (9;23) Adult a chunky, short-tailed, glossy black bird with heavy, slightly curved bill. Iris yellow. Immatures duller, brownish above with pale streaking underneath, the amount of which varies geographically and with feather wear. Iris brown at first, gradually changing to yellow.

Habits: Found in most habitats from seacoast to mountaintop on high islands, and also on atolls. Often in flocks. Bold and noisy.

Voice: Highly varied, with loud slurred whistles and gurgling notes. Song an elaboration of call notes with no consistent pattern. Typical note a harsh, rolling *brleeep.*

Identification: Usually the only all-black species present. On Guam and Rota, note that Mariana Crow is much larger with brown iris, Black Drongo slightly larger with long forked tail. See Pohnpei Mountain Starling, Kosrae Mountain Starling.

Occurrence: Abundant throughout c. and w. MICRONESIA from Palau and the Marianas E to Kosrae including many atolls in the c. Carolines. Declining on Guam, where proposed as an Endangered Species.

[**MYSTERIOUS STARLING**   *Aplonis mavornata*   See Appendix A]

EUROPEAN STARLING   *Sturnus vulgaris*   PLATE 4

Appearance: (8;20) A small black bird glossed with purple and green. Tail short, wings pointed. Bill long, pointed, varying seasonally from brown (nonbreeding) to yellow with blue base (breeding). Recently molted birds heavily speckled with white, but the spots wear off eventually so that a worn bird is almost all black. Juveniles dull brown, slightly streaked below with whitish throat, dark bill. Timing of plumage cycle not well known for Pacific island populations.

Habits: Gregarious except when breeding, often in very large flocks.

Noisy and garrulous, frequenting villages and gardens where sometimes a pest. Often feeds on the ground.

Voice: Call a whistled *seeoo*. Song variable and often harsh, with whistles, clicks, gurgles, and rattles. Imitates other birds.

Identification: Distinguished from Polynesian Starling by entirely glossy black or white-speckled plumage, longer, pointed bill.

Occurrence: Native to Eurasia and N. Africa. Introduced almost worldwide including extreme se. FIJI (Vatoa, Ono-i-lau) and TONGATAPU (Tonga). Common. Has been seen twice in the HAWAIIAN IS. (Oahu, Hawaii), origin and status unknown.

Reference: Donaldson, P. 1984. A European Starling on Oahu and its possible origin. *'Elepaio* 45:25-27.

Watling, D. 1982. Fiji's sedentary starlings. *Notornis* 29:227-30.

RED-CHEEKED STARLING   *Sturnus philippensis*

An immature female of this starling was taken once at PALAU. The species breeds in Japan, winters in the Philippines. Female plain pale tan, with black wings and tail and brown back. Male has irregular chestnut patch on side of head and neck, buffy rump, and bold single white wing bars. For illustration, see WBSJ (1982). Other names: Violet-backed Starling, Chestnut-cheeked Starling.

ASHY STARLING   *Sturnus cineraceus*

A one-time vagrant to SAIPAN (Mariana Is.), this species breeds in e. Asia, winters S to the Philippines. It is basically grayish brown with white cheek patch, rump, and tips to outer tail feathers. Head and breast darker, with irregular white streaks. Bill orange, tipped black. Juveniles less streaked, duller. Illustrated in WBSJ (1982) and Flint et al. (1984). Other names: Gray Starling, White-cheeked Starling.

COMMON MYNA   *Acridotheres tristis*   PLATE 41

Appearance: (10;25) A plump brown bird with black head and tail. Belly, undertail coverts, tail tip, and large wing patch white, the latter two conspicuous in flight. Bill, legs, and bare skin around eye yellow.

Habits: Gregarious, often in noisy flocks particularly at roosts. Walks rather than hops. Found in variety of habitats from seacoast to forest edge including open countryside, agricultural areas, residential gardens, and city streets. Often associates with domestic animals. Avoids dense forests.

Voice: A variety of harsh gurgles, whistles, grating sounds, and liquid notes. Occasionally mimics other sounds. Flocks at a roost produce a deafening cacophony.

Identification: Distinguished from Jungle Myna by brown, not gray, body, yellow orbital skin, and lack of crest. Other birds with bold wing patches include Northern Mockingbird, Polynesian Triller.

Occurrence: Native to India. Introduced to the HAWAIIAN IS. (all main islands, Midway), FIJI (Viti Levu, Taveuni), the COOK IS. (Rarotonga, Aitutaki, Manuae, Atiu, Mauke, Mangaia), the SOCIETY IS. (Tahiti, Moorea, Raiatea), and HIVAOA (Marquesas Is.). Abundant everywhere. A single bird seen on Tutuila (A. Samoa) may have been an escape. A breeding population on Kwajalein (Marshall Is.) died out.

Other names: Indian Myna, House Myna.

JUNGLE MYNA   *Acridotheres fuscus*   PLATE 41

Appearance: (9;23) Similar to Common Myna but gray rather than brown, with short bristly crest. Wing dull brown with white patches, tail tipped white. Bill yellow with blue base, iris yellow. No bare skin around eye.

Habits: Like those of Common Myna. The two often flock together. Jungle Myna more likely to be seen in rural areas, but is also found in urban residential areas and parks. Noisy and gregarious.

Voice: Similar to that of Common Myna.

Identification: Distinguished from Common Myna by slightly smaller size, gray, not brown, body, short crest, blue base to bill, and yellow iris not surrounded by bare skin. Despite obvious differences, easily overlooked in a flock of Common Mynas.

Occurrence: Native to India. Introduced to VITI LEVU (Fiji) and UPOLU (W. Samoa). Common in Fiji, increasing on Upolu around Apia. Samoan population first reported incorrectly as Common Myna.

[**HILL MYNA**   *Gracula religiosa*   See Appendix A]

FAMILY MELIPHAGIDAE: Honeyeaters

HONEYEATERS comprise a large family found mainly in the Australian region, including the larger islands of Micronesia, central Polynesia, and Hawaii. As the name implies, most species feed at least partly on nectar. They have a characteristic four-branched, brush-tipped tongue that serves as a "drinking straw." Some species serve as pollinators for the flowers upon which they feed. Most Pacific island honeyeaters have sharp-pointed, slightly downcurved bills. Many are brightly colored in red, yellow, and black. They tend to be highly vocal and often dominate the forest sounds. Their songs have a melancholy, hollow, echoing or bell-like quality, often very pleasing to human ears.

CARDINAL HONEYEATER   *Myzomela cardinalis*   PLATE 32

Appearance: (5;13) Male small, scarlet above and on breast, black on wings, tail, and belly. Female grayish olive with scarlet rump. Juvenile sooty olive with scarlet head (male). Bill thin, black, downcurved.

Habits: Found in flowering trees and shrubs throughout lowland coastal areas such as plantations and forest edge. Takes nectar and insects. Active and acrobatic.

Voice: A short song of slurred whistles and a characteristic twittering call. Dawn song louder, with clear whistled phrases.

Occurrence: Widely distributed in Vanuatu, Santa Cruz Is., Solomon Is., and SAMOA (Savaii, Upolu, Tutuila). Common.

Other name: Cardinal Myzomela.

MICRONESIAN HONEYEATER   *Myzomela rubratra*   PLATE 23

Appearance: (5;13) Similar to Cardinal Honeyeater, but males with red and black parts of plumage intermingled, not clearly demarcated, and red extending further along flanks. Females like dull versions of males, with black replaced by sooty brown, but showing much more variation from island to island. On Kosrae and Truk females are almost identical to males. On Pohnpei, they are more brownish gray, with a touch of red on throat, breast, and rump. Yap females have the same areas brighter red and are more olive-brown elsewhere. Females of Palau and the Mariana Is. are similar to Yap females but have red also on the crown.

Habits: Conspicuous in lowland habitats such as forest edge, roadsides, and plantations. Also in flowering trees of towns. Feeds on nectar and insects.

Voice: A long dawn song with a complex series of chirps and tweets, usually in pairs. Daytime calls very different, with wheezy chirps, buzzy notes, and whistles.

Occurrence: Widespread among high islands of Micronesia including PALAU (*M. r. kobayashii*), YAP (*M. r. kurodai*), the larger MARIANAS (*M. r. saffordi*), TRUK (*M. r. major*), POHNPEI (*M. r. dichromata*), and KOSRAE (*M. r. rubratra*). Common to abundant in most of range, but less so in the Marianas. Has declined rapidly on Guam in the last decade and is now a proposed Endangered Species there.

Note: This complex of subspecies is usually included in the Cardinal Honeyeater species on the basis of old studies of museum skins. We believe the group's morphological and vocal differences along with its geographic isolation argue for separate species status.

ROTUMA HONEYEATER   *Myzomela chermesina*   PLATE 32

Appearance: (5;13) Resembles Cardinal Honeyeater but male mostly black, including top of head, with red patches on throat, breast, back, and rump. Female olive-brown, shading to dull yellow on belly, with red tinge in throat.

Habits: Similar to other members of this genus. A nectar-feeder found in forest edge and plantations. Voice unreported.

Occurrence: Endemic to ROTUMA (Fiji).

Other name: Rotuma Myzomela.

Note: Sometimes considered conspecific with Cardinal Honeyeater.

ORANGE-BREASTED HONEYEATER   PLATE 32
Myzomela jugularis

Appearance: (4;10) A tiny black, red, and yellow bird with thin, down-curved bill. Tail tipped white. Female patterned like male but duller, with no red on crown or rump, black areas suffused with olive.

Habits: Inhabits open country and forest edge, feeds in flowering trees and shrubs. Often seen in village gardens and town parks. Active.

Voice: Song a high, squeaky *tsee-oop-tee-dee*. Flight call *tee-too, tee-too-tee*, etc.

Occurrence: Common throughout FIJI (except Rotuma).

Other name: Orange-breasted Myzomela.

WATTLED HONEYEATER   *Foulehaio carunculata*   PLATE 33

Appearance: (7;18) A medium-sized, dull olive green bird with a naked orange-yellow wattle extending from base of bill along malar region. Darker above, grayish on underparts. Bill black, slightly downcurved. Females smaller and more yellowish. From the Lau Arch. (Fiji) to Samoa and Tonga birds have large wattles, surrounded by large yellow patch. In most of Fiji, wattle small and surrounded by black; breast feathers have a scaly look.

Habits: Found from coastal scrub to montane forest. Often seen in residential areas and parks. Noisy, conspicuous, aggressive, and quarrelsome; may harass even much larger birds. Feeds on nectar, insects, and occasionally lizards.

Voice: A short barking call and a dry chatter. Song difficult to describe, a jumbled series of gurgling whistles: *churwee-churwee-churdle-twee-twur; tweer, twur, tee-wurdle;* or *chee-wurdle-chee-wurdle-chee.*

Occurrence: Endemic to c. Polynesia. Nominate subspecies abundant throughout WALLIS AND FUTUNA, SAMOA, and TONGA. Two similar-looking subspecies inhabit w. FIJI: *F. c. procerior* on Viti Levu and nearby islands; *F. c. taviunensis* on Vanua Levu, Taveuni, and environs.

Other name: Carunculated Honeyeater.

KADAVU HONEYEATER   *Xanthotis provocator*   PLATE 33

Appearance: (7;18) A medium-sized, olive-brown bird with golden yellow patch of bare skin around eye. Forehead, lores, and malar streak black. Lightly streaked above and below.

Habits: Mainly a nectar-feeder, found in a variety of habitats from coastal scrub to mountain forests.

Voice: Mellow whistles; similar to song of Wattled Honeyeater.

Identification: Compare Wattled Honeyeater (recorded once on Kadavu).

Occurrence: Endemic to KADAVU (Fiji). Common.

Other name: Yellow-faced Honeyeater.

GIANT FOREST HONEYEATER   *Gymnomyza viridis*   PLATE 33

Appearance: (10;25) A large olive green bird with long, curved, black (Viti Levu) or yellow (Vanua Levu, Taveuni) bill.

Habits: A shy honeyeater found in the canopy of original rain forests. More often heard than seen, but sometimes perches in the open.

Voice: A loud, conspicuous, ringing yodel that swells in intensity: *keeyow, kee-yow, kee-yow,* etc. Rather like a double-noted version of the call of the Laughing Kookaburra (*Dacelo novaeguineae*), familiar to moviegoers as the Tarzan jungle bird. Has some of the quality of the electronic "whoopee" sirens used on many emergency vehicles. Hard to miss.

Identification: Distinguished from other Fijian honeyeaters by larger size and more uniform color.

Occurrence: Endemic to FIJI (*G. v. brunneirostris* on Viti Levu; *G. v. viridis* on Vanua Levu, Taveuni). Fairly common in appropriate habitat.

Other name: Green Honeyeater.

MAO   *Gymnomyza samoensis*   PLATE 33

Appearance: (12;31) A large bird that looks all dark at a distance. Black of head shades to dull olive posteriorly. Olive streak under eye. Bill long, black, decurved. Female smaller than male.

Habits: A shy inhabitant of mountain forests. Keeps to the subcanopy and forages among moss-covered branches. Occasionally hangs upside down. Wags tail up and down.

Voice: Call a loud mechanical *chlip* or a squeaky short note. Also a catlike series of squeaky wailing cries with low hoarse notes and calls interspersed. Orenstein (see Reference) has likened it to the sound of a catfight.

Identification: Superficially rather similar to the Samoan Starling.

Mao's bill thinner and more decurved. The starling never appears to have a two-toned plumage, but in its characteristic shady habitat, the Mao may look all black.

Occurrence: Endemic to larger islands of SAMOA (Savaii, Upolu, Tutuila). Generally rare, nearly extinct on Tutuila (last seen 1977, *fide* P. L. Bruner). More common at highest elevations.

Reference: Orenstein, R. I. 1979. Notes on the Ma'o (*Gymnomyza samoensis*), a rare Samoan honeyeater. *Notornis* 26:181-84.

Other names: Mao Honeyeater, Black-breasted Honeyeater.

KAUAI OO   *Moho braccatus*   PLATE 36

Appearance: (8;20) Mostly sooty black with prominent white patch at bend of wing, especially evident in flight. Malar region and throat also spotted irregularly with white. Yellow thighs often concealed. Pollen clinging to the forehead can produce a frosty effect. The short, pointed tail frequently cocked up.

Habits: An acrobatic, aggressive bird that dominates all other nectar-feeders. A pair will defend a favored blooming ohia tree against all comers. Nests in tree cavities.

Voice: One of the finest singers of Hawaii's native birds. Calls are haunting, flutelike notes: *oak* or *keek-oh*. Song is variable but always with a hollow or echoing quality. The pitch may rise or fall. One bird may answer another in a duet: *Take-a-looky-now* then *Take-a-look-over-here!* Other variations may remind the birder of the song of the Western Meadowlark, but with fewer slurs: *kay-kittle-keedle-o-coo*, etc.

Identification: Kauai Oo looks like no other bird in the Alakai Swamp. Some calls of the Iiwi might be mistaken for those of this species.

Occurrence: Endemic to KAUAI (Hawaiian Is.). The only oo to survive in numbers into the 20th century. Declined drastically in the 1970s in its last stronghold in the Alakai Swamp. At this writing (1985) only a few individuals known to survive. An Endangered Species.

Other name: 'ō'ō'ā'ā.

OAHU OO   *Moho apicalis*   PLATE 36

The oo that inhabited OAHU (Hawaiian Is.) has not been seen since 1837 and is presumed extinct. It was of the same size and general shape as Bishop's Oo and Hawaii Oo, with a long, graduated tail. The tail feathers were tipped white except for the long, narrow, tapering upturned central pair. Flank feathers were yellow, and probably puffed out to form a conspicuous tuft on each side. A white patch under the wing would probably be conspicuous in flight. Nothing is known of this bird's habits. Beginning birders sometimes report oos o

Oahu, but the birds always turn out to be some mostly black exotic such as bulbuls, shamas, or even mynas.

BISHOP'S OO   *Moho bishopi*   PLATE 36

Appearance: (12;31) A large bird with long bill and tail, mostly brownish black with narrow, pale streaks along feather shafts. Undertail coverts yellow, as are wispy plumes on sides of head and under wings.

Habits: A nectar-feeder that keeps to the upper canopy of dense rain forest.

Voice: A loud, echoing *oh-oh* with a flutelike quality.

Identification: Immature Akohekohe similar to an oo in being a nearly all black, nectar-feeding bird with a thin, downcurved bill, but without yellow plumes and smaller, with much shorter fan-shaped tail.

Occurrence: On the HAWAIIAN IS. of Molokai (last seen 1904) and Maui where it was rediscovered (1981) after a lapse of about 80 years, to the amazement of the birding world. Very rare in the dense rain forests of the NE slope of Haleakala.

Reference: Sabo, S.R. 1982. The rediscovery of Bishop's O'o' [sic] on Maui. *'Elepaio* 42:69-70. (Correct Hawaiian spelling is *'o'o*.)

HAWAII OO   *Moho nobilis*   PLATE 36

Appearance: (12;31) Glossy black, with long, graduated tail and yellow axillary plumes conspicuous in flight. Undertail coverts yellow, shorter outer tail feathers white. Central tail feathers twisted and extending beyond other rectrices. Immature entirely black.

Habits: A nectar-feeder of the forest canopy. Flight undulating. Jerks tail up and down when perched.

Voice: A loud, harsh *oh-oh*.

Identification: Other mostly black birds known from Hawaii include the much larger Hawaiian Crow and smaller Hawaii Mamo. The latter shows more extensive yellow on underparts, has shorter tail and much longer, sickle-shaped bill. Neither of these species would cause much confusion.

Occurrence: Endemic to HAWAII (Hawaiian Is.). Possibly extinct, but rumors of its existence persist. In light of recent rediscovery of Bishop's Oo, birders should be alert to the possibility that this species may also survive in some remote area in very low numbers. Recent thorough USFWS surveys failed to find it.

KIOEA   *Chaetoptila angustipluma*   PLATE 36

This very large (13;33) honeyeater was found in historic times only on the island of HAWAII, but fossil remains of it have been found on other islands. It has not been reported since the 1860s and is presumed extinct. It was apparently a canopy nectar-feeder with a loud melodious voice, but little else is known about it. It was heavily streaked with olive and white, had a prominent black ear patch, and a long, tapering tail.

FAMILY ZOSTEROPIDAE: White-eyes

THE white-eyes are a relatively uniform family of small passerines. Their name derives from the ring of white feathers that surrounds the eye in most species. The typical white-eyes (*Zosterops*) are mostly green and yellow, move about in noisy, active flocks, and have simple, high-pitched calls. A few species are good singers. White-eyes feed on insects and nectar among foliage and flowers. Several atypical members of this family are found in Micronesia. They may lack the white eye-ring and may be much larger than typical white-eyes.

The taxonomy we use here is based mainly on our own field studies. We believe traditional classifications have been based more on political boundaries than on biological considerations. Our classifications, where they differ from those given in other recent works, are discussed under the species accounts.

JAPANESE WHITE-EYE *Zosterops japonicus* PLATE 42

Appearance: (4;10) Green above with a yellow throat and white belly. Eye-ring very prominent.

Habits: In Hawaii found in virtually every available habitat, usually in small flocks. Very active, moving quickly through the foliage. Often feeds in flowers.

Voice: Call notes include a high-pitched *teee* and a nervous twitter. The song is high-pitched and squeaky but complex, resembling in pattern the song of the House Finch. Often includes mimicry of other species.

Identification: White-eyes are a source of much frustration for first time birders in Hawaii. They resemble, in size, color, and behavior many small green native honeycreepers (see Table 4). White-eyes are usually more active than the native birds, and are much more easily "squeaked up." Hawaiian honeycreepers only rarely respond to squeaking. The white eye-ring is diagnostic, but can be difficult to see on an actively feeding bird.

Occurrence: Native to e. Asia. Introduced to the HAWAIIAN IS (Oahu) about 1930, whence it spread throughout the main islands, and has even been seen far at sea and on JOHNSTON ATOLL. Probably the most abundant bird in Hawaii today.

BRIDLED WHITE-EYE   *Zosterops conspicillatus*   PLATE 23

Appearance: (4;10) A typical *Zosterops*. The three subspecies are well marked: *Z. c. conspicillatus* (Guam) largest of the three with gray crown and very prominent "spectacles"; *Z. c. saypani* (Saipan, Tinian) smaller, greener, with less prominent loral streak; *Z. c. rotensis* (Rota) with plumage suffused with yellow throughout, bill, legs, and feet yellow-orange.

Habits: Found in shrubby forests, including native *Pandanus* woods and limestone forest as well as thickets of introduced tangan-tangan. When common, forms large noisy flocks.

Voice: Varies from island to island. All subspecies utter rolling chirps, distinguishable among themselves but all similar to and higher pitched than call of Eurasian Tree Sparrow. On Guam the chirp is a buzzy *cheep* or *tszeeip*, the song a lilting series of buzzy notes, *zeeip-zee-zee-zoo-zip*. The Saipan-Tinian birds' notes are all higher pitched and less buzzy, the chirps often rapidly uttered and organized into a loose song. Sometimes mimics other species. The population on Rota gives a harsh, rolling, low-pitched *tsheip*, a buzzy *zee-zee-zeee-e-e*, and a less buzzy *see-tseep*.

Occurrence: Endemic to the larger MARIANA IS. Abundant on Saipan, Tinian and Agiguan; apparently declining on Rota with patchy distribution on central plateau; an Endangered Species nearing extinction on Guam where a few individuals may still exist in forests near Ritidian Point. The reasons for the recent sudden decline on Guam are not known.

Notes: In all other recent sources on Micronesian birds, this species includes all the "typical" *Zosterops* in the region. Our field studies reveal that the complex is far more diverse than previous museum-based investigations could have determined. The forms in the Mariana Islands and on Yap (*hypolais*) all have relatively complex songs as well as simpler flock calls. We believe they are most likely derived from continental forms to the north, which also sing. The Caroline Islands forms (*semperi* of Palau, *owstoni* of Truk, *takatsukasai* of Pohnpei) are less "bridled," are bright yellow below, and lack complex songs. We think they are more likely to be related to a Melanesian ancestor than to the Bridled White-eye complex of the Marianas and Yap. If, as we hypothesize, the two groups resulted from colonizations of Micronesian islands from two directions, they cannot be conspecific. The differences described above for the subspecies inhabiting the Marianas are as great as among many sympatric species of *Zosterops* elsewhere (e.g. *Z. lateralis* and *Z. explorator* in Fiji). The Rota form superficially resembles the Caroline Islands birds because of much yellow in the plumage and soft parts, but behaviorally is more like other Mariana Islands white-eyes. At present, we regard all three Mariana forms as conspecific under the name Bridled White-eye. The peculiarities of the Yap bird, both morphologically and behaviorally, are so great that we regard it as a monotypic species. The three Caroline Islands forms differ only slightly among themselves morphologically and thus may be considered a single polytypic species pending further field studies.

PLAIN WHITE-EYE *Zosterops hypolais* PLATE 24

Appearance: (4;10) Very nondescript, plain greenish gray above, white below, tinged yellow. Eye-ring very thin, iris white. (One of the few *Zosterops* that really has a white eye.) Crown feathers often ruffled to produce a big-headed profile.

Habits: Slower and more deliberate in feeding than other *Zosterops*. Found in a wide variety of habitats from forest canopy to grassy fields. Often in small flocks, but not so noisy or conspicuous as more typical *Zosterops*.

Voice: Thin, trilled *chee* notes, a buzzy *zee-up*, and a song of short, chirpy phrases: *chee-twee-chulip-*, etc.

Identification: The smallest and plainest bird on Yap. Olive White-eye much larger, darker, and with more prominent eye-ring.

Occurrence: Endemic to YAP, widespread and common.

Note: Previous references include this form in the Bridled White-eye (which see).

CAROLINE ISLANDS WHITE-EYE PLATES 24, 25
Zosterops semperi

Appearance: (4;10) A typical *Zosterops*, dark green above, yellow below, with very prominent eye-ring.

Habits: Typical *Zosterops* behavior. Feeds in foliage of small trees. Usually in flocks, sometimes with Dusky or Gray White-eyes, in a variety of forest and scrub habitats.

Voice: Only a squeaky, high-pitched contact call. Apparently lacks song.

Identification: Much yellower than Dusky White-eye, which lacks white eye-ring, but similar in behavior. Gray White-eye much duller throughout, eye-ring very narrow; only occasionally joins flocks.

Occurrence: Widespread and common at PALAU (*Z. s. semperi* on all main islands except Angaur), TRUK (*Z. s. owstoni*), and POHNPEI (*Z. s. takatsukasai*).

Note: Usually included as subspecies of Bridled White-eye, but possibly more closely related to a Melanesian species. See Bridled White-eye.

SAMOAN WHITE-EYE *Zosterops samoensis* PLATE 32

Appearance and Identification: (4;10) Green above, dingy white below, tinged yellow in throat. Eye-ring complete, prominent. Iris pale. The only white-eye in Samoa.

Habits and Voice: Highly gregarious and apparently noisy, but voice never described. Feeds in low bushes of alpine zone.

Occurrence: Endemic to SAVAII (W. Samoa), where restricted to mountaintops above 900 m. Rare.

Other name: Savaii White-eye.

LAYARD'S WHITE-EYE   *Zosterops explorator*   PLATE 32

Appearance: (4;10) A typical *Zosterops*, olive green above with bright yellow throat and breast. White eye-ring complete.

Habits: Gleans foliage of small trees and shrubs. Found in many habitats, sometimes in mixed flocks with Silvereyes. Layard's tends to be more common in heavily forested areas, but overlaps broadly with the other species.

Voice: Call a reedy, high-pitched *seeu-seeu* or *pleeu* and a squeaky *seee*. Song a rambling series of the same notes. Also a short *zick*.

Identification: Very similar to Silvereye. At a glance, Layard's is much yellower overall, but without the yellow-hooded look of Silvereye, and is chunkier and shorter-tailed. At close range, note Layard's complete eye-ring (Silvereye's is broken in front of the eye). Behaviorally, the two are virtually identical.

Occurrence: Endemic to FIJI (Viti Levu, Vanua Levu, Taveuni, Kadavu, Ovalau). Common.

SILVEREYE   *Zosterops lateralis*   PLATE 32

Appearance: (4;10) A typical *Zosterops*. Appears yellow-headed because the yellow of the throat ends abruptly at the breast and the back is gray. Society Is. birds tinged cinnamon on the flanks and with less yellow in the throat.

Habits: A foliage and flower gleaner, often in flocks. Varied habitats.

Voice: Call very similar to that of Layard's White-eye, a high, thin *seer*. Also a dry *rick*. Song a loosely organized series of whistles.

Identification: See Layard's White-eye.

Occurrence: Ranges from w. Australia to New Zealand and FIJI (throughout except Lau Arch.). Introduced (1939) from New Zealand to the SOCIETY IS. (Tahiti, Moorea, Raiatea, Bora Bora) and more recently to the TUBUAI IS. (Raivavae, Tubuai, Rurutu). Common to abundant.

Other names: Gray-backed White-eye, Gray-breasted White-eye.

DUSKY WHITE-EYE   *Zosterops finschii*   PLATE 24

Appearance and Identification: (4;10) A dull gray, nondescript bird, smaller and duller than any other Palau species. One of the few *Zosterops* to lack a contrasting eye-ring altogether.

Habits: Highly gregarious. Moves about in small to large flocks in virtually every habitat. Sometimes feeds in the same trees as Caroline Islands White-eyes.

Voice: Flocks are very noisy, the contact call being a frequently uttered nasal *cheee*, louder and lower pitched than similar calls of Caroline Islands White-eye. In flight and sometimes perched, the birds give a rollicking *CHEE-che-che-CHE* that will remind N. Americans of the flight calls of the American Goldfinch.

Occurrence: Endemic to PALAU, and abundant on all main islands except Angaur. More common than Caroline Islands White-eye.

Note: In other sources includes Gray White-eye.

GRAY WHITE-EYE   *Zosterops cinereus*   PLATE 25

Appearance: (4;10) A tiny gray bird with a very narrow white eye-ring. Pohnpei birds have a tinge of olive-brown on the flanks.

Habits: Often solitary, but small family groups may accompany flocks of Caroline Islands White-eyes. Widespread in many different habitats; actively gleans leaves and branches.

Voice: A hissing chatter *feet-chr-chr* or *scheee-scheee*.

Identification: Distinguished by small size and all-gray plumage, lacking yellow. See Long-billed White-eye.

Occurrence: Endemic to and common on POHNPEI (*Z. c. ponapensis*) and KOSRAE (*Z. c. cinereus*).

Note: Other recent authors combine this form with the Dusky White-eye. The very different foraging behavior and vocalizations of this form, as well as its much smaller bill, argue against combining it with the distantly separated Palau species. The two forms may represent separate species, but have not yet been adequately studied to determine their status with certainty.

GOLDEN WHITE-EYE   *Cleptornis marchei*   PLATE 23

Appearance: (5½;14) A bright golden yellow bird with orange bill and feet. Immature paler, with dusky bill.

Habits: Travels about in small flocks in almost every type of habitat, including urban areas. Feeds on insects picked from bark and leaves of trees. Curious and bold.

Voice: Flock calls include a harsh, raspy *tchup* or *schick* and a quick, loud whistle. Song is an extended rambling warble: *SEE ME-can you SEE ME-I can SEE YOU-can you SEE ME*, etc.

Identification: Resembles no other bird where it occurs, but song could be confused with that of the Nightingale Reed-Warbler.

Occurrence: Endemic to the MARIANA IS. (Saipan and Agiguan). Common to abundant at least on Saipan.

Note: Until now, this species has been classified as an aberrant honey-eater (Meliphagidae). Pratt's hypothesis, based on behavioral, eco-logical, and zoogeographical considerations, that the "Golden Honey-eater" is really a white-eye (Zosteropidae) has, as we go to press, been confirmed by biochemical studies in the laboratory of C. G. Sibley (in litt.) at the Yale Peabody Museum. The details of Pratt's and Sibley's research will be published in due course. Among the white-eyes, *Cleptornis* appears closest to *Rukia*.

GREAT TRUK WHITE-EYE   *Rukia ruki*   PLATE 25

Appearance and Identification: (5½;14) Uniformly dark brown with orange legs and a white "teardrop" below the eye. No other Truk pas-serine resembles it.
Habits: Keeps to the outer canopy of dense native montane forest. Feeds by probing among tangles of vines and leaves.
Voice: A loudly whistled, lilting warble.
Occurrence: Endemic to TRUK. Locally common at summit of Tol I., rare on Polle, Onei, and Pata. Endangered Species.
Other names: Large Truk White-eye, Truk Greater White-eye, Truk White-eye.

OLIVE WHITE-EYE   *Rukia oleaginea*   PLATE 24

Appearance: (5;13) A dark olive green bird with yellow-orange legs and bill, and very prominent white eye-ring.
Habits: Solitary or in small groups. A foliage gleaner usually seen in the tops of small to medium-sized trees. Often hangs head downward to pick at the undersides of branches. Not confined to native vegetation.
Voice: Call a shrill, harsh *cheee*. The song comprises loudly whistled, monotonously repeated phrases, *Tickle me, Peter* or *Fickle-EE-feedle-DEE*.
Identification: See Plain White-eye. More similar behaviorally and in plumage color to female and immature Micronesian Honeyeater, but note straight yellow bill.
Occurrence: Endemic to YAP. Fairly common and widespread.
Other names: Yap Greater White-eye, Large Yap White-eye.

LONG-BILLED WHITE-EYE   *Rukia longirostra*   PLATE 25

Appearance: (6;15) A drab olive-brown white-eye with reduced eye-ring, conspicuous flesh-colored legs, and long, decurved bill.
Habits: Usually in small flocks that dash rapidly and wildly through for-est understory. Feeds quietly in the canopy, often in the company of Gray White-eyes.
Voice: Contact call a loud series of clear downslurred whistles: *peer-peer-*

peer, less nasal than calls of other white-eyes. Song comprises an introductory downslurred whistle followed by a short warble and a burry chatter: *peer-cheturdle-tr-r-r-r-r-r* (J. T. Marshall, J. Engbring; unpubl. notes).

Identification: Larger and more olive than Gray White-eye, less yellow than, and without prominent eye-ring of, Caroline Islands White-eye. Note particularly the long bill. Caroline Islands Reed-Warbler superficially similar, and also feeds sometimes in forest canopy, but note its pale eyebrow, white-tipped tail, and darker legs.

Occurrence: Endemic to POHNPEI, where widespread but uncommon and easily overlooked. An Endangered Species.

Other names: Ponape Greater White-eye, Large Ponape White-eye.

GIANT WHITE-EYE   *Megazosterops palauensis*   PLATE 24

Appearance: (5½;14) Generalizations about white-eyes should be ignored in the case of this species. Olive-green above, olive-yellow below, with a yellow eyebrow and obscurely *streaked* auriculars. Base of bill and mouth lining orange-yellow. Bill heavy but not finchlike. Legs dark.

Habits: Found in both canopy and understory in native forests and *Leucaena* thickets. Often solitary, but also in small flocks. Noisy, curious, and conspicuous, these birds gather about an observer and create a loud, scolding commotion. When scolding, the bird holds the bill open constantly, revealing the bright mouth lining.

Voice: Calls include a rasping *scheee* and a dry rattle. Song totally unlike that of any other Micronesian bird. A solo performance sounds like a chorus. Has a mechanical quality with abrupt starts and stops, as if the bird is being turned on and off by a switch. Underlying the louder parts of the song is a rhythmic rattling or clicking sound. Simultaneously the bird utters a vaguely canary-like series of short whistles, trills, and descending, sirenlike slurs. One of the most bizarre bird songs known to the authors.

Identification: Very similar in color pattern to Palau Bush-Warbler, but postures and behavior very different. The bush-warbler is solitary, secretive, and difficult to see; the Giant White-eye is hard to miss. The warbler is slimmer with a much thinner bill, a pronounced dark streak through the eye, unstreaked auriculars, and orange-yellow legs.

Occurrence: Endemic to PALAU, where unevenly distributed. Abundant on Peleliu, common on Urukthapel, and recorded once on Babelthuap, but curiously absent from Koror, Eil Malk, and other seemingly suitable islands.

Other names: Palau Greater White-eye, Palau White-eye, Large Palau White-eye.

Note: For comments on the taxonomy of this species, see Pratt et al. (1979).

FAMILY EMBERIZIDAE: Emberizine Finches and Their Relatives

This large family as currently constituted includes such a variety of superficially different kinds of birds that no single collective name can be applied to it. Research has shown that the several groups of thick-billed seedeating birds called finches are not necessarily closely related to each other. They have evolved their seedeating adaptations from several different ancestral stocks, and are now distributed among several families. Some of them (e.g. cardinals, most grosbeaks, buntings, New World sparrows) are grouped here with several diverse New World groups (wood warblers, tanagers, blackbirds, orioles, meadowlarks, etc.) believed to be related to them. Only a few of these are represented in the tropical Pacific, mostly as introduced populations. A few have been recorded as migratory stragglers.

CRIMSON-BACKED TANAGER   Plate 40
Ramphocelus dimidiatus
Appearance: (6;15) A medium-sized, dark velvety red and black bird with prominent silver lower mandible. Female duller brownish red, with bright red rump and undertail coverts.
Habits: A resident of lowland gardens and forest edge. Usually seen in pairs.
Voice: A short clear whistle.
Occurrence: Native to Panama and nw. S. America. Introduced prior to 1940 to TAHITI (Society Is.) and established uncommonly in w. coastal areas.

NORTHERN CARDINAL   *Cardinalis cardinalis*   Plate 40
Appearance: (9;23) A thick-billed, crested finch. Male red with black mask around base of bill, female buffy tan with red in wing, tail, and crest. Bill orange-red in both sexes. Juvenile like female but bill dull brown.
Habits: A seedeating bird of thickets, suburban lawns, and forests. One of the few introduced birds in Hawaii to have penetrated deeply into native forests, but more common in disturbed habitats. Bold and curious, usually seen near the ground.

Voice: Call a distinctive metallic *speet*. Songs loud, whistled melodies and trills: a slow trill followed by several slower, downslurred notes, *weet-weet-weet-weet-weet-tew-tew-tew*; a loud *sweet-teeoo-wheet-wheet-wheet*; and a long trill of liquid notes, dropping in pitch at the end.

Identification: Red-crested Cardinal red only on head and breast, bill blue-gray. Yellow-billed Cardinal smaller, black-backed, without crest. Smaller native red birds (Apapane, Iiwi, Akepa) are mostly canopy-feeders whereas cardinal found in understory.

Occurrence: Native to N. America. Introduced (1929) and established on all main HAWAIIAN IS. from sea level to tree line. Common. Vagrant to Nihoa. Reports of Northern Cardinals in Tahiti probably erroneous.

RED-CRESTED CARDINAL   *Paroaria coronata*   PLATE 40

Appearance: (7½;19) A thick-billed, crested finch with bold pattern of red head and breast, blue-gray back, white underparts, and blue-gray bill. Sexes similar. Juveniles have darker bills, shorter crests, and red replaced by yellow-brown.

Habits: Found in dry thickets, suburban lawns, and city parks. Rarely enters native forests. A seedeater often seen on the ground, but equally at home in shrubs and trees.

Voice: Call a buzzy *chink*. Song a loudly whistled melody with evenly spaced lilting slurs and warbles: *wheet-cheer-up, sweet-chew*, or *tweer, cheerio, tweet, tew*. A greeting pair may utter an excited jumble of liquid whistles, chirps, and slurs.

Identification: See Northern Cardinal and Yellow-billed Cardinal.

Occurrence: Native to S. America. Introduced to the HAWAIIAN IS. in 1929. Now common and widespread on Oahu, less common and localized on Kauai, Lanai, Molokai, and Maui (Lahaina area). Reports from Hawaii have not been confirmed.

Other name: Brazilian Cardinal.

YELLOW-BILLED CARDINAL   *Paroaria capitata*   PLATE 40

Appearance: (7;18) A boldly patterned finch, glossy blue-black above, white below with red head and black throat. Bill and legs yellow-orange. No crest. Juvenile gray-brown above, with orange-brown head and dusky bill.

Habits: Inhabits dry kiawe thickets often near coastal fish ponds. Forages at all levels in the woods, most often in the underbrush.

Voice: Call note a soft *ent*. Song a series of lilting whistles uttered in pairs: *sweet-seet, sweet-seet, sweet-tew, sweet-tew*, etc. Like song of Red-crested Cardinal but weaker.

Identification: Distinguished from Red-crested Cardinal by lack of crest, darker back, and black throat. At present the two species are not found together.

Occurrence: Native to S. America. Introduced on HAWAII about 1930 and established in dry scrub along the Kona Coast from Kawaihae Bay to Honaunau. Most common at Honokohau.

Reference: Collins, M. S. 1975. South American cardinal populations on the Big Island. *'Elepaio* 37:1-2.

YELLOW-FACED GRASSQUIT *Tiaris olivacea* PLATE 42

Appearance: (4;10) A small dark finch, olive green above, gray below, with yellow throat and eyebrow. Male black on head and breast. Female duller, without black, yellow markings less prominent.

Habits: Usually found in grassy areas at forest edge. Prefers wetter habitats than most other small finches in Hawaii.

Voice: Call a thin *tzip*. Song a buzzy, insectlike trill.

Identification: Yellow-fronted Canary has vaguely similar face pattern but is bright yellow below.

Occurrence: Native to C. America. Introduced about 1974 to OAHU (Hawaiian Is.) and established in low numbers in highlands of central Koolau Mts.

SAFFRON FINCH *Sicalis flaveola* PLATE 42

Appearance: (7;18) Male bright golden yellow with orange crown and lightly streaked back. Female duller, with more streaks and yellow only on breast, upperparts, and undertail coverts. Immatures olive with yellow tinge to upper breast.

Habits: A seedeater usually seen on or near the ground. Forages on grassy lawns and golf courses as well as weedy roadsides. May roam in large flocks.

Voice: Call a loud metallic *teek*. Song a musical series of chips and short whistles: *chip-brrr-chipchip-brree-chip*.

Identification: Avoid making a Saffron Finch into one of the supposedly extinct native koa-finches, which had darker bills, no streaks, and olive green body plumage. Palila has black face, gray back, no streaks. Yellow-fronted Canary smaller, more lemon yellow, with pronounced face pattern.

Occurrence: Native to S. America. Introduced (1960s) to the HAWAIIAN IS. and established on Hawaii (common in Kona and Kohala) and possibly Oahu (apparently established in Kapiolani Park for at least 15 years, but now may be dying out).

SAVANNAH SPARROW   *Passerculus sandwichensis*

A small (5½;14), heavily streaked sparrow with a pale yellow superciliary, prominent dark malar streak, and pink legs. Breeds throughout N. America, northern populations migratory. Has straggled once to KURE (NW Hawaiian Is.). Illustrated in N. American field guides.

BLACK-HEADED BUNTING   *Emberiza melanocephala*

A medium-sized (7;18) finch with yellow underparts, chestnut back, and black top and sides of head. Breeds from s. Europe to Iran. Straggler to SE. Asia and once to PALAU. Illustrated in WBSJ (1982).

SNOW BUNTING   *Plectrophenax nivalis*

A medium-sized (7;18), mostly white finch. Upperparts marked and scaled with black and tinged with rusty. Wing tips and tail black, with white in outer rectrices. Breeds around the Arctic and winters S to temperate regions. Straggler to KURE (NW Hawaiian Is.). Illustrated in Eurasian and N. American field guides.

WESTERN MEADOWLARK   *Sturnella neglecta*   PLATE 42

Appearance: (9½;24) A chunky, long-billed bird, streaked brown above, yellow below with bold black V on upper breast. White outer tail feathers show prominently in flight.

Habits: Found in fallow fields, pastures, golf courses, and other open areas. Often sits on fences, power lines, or other exposed perches.

Voice: Call a low, throaty *chuck*; flight call a rattle. Song a flutelike gurgling melody, *urg-leedle-eedle-oh*, or variants thereof.

Identification: Note the long, sharply pointed bill and short tail. Yellow breast diagnostic but often hard to see. Bold white sides of tail distinguish meadowlarks from Japanese Quail and Lesser Golden-Plover, which might flush from the ground in the same habitat.

Occurrence: Native to N. America. Introduced (1931) to KAUAI (Hawaiian Is.), now common in lowland fields throughout the island.

[**GREAT-TAILED GRACKLE**   *Quiscalus mexicanus*   See Appendix A]

FAMILY FRINGILLIDAE: CARDUELINE FINCHES AND HAWAIIAN HONEYCREEPERS

THIS family comprises two groups of finches and their derivatives, a group of species endemic to the Hawaiian Islands. Only one of the finch groups is represented in the tropical Pacific—by a single migratory straggler and several introduced species. The Hawaiian honeycreepers and finches, however, are probably the most interesting native birds in the region from an evolutionary standpoint.

CARDUELINE FINCHES: Subfamily Carduelinae

CARDUELINE finches differ from other finch groups in internal anatomy, in having nine instead of ten primaries, and in details of reproductive biology. Many are fine singers with brightly colored plumage and thus are popular as cage birds. Several such cage birds have been released and have become established in the Hawaiian Islands.
Reference: Newton, I. 1973. *Finches.* New York: Taplinger Publ. Co.

HOUSE FINCH   *Carpodacus mexicanus*   PLATE 42

Appearance: (6;15) A streaked, sparrowlike finch. Male's eyebrow, forehead, throat, and breast vary from bright red to orange to dull yellow. Hawaiian birds more variable than those on mainland. Female streaked all over, male streaked below only.

Habits: Highly adaptable, nesting in city high-rises as well as forests. Most common in relatively open groves of trees. Seen singly or in flocks. Particularly fond of seed cones of ironwood trees.

Voice: Calls vary from simple chirps to upslurred whistles. Song long, complex, canary-like. Characteristically ends with one or two upslurred buzzy notes.

Identification: Note short finch bill, streaks on underparts. These eliminate House Sparrow and all native finchlike birds. Avoid letting wishful thinking make a Palila out of a yellow-headed House Finch (which are abundant in Palila habitat). Skylark also streaked below, but note white tail sides and distinctive behavior.

Occurrence: Native to N. America. Introduced (19th century) to the HAWAIIAN IS. and now abundant on all main islands. Vagrant to Nihoa.

References: Hirai, L. T. 1975. The nesting biology of the House Finch in Honolulu, Hawaii. *Western Birds* 6:33-44.
van Riper III, C. 1976. Aspects of House Finch breeding biology. *Condor* 78:224-29.

COMMON REDPOLL   *Carduelis flammea*

A small (5;13) brownish finch with crimson cap and black throat. Streaked with brown above and on flanks. Breast tinged pink. Breeds in the Arctic, and winters S to temperate regions. Rare fall vagrant to the NW HAWAIIAN IS. (Kure, Midway). Illustrated in Eurasian and N. American field guides.

YELLOW-FRONTED CANARY   *Serinus mozambicus*   PLATE 42

Appearance: (4½;11) A tiny finch with bright lemon yellow breast, rump, throat, forehead, and eyebrow. Dark auriculars, lores, and malar streak produce characteristic facial expression. Back dark olive green, crown and nape gray.

Habits: Forages in foliage of small trees, or sometimes on grassy lawns. Found in city parks or open, parklike dry forests. May wander occasionally into denser forests. Flocks roam widely during the nonbreeding season.

Voice: A sweet, lilting song similar to that of Common Canary, but less powerful and with a piercing or ringing quality. Call a low *chiv-chiv*.

Identification: Smaller and much brighter yellow than any variant of House Finch. Saffron Finch larger, lacks dark facial streaks.

Occurrence: Native to Africa. Introduced about 1964 to the HAWAIIAN IS. and established on Oahu (Kapiolani Park area) and Hawaii (most common near Puu Waa Waa but flocks could turn up anywhere on the island).

Reference: Paton, P.W.C. 1981. Yellow-fronted Canary extends range into 'ohi'a forest on the Big Island. *'Elepaio* 42:11-12.

Other names: Green Singing Finch, Yellow-eyed Canary.

[**GRAY CANARY**   *Serinus leucopygius*   See Appendix A]

COMMON CANARY   *Serinus canaria*   PLATE 42

Appearance: (6;15) Uniformly pale yellow with nearly white wings and tail, pink bill. Pacific island birds are descendants of domestic stock and lack the dark sparrowlike streaks of the wild parent population. Some individuals have small patches of darker plumage.

Habits: Found primarily in groves of ironwood trees, but may also be seen on the ground. Feeds mostly on seeds.

Voice: The song of this familiar cage bird is the one to which other bird songs are most often compared. The term "canary-like" means a long complex song comprising whistles and trills.

Occurrence: Native to the Canary Is. Cage birds were first released in 1911 on MIDWAY (NW Hawaiian Is.) and have become fairly common. Releases on Kure failed to become established.

HAWAIIAN HONEYCREEPERS AND FINCHES:
Subfamily Drepanidinae

THIS subfamily, now known to be derived from the same source as the cardueline finches, is endemic to the Hawaiian Islands. It is the only group of such high taxonomic rank to be confined to the tropical Pacific. Long ago, a finchlike bird colonized the Hawaiian chain and, finding few other birds present, was able to take advantage, through its descendants, of various ecological opportunities. As new islands were colonized, new species were formed that could then reinvade the parent island. Since each new species had to adapt to a slightly different niche in order to coexist with an older species, an array of varying forms developed that eventually almost covered the spectrum of passerine bird adaptations. When first discovered by ornithologists, they were thought to belong to several families. The drepanidines are thus the finest example known of the process called adaptive radiation, wherein a varied array of species evolves from a single ancestor. Hawaii, because it is an isolated chain of large islands, provided the perfect natural laboratory for such an evolutionary experiment.

Unfortunately, we may never know the full extent of adaptive radiation among Hawaiian birds. From their earliest contact with man, the honeycreepers and other native birds have fought a losing battle. When the ancient Polynesian colonists destroyed most of the lowland forests, many bird species perished; we know them only as fossils. Many more species succumbed to changes wrought by the coming of European man. The most significant event of that contact was the introduction of mosquitoes in the 1820s. This unfortunate event allowed avian blood diseases to be transferred to endemic species that had never before had to deal with them. Many could not cope. Today, the survivors of this catastrophe are found mainly above 600 m elevation, where mosquitoes are less numerous. Many species, for whom these high refuges are only marginal habitat, cling to a very precarious existence. Over half of the surviving species are considered Endangered. Their limited ranges are still deteriorating because of the ongoing destruction of upland native forests, primarily by logging and cattle grazing.

The taxonomy we use here is new, based on recent extensive research by the senior author. Pratt's (1979) taxonomy at the generic level was followed by A. J. Berger in the second edition (1981) of *Hawaiian Birdlife* and subsequently by the 1983 AOU Check-list. Berger did not adopt all of Pratt's findings at the species level, however, and the AOU followed Berger. Thus the species limits given here differ in a few cases from those of the AOU.

The Hawaiian honeycreepers include three fairly well defined groupings plus an assortment of unique species. One group includes finches not very different from the thick-billed seedeaters of other taxonomic groups. The Hawaiian finches are medium to large passerines, usually with brightly colored heads (red or yellow). They are accomplished singers with pleasing, canary-like songs.

A second group comprises an array of nectar-feeders that are strongly associated with the red-flowering ohia-lehua tree (Plate 44), as well as other native and exotic flowering trees. This group is also vocally adept, but their songs are unlike those of the Hawaiian finches, and instead are complex concerts of reedy, squeaky, raspy, or whistled notes. Many of them resemble songs of the unrelated honeyeaters (Meliphagidae). Members of this group are clad in red, black, and white.

A third group includes an array of species, some of which may not be closely related to the others, but all of which can be characterized as "little green birds" (see Table 4). Many are so superficially similar that they present very difficult problems of field identification. This latter group includes mostly thin-billed species that feed on both nectar and insects. Several are bark-pickers, and most feed at least occasionally in flowers of ohia.

LAYSAN FINCH   *Telespyza cantans*   PLATE 37

Appearance: (7½;19) A large, yellow-headed, gray-backed finch with a heavy, hooked bill. Females somewhat streaked, especially on the back.

Habits: An omnivore, the Laysan Finch is said to have escaped extinction by feeding on seabird eggs when rabbits destroyed all vegetation on Laysan. Nests in grass tussocks.

Voice: A complex, canary-like warbling song. Calls are rather like those of House Finches or House Sparrows.

Identification: Not likely to be confused with any other bird on Laysan, but note that the Savannah Sparrow has been recorded once in the NW Hawaiian Islands.

Occurrence: Endemic to LAYSAN (NW Hawaiian Is.). An introduced population on Midway was destroyed by rats during World War II; a small population survives at Pearl and Hermes Reef from an introduction in 1967. An Endangered Species.

Reference: Banks, R. C., and R. C. Laybourne. 1977. Plumage sequence and taxonomy of Laysan and Nihoa Finches. *Condor* 79:343-48.

NIHOA FINCH   *Telespyza ultima*   PLATE 37

Appearance: (6½;17) Similar to Laysan Finch but noticeably smaller, with proportionally smaller bill without overhanging hook at tip. Females and immatures heavily streaked above and below with dark brown.

Habits: Omnivorous. Nests in rock crevices.

Voice: A loud canary-like song and several varied chirping calls.

Identification: The House Finch has been recorded as a straggler on Nihoa. It is much smaller than Nihoa Finch, with males usually redder, females duller than the residents.

Occurrence: Endemic to NIHOA in the NW Hawaiian Is., where common. A population introduced to French Frigate Shoals in 1967 did not survive. An Endangered Species.

Reference: See Laysan Finch.

OU *Psittirostra psittacea* PLATE 37

Appearance: (6½;17) A heavy-set green bird with thick, pink, hooked beak. Male has bright yellow head. Perches horizontally, appearing quite pot-bellied.

Habits: A rather lethargic bird when perched. Often sits for long periods in a high tree over the forest canopy where only the loud calls betray the bird's presence. Flight is strong and direct. A fruiteater. Found only in wet ohia forests.

Voice: Call a plaintive, far-carrying, upslurred whistle. The canary-like song is loud and complex, comprising whistles, warbles, and trills.

Identification: Male unmistakable; no other Hawaiian bird has bright yellow head sharply set off from the rest of the plumage (but compare Lesser Koa-Finch). Females strongly resemble female koa-finches, but the pink hooked bill of the Ou is distinctive.

Occurrence: Originally widespread on the six largest HAWAIIAN IS., but now an Endangered Species. Reduced to about 400 birds on Hawaii (1300-1500 m elevation Hamakua region to Volcanoes National Park) and a few individuals in the remotest part of the Alakai Swamp on Kauai (USFWS survey data). Noticeably declining on Hawaii.

Other name: 'ō'ū.

PALILA *Loxioides bailleui* PLATE 37

Appearance: (7½;19) A large finch with yellow hood and gray back, the yellow brighter and more extensive in males. A black mask and dark bill impart a distinctive facial expression.

Habits: Found only in mamane and mamane/naio forests, often in small flocks, the birds feed almost exclusively on green mamane seed pods (Plate 44) held in the feet and ripped open with the bill.

Voice: Call a distinctive, rather bell-like *chee-clee-o* or *tee-cleet*. Song a pleasing, canary-like, but quiet series of whistles, warbles, and trills.

Identification: House Finches of the orange or yellow types can be confusing to a birder in search of the rare Palila, but the native bird is much larger and the black face shows at a considerable distance.

Occurrence: An Endangered Species restricted to the island of HA-

WAII. The remnant population fluctuates between about 2000 and 6000 individuals on the upper slopes (2000-3000 m) of Mauna Kea.

References: Scott, J. M., S. Mountainspring, C. van Riper III, C. B. Kepler, J. D. Jacobi, T. A. Burr, and J. G. Giffin. 1984. Annual variation in the distribution, abundance, and habitat response of the Palila (*Loxioides bailleui*). *Auk* 101:647-64.

van Riper III, C. 1980. Observations on the breeding of the Palila *Psittirostra bailleui* of Hawaii. *Ibis* 122:462-75.

LESSER KOA-FINCH   *Rhodacanthis flaviceps*   PLATE 37

Appearance: (7½;19) Similar to Greater Koa-Finch but smaller with yellow, not orange, head (male). Female probably indistinguishable from Greater Koa-Finch except in hand.

Habits: Apparently identical to those of Greater Koa-Finch.

Identification: Young male Greater Koa-Finches are yellower than adults, but never as clearly yellow on the whole head as this species. Palila has gray, not green back, Ou has hooked pink bill. Kona Grosbeak like female, but with huge pinkish bill.

Occurrence: Known from a few specimens collected in 1891 at one locality in Kona, HAWAII. Extinct.

GREATER KOA-FINCH   *Rhodacanthis palmeri*   PLATE 37

Appearance: (9;23) Male bright golden orange on head and breast, dull olive-brown elsewhere. Female dull green. Bill very thick, steel gray. Largest of the Hawaiian native finches to have lived in historic times.

Habits: Apparently fed exclusively in koa trees. Not particularly active, keeping to upper branches of trees.

Voice: A clear whistle, not very loud, and "several whistled flute-like notes, the last ones prolonged" (Munro 1960).

Identification: Very large size and orange color distinguish males from all other Hawaiian birds. Females resemble female Ou, but bill much larger, gray rather than pink. See Lesser Koa-Finch.

Occurrence: Known historically only from above 1000 m in Kona and Kau districts, HAWAII. Last seen about 1896. Extinct.

KONA GROSBEAK   *Chloridops kona*   PLATE 37

Appearance: (6;15) A dull green chunky bird with a huge buffy pink bill. The bill was usually smeared with a sticky brown substance from the fruit of the naio tree (Plate 44).

Habits: A very sluggish bird that fed on the hard dried fruits of naio growing on medium-aged lava flows. The cracking sounds of its feeding could be used to locate the bird.

Voice: Usually silent. Early accounts describe a low *cheep* and a clear but quiet whistled song.
Occurrence: Known only from a small area in the Kona District of HAWAII, where last seen about 1894. Extinct.
Other names: Grosbeak Finch, Kona Finch.

MAUI PARROTBILL *Pseudonestor xanthophrys* PLATE 39

Appearance: (5½;14) A stocky, short-tailed, yellow and green bird with enormous parrotlike bill. Yellow superciliary stripe a good field mark. Females duller with considerably smaller bills.
Habits: Feeds in a deliberate manner along trunks and branches of trees and low shrubs, wrenching away chunks of bark and crushing twigs in search of insect prey. Rather parrotlike in movements, often hanging upside down. The cracking sounds of its feeding are useful in locating the bird. Often accompanies groups of Maui Creepers. Prefers forest with open canopy, heavy undergrowth.
Voice: Call a loud *kzeet*, louder than the chips of Maui Creeper or Poouli. Also utters a thin, upslurred *queet*. Song a descending cascade of notes: *twee-twee-twee-twee-twee*.
Identification: The larger size and huge bill of the parrotbill separate it from all other greenish, bark-creeping birds on Maui.
Occurrence: Endemic to MAUI (Hawaiian Is.) A population of about 500 individuals of this Endangered Species survives between 1200 and 2150 m elevation on the e. slopes of Haleakala from Waikamoi Preserve to Kipahulu Valley (USFWS survey data).

COMMON AMAKIHI *Hemignathus virens* PLATE 39

Appearance: (4½;11) Males are small, bright yellow-green birds with short downcurved bills. Interisland variation of males slight, but immatures and females vary considerably: on Oahu, greenish gray above, yellowish white below with two more or less prominent white wing bars; on Maui, Molokai, and Lanai dull grayish green with greenish wing bars; on Hawaii, greener still, wing bars very indistinct. Female's bill smaller than that of male.
Habits: Feeds in a variety of ways from sipping nectar to picking over the bark of trees. Often in small flocks. Prefers drier forest types.
Voice: Call notes variable, including a buzzy *zheck*, an upslurred *queet*, and a thin *zeek*. Song a loud trill on level pitch, swelling in intensity in the middle. Also a complex, canary-like whisper song.
Identification: This species is the commonest of the native little green birds (see Table 4) in Hawaii. It resembles many other natives as well as the introduced Japanese White-eye. The white-eye's brighter, more

yellow-green back and prominent white eye-ring will separate it. For comparisons with Oahu Creeper, Maui Creeper, Akiapolaau, Nukupuu, Greater Amakihi, Hawaii Creeper, and female Akepa, see those accounts and Figures 47 and 48.

Occurrence: Endemic to the HAWAIIAN IS. with distinct subspecies on Oahu (*H. v. chloris*), Maui and its neighbors (*H. v. wilsoni*), and Hawaii (*H. v. virens*). Probably the most adaptable of the native forest birds. Abundant Hawaii, Maui; locally common Molokai; uncommon to rare Oahu; extirpated Lanai (USFWS data). May be found at lower elevations than most other honeycreepers.

References: Berger, A. J. 1969. The breeding season of the Hawaii 'Amakihi. Occ. Pap. Bernice P. Bishop Mus. 24:1-8.

Russell, S. M., and C. J. Ralph. 1981. The first observation of the nest of the Oahu 'Amakihi. '*Elepaio* 42:53-54.

van Riper III, C. 1984. The influence of nectar resources on nesting success and movement patterns of the Common Amakihi (*Hemignathus virens*). *Auk* 101:38-46.

Note: This species is restricted here to the islands from Oahu to Hawaii. The Kauai Amakihi is regarded by Berger (1981) and the 1983 AOU Check-list as conspecific. The Kauai form has a much larger bill (not just on average; measurements do not overlap), fills a different feeding niche (primarily a bark-picker), and has somewhat different vocalizations. Playback experiments (Pratt 1979) were inconclusive, but showed some lack of vocal recognition between Kauai and Hawaii populations.

KAUAI AMAKIHI   *Hemignathus stejnegeri*   PLATE 39

Appearance: (4½;11) Similar to Common Amakihi but with much larger bill, sex for sex. Female not as brightly colored as male and has smaller bill.

Habits: Forages by creeping over smaller branches of large trees, often hanging upside down to peer underneath a branch. Also feeds among leaves and flowers. When creeping, does not crouch in the manner of the Akikiki (Kauai Creeper). Most common in mixed koa/ohia forests.

Voice: Call note a loud *clerk*. Sings a variety of trills, some on level pitch some trailing downward toward the end. One variation almost identical to song of Akikiki (Kauai Creeper), but somewhat louder. Also possesses an elaborate whisper song that includes imitations of songs of other Kauai birds.

Identification: Distinguished from Akekee (Kauai Akepa) by longer darker bill and less black in face. Anianiau smaller with straighter bill and no black in lores, has yellower plumage and does not creep. Nu kupuu yellower on the head (male only), has very long upper mandible.

Occurrence: Endemic to KAUAI (Hawaiian Is.) and abundant in the Kokee area, common in the Alakai Swamp. Also present on outlying mountain ridges.

Note: Considered a subspecies of Common Amakihi in the 1983 AOU Check-list.

ANIANIAU *Hemignathus parvus* PLATE 39

Appearance: (4;10) A tiny yellow bird with thin, slightly curved bill. No black in lores, bill pinkish at base. Female duller than male.

Habits: Feeds mostly in flowers of ohia but also forages among leaves of trees and shrubs. May also be found at flowers of introduced plants.

Voice: A characteristic 2-note call, *tew-weet*, with rising inflection. Song variable, but always a trill composed of doubled or tripled notes: *weesee-weesee-weesee-*, etc. or *weesity-weesity-weesity*, etc. Occasionally utters a slower song of doubled whistles and chirps, and also sings a faint whisper song from the concealment of shrubbery.

Identification: No other yellow bird on Kauai lacks black in lores. Males can be identified at a glance by their golden yellow color and small size. Females may require more careful study; note short, thin bill and small size.

Occurrence: Endemic to KAUAI (Hawaiian Is.) where found in all mountains above 600 m elevation. Abundant at Kokee and in the Alakai Swamp (USFWS survey data).

Reference: Berger, A.J., C. R. Eddinger, and S. C. Frings. 1969. The nest and eggs of the Anianiau. *Auk* 86:183-87.

Other name: Lesser Amakihi.

GREATER AMAKIHI *Hemignathus sagittirostris* PLATE 39

Appearance: (6½;17) A plain olive green bird with long straight bill, bluish at base. Sexes similar.

Habits: Probes for insects among leaves, vines, and ferns. Apparently does not creep in the manner of other small green birds on Hawaii.

Voice: Call a repeated *chirrup*. Song very similar to that of Common Amakihi but with several additional notes at the end.

Identification: This bird could easily be overlooked as it is similar in both general appearance and voice to the Common Amakihi. Note the larger size and straight, not curved bill.

Occurrence: Known only from the dense rain forests of the Hamakua coast of HAWAII above 800 m. Last seen early in this century, and probably extinct.

AKIALOA   *Hemignathus obscurus*   PLATE 39

Appearance: (6½-7½; 17-19) A stocky green bird with very long, down-curved bill and black lores. Hawaii form smaller and more olive than others, with a proportionally smaller and more sharply downcurved bill.

Habits: Akialoas are bark-creepers, picking their insect food from cracks and crevices or probing in clumps of moss and lichen. Early observers reported that they also pecked at the bark in the manner of Akiapolaau and Nukupuu, but the sound produced was not loud.

Voice: Call note louder and deeper than those of amakihis. Song a trill intermediate between songs of Akiapolaau and amakihis. A few early writers described Kauai form's song as canary-like.

Identification: Akialoas on all islands look basically like overgrown, long-billed amakihis. The Kauai representative is so much larger than any other green bird on the island that it presents few problems. On Hawaii, Akialoa is less yellow than Akiapolaau but resembles Common Amakihi closely in coloration.

Occurrence: Known from all the larger HAWAIIAN IS. except Maui. Extinct on most islands by the 20th century. Kauai form survived into the 1960s in the Alakai Swamp, but has not been reliably reported since. Possibly now extinct everywhere.

Note: Until 1950, only one species of akialoa was recognized. Then D. Amadon [1950. The Hawaiian honeycreepers (Aves, Drepaniidae). *Bull. American Mus. Nat. Hist.* 95:151-262] classified the Kauai form as a species separate from the other three subspecies (on Oahu, Lanai, and Hawaii). The Kauai Akialoa (*H. procerus*) supposedly stood apart by having a longer bill and larger size than the other forms. However, Amadon saw only immature specimens (which have shorter bills than adults) from Lanai and none from Oahu. Pratt (1979) and Olson and James (1982) determined that akialoas from Oahu, Lanai, and Molokai (fossils) are morphologically close to the Kauai form, and that the Hawaii one is the atypical member of the group. If two species of akialoa are to be recognized, the separation must be between Lanai and Hawaii rather than between Kauai and Oahu as in Amadon's classification. This creates a taxonomic tangle, because *procerus* is not the oldest name available for the larger species, which must be called *H. ellisianus* based on the 1860 name for the Oahu population. The smaller species would be *H. obscurus* sensu stricto. Thus the 1983 AOU Check-list names "Kauai Akialoa" and "Hawaiian Akialoa" are unusable. We recommend the names Greater Akialoa and Lesser Akialoa respectively for *H. ellisianus* and *H. obscurus*, but for the moment prefer to treat them as conspecific, as do Olson and James (1982).

NUKUPUU *Hemignathus lucidus* PLATE 39

Appearance: (5½;14) A thick-headed, short-tailed bird with bright yellow head (males) and black lores. Females and immatures less yellow, with shorter bills. The long, downcurved upper mandible twice the length of the lower. Undertail coverts white (Kauai) or yellow (Maui).

Habits: A bark-picker; forages in a manner similar to that of Kauai Amakihi, Akikiki (Kauai Creeper), and sometimes Common Amakihi. Nukupuu also said to tap at bark in manner of Akiapolaau but less vigorously. Rarely takes nectar. Inhabits dense, wet ohia forests.

Voice: Call a loud *kee-wit*. Song similar to, but less vigorous than, that of Akiapolaau. Also has a song said to resemble that of the House Finch.

Identification: The unusual bill distinguishes this from all other Hawaiian birds except Akiapolaau, but the long upper mandible can be hard to see. Note thick, straight lower mandible of Akiapolaau. Nukupuu's bright yellow head sharply set off from green back distinguishes it from amakihis as well as akialoas. On Kauai, Akialoa is much larger, longer-billed, and greener, with yellow eye stripe.

Occurrence: Endemic to the HAWAIIAN IS. An Endangered Species, extinct on Oahu (*H. l. lucidus*), very rare on Kauai (*H. l. hanapepe*) in the Alakai Swamp and on Maui (*H. l. affinis*) at high elevations on the ne. slope of Haleakala. Reported recently from Kohala Mt., Hawaii (van Riper 1982). The species' occurrence on Hawaii has been confirmed by a specimen overlooked until recently (S. L. Olson, pers. comm.).

AKIAPOLAAU *Hemignathus munroi* PLATE 39

Appearance: (5½;14) A stocky, short-tailed, big-headed bird. Head bright golden yellow (male) or dull gray-green (female and immature). Lores black in males, gray in females and immatures. The bill, with long, thin, sickle-shaped upper mandible and stout, straight lower one, unique among birds. Females have somewhat smaller bills.

Habits: The amazing bill is used to extract insect larvae from trunks and branches of large trees. The mandibles are held apart while the lower one is used to chisel openings in the bark, then the exposed larvae are picked out with the upper one. The tapping sounds can sometimes be used to locate a feeding bird. Often found in groups of three, one bright male and two dull-plumaged birds. Partial to koa trees, they move creeperlike over the branches. Found primarily in koa/ohia forests, but also inhabits mamane/naio parklands.

Voice: Males utter a loud *chip* while foraging, as well as an upslurred *squeet*. Call notes of females weaker. Song a lively series of whistled notes: *You-don't-see-me-but-I-SEE-you!* The last two notes, with a rising then falling inflection, are particularly distinctive. Young birds following adults utter a loud *chirp*.

Identification: Similarly colored but smaller Common Amakihi sometimes creeps over trunks and branches but never produces loud tapping sounds. The bill of Akiapolaau looks thicker at the base than that of the amakihi even when the very thin, hooked upper mandible cannot be seen.

Occurrence: Endemic to the island of HAWAII. An Endangered Species with fragmented distribution in the Hamakua-Volcano region, Kau Forest Reserve, leeward Mauna Kea, and upper Kona (a few). Population about 1500, mostly in Kau and the Hamakua area (USFWS survey data).

Other names: '*akiapōlā'au*, Hawaii Nukupuu.

AKIKIKI (KAUAI CREEPER) *Oreomystis bairdi*   PLATE 39

Appearance: (5;13) A fluffy ball of gray and white feathers, dark above, light below. Tail very short. Bill pale dull pink, short, slightly curved. Legs and feet dull pink. Adults with dark cheeks and lores, immatures with white "spectacles."

Habits: Almost invariably seen creeping over the trunks and larger branches of trees, especially koa. Rarely feeds among flowers. Clings closely to the bark but does not brace with the tail.

Voice: Usual call a thin *sweet*. Occasionally utters a loud *whit*. The song, rarely given, a trill that trails off and drops in pitch, very similar to one of the songs of the Kauai Amakihi. Also utters a complex whisper song of trills and chirps.

Identification: All other bark-creeping birds on Kauai have some yellow or green in plumage. Pink bill of Akikiki diagnostic.

Occurrence: Endemic to KAUAI (Hawaiian Is.). Uncommon in high native forests. Can be seen along roads and trails in the Kokee and Alakai Swamp areas. Listed as rare by the ICBP (King 1981).

Reference: Eddinger, C. R. 1972. Discovery of the nest of the Kauai Creeper. *Auk* 89:673-74.

HAWAII CREEPER *Oreomystis mana*   PLATE 39

Appearance: (4½;11) Adults olive green above, paler below, chin and throat white. Dark mask from base of bill to behind eye. Sexes similar. Immatures and females lack dark mask, immatures have broad whitish superciliary line. Bill pale, only slightly curved.

Habits: Picks over bark of trunks and branches of trees. Often solitary but may form small flocks (probably family groups). Prefers mixed koa/ohia forests.

is indicated by as yet unpublished research by the senior author, the AOU recommends the names Common Akepa and Kauai Akepa for them respectively. We prefer one of the two native Hawaiian names for the Kauai form because that allows "Akepa" to stand unmodified for *L. coccineus*. We were surprised that the AOU Check-list committee applied the epithet "common" *de novo* to an Endangered Species that may be less common than the form from which the name is intended to distinguish it.

The two *Loxops* differ not only in plumage color and degree of sexual dimorphism but also in many other ways. The bill of the Akekee is larger and thicker at the base than that of the other form, and the bird has somewhat different feeding behavior. The songs of the two are similar but differ in noticeable ways (see above) and are apparently perceived as different by the birds themselves (based on playback experiments). Furthermore, the Akekee builds its nest on the branches of trees, but the Akepa (on Hawaii at least) nests in cavities.

ULA-AI-HAWANE   *Ciridops anna*   PLATE 38

Appearance: (4½;11) A small bird patterned in black, gray, and red. Immature dull greenish brown above, paler below, with buff cheeks. Bill short, thick, somewhat finchlike. Habits and voice unknown.
Occurrence: Found in historic times only on the island of HAWAII. Last seen in the early 1890s in Kohala. Extinct.

IIWI   *Vestiaria coccinea*   PLATE 38

Appearance: (6;15) Brilliant scarlet with black wings and tail and long, deeply decurved, peach-colored bill. Immature dull yellow with black spots. Bill dusky brown at first, becomes brightly colored with age.
Habits: A nectar-feeder often found in flowering ohia-lehua, mamane, and many introduced plants such as banana poka. Slow and deliberate in movements, keeps to the interior of leafy branches, and rarely in the open. More difficult to see than Apapane, with which it often feeds. Wings produce an audible flutter in flight.
Voice: An almost infinitely varied repertoire of creaks, whistles, gurgles, and reedy notes often joined into a halting song. Some random calls sound like a child playing with a rusty harmonica. A loud rusty-hinge call diagnostic. May give humanlike whistles, or imitate other native birds such as Elepaio.
Identification: Long sickle-shaped bill unique among Hawaiian red birds. Iiwi more orange-red than Apapane, without white under tail. Larger and redder than Akepa. Vocalizations can be very confusing because of wide variation and occasional imitations of other species.
Occurrence: Endemic to the HAWAIIAN IS. (six largest). In native for-

ests above 600 m. Common to abundant Hawaii, Maui, Kauai; uncommon and local Molokai, Oahu; extirpated Lanai.

HAWAII MAMO   *Drepanis pacifica*   PLATE 38

Appearance: (9;23) A large sickle-billed bird, glossy black with yellow rump and undertail coverts. Wing linings and spot at bend of wing white. Tail short, rounded.

Habits: A shy dweller of the forest canopy that fed on nectar of lobelioid flowers with curved tubular corollas.

Voice: A long plaintive whistle.

Identification: Hawaii Oo, the only other black and yellow bird on Hawaii, all black above, with long tapering tail, short bill.

Occurrence: Endemic to the island of HAWAII. Last seen in 1899 near Kaumana. Presumed extinct.

BLACK MAMO   *Drepanis funerea*   PLATE 38

Appearance: (8;20) Entirely dull sooty black with extremely long, sickle-shaped bill. Outer primaries edged white. Base of upper mandible (operculum) yellow. Forehead often coated with pollen, appearing pale.

Habits: Fed in flowers of lobelias and ohia-lehua. A curious bird that would approach an observer.

Voice: A clear flutelike whistle and a 5- or 6-note rollicking whistle.

Identification: Immature Akohekohe (Crested Honeycreeper) and Bishop's Oo are also mostly black, but bill of both is much shorter than that of Black Mamo.

Occurrence: Known only from MOLOKAI (Hawaiian Is.). Last seen in 1907. Presumed extinct.

Other name: *hoa*.

AKOHEKOHE (CRESTED HONEYCREEPER)   PLATE 3
Palmeria dolei

Appearance: (7;18) A medium-sized dark bird with bright orange nape and peculiar pale, recurved, bushy crest. Fan-shaped tail tipped white, undertail coverts pale gray. Plumage basically black, streaked and spotted with gray and red. Immature nondescript, plain brownish gray without markings of adult, but nape may be buffy.

Habits: A comical, boisterous bird that feeds on nectar in tops of tall flowering trees, especially ohia-lehua. Sometimes flies high in the air from one ridge to the next.

Voice: Highly vocal with many different calls, including upslurred and downslurred humanlike whistles, a rolling *chirk*, and a song of whee notes and guttural buzzy sounds. Typical phrases might be written *ah-churg-churg-churg* or *greee-tawk-tawk*.

Identification: A very distinctive bird. In misty weather (which is frequent), when colors are hard to see, Akohekohe can resemble the much smaller Apapane, which has similar shape and postures. Note white tail tip of Akohekohe. Immature could be mistaken for Bishop's Oo.

Occurrence: Endemic to the HAWAIIAN IS. (Maui, Molokai). Believed extinct on the latter, but still common locally in upper rain forests of East Maui. An Endangered Species.

APAPANE   *Himatione sanguinea*   PLATE 38

Appearance: (5;13) Adult bright crimson with dark wings and tail and prominent white undertail coverts. Head usually brighter than the rest of the plumage. The brush-tipped tongue usually protrudes slightly, making bill tip look white. Juvenile yellow-brown with white undertail coverts. Laysan subspecies was more orange, with dingy undertail feathers.

Habits: Always found around flowering trees, particularly ohia-lehua. Often perches conspicuously on the outer clusters of flowers to feed on the nectar. The tail is characteristically cocked up. Small flocks of Apapane frequently fly high over forested ridges.

Voice: Incredibly varied calls and songs, including squeaks, whistles, rasping notes, clicking sounds, and melodic trills. Some songs are pleasant and rather canary-like; others are harsh and mechanical-sounding. The songs vary from place to place.

Identification: White undertail coverts distinguish Apapane from all other red birds in Hawaii. Dull-colored juveniles best distinguished by slightly curved black bill and tail-up posture.

Occurrence: Most abundant native bird in the HAWAIIAN IS. Present in varying numbers on all main islands in mountain forests above 600 m and rarely in the lowlands. Abundant Kauai, Maui, and Hawaii; locally common Oahu; scarce Molokai; rare Lanai. Laysan form (*H. s. freethi*), last seen in 1923.

OO-ULI   *Melamprosops phaeosoma*   PLATE 39

Appearance: (5½;14) A chunky, short-tailed bird, brown above, pale buff below with prominent black mask. A pale band behind and below the mask on each side of the head a good field mark. Bill thick but not strongly hooked.

Habits: Creeps over the bark of trees, apparently feeding on snails and other invertebrates. Often joins small groups that include Maui Creeper and Maui Parrotbill. A bold and curious bird.

Voice: Call is a loud *chip*, lower in pitch than that of the Maui Creeper. Also a series of 4 rapid chips, the third lower in pitch: *chi-chit-chu-chip*. No song has yet been ascribed to this bird.

Occurrence: Known only from MAUI (Hawaiian Is.). Rare and local in a single locality on ne. slope of Haleakala. Discovered 1973. An Endangered Species.

Reference: Baldwin, P. H., and T.L.C. Casey. 1983. A preliminary list of foods of the Po'o-uli. '*Elepaio* 43: 53-56.

Casey, T.L.C., and J. D. Jacobi. 1974. A new genus and species of bird from the island of Maui, Hawaii (Passeriformes: Drepanididae). Occ. Pap. Bernice P. Bishop Mus. 24:216-26.

Other names: Black-faced Honeycreeper, *po'o-uli*.

FAMILY PASSERIDAE: Old World Sparrows

THIS family of streaky brown birds with finch bills originated in the Old World, but has now been introduced virtually worldwide. They are closely associated with human activities; the House Sparrow has even been called a feathered mouse. Two species are now established in the tropical Pacific.

HOUSE SPARROW   *Passer domesticus*   PLATE 42

Appearance: (6;15) A mousy brown sparrow, streaked above, plain below. Adult male has black bib, gray cap, grayish white cheeks. In flight, plain gray rump distinctive.

Habits: Closely associated with man, and rarely found in the countryside. Feeds on scraps and garbage as well as on seeds. Large, bulky communal nests often placed in buildings.

Voice: A rolling chirp.

Identification: Much larger than any of the mannikins or waxbills in Hawaii. Female House Finch is streaked below. See Eurasian Tree Sparrow.

Occurrence: Native to Eurasia, Africa, India. Introduced almost worldwide, including all main HAWAIIAN IS. Common to abundant in cities and towns.

EURASIAN TREE SPARROW   *Passer montanus*   PLATE 4

Appearance: (5½;14) Similar to House Sparrow but cap brown, throat patch smaller. Black spot on ear coverts. Sexes similar.

Habits: In tropical Pacific confined to towns and villages. Often perched on power lines.

Voice: A simple *chirrup*.

Identification: Told from House Sparrow by brown cap, ear spot. The two do not occur together in the tropical Pacific, but some island populations have been misidentified in the past.

Occurrence: Native to temperate Eurasia. Introduced (probably in 1940s) to the MARIANA IS. (common on Guam; uncommon Saipan, Tinian, Rota) and KWAJALEIN (Marshall Is.; first identified as House Sparrows), and after 1978 to YAP.

FAMILY ESTRILDIDAE: Waxbills, Mannikins, and Parrotfinches

These are tiny finches often kept as cage birds. They are easy to breed in captivity, and thus excellent candidates for avian introductions. Many species have been released on islands of the tropical Pacific. Several are well established, others are of uncertain status. A few have become established for several years only to die out eventually. The origin of a few populations is unknown; some may be native. Most are "weed" birds in the sense that they are likely to be found in weedy roadsides, abandoned military installations, or vacant city lots. They rarely penetrate native forests, and usually fill niches not occupied by native birds. All species are highly gregarious seedeaters that can become serious agricultural pests. Mixed flocks are common where more than one species are established. A few species, the parrotfinches of the genus *Erythrura*, are native to islands of the tropical Pacific.

Reference: Goodwin, D. 1982. *Estrildid finches of the world*. British Mus. (Nat. Hist.), Comstock Publ. Assoc.; Ithaca: Cornell Univ. Press.

RED-CHEEKED CORDONBLEU   Plate 43
Uraeginthus bengalus

Appearance: (5;13) A small, crimson-billed finch with a peculiar color combination of dusty brown and pale sky blue. Males have a bright crimson patch on auriculars.

Habits: Like those of other small finches and waxbills. Often joins mixed flocks.

Voice: Call a thin, inconspicuous *see-seee*. Song is a hummingbird-like jumble of squeaky, high-pitched, and buzzy notes.

Identification: Unmistakable. Two close relatives, Blue-headed Cordonbleu (*U. cyanocephalus*) and Angolan Cordonbleu (*U. angolensis*), also released in Hawaii in 1960s, apparently did not become established. Angolan lacks crimson cheek patch, and Blue-headed has entire head blue (males). Females of all three virtually identical, but Blue-headed has more blue on sides of head and forehead.

Occurrence: Native to Africa. Introduced (mid-1960s) to the HA-WAIIAN IS. and established on Hawaii (Puu Waa Waa area) and possibly Oahu (seemed established in mid-1970s, but observations have tapered off since; Kapiolani Park area only).

LAVENDER WAXBILL   *Estrilda caerulescens*   PLATE 43

Appearance: (4½;11) A pearly gray finch with crimson rump and tail. Bill purplish red, flanks black with small white spots.

Habits: A flocking species often found near the ground in grass or weeds.

Voice: A metallic chip note and a thin squeaky song: *seee-see-see-sweee*.

Identification: Orange-cheeked Waxbill also has red rump, but is brown, not gray. Red-cheeked Cordonbleu vaguely similar in color, but lacks red rump and tail.

Occurrence: Native to Africa. Introduced (early 1960s) to the HA-WAIIAN IS. Established on Hawaii (Puu Waa Waa area) and probably Oahu (Diamond Head). For several years was the most common of the "Diamond Head finches" but has declined since about 1980 and may not survive much longer in that area.

Note: Sometimes placed in genus *Lagonosticta* and called Lavender Firefinch.

ORANGE-CHEEKED WAXBILL   *Estrilda melpoda*   PLATE 43

Appearance: (4½;11) A red-billed brown finch with orange cheeks and red rump.

Habits: Feeds near the ground on grass seeds. May perch in low bushes. Usually in mixed-species flocks with other waxbills or mannikins.

Voice: A thin chip note and a light whistled song: *wheee-tititi-whee-tititi-wheee-* etc.

Identification: The general dusty brown color of this species is unlike the paler color of the Warbling Silverbill or the darker tone of the Nutmeg Mannikin. Immatures of Chestnut Mannikin and Nutmeg Mannikin are nearly the same color, but have no red in the plumage, and dark bills.

Occurrence: Native to W. Africa. Introduced (1960s) to the HA-WAIIAN IS. and established on Hawaii (Puu Waa Waa area) and scattered localities on Oahu (Diamond Head, Kapiolani Park, Kaneohe). Generally rare and local.

[BLACK-RUMPED WAXBILL   *Estrilda troglodytes*   See Appendix A]

COMMON WAXBILL   *Estrilda astrild*   PLATE 43

Appearance: (4;10) A small, red-billed, brown finch with a prominent red streak from the bill through the eye. Rump brown, undertail coverts black. Tail long and graduated.

Habits: Flocks in weedy grassy areas, usually near water. Feeds on grass seeds.

Voice: A weak twittering. Song *chip-chip-tooee, chip-chip-tooee*, etc.

Identification: Very similar to the Black-rumped Waxbill (Appendix A) which was present for a few years on Oahu. Black-rumped is correctly named, and also has white, not black, undertail coverts, and squarish black tail.

Occurrence: Native to Africa. Introduced earlier this century to OAHU (Hawaiian Is.) and TAHITI (Society Is.). Common on Tahiti, locally common on Oahu (Pearl Harbor, Kahuku area) and apparently expanding its range.

Reference: Ord, W. M. 1982. Red-eared and Common Waxbills on Oahu. '*Elepaio* 42:89-90.

Other names: St. Helena Waxbill, Astrild.

RED AVADAVAT   *Amandava amandava*   PLATE 43

Appearance: (4½;11) A tiny finch with a red rump. Males are red all over with white speckles. Females and immatures yellowish brown with red bill.

Habits: A highly gregarious inhabitant of grassy and weedy places, often around human habitation or agricultural fields.

Voice: A high-pitched twitter.

Identification: In Hawaii, two other introduced finches (Orange-cheeked Waxbill, Lavender Fire-finch) have red rumps, but no red on the body. Chestnut Mannikin is found in the same localities as this species in Hawaii and is much more abundant. Wishful thinking can make it look redder than it is.

Occurrence: Native to SE. Asia. Introduced (early 1900s) and established in FIJI (common to abundant on Viti Levu and Vanua Levu) and the HAWAIIAN IS. Common but very local in the Pearl Harbor area, Oahu; occasionally seen on the windward side. Reported 1983 in North Kohala District, Hawaii, and 1984 on Kauai, but not known to be established as yet on those islands.

Other names: Strawberry Finch, Red Munia, Red Waxbill.

[**ZEBRA FINCH**   *Poephila guttata*   See Appendix A]

RED-BROWED FIRETAIL   *Emblema temporalis*   PLATE 43

Appearance: (4½;11) A small gray finch with red bill, eyebrow, and rump. Back olive, tail black.

Habits: Usually in flocks in lowland grasslands and roadsides, mostly near settled areas. May associate with Common Waxbill.

Voice: A high-pitched metallic peep. Flocks produce a dry chatter.

Identification: Common Waxbill also has red bill and eyebrow, but firetail is distinguished by red rump and paler underparts.

Occurrence: Native to e. Australia. Introduced (1800s) to the SOCIETY IS. (Tahiti, Moorea), and subsequently to the MARQUESAS IS. (Nukuhiva, Uahuka; possibly Hivaoa). Common but less numerous than Common Waxbill.

Other names: Sydney Waxbill, Red-browed Finch, Red-browed Waxbill.

BLUE-FACED PARROTFINCH *Erythrura trichroa* PLATE 25

Appearance: (4½;11) A tiny, dark green finch with blue face, red rump and tail. Bill black. Females and immatures similar but duller.

Habits: Usually found in small flocks, which forage in grasses or in the tops of trees. At Palau, found most often in ironwood groves.

Voice: A thin metallic *tink*, like the sound of coins clicked together. Easily overlooked or mistaken for the sound of an insect.

Occurrence: Widespread in ne. Australia, Melanesia, E. Indies, and MICRONESIA (Palau, Truk, Pohnpei, Kosrae). Fairly common in the e. Carolines but uncommon and hard to find at Palau, where restricted to the limestone islands from s. Babelthuap to Eil Malk.

RED-HEADED PARROTFINCH *Erythrura cyaneovirens* PLATE 32

Appearance: (4;10) A tiny, blue-green finch with scarlet face and crown, red rump and tail. Throat and breast with variable blue suffusion. Immatures may lack red on a bluish head, or may show patches or flecks of red, particularly in the crown.

Habits: In Fiji, a tame and confiding bird found in small flocks in a variety of habitats including city parks and gardens. Gleans unripe grass seeds near the ground or feeds in trees, where it seeks flowers and buds or picks at the bark for insects. Samoan birds much shyer, less gregarious, and found mainly in montane rain forest.

Voice: Call a high, thin *seep*. Song a "persistent double note" like that of the Orange-breasted Honeyeater but not so loud (Watling 1982).

Occurrence: Resident in Vanuatu, FIJI (Viti Levu, Vanua Levu, Taveuni, Kadavu, Yasawa Is.), and W. SAMOA (Savaii, Upolu). Common in Fiji, uncommon in Samoa.

Note: The Fiji subspecies (*E. c. pealii*) has been treated as a full species in some recent works, but on what basis we cannot say. All populations are very similar except for the ecological differences noted above. Recognition of the Fiji Parrotfinch as a species, with the Vanuatu and Samoan forms remaining conspecific, makes little zoogeographical sense.

PINK-BILLED PARROTFINCH   *Erythrura kleinschmidti*   PLATE 32

Appearance: (4½;11) A chunky, dark green finch with black face, dark blue crown and nape, and red rump. Adults have large, glossy pink bills, immatures orange-buff bills with black tips.

Habits: Primarily insectivorous. Forages at mid-height along tree trunks and branches, probing and crushing stems and bark. Usually seen alone or in pairs but also joins mixed-species flocks. Prefers mature forest up to 1000 m. Occasionally seen in secondary forest.

Voice: Clicking sounds and a high-pitched *zee* or *chee*.

Identification: Similar to Red-headed Parrotfinch but has much larger pink bill and no red on head.

Occurrence: Endemic to VITI LEVU (Fiji), where formerly considered very rare but recently found to be locally common.

Reference: Clunie, F. 1973. Pink-billed Parrotfinches near Nailagosakelo Creek, Southern Viti Levu. *Notornis* 20:202-209.

WARBLING SILVERBILL   *Lonchura malabarica*   PLATE 43

Appearance: (4½;11) A tiny, sandy-colored finch with black rump and tail and metallic blue-gray bill.

Habits: Highly gregarious, nesting colonially. Found in very dry habitats such as kiawe thickets or open brushy grasslands. Often attracted to water sources.

Voice: Flock calls are metallic chips rather like the sound of coins clicked together. Song a quiet *whee-too-whee-too-whee-whee-wheer*, etc.

Identification: The pale color and black tail distinguish this species from Nutmeg Mannikin, which often flocks with it, as well as from other small finches.

Occurrence: Native to Africa. Introduced to the HAWAIIAN IS. on Hawaii, whence it has spread to Kahoolawe, Lanai, Maui (Makena area), Molokai, Oahu (dry se. end), and Kauai (Poipu). Abundant in N. and S. Kohala and N. Kona districts, Hawaii. Recent arrival on n. islands, status unknown.

Reference: Berger, A. J. 1975. The Warbling Silverbill, a new nesting bird in Hawaii. *Pacific Science* 29:51-54.

[**WHITE-BACKED MANNIKIN**   *Lonchura striata*   See Appendix A]

NUTMEG MANNIKIN   *Lonchura punctulata*   PLATE 43

Appearance: (4½;11) A tiny, dark brown finch with black bill. The face often looks darker than rest of plumage. Breast scalloped with dark brown, but pattern difficult to see in the field. Juvenile plain buffy brown, paler below, with black bill.

Habits: Usually found in small flocks in open grassy areas of lawns, parks, and rural areas, occasionally in openings in forest. Less confined to dry habitats than other small finches. Feeds on green grass seeds gleaned by weighting down tall stems. Difficult to see well; flocks are very nervous and flighty. Often forms the nucleus of mixed flocks of mannikins and waxbills.

Voice: A characteristic low-pitched, reedy *chee, ba-hee*, different in quality from the calls of most other small finches.

Identification: Can be picked out of mixed flocks by the low-pitched call, medium brown (not pale sandy, not chestnut) color, and greenish rump and tail. Juvenile very similar to same-aged Chestnut Mannikin, but with black (not blue) bill.

Occurrence: Native from India to Indonesia and the Philippines. Common on YAP (introduced?) and on all main HAWAIIAN IS. (introduced 1865). The most abundant and widespread of the introduced small finches in Hawaii. Formerly present at PALAU (Koror; last seen in 1940s).

Other names: Ricebird, Spice Finch, Scaly-breasted Munia, Spotted Munia.

CHESTNUT MANNIKIN *Lonchura malacca* PLATE 43

Appearance: (4½;11) A tiny dark finch with a relatively large, silvery bill. In flight, chestnut body plumage may look quite red. Immatures warm buff below, brown above, with blue-gray bill and chestnut tail.

Habits: Usually found in weedy roadsides in small to large flocks, often near sugar cane or pineapple fields, or in open grasslands. Feeds on grass seeds near the ground.

Voice: A weakly whistled *tee, tee*.

Identification: The silvery bill and chestnut plumage are very distinctive, but see Red Avadavat. Immature similar to young Nutmeg Mannikin, but with blue bill and chestnut tail.

Occurrence: Native from India to Indonesia and the Philippines. Introduced and well established at PALAU (Koror complex, s. Babelthuap), GUAM, and the HAWAIIAN IS. Abundant on Oahu (Pearl Harbor and central valley but spreading), common but local on Kauai (Koloa area). Reported from Hawaii (Honaunau) but not known to be established.

Other names: Black-headed Munia, Black-headed Mannikin, Chestnut Munia.

HUNSTEIN'S MANNIKIN *Lonchura hunsteini* PLATE 2?

Appearance: (4½;11) A tiny, mostly black finch with rusty tan rump and tail. The crown and back of head are variably scaled pearly white. Juveniles yellowish brown with black head and a few dark breast streaks.

Habits: Usually seen in huge flocks along roadsides, in grassy fields, and in cultivated areas. A major agricultural pest.

Voice: High, thin *peep-peep, peep* etc. and flutelike *pee* or *pee-up*.

Identification: Blue-faced Parrotfinch has green plumage at all stages. No other finches are found on Pohnpei.

Occurrence: Native to New Ireland (Papua New Guinea). Introduced (1920s) to POHNPEI, where abundant in the northern and eastern parts of the island.

Other names: Black-breasted Weaver-finch, Hunstein's Munia.

CHESTNUT-BREASTED MANNIKIN   PLATE 43
Lonchura castaneothorax

Appearance: (4½;11) A small, brown-faced finch with a silvery gray cap and bill, golden breast with black band, pale underparts, and short, yellowish tail.

Habits: Forages in large flocks in moist grasslands, roadsides, and fern brakes. Tame and easily approached.

Voice: High-pitched *tit*.

Identification: Light bill and crown plus prominent black breast band easily distinguish this finch from others with which it is found.

Occurrence: Native to Australia and parts of New Guinea. Introduced to the SOCIETY IS. (Bora Bora, Raiatea, Moorea, Tahiti) in the 1800s and now common. Also in the MARQUESAS (Hivaoa, Tahuata, Mohotani).

Other name: Chestnut-breasted Finch.

JAVA SPARROW   *Padda oryzivora*   PLATE 43

Appearance: (6;15) A tiny, boldly patterned finch with huge pink bill and prominent white cheeks. Juvenile brownish, with less pronounced pattern and dark bill.

Habits: Highly gregarious, often seen in open grassy areas of lawns and parks, but also perches in trees. Mostly in urban areas in Hawaii. Can be a serious agricultural pest.

Voice: A series of chirps similar to but softer than those of House Sparrow.

Occurrence: Native to SE. Asia. Introduced to FIJI (established in wetter areas of Viti Levu, Vanua Levu, and Taveuni) and the HAWAIIAN IS. (abundant and spreading from Honolulu area on Oahu, less numerous but increasing in Keauhou-Kona area of Hawaii and on Kauai. Bred for a short time in early 1960s on Guam, but apparently died out there.

PIN-TAILED WHYDAH   *Vidua macroura*   See Appendix A]

APPENDIX A. HYPOTHETICAL, ENIGMATIC, AND TEMPORARILY ESTABLISHED SPECIES

THIS compilation includes birds that have been reported from the tropical Pacific but which, for a variety of reasons, cannot be unequivocally included in the avifauna. "Hypothetical" species are those that have been reported with inadequate supporting details. They include sight records by single observers unfamiliar with the species in question, sightings of species difficult to identify in the field, or even collected specimens that cannot be definitely assigned to a species. Inclusion of these sightings here does not in any way denigrate the observers' abilities (note that we list some of our own sightings as hypothetical), but rather shows the need for better documentation of observations. Some of these sightings undoubtedly represent valid occurrences. Also included here are "enigmatic" species indigenous to the tropical Pacific. They are names based on old descriptions or illustrations only, on poorly documented specimens, or on specimens that are unique. Thus their relationships and status cannot be determined with certainty. The list also includes introduced species that have been reported as established in the past but that now appear to have died out or to have failed to establish self-sustaining wild populations.

ROYAL ALBATROSS *Diomedea epomophora*
One unconfirmed sight record from FIJI, listed with a question mark by duPont (1976) with no details.

SOLANDER'S PETREL *Pterodroma solandri*
This large, dark gray petrel has reportedly been seen near the Hawaiian Is. It is so similar to Murphy's, Herald, and Kermadec petrels, however, that identification by sight alone must be considered tentative. The tail is wedge-shaped (as in Murphy's) but underwing has white markings (as in dark-phase Kermadec and Herald). Body of Solander's is contrastingly grayer above and below than that of Herald or Kermadec. Also called Providence Petrel, it breeds on Lord Howe I. (Australia) and disperses to adjacent seas and in low numbers to the temperate N. Pacific E of Japan. Migrants to the north obviously pass through the tropics, but the above report is the only one for the area of this guide.

GREAT-WINGED PETREL   *Pterodroma macroptera*

A cold-water species that breeds on islands off New Zealand and wanders northward. No substantiated records from the tropics. A sighting in the Phoenix Is. is questionable.

ORIENTAL DARTER   *Anhinga melanogaster*

S. D. Ripley (1948. First record of Anhingidae in Micronesia. *Auk* 65:454-55) reported observing a small colony of this species at Palau in 1946. The account provides no details as to how the birds were identified, and nothing in the account is inconsistent with the likely possibility that the birds seen were Little Pied Cormorants. Darters have not been reported again from Palau. Because this record does not meet even minimal standards for acceptance of unsubstantiated sight records, we consider it hypothetical.

GLOSSY IBIS   *Plegadis falcinellus*

A juvenile female *Plegadis* ibis was collected recently in Fiji. It probably belonged to this species rather than to *P. chihi*, the White-faced Ibis, which has been found in Hawaii, but the two species are indistinguishable as juveniles, even in the hand. Reference: Clunie, F., F. C. Kinsky, and J.A.F. Jenkins. 1978. New bird records from the Fiji Archipelago. *Notornis* 25:118-27.

WHITE-EYED DUCK   *Aythya australis*

This Australian species is listed for Guam in unpublished field notes in the files of the Guam Div. of Aquatic and Wildlife Resources. Several individuals were reportedly seen in 1963. This species is irruptive in Australia, and could have reached Guam. Equally likely, however, is the Ferruginous Duck or White-eyed Pochard (*A. nyroca*), which has been recorded in Japan. The two species are very similar and possibly indistinguishable in the field. Drakes are rich mahogany with white wing stripes, belly, and undertail coverts, and white eyes. Hens are similarly patterned but with duller colors and dark eyes.

COMMON BUZZARD   *Buteo buteo*

This species has been reported from Palau (Pratt and Bruner 1981) and by T. O. Lemke (unpubl.) from the Marianas (Anatahan, Sarigan; possibly same individual both places). Marshall (1949) saw an unidentified *Buteo* at Palau. In the absence of specimens or good photographs, these records of this highly variable hawk must be regarded as hypothetical. The Common Buzzard is the most likely *Buteo* to visit Micronesia, but some other e. Asian hawks are shaped rather like *Buteo*s and could be confused with them. Illustrated in WBSJ (1982).

AMERICAN KESTREL   *Falco sparverius*

An individual of this species that was present for a short time on Oahu (Hawaiian Is.) and was reported as a natural vagrant is now believed to have been an escape.

NORTHERN HOBBY   *Falco subbuteo*

Sightings of this small falcon have been reported on Guam (unpubl. notes of Div. of Aquatic and Wildlife Resources) and Pagan in the Marianas (T. K. Pratt and T. O. Lemke, unpubl. report of Dept. of Natural Resources, CNMI). The Pagan bird was not seen well enough to positively distinguish it from an immature Amur Red-footed Falcon (*F. amurensis*). Adult Northern Hobby is black above with a black whisker mark in front of white cheeks. The underparts are heavily streaked on the white breast, with chestnut thighs and undertail coverts. Immatures lack chestnut. Immature Amur Red-footed Falcons differ mainly in being buffy throughout the underparts, with red cere. Both are illustrated in WBSJ (1982).

ORIENTAL HOBBY   *Falco severus*

Owen (1977a) reported a sighting of this species at Palau. Further confirmation is needed before this falcon can be unequivocally added to the avifauna of the tropical Pacific. It differs from the Northern Hobby in having entirely black cheeks and dark chestnut underparts. Illustrated in King and Dickinson (1975) and WBSJ (1982).

COMMON QUAIL   *Coturnix coturnix*

This species is listed among other birds introduced and established in e. Polynesia (Thibault and Thibault 1973), but no exact locality or other details are given. We find no other reference to its presence in the tropical Pacific, although it is sometimes considered conspecific with the Japanese Quail established in the Hawaiian Is.

STUBBLE QUAIL   *Coturnix pectoralis*

A *Coturnix* of some sort was introduced to Niihau (Hawaiian Is.) in the 1930s and persisted at least until 1947, when naturalists were last allowed to visit the island (Fisher 1951). The bird was called "Australian Bush Partridge" by the landowners, and thus was listed as *C. pectoralis* in several publications. More likely the introduced quail were Japanese

Quail, which are established on nearby Kauai. Present status on Niihau unknown.

PRAIRIE CHICKEN (sp. ?)   *Tympanuchus* sp.

Prairie chickens of unknown species (Greater, *T. cupido*; or Lesser, *T. pallidicinctus*) were introduced to Niihau (Hawaiian Is.) in the 1930s and persisted at least until 1947 (Fisher 1951), the last time any ornithologist was allowed on the island. Present status unknown.

HELMETED GUINEAFOWL   *Numida meleagris*

Widely kept in domestication and introduced on several of the Hawaiian Is. Feral populations persisted on private ranches for years, but always died out unless the populations were augmented by new releases. We know of no presently established populations.

TAHITI RAIL   *Rallus pacificus*

A small, brightly colored rail, probably related to the Banded Rail. Known only from descriptions and a drawing by Forster from Cook's second voyage (ca. 1773). Dark above, white below with white eyebrow, red legs and bill. Undoubtedly extinct.

WATERCOCK   *Gallicrex cinerea*

R. P. Owen (pers. comm.) saw what he believed to be an individual of this species once at Palau. The record is not outlandish, as this species migrates from e. Asia to Celebes. Size of Purple Swamphen, but black with prominent red "horn" (male) or brownish with streaked back (female).

GREEN SANDPIPER   *Tringa ochropus*

Very similar to Solitary Sandpiper but with dark underwings. An unconfirmed sighting from Palau (Owen 1977). Illustrated in Eurasian field guides and NGS (1983).

UPLAND SANDPIPER   *Bartramia longicauda*

Maben and Wiles's 1981 report (*Micronesica* 17:193) of this species on Guam is apparently based on an incorrect identification of Ruff. Their description fits that much more likely species better than it does this c. N. American bird.

SMALL PRATINCOLE   *Glareola lactea*

Unpublished reports of sightings of this species on Guam and Saipan (Mariana Is.) must be regarded with suspicion; no details have been given. The occurrence of this sedentary SE. Asian species in the Marianas would be highly improbable, as the bird has not been recorded in any intervening localities. If the birds seen were not simply juvenile Oriental Pratincoles, they might have been Australian Pratincoles (*Stiltia isabella*), which regularly migrate to the E. Indies and could easily overshoot and reach the Marianas.

SILVER GULL   *Larus novaehollandiae*

A medium-sized gull with pearly gray back, black wing tips, and bright red bill. Reported, probably erroneously, from the Marquesas and Society Is. in the 19th century. Indigenous to s. oceans from Africa to New Zealand.

MEW GULL   *Larus canus*

An unconfirmed sight record for Palau (Owen 1977). For descriptions and illustrations, see Eurasian and N. American field guides.

GULL-BILLED TERN   *Sterna nilotica*

This species was reported by King (1967) from the Hawaiian Is., but we can find no documentation of the record and the author (pers. comm.) does not recall its source. The only other report for the tropical Pacific is of two birds seen on Saipan, fall 1984 (T. K. Pratt, unpubl.). The latter record needs further substantiation. Illustrated in Eurasian and N. American field guides.

ROSEATE TERN   *Sterna dougalii*

This species is reported, without documentation, by King (1967), du-Pont (1976), Watling (1982), and others for Tonga and the Tuamotu Arch. We do not know the origin of these reports, and consider this species, which closely resembles both the Common and Arctic Tern, hypothetical in the tropical Pacific. This tern has a patchy, discontinuous worldwide distribution.

PALE-HEADED ROSELLA   *Platycercus adscitus*

This Australian parakeet was established on Maui (Hawaiian Is.) for at least 50 years (1877-1928 +), but has not been reported for several decades. It could still be present, since observers have spent very little time in low-elevation exotic forest on Maui. Look for it around Olinda, where it was reportedly numerous in the 1890s. It is a nearly white-headed small parrot with pale blue belly, red undertail coverts, long green tail, and scaly-looking, black and yellow back. Illustrated in Australian field guides.

COMMON KOEL   *Eudynamis scolopacea*

A large, long-tailed, black bird reported on Tobi (Palau) in 1978 was probably this species (Engbring 1983), but confirmation is needed.

BROWN HAWK-OWL   *Ninox scutulata*

This small, hawklike owl has been reported twice from Helen I. (Palau) and once from Rota (Mariana Is.) but no sighting has been documented sufficiently for the species to be added unequivocally to the list of Micronesian birds. This owl ranges from s. and e. Asia to Celebes, with n. populations migratory. It has a chocolate brown head and upperparts, white underparts with bold brown streaks, and yellow eyes. Illustrated in King and Dickinson (1975) and WBSJ (1982).

RED-BILLED BLUE MAGPIE   *Urocissa erythrorhyncha*

A striking, large, long-tailed bird with red bill, black head, blue upperparts, and white underparts and tail tip. Escaped from captivity on windward Oahu (Hawaiian Is.) in mid-1960s, and appeared to be established in Kahana Valley by 1970. Attempts by State Fish and Game officials to exterminate this potential agricultural pest appear to have succeeded.

VARIED TIT   *Parus varius*

A Japanese species apparently established for a time on Kauai and Oahu (Hawaiian Is.). Not reported since 1963. A small arboreal bird with bold pattern of black, white, and chestnut. For illustration, see Peterson (1961) or WBSJ (1982).

GREAT REED-WARBLER   *Acrocephalus arundinaceus*

An unidentified reed-warbler was seen once at Palau by J. Engbring and R. P. Owen (pers. comms.). Reed-warblers do not breed at Palau. Most likely the bird seen was of this species, which migrates from ne. Asia to the E. Indies. Should be looked for at Palau during winter months. Resembles Caroline Islands Reed-Warbler. Illustrated in Eurasian field guides.

MAGPIE-ROBIN   *Copsychus saularis*

A glossy black and white thrush, introduced to Kauai and Oahu (Hawaiian Is.) several times but not believed to be established. Reported occasionally on both islands during the past two decades. Similar to White-rumped Shama but with shorter tail, dark rump, and no rufous below. Also called Dyal Thrush. Illustrated in Peterson (1961).

ULIETA MYSTERY THRUSH *"Turdus ulietensis"*

See Mysterious Starling, below.

WHITE-THROATED LAUGHING-THRUSH *Garrulax albogularis*

This species was reported as established on Kauai (Hawaiian Is.) in the early 1960s. These reports were probably based on mistaken identifications of Greater Necklaced Laughing-thrush, which was not then known to be on Kauai. Both species have white throats, so the name could easily have been incorrectly applied to the latter species.

WHITE WAGTAIL *Motacilla alba*

This species was reported as a straggler to Palau before the equally likely Black-backed Wagtail (*M. lugens*) was recognized as a distinct species. The bird was an immature, and criteria for distinguishing these two species at that age have not been worked out. Both species are illustrated in WBSJ (1982) and NGS (1983).

MYSTERIOUS STARLING *"Aplonis mavornata"*

This species is known from a single specimen supposedly collected on one of Cook's voyages somewhere in the Pacific. Some have suggested that it came from Raiatea (Society Is.). If so, the species is now extinct. It is a small, brown, starlinglike bird with a faint gloss on the head. A bird described by Forster from Raiatea and named *"Turdus ulietensis"* may have been this species. His description sounds much more like a starling of the *Aplonis* group than a thrush. *Turdus ulietensis* is known only from his descriptions.

HILL MYNA *Gracula religiosa*

The "talking myna" of the pet trade, this species has escaped numerous times and bred in the wild on Oahu (Hawaiian Is.), but is not presently believed to be established; a small population persists in Lyon Arboretum. The Hill Myna is a large, chunky, glossy black bird with big, yellow-tipped red bill, yellow wattles behind the eye, and white wing patches. Utters loud humanlike whistles in the wild. See Plate 41.

GREAT-TAILED GRACKLE *Quiscalus mexicanus*

A female of this species was seen several times in the 1980s on Waipio Peninsula in Pearl Harbor, Oahu (Hawaiian Is.). The bird was almost certainly an escape from the Honolulu Zoo (where the species has bred in captivity) or a ship-assisted traveller. Illustrated in NGS (1983).

GRAY CANARY *Serinus leucopygius*

This W. Africa native was released in the 1960s and persisted for several years in the Kapiolani Park/Diamond Head area of Oahu (Hawaiian Is.), but is now believed to have died out. Looks like a Yellow-fronted Canary with all the yellow removed. Also called Gray Singing Finch and White-rumped Serin.

BLACK-RUMPED WAXBILL *Estrilda troglodytes*

This species was released in the mid-1960s near the base of Diamond Head on Oahu (Hawaiian Is.) and a small population built up there into the mid-1970s. Those birds appear to have died out. All birds of this species reported elsewhere on Oahu have, upon investigation, turned out to be misidentified Common Waxbills. A 1975 report of a flock of nine Black-rumped Waxbills in N. Kohala, Hawaii, may also be erroneous; neither species has been reported on Hawaii since. See Plate 43.

ZEBRA FINCH *Poephila guttata*

A small, red-billed finch with a bold black and white whisker mark and prominent white spots on central tail feathers. Male has rufous cheeks and flanks. Established for a time on Nauru, but not found there recently. Has probably died out.

WHITE-BACKED MANNIKIN *Lonchura striata*

A report of this SE. Asian finch for Johnston Atoll is almost surely based on escaped pet(s).

PIN-TAILED WHYDAH *Vidua macroura*

A small, red-billed finch. Male black and white with extremely long central tail feathers. Female sparrowlike, heavily streaked with dark brown. A popular cage bird released in Kapiolani Park, Honolulu, Oahu (Hawaiian Is.) in the 1960s. A brood parasite on waxbills, it appeared established by the mid-1970s but has since apparently died out. "Whydah" is a corruption of "widow" and is pronounced "whidda." Illustrated in Shallenberger (1984).

APPENDIX B. REGIONAL CHECKLISTS

SYMBOLS USED IN CHECKLISTS

R – Resident. Present all year, but not necessarily breeding.

M – Migratory breeder. Breeds at the locality, but departs for rest of year.

V – Visitor. Includes passage migrants as well as vagrants.

W – Winter resident. Resident in the islands during the nonbreeding season. Designates the season from the bird's perspective, i.e. the same symbol is used for Long-tailed Cuckoo (which visits during the austral winter) and Lesser Golden-Plover (which is a northern breeder).

X – Extinct.

? – Uncertain. Used alone designates records that are unconfirmed.

CHECKLIST 1. HAWAIIAN ISLANDS

	Kure, Midway	Other NW Hawaiian Is.	Kauai	Oahu	Molokai	Lanai	Maui
Arctic Loon				V			
Pied-billed Grebe			V	V			
Horned Grebe			V				
Eared Grebe				V			
Short-tailed Albatross	V	V					
Black-footed Albatross	M	M	V	V		V	V
Laysan Albatross	M	M	M	V			
Wedge-tailed Shearwater	M	M	M	M			M
Sooty Shearwater	V	V		V			
Christmas Shearwater	M	M		M	V		
Newell's (Townsend's) Shearwater			M	M?	M	M?	
Little Shearwater	V						
Bulwer's Petrel	M	M		M		M	M
Jouanin's Petrel		V					
Northern Fulmar	V	V		V			
Black-winged Petrel				V			
Mottled Petrel			V	V	V		
Bonin Petrel	M	M					
Stejneger's Petrel						V	
Herald Petrel		V					
Hawaiian (Dark-rumped) Petrel			M?		M?	M	M
Kermadec Petrel	V						
Juan Fernandez Petrel				V			
Murphy's Petrel	V	V					
Leach's Storm-Petrel	V		V	V			

	KM	NW	KA	OH	MO	LN	MA	HA
Band-rumped Storm-Petrel			M				M?	M?
Tristram's (Sooty) Storm-Petrel	M	M						
White-tailed Tropicbird	M		R	R	R	R	R	R
Red-billed Tropicbird		V	V					
Red-tailed Tropicbird	R	R	M	M	M	M	V	V
Masked Booby	M	M		R				
Brown Booby	M	M	M	R				V
Red-footed Booby	M	M	M	R				
Pelagic Cormorant		V						
Great Frigatebird	R	R	R	R	V		R	V
Lesser Frigatebird	V	V						
Great Blue Heron			V	V			V	V
Great Egret				V			V	
Snowy Egret				V			V	V
Little Blue Heron				V				V
Cattle Egret	V	V	R	R	R	R	R	R
Little (Green-backed) Heron								V
Black-crowned Night-Heron			R	R	R	R	R	R
White-faced Ibis				V	V			V
Fulvous Whistling-Duck				R				
Tundra Swan	V							
Greater White-fronted Goose	V			V	V			V
Snow Goose	V			V	V			V
Emperor Goose	V	V	V	V		V	V	V
Brant		V		V	V		V	V
Canada Goose	V			V	V		V	V
Hawaiian Goose							R	R
Green-winged Teal	V	V	V	V	V	V	V	V
Mallard	V	V	R	R	V	V	V	V
Hawaiian Duck			R	R	X	X	X	R
Laysan Duck		R						
Northern Pintail	W	W	W	W	W	W	W	W
Garganey	V			V	V			V
Blue-winged Teal			V	V	V		V	V

	KM	NW	KA	OH	MO	LN	MA	HA
Cinnamon Teal			V				V	
Northern Shoveler	W	W	W	W	W	W	W	W
Gadwall	V	V		V	V			
Eurasian Wigeon	V			V				V
American Wigeon	W	W	W	W	W	W	W	W
Common Pochard	V							
Canvasback				V	V		V	V
Redhead				V				
Ring-necked Duck				V				V
Tufted Duck	V			V				V
Greater Scaup		V	V	V				V
Lesser Scaup			W	W	W	W	W	W
Harlequin Duck	V	V						
Oldsquaw	V							
Black Scoter	V							
Surf Scoter				V				
Bufflehead	V			V			V	V
Hooded Merganser				V				V
Red-breasted Merganser				V	V			V
Ruddy Duck				V				V
Osprey			V	V	V		V	V
Steller's Sea-Eagle	V	V						
Northern Harrier	V			V				
Hawaiian Hawk				V			V	R
Golden Eagle			V					
Peregrine Falcon	V	V	V	V				V
Black Francolin					R	R	R	R
Gray Francolin			R	R	R	R	R	R
Erckel's Francolin			R	R	R	R	R	R
Chukar			R		R	R	R	R
Japanese Quail			R		R	R	R	R
Kalij Pheasant								R
Red Junglefowl			R	R	X	X	X	
Common (Ring-necked) Pheasant			R	R	R	R	R	
Common Peafowl				R			R	

	KM	NW	KA	OH	MO	LN	MA	HA
Wild Turkey						R	R	R
Gambel's Quail						R		R?
California Quail			R			R	R	R
Hawaiian Rail								X
Laysan Rail	X	X						
Common Moorhen			R	R	R		X	X
American Coot			V					V
Hawaiian Coot	V	V	R	R	R		R	R
Gray (Black-bellied) Plover	V	V	W	W	W	W	W	W
Lesser Golden-Plover	W	W	W	W	W	W	W	W
Mongolian Plover		V						
Common Ringed Plover	?							
Semipalmated Plover	V	V		W			W	V
Killdeer				V			V	V
Eurasian Dotterel	V							
Black-necked Stilt			R	R	R	V	R	R
Greater Yellowlegs		V		V				
Lesser Yellowlegs	V	V	W	W		V	W	
Wood Sandpiper	V							
Solitary Sandpiper								V
Willet				V			V	
Wandering Tattler	W	W	W	W	W	W	W	W
Siberian (Gray-tailed) Tattler	V							
Common/Spotted Sandpiper			V	V				
Whimbrel	V			V				
Bristle-thighed Curlew	W	W	V	V				V
Hudsonian Godwit				V?				
Bar-tailed Godwit	V	V		V			V	V
Marbled Godwit		V						
Ruddy Turnstone	W	W	W	W	W	W	W	W
Red Knot	V	V		V			V	
Sanderling	W	W	W	W	W	W	W	W
Semipalmated Sandpiper				V				
Western Sandpiper	V			V			V	
Rufous-necked Stint	V							V

	KM	NW	KA	OH	MO	LN	MA	HA
Little Stint	V							
Long-toed Stint	V							
Least Sandpiper				W			W	W
Baird's Sandpiper				V				
Pectoral Sandpiper	W	V		W			W	W
Sharp-tailed Sandpiper	W	W	W	W	W	W	W	W
Dunlin	V	V		V				
Curlew Sandpiper				V				
Buff-breasted Sandpiper	V		V	V				
Ruff	V	V		W			V	
Short-billed Dowitcher	V			V?				
Long-billed Dowitcher	V	V	V	V			V	
Common Snipe	V	V	V	V	V		V	V
Pin-tailed Snipe	V							
Wilson's Phalarope			V	V			V	
Red-necked Phalarope		V	V	V				
Red Phalarope		W	W	W				
Pomarine Jaeger				W	W	W		W
Laughing Gull			V	V			V	
Franklin's Gull		V	V	V			V	V
Common Black-headed Gull	V			V				
Bonaparte's Gull	V	V	V	V			V	V
Ring-billed Gull		V		V	V		V	V
California Gull				V			V	V
Herring Gull	V	V		V			V	
Slaty-backed Gull	V							
Western Gull				V				
Glaucous-winged Gull	V	V		V		V	V	V
Glaucous Gull	V		V	V		V	V	V
Black-legged Kittiwake	V	V		V				
Caspian Tern				V			V	V
Common Tern				V			V	V
Arctic Tern				V				V
Little/Least Tern	V	V	V	V				

	KM	NW	KA	OH	MO	LN	MA	HA
Spectacled (Gray-backed) Tern	M	M		M				
Sooty Tern	M	M		M				
Black Tern	V			V			V	V
Brown Noddy	R	R	R	R	R	R	R	R
Black Noddy	R	R	R	R	R	R	R	R
Blue-gray Noddy		R						
Common Fairy-Tern	R	R		R				
Parakeet Auklet	V	V						
Tufted Puffin		V						
Horned Puffin	V	V						
Chestnut-bellied Sandgrouse								R
Rock Dove	R	V	R	R	R	R	R	R
Spotted Dove			R	R	R	R	R	R
Zebra Dove			R	R	R	R	R	R
Mourning Dove								R
Rose-ringed Parakeet			R	R				R
Common Barn-Owl			R	R	R		R	R
Short-eared Owl	V	V	R	R	R	R	R	R
Island (Gray) Swiftlet				R				
Belted Kingfisher							V	V
Eurasian Skylark	V			R	R	R	R	R
Barn Swallow	V							V
Hawaiian Crow								R
Red-vented Bulbul				R	R?			R?
Red-whiskered Bulbul				R				
Elepaio			R	R				R
Japanese Bush-Warbler			R?	R	R	R	R	
Millerbird		R						
White-rumped Shama			R	R				
Kamao			R					
Amaui				X				
Olomao					R	X		
Omao								R
Puaiohi			R					

	KM	NW	KA	OH	MO	LN	MA	HA
Greater Necklaced Laughing-thrush			R					
Gray-sided Laughing-thrush				R				
Melodious Laughing-thrush			R	R	R		R	R
Red-billed Leiothrix			R	R	R		R	R
Northern Mockingbird		V	R	R	R	R	R	R
Olive Tree-Pipit	V							
Red-throated Pipit	V							
Water Pipit	V							
Common Myna	R		R	R	R	R	R	R
Kauai Oo			R					
Oahu Oo				X				
Bishop's Oo					X		R	
Hawaii Oo								X
Kioea								X
Japanese White-eye			R	R	R	R	R	R
Northern Cardinal		V	R	R	R	R	R	R
Red-crested Cardinal			R	R	R	R	R	R?
Yellow-billed Cardinal								R
Yellow-faced Grassquit				R				
Saffron Finch				R				R
Savannah Sparrow	V							
Snow Bunting	V							
Western Meadowlark			R					
House Finch		V	R	R	R	R	R	R
Common Redpoll	V							
Yellow-fronted Canary				R				R
Common Canary	R							
Laysan Finch	X	R						
Nihoa Finch		R						
Ou			R	X	X	X	X	R
Palila								R
Lesser Koa-Finch								X
Greater Koa-Finch								X
Kona Grosbeak								X

	KM	NW	KA	OH	MO	LN	MA	HA
Maui Parrotbill							R	
Common Amakihi				R	R	R?	R	R
Kauai Amakihi			R					
Anianiau			R					
Greater Amakihi								X
Akialoa			X?	X		X		X
Nukupuu			R	X			R	R
Akiapolaau								R
Akikiki (Kauai Creeper)			R					
Hawaii Creeper								R
Maui Creeper						X	R	
Kakawahie (Molokai Creeper)					X?			
Oahu Creeper				R				
Akepa				R?			R	R
Akekee (Kauai Akepa)			R					
Ula-ai-hawane								X
Iiwi			R	R	R	X	R	R
Hawaii Mamo								X
Black Mamo					X			
Akohekohe (Crested Honeycreeper)					X		R	
Apapane		X	R	R	R	R	R	R
Oo-uli							R	
House Sparrow			R	R	R	R	R	R
Red-cheeked Cordonbleu				R?				R
Lavender Waxbill				R?				R
Orange-cheeked Waxbill				R				R
Common Waxbill				R				
Red Avadavat			R?	R				R?
Warbling Silverbill			R?	R?	R	R	R	R
Nutmeg Mannikin				R	R	R	R	R
Chestnut Mannikin			R	R				
Java Sparrow			R	R				R

CHECKLIST 2. MICRONESIA (HIGH ISLANDS ONLY)

	Saipan, Tinian, Agiguan	Rota	Guam	Yap	Palau	Truk	Pohnpei	Kosrae
Laysan Albatross							V	
Streaked Shearwater	V			V	V	V		
Wedge-tailed Shearwater	R		X	V	V	V	V	V
Short-tailed Shearwater	V		V				V	
Christmas Shearwater	V							V
Newell's (Townsend's) Shearwater	V		V					
Audubon's Shearwater	V		V	V	R	R	R	R
Bulwer's Petrel						V?	V?	
Tahiti Petrel						V		
Leach's Storm-Petrel	V		V					
Matsudaira's Storm-Petrel	V		V		V		?	?
White-tailed Tropicbird	R	R	R	R	R	R	R	R
Red-tailed Tropicbird	R	R			V	V	V	
Masked Booby	R	V	?		V			
Brown Booby	R	R	V	V	R	R	R	V
Red-footed Booby	V	R	V		R	R	R	
Australian Pelican					V			
Little Pied Cormorant	V				R			
Great Frigatebird	V	V	V	V	R	R	R	
Lesser Frigatebird	V		?	V	V			
Yellow Bittern	R	R	R	R	R	R		
Schrenck's Bittern					V			
Black Bittern			V					
Gray Heron	V				V?			
Intermediate Egret	V	V	V	V	V	V		
Little Egret	V			V	V			
Pacific Reef-Heron	R	R	R	R	R	R	R	

	ST	RT	GU	YP	PA	TK	PO	KS
Cattle Egret	V	V	V	V	V	V	V	
Little (Green-backed) Heron	V		?		V	V		
Black-crowned Night-Heron	V			V	V	V	V	
Rufous Night-Heron	?			?	R	R		
Japanese Night-Heron					V			
Malayan Night-Heron					V			
Green-winged Teal	V				V			
Mallard	X		X	?				
Gray Duck					R	R		
Northern Pintail	V		V		V	V		
Garganey	V		V		V			
Northern Shoveler	V		V				V	V
Eurasian Wigeon	V		V	V	V	V		
American Wigeon			V					
Common Pochard			V					
Tufted Duck	V		V	V	V			
Osprey			V		V			
Brahminy Kite					V			
Japanese Sparrowhawk			V					
Chinese Goshawk		V	V	V	V			
Eurasian Kestrel	V							
Peregrine Falcon			V	V	V			
Micronesian Megapode	R	X	X		R			
Black Francolin			R					
Blue-breasted Quail			R					
Red Junglefowl		R		R	R	R	R	R
Banded Rail					R			
Guam Rail			R					
Banded Crake					R			
Red-legged Crake					V			
White-browed Crake			X	R	R	R	R	
Kosrae Crake								X
Common Moorhen	R		X		R			
Bush-hen					V			
Purple Swamphen					R			

	ST	RT	GU	YP	PA	TK	PO	KS
Eurasian Coot	V		V					
Gray (Black-bellied) Plover	V	V	V	V	V	V		
Lesser Golden-Plover	W	W	W	W	W	W	W	W
Mongolian Plover	W	W	W	W	W	W	W	W
Great Sand-Plover	V		V	V	W	V		V
Snowy Plover	V				V			
Common Ringed Plover			V		V			
Little Ringed Plover			?	V	V			
Oriental Plover					V			
Eurasian Oystercatcher			V					
Black-winged Stilt					V			
Common Greenshank	V		W	W	W	W		
Nordmann's Greenshank			V					
Marsh Sandpiper	V		V	V	V	V		
Common Redshank				V	V			
Spotted Redshank			V			V		
Wood Sandpiper	W		W	W	W	W		
Wandering Tattler	W	W	W	W	W	W	W	
Siberian (Gray-tailed) Tattler	W	W	W	W	W	W	W	
Common Sandpiper	V?	W	W	W	W	W	W?	
Terek Sandpiper	V		V	V	V			
Little Curlew			V		V			
Whimbrel	W	W	W	W	W	W	W	
Bristle-thighed Curlew	V		?	?		V	V	
Far Eastern Curlew			?	V	V	V		
Eurasian Curlew	V							
Black-tailed Godwit			V	V	V	V		
Bar-tailed Godwit	V		V		W	W	W	
Ruddy Turnstone	W	W	W	W	W	W	W	
Great Knot					V	V		
Red Knot					V			
Sanderling	V		W	W	W	W	W	
Rufous-necked Stint	W		W	W	W	W		
Little Stint	?							
Temminck's Stint	V							
Long-toed Stint			V	V	V	V		

	ST	RT	GU	YP	PA	TK	PO	KS
Pectoral Sandpiper	V		V		V		V	
Sharp-tailed Sandpiper	V	V	W	W	W	W	V	V
Dunlin	V		V		V		V	
Curlew Sandpiper				V	V			
Broad-billed Sandpiper					V			
Buff-breasted Sandpiper							V	
Ruff	V		V		V	V		
Common Snipe	V							
Pin-tailed Snipe	?	?						
Swinhoe's Snipe	V	V	V	V	W	V		
Oriental Pratincole				V	V	V		
Long-tailed Jaeger					V			
Franklin's Gull						V		
Common Black-headed Gull	V		V		W			
Herring Gull					?			
Great Crested Tern	V		V	R	R	R	R	V
Common Tern	V		V	V	V	V	V	
Black-naped Tern			V	R	R	R	R	
Little Tern	V		V		V	V	V	?
Spectacled (Gray-backed) Tern				?	?			
Bridled Tern					R			
Sooty Tern	R	V	V	V	R	R	R	V
Whiskered Tern				V				
White-winged Tern	V		V		V			
Brown Noddy	R	R	R	R	R	R	R	R
Black Noddy	R	V		R	R	R	R	R
Common Fairy-Tern	R	R	R	R	R	R	R	R
Rock Dove	R	R	R			R	R	R
Philippine Turtle-Dove	R	R	R					
Nicobar Pigeon					R			
White-throated Ground-Dove	R	R	R	R				
Caroline Islands Ground-Dove						R	R	
Palau Ground-Dove					R			
Purple-capped Fruit-Dove						R	R	R
Palau Fruit-Dove					R			
Mariana Fruit-Dove	R	R	R					

	ST	RT	GU	YP	PA	TK	PO	KS
Micronesian Pigeon				R	R	R	R	R
Pohnpei Lory							R	
Greater Sulphur-crested Cockatoo					R			
Eclectus Parrot					R			
Chestnut-winged Cuckoo					V			
Hodgson's Hawk-Cuckoo					V			
Common Cuckoo					V			
Oriental Cuckoo				V	W			
Brush Cuckoo					V			
Long-tailed Cuckoo				V	V	W	W	W
Palau Owl					R			
Short-eared Owl	V		V	?			R	V
Jungle Nightjar					R			
Island (Gray) Swiftlet	R	X	R	?	R	R	R	R
Collared Kingfisher	R	R			R			
Micronesian Kingfisher			R		R		R	
Rainbow Bee-eater					V			
Dollarbird				V	V		V	
Barn Swallow	W	W	W	W	W	W	W	
Asian House-Martin					V			
Black Drongo		R	R					
Mariana Crow		R	R					
Cicadabird				R	R		R	
Morningbird					R			
Yap Monarch				R				
Tinian Monarch	R							
Truk Monarch						R		
Mangrove Flycatcher					R			
Guam Flycatcher			R					
Oceanic Flycatcher						R		
Pohnpei Flycatcher							R	
Palau Fantail					R			
Rufous Fantail	R	R	R	R				
Pohnpei Fantail							R	
Palau Bush-Warbler					R			

	ST	RT	GU	YP	PA	TK	PO	KS
Lanceolated Grasshopper-Warbler					V			
Nightingale Reed-Warbler	R		X					
Caroline Islands Reed-Warbler						R	R	X
Narcissus Flycatcher					V			
Gray-spotted Flycatcher					V			
Siberian Rubythroat					V			
Blue Rock-Thrush					V			
Eye-browed Thrush					V			
Yellow Wagtail		V		W	W			
Gray Wagtail			V		V			
Red-throated Pipit					V			
White-breasted Woodswallow					R			
Brown Shrike					V			
Pohnpei Mountain Starling							X?	
Kosrae Mountain Starling								X
Micronesian Starling	R	R	R	R	R	R	R	R
Red-cheeked Starling					V			
Ashy Starling	V							
Micronesian Honeyeater	R	R	R	R	R	R	R	R
Bridled White-eye	R	R	R					
Plain White-eye				R				
Caroline Islands White-eye					R	R	R	
Dusky White-eye					R			
Gray White-eye							R	R
Golden White-eye	R							
Great Truk White-eye						R		
Olive White-eye				R				
Long-billed White-eye							R	
Giant White-eye					R			
Black-headed Bunting					V			
Eurasian Tree Sparrow	R	R	R	R				
Blue-faced Parrotfinch					R	R	R	R
Nutmeg Mannikin			R	X				
Chestnut Mannikin			R		R			
Hunstein's Mannikin							R	

CHECKLIST 3. CENTRAL PACIFIC ISLANDS

	Wake I.	Marshall Is.	Nauru	Gilbert Is.	Phoenix Is.	Line Is.	Tuvalu	Tokelau
Black-footed Albatross	V	V						
Laysan Albatross	V	V						
Pink-footed Shearwater						V		
Flesh-footed Shearwater		V						
Wedge-tailed Shearwater		R			R	M		
Sooty Shearwater		V			V	V		
Short-tailed Shearwater		V		V	V	V		
Christmas Shearwater	V	R		V	R	R	V	
Audubon's Shearwater			V		R	M	V	
Bulwer's Petrel		V			R			
Black-winged Petrel		V			V	V		
White-naped (White-necked) Petrel		?		V	V	V		
Mottled Petrel					V	V		
Bonin Petrel		V			V	V		
Stejneger's Petrel		V			V	V		
Collared Petrel					V	V		
Cook's Petrel					V	V		
Phoenix Petrel					R	R		
Kermadec Petrel		V						
Juan Fernandez Petrel		V		V	V	V		
Wilson's Storm-Petrel		V			V			
Polynesian Storm-Petrel				V	R	M		
Leach's Storm-Petrel		V			V	V		
Band-rumped Storm-Petrel		V			V			
White-tailed Tropicbird	R	R	R	R	V	R	R	
Red-billed Tropicbird		?						
Red-tailed Tropicbird	R	R	V	V	R	R	V	

	WI	MI	NU	GI	PH	LI	TU	TO
Masked Booby	R	R		V	R	R	V	
Brown Booby	R	R	V	R	V	R	V	V
Red-footed Booby	R	R		R	R	R	V	?
Great Frigatebird	R	R	V	R	R	R	V	V
Lesser Frigatebird		V		V	R	R	V	V
Pacific Reef-Heron		R	R	R	R	R	R	
Cattle Egret		V						
Snow Goose		V						
Canada Goose		V		V				
Green-winged Teal		V				V		
Mallard		?		?				
Northern Pintail	V	V				V		
Garganey	V							
Northern Shoveler	V	V		V		V		
Gadwall		V				X		
Eurasian Wigeon		V			V			
Canvasback		V						
Tufted Duck		V						
Wake Rail	X							
White-browed Crake		V						
Gray (Black-bellied) Plover		V	V	V				
Lesser Golden-Plover	W	W	W	W	W	W	W	W
Mongolian Plover		V	V					
Great Sand-Plover			V					
Semipalmated Plover							?	
Stilt (sp. ?)				V				
Greater Yellowlegs	?	V						
Wood Sandpiper		V						
Wandering Tattler	W	W	W	W	W	W	W	W
Siberian (Gray-tailed) Tattler		W	W	W			W	
Common Sandpiper					V			
Spotted Sandpiper		V						
Tuamotu Sandpiper						X		
Whimbrel		V	V	V			V	
Bristle-thighed Curlew	V	W		W	W	W	W	W

	WI	MI	NU	GI	PH	LI	TU	TO
Black-tailed Godwit		V		V				
Bar-tailed Godwit		W	W	V				
Ruddy Turnstone	W	W	W	W	W	W	W	W
Sanderling	V	W		W	W	W	W	W
Rufous-necked Stint		V						
Pectoral Sandpiper		V			V			
Sharp-tailed Sandpiper	V	V	V		V	V		
Dunlin	V							
Buff-breasted Sandpiper		V						
Ruff		V						
Common Snipe	V							
Japanese Snipe		V						
Red Phalarope						V		
Oriental Pratincole		V						
Pomarine Jaeger					V	V		
Long-tailed Jaeger					V	V		
South Polar Skua				?	V	V		
Laughing Gull					V	V		
Franklin's Gull		V				V		
Ring-billed Gull						V		
Great Crested Tern		R		R	V	R	R	
Common Tern		V						
Arctic Tern		V						
Black-naped Tern		R	R	R		V	R	R
Little Tern		V		V				
Spectacled (Gray-backed) Tern	V	V		V	R	R	V	
Bridled Tern		V						
Sooty Tern	R	R	R	R	R	R	R	R
Brown Noddy	R	R	R	R	R	R	R	R
Black Noddy	V	R	R	R	R	R	R	R
Blue-gray Noddy		R		R	R	R	V	?
Common Fairy-Tern	V	R	R	R	R	R	R	R
Little Fairy-Tern					?	?		
Rock Dove				R				

	WI	MI	NU	GI	PH	LI	TU	TO
Polynesian Ground-Dove				?				
Shy Ground-Dove				R?				
Purple-capped Fruit-Dove		X						
Pacific Pigeon					R		R	
Micronesian Pigeon		R	R	R				
Kuhl's Lorikeet						R		
Long-tailed Cuckoo		W	W	W	W		W	W
Short-eared Owl		V						
Fork-tailed Swift		V						
Sacred Kingfisher		V	?					
Barn Swallow		V						
Nauru Reed-Warbler			R					
Bokikokiko						R		
Eurasian Tree Sparrow		R						

CHECKLIST 4. CENTRAL POLYNESIA

	Savaii	Upolu	American Samoa	Wallis and Futuna	Northern Tonga	Ha'apai	Southern Tonga	Niue
Wedge-tailed Shearwater	R	R	R	V	R	R	R	R
Short-tailed Shearwater	V	V	V					
Christmas Shearwater			R					
Audubon's Shearwater	R	R	R	R?	M	M	V	
Tahiti Petrel			R					
Giant-Petrel (sp. ?)						V		V
Black-winged Petrel						V		
White-naped (White-necked) Petrel			V					
Collared Petrel	V	V	R					
Phoenix Petrel					R	R	R	
Herald Petrel					R	R	R	
White-bellied Storm-Petrel	V	V	V					
Black-bellied Storm-Petrel	V	V	V					
Polynesian Storm-Petrel	R	R	R					
White-tailed Tropicbird	R	R	R	R?	R	R	R	R
Red-tailed Tropicbird	R	R	R		R	R		V
Masked Booby			R	V?	V			
Brown Booby	V	V	R	V?	R	V	V	
Red-footed Booby	R	R	R	V?	R	V	V	R
Great Frigatebird	R	R	R	V?	V	V	V	V
Lesser Frigatebird	V	V	R	V?	V	V	V	
White-faced Heron								V
Snowy Egret			V					
Pacific Reef-Heron	R	R	R	R?	R	R	R	V
Cattle Egret			V					
Gray Duck	R	R	R		R	R	R	R?
Swamp Harrier						R		

	SA	UP	AS	WF	NT	HP	TN	NI
Peregrine Falcon	V							
Niuafo'ou Megapode					R			
Red Junglefowl	R	R	X		R	R	R	R
Banded Rail	R	R	R	R	R	R	R	R
White-browed Crake	R	R						
Spotless Crake	R		R?		R	R?	R?	R
Samoan Woodhen	X							
Purple Swamphen	R	R	R		R	R	R	R
Lesser Golden-Plover	W	W	W	W	W	W	W	W
Wandering Tattler	W	W	W	W?	W	W	W	W
Common Sandpiper		V						
Whimbrel	V	V	V					
Bristle-thighed Curlew	W	W	W		V			W
Far Eastern Curlew	V							
Eurasian Curlew								V
Bar-tailed Godwit		V	V		W	W	W	V
Ruddy Turnstone	W	W	W		V			W
Sanderling			V					
Pectoral Sandpiper								V
Laughing Gull		V						
Great Crested Tern			V		R	R	R	
Black-naped Tern	V	V	V		V	R	V	
Little Tern		V						
Spectacled (Gray-backed) Tern	V	V	M					
Sooty Tern	M	M	M		M	V	V	
Brown Noddy					R	R	R	V
Black Noddy					R	R	R	
Blue-gray Noddy	R	R	R		R			
Common Fairy-Tern	R	R	R	R?	R	R	R	R
Rock Dove	R	R	R					
White-throated Pigeon	R	R						
...hy Ground-Dove	R	R	R	R	R	R		
...ooth-billed Pigeon	R	R						
...any-colored Fruit-Dove	R	R	R		R	R	R	
...urple-capped Fruit-Dove	R	R	R	R	R	R	R	R

	SA	UP	AS	WF	NT	HP	TN	NI
Pacific Pigeon	R	R	R	R	R	R	R	R
Blue-crowned Lorikeet	R	R	R		R	R	X	R
Red Shining-Parrot							R	
Long-tailed Cuckoo	W	W	W	W	W	W	W	W
Common Barn-Owl	R	R	R	R	R	R	R	R
White-rumped Swiftlet	R	R	R	R	R	R	R	R
Collared Kingfisher			R		R	R	R	
Sacred Kingfisher				R				
Flat-billed Kingfisher	R	R						
Pacific Swallow						R		
Polynesian Triller	R	R		R	R	R	R	R
Samoan Triller	R	R						
Red-vented Bulbul	R	R	R		R		R	
Scarlet Robin	R	R						
Tongan Whistler					R			
Samoan Whistler	R	R						
Fiji Shrikebill			R		R	R	X	
Samoan Flycatcher	R	R						
Samoan Fantail	R	R						
Island Thrush	R	R						
Samoan Starling	R	R	R					
Polynesian Starling	R	R	R	R	R	R	R	R
European Starling							R	
Jungle Myna		R						
Cardinal Honeyeater	R	R	R					
Wattled Honeyeater	R	R	R	R	R	R	R	
Mao	R	R	X?					
Samoan White-eye	R							
Red-headed Parrotfinch	R	R						

CHECKLIST 5. SOUTHEASTERN POLYNESIA

	Cook Is.	Leeward Society Is.	Tahiti and Moorea	Tuamotu Arch.	Marquesas Is.	Northern Tubuai Is.	Rapa	Pitcairn Is.
Wandering Albatross					V			
Black-browed Albatross				V				V
Light-mantled Albatross					V			
Wedge-tailed Shearwater	V	R	R	R	R	R	R	R
Sooty Shearwater	V	V	V		V			
Short-tailed Shearwater		V	V	V				
Christmas Shearwater				R	R	V	R	R
Little Shearwater					V		M	
Audubon's Shearwater	V	R	V	R	R			
Bulwer's Petrel		V	V		R			
Tahiti Petrel	V	R	R		R			
Antarctic Giant-Petrel			V	V		V		
Hall's Giant-Petrel	V							
Cape Petrel	V				V			
Black-winged Petrel	V	V	V		V	V	M	
White-naped (White-necked) Petrel	V							
Collared Petrel	V			V				
Phoenix Petrel	?			R	R			R
Herald Petrel	M			R	R			M
Kermadec Petrel	V			R		R	R	M
Murphy's Petrel		V	V	R			R	R
White-bellied Storm-Petrel	V	V	V		V	V	R	
Black-bellied Storm-Petrel					V			
Polynesian Storm-Petrel	V	V	V	M	R	V	R	
Leach's Storm-Petrel					V			
White-tailed Tropicbird	R	R	R	R	R	R	R	V
Red-billed Tropicbird					V?			

	CI	LS	TM	TA	MQ	TB	RP	PT
Red-tailed Tropicbird	R	R	R	R	V	R	R	R
Masked Booby	R	V	V	R	V			R
Brown Booby	R	R	R	R	R	R	R	V
Red-footed Booby	R	R	R	R	R	R	R	R
Great Frigatebird	R	R	R	R	R	R	R	R
Lesser Frigatebird	R	R	R	R	R	R	R	
Pacific Reef-Heron	R	R	R	R	R	R		
Little (Green-backed) Heron			R					
Mallard	V							
Gray Duck	R	R	R			R	R	
Northern Pintail	V		V		V			
Northern Shoveler				V				
Swamp Harrier		R	R					
Red Junglefowl		R	R	R	R			
Spotless Crake	R	R	R	R	R	R	R	R
Henderson Island Crake								R
Gray (Black-bellied) Plover	V							
Lesser Golden-Plover	W	W	W	W	W	W	W	
Wandering Tattler	W	W	W	W	W	W	W	W
Siberian (Gray-tailed) Tattler	V							
Tuamotu Sandpiper				R				
Tahitian Sandpiper			X					
Bristle-thighed Curlew	W	W	W	W	W			W
Ruddy Turnstone	V	V	V	V				
Sanderling	V	V		V	V			V
Pectoral Sandpiper		V					V	
Buff-breasted Sandpiper							V	
Franklin's Gull				V				
Great Crested Tern	V	R	R	R				
Common Tern	V							
Black-naped Tern	R							
Spectacled (Gray-backed) Tern				R	V			
Sooty Tern	R	V	V	R	R	R	R	R
Brown Noddy	R	R	R	R	R	R	R	R
Black Noddy	R	V	V	R	R	R	R	

	CI	LS	TM	TA	MQ	TB	RP	PT
Blue-gray Noddy	R			R	R			R
Common Fairy-Tern	R	R	R	R	R	R	R	R
Little Fairy-Tern					R			
Rock Dove	R	R	R	R	R			
Zebra Dove			R					
Polynesian Ground-Dove			X	R				
Marquesas Ground-Dove					R			
Cook Islands Fruit-Dove	R							
Henderson Island Fruit-Dove								R
Gray-green Fruit-Dove		R	R					
Atoll Fruit-Dove				R				
Makatea Fruit-Dove				R				
White-capped Fruit-Dove					R			
Red-mustached Fruit-Dove					X?			
Rapa Fruit-Dove							R	
Pacific Pigeon	R							
Polynesian Pigeon			R	R				
Nukuhiva Pigeon					R			
Kuhl's Lorikeet						R		
Stephen's Lorikeet								R
Blue Lorikeet	R	R	X	R				
Ultramarine Lorikeet					R			
Black-fronted Parakeet			X					
Raiatea Parakeet		X						
Long-tailed Cuckoo	W	W	W	W	W	W	W	W
Tahiti Swiftlet			R					
Atiu Swiftlet	R							
Marquesas Swiftlet					R			
Chattering Kingfisher	R	R	R					
Mangaia Kingfisher	R							
Tuamotu Kingfisher				R				
Marquesas Kingfisher					R			
Tahiti Kingfisher			R					
Pacific Swallow			R					
Red-vented Bulbul			R					

	CI	LS	TM	TA	MQ	TB	RP	PT
Rarotonga Monarch	R							
Tahiti Monarch		X	R					
Iphis Monarch					R			
Marquesas Monarch					R			
Fatuhiva Monarch					R			
Tahiti Reed-Warbler		R	R					
Marquesas Reed-Warbler					R			
Tuamotu Reed-Warbler				R				
Cook Islands Reed-Warbler	R							
Pitcairn Reed-Warbler						R		R
Rarotonga Starling	R							
Common Myna	R	R	R		R			
Silvereye		R	R			R		
Crimson-backed Tanager			R					
Common Waxbill			R					
Red-browed Firetail			R		R			
Chestnut-breasted Mannikin		R	R		R			

CHECKLIST 6. FIJI

(Asterisk indicates seabirds that are widespread in the islands and whose exact distribution is not well documented.)

	Viti Levu	Vanua Levu	Taveuni	Kadavu	Gau	Ovalau	Lau Archipelago	Rotuma
Wandering Albatross				V				
Wedge-tailed Shearwater*	R	R	R	R	R	R	R	R
Buller's Shearwater			V	V			V	
Sooty Shearwater	V				V	V		
Short-tailed Shearwater	V				V	V	V	
Audubon's Shearwater*	R	R	R	R	R	R	R	
Fiji Petrel					R			
Antarctic Giant-Petrel	V							
Cape Petrel					V			
White-naped (White-necked) Petrel	V							
Mottled Petrel					V			
Collared Petrel*	R	R	R	R	R	R	R	
Polynesian Storm-Petrel*	R	R	R	R	R	R		
White-tailed Tropicbird*	R	R	R	R	R	R	R	R
Red-tailed Tropicbird*	R	R	R	R	R	R	R	R
Masked Booby*	R	R	R	R	R	R	R	R
Brown Booby*	R	R	R	R	R	R	R	R
Red-footed Booby*	R	R	R	R	R	R	R	R
Australian Pelican	V							
Great Frigatebird*	R	R	R	R	R	R	R	R
Lesser Frigatebird*	R	R	R	R	R	R	R	R
White-faced Heron	V							
Pacific Reef-Heron	R	R	R	R	R	R	R	R
Little (Green-backed) Heron	R	R	R	R	R	R	R	

	VI	VN	TV	KD	GA	OV	LA	RM
Wandering Whistling-Duck	V							
Gray Duck	R	R	R	R	R	R	R	
Swamp Harrier	R	R	R	R	R	R	R	
Fiji Goshawk	R	R	R	R	R	R		
Peregrine Falcon	R	R	R		R	R		
Brown Quail	R	R						
Red Junglefowl	X	X	R	R	R	R	R	R
Banded Rail	X	X	R	R	R	R	R	R
Bar-winged Rail	R?					X		
White-browed Crake	R	R	R	R	R	R		
Spotless Crake	R	R	R	R	R	R	R	
Purple Swamphen	X	X	R	R	R	R	R	R
Lesser Golden-Plover	W	W	W	W	W	W	W	W
Mongolian Plover	V							
Double-banded Dotterel	V						V	
Wandering Tattler	W	W	W	W	W	W	W	W
Siberian (Gray-tailed) Tattler	W	W	W	W	W	W	W	W
Terek Sandpiper	V							
Whimbrel	W	W	W	W	W	W	W	W
Bristle-thighed Curlew	W	W	W	W	W	W	W	W
Far Eastern Curlew	V							
Hudsonian Godwit	V							
Bar-tailed Godwit	W	W	W	W	W	W	W	W
Ruddy Turnstone	W	W	W	W	W	W	W	W
Red Knot	V	V						
Sanderling	V	V						
Rufous-necked Stint	V							
Sharp-tailed Sandpiper	V							
Pomarine Jaeger				V				
Parasitic Jaeger				V				
Great Crested Tern*	R	R	R	R	R	R	R	R
Common Tern*	V	V	V	V	V	V		
Black-naped Tern*	R	R	R	R	R	R	R	
Spectacled (Gray-backed) Tern	V	V						

	VI	VN	TV	KD	GA	OV	LA	RM
Sooty Tern*	R	R	R	R	R	R	R	R
Brown Noddy*	R	R	R	R	R	R	R	R
Black Noddy*	R	R	R	R	R	R	R	R
Blue-gray Noddy*	R	R	R	R	R	R	R	R
Common Fairy-Tern*	R	R	R	R	R	R	R	R
Rock Dove	R	R	R					
White-throated Pigeon	R	R	R	R	R	R	R	
Spotted Dove	R	R	R				R	
Shy Ground-Dove	R	R	R	R	R	R	R	
Many-colored Fruit-Dove	R	R	R	R	R	R	R	
Purple-capped Fruit-Dove							R	R
Whistling Dove			R					
Golden Dove	R				R	R		
Orange Dove		R	R					
Pacific Pigeon					R	R	R	R
Peale's Pigeon	R	R	R	R	R	R	R	
Collared Lory	R	R	R	R	R	R	R	
Red-throated Lorikeet	R	R	R			X		
Blue-crowned Lorikeet							R	
Red Shining-Parrot	R	R	R	R	R			
Masked Shining-Parrot	R							
Fan-tailed Cuckoo	R	R	R	R	R	R		
Long-tailed Cuckoo	W	W	W	W	W	W	W	W
Eastern Grass-Owl	X?							
Common Barn-Owl	R	R	R	R	R	R	R	R
White-throated Needletail	V							
White-rumped Swiftlet	R	R	R	R	R	R	R	
Collared Kingfisher							R	
Sacred Kingfisher	R	R	R	R	R	R		
Pacific Swallow	R	R	R	R	R	R	R	
Australian Magpie		V	R					
Polynesian Triller	R	R	R	R	R	R	R	R
Red-vented Bulbul	R					R		
Scarlet Robin	R	R	R	R				

	VI	VN	TV	KD	GA	OV	LA	RM
Golden Whistler	R	R	R	R	R	R	R	
Fiji Shrikebill	R	R	R	R	R	R	R	R
Black-faced Shrikebill	R	R	R	R		R		
Slaty Flycatcher	R	R	R	R	R	R	R	
Versicolor Flycatcher							R	
Vanikoro Flycatcher	R	R	R	R	R	R	R	
Blue-crested Flycatcher	R	R	R					
Silktail		R	R					
Streaked Fantail	R	R	R			R		
Kadavu Fantail				R				
Fiji Bush-Warbler	R	R	R	R				
Long-legged Warbler	R	R						
Island Thrush	R	R	R	R	R	R		
White-breasted Woodswallow	R	R	R		R			
Polynesian Starling	R	R	R	R	R	R	R	R
European Starling							R	
Common Myna	R	R	R	R	R	R		
Jungle Myna	R							
Rotuma Honeyeater								R
Orange-breasted Honeyeater	R	R	R	R	R	R	R	
Wattled Honeyeater	R	R	R		R	R	R	
Kadavu Honeyeater				R				
Giant Forest Honeyeater	R	R	R					
Layard's White-eye	R	R	R	R		R		
Silvereye	R	R	R	R	R	R		
Red Avadavat	R	R						
Red-headed Parrotfinch	R	R	R	R				
Pink-billed Parrotfinch	R							
Java Sparrow	R	R	R					

APPENDIX C. REGIONAL MAPS

THE maps presented here are intended primarily as an aid to understanding bird distributions. All islands that are mentioned in the text are labelled on one of the following maps. Some minor inaccuracies are inherent. Island shapes often are not precise, but should provide a general idea of the outlines of the larger islands. Sizes of small islands must be exaggerated for clarity; even the smallest possible ink dot would be too large for some of these tiny bits of land. Coral reefs and atolls are indicated by dotted lines that only approximate the actual shapes of the reefs. Finally, scales are only approximations inasmuch as such measurements vary progressively as one travels further from the equator. We have labelled mostly geographical rather than political entities, although some of the latter are indicated.

The five maps labelled A through E are those referred to by the circled letters on the map of the Tropical Pacific (pp. xvi-xvii), and cover fairly broad regions. The remaining maps are of those island groups in which birds are unevenly distributed. All islands, however small, that are mentioned in the text are labelled.

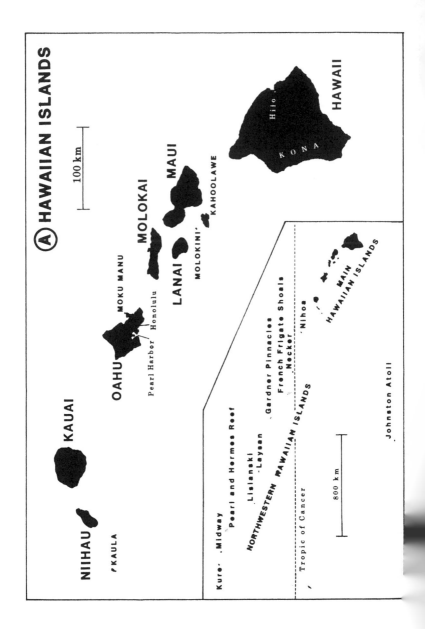

Ⓐ HAWAIIAN ISLANDS

100 km

KAUAI

NIIHAU

KAULA

OAHU

MOKU MANU

Pearl Harbor   Honolulu

MOLOKAI

LANAI

MAUI

MOLOKINI

KAHOOLAWE

KONA

Hilo

HAWAII

Kure   Midway

Pearl and Hermes Reef

Lisianski   Layaan   Gardner Pinnacles

French Frigate Shoals

NORTHWESTERN HAWAIIAN ISLANDS   Necker

Nihoa

NiNoa   MAIN

HAWAIIAN ISLANDS

Tropic of Cancer

800 km

Johnston Atoll

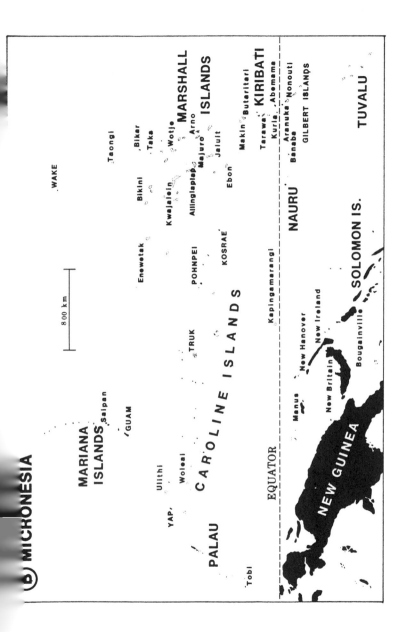

(b) MICRONESIA

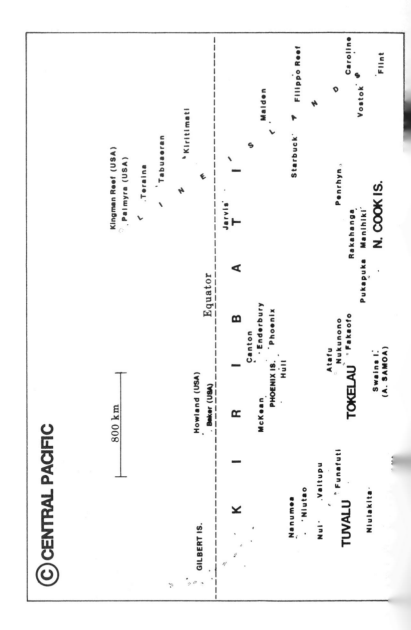

© CENTRAL PACIFIC

800 km

GILBERT IS.

Howland (USA)
Baker (USA)

Kingman Reef (USA)
Palmyra (USA)
Teraina
Tabuaeran
Kiritimati

Equator

K I R I B A T I

Nenumea
Niutao
Nui   Vaitupu
Funafuti
TUVALU
Niulakita

McKean   Canton
Enderbury
PHOENIX IS.   Phoenix
Hull

Atafu
Nukunono
TOKELAU   Fakaofo

Swains I.
(A. SAMOA)

Jarvis

Malden

Starbuck   Filippo Reef

Pukapuka   Manihiki
Rakahanga   Penrhyn

N. COOK IS.

Caroline
Vostok
Flint

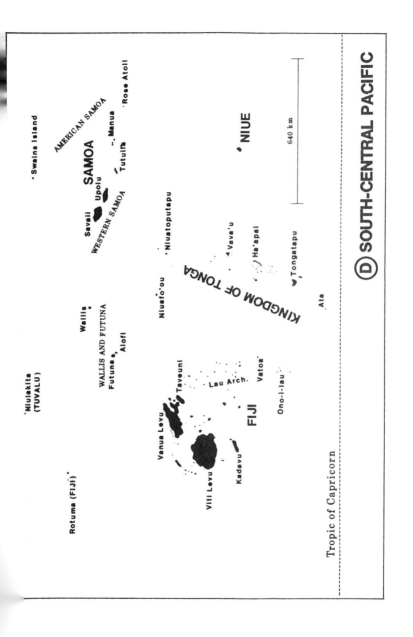

Niulakita (TUVALU)

Rotuma (FIJI)

Swains Island

AMERICAN SAMOA

SAMOA

Savaii   Upolu
WESTERN SAMOA

Menua   Rose Atoll
Tutuila

Wallis
WALLIS AND FUTUNA
Futuna   Alofi

Niuafo'ou

Niuatoputapu

KINGDOM OF TONGA

Vava'u
Ha'apai
Tongatapu

Ata

NIUE

640 km

Venua Levu
Taveuni

Lau Arch.

Vatoa

FIJI

Viti Levu

Ono-i-lau

Kadavu

Tropic of Capricorn

Ⓓ SOUTH-CENTRAL PACIFIC

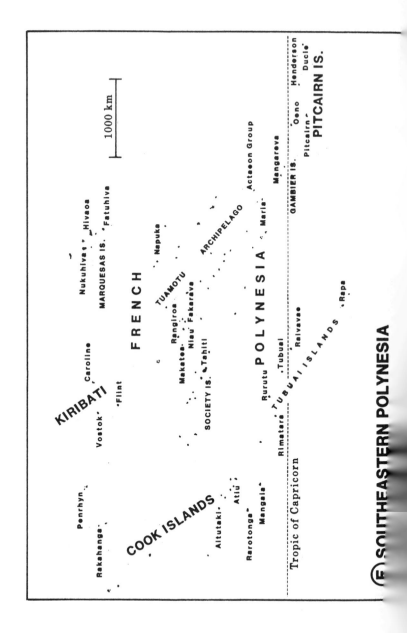

SOUTHEASTERN POLYNESIA

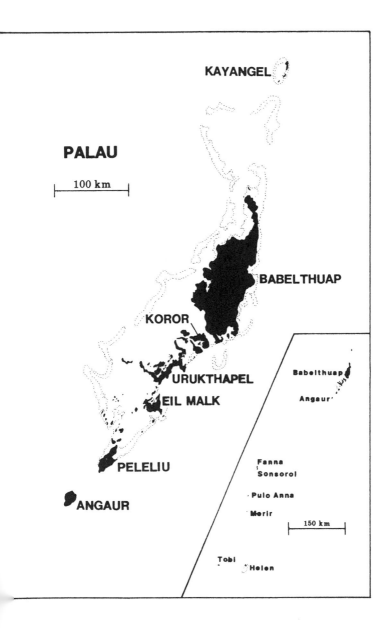

PALAU

100 km

KAYANGEL

BABELTHUAP

KOROR

URUKTHAPEL

EIL MALK

PELELIU

ANGAUR

Babelthuap

Angaur

Fanna
Sonsorol

Pulo Anna

Merir

150 km

Tobi   Helen

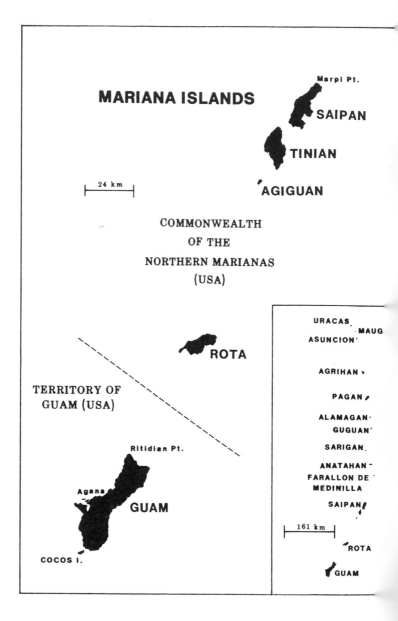

MARIANA ISLANDS

Marpi Pt.

SAIPAN

TINIAN

'AGIGUAN

24 km

COMMONWEALTH
OF THE
NORTHERN MARIANAS
(USA)

ROTA

TERRITORY OF
GUAM (USA)

Ritidian Pt.

Agana

GUAM

COCOS I.

URACAS
MAUG
ASUNCION

AGRIHAN

PAGAN

ALAMAGAN
GUGUAN

SARIGAN

ANATAHAN
FARALLON DE
MEDINILLA

SAIPAN

161 km

ROTA

GUAM

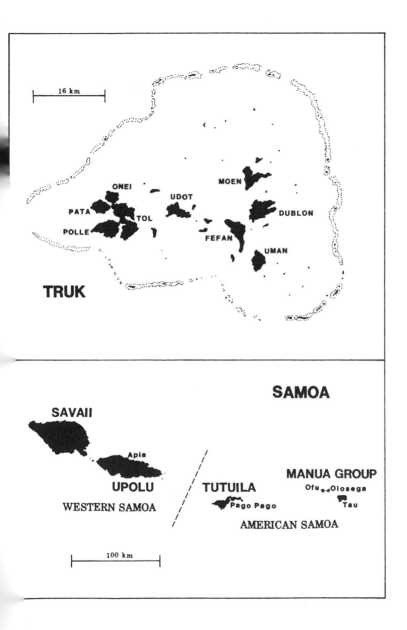

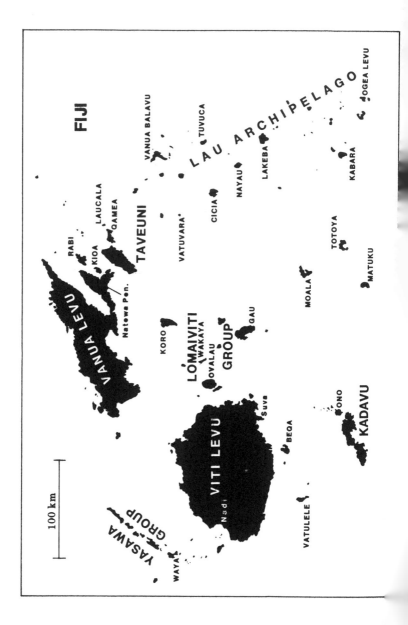

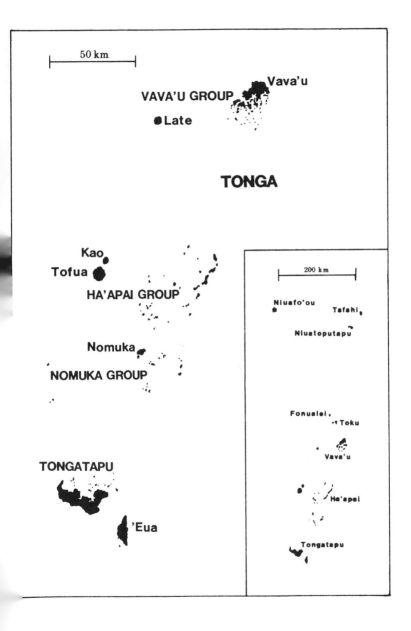

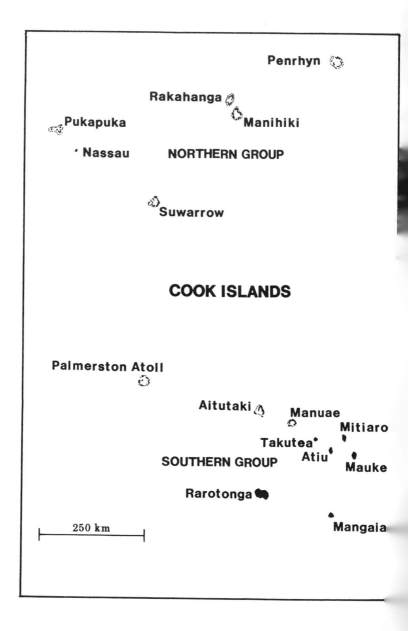

Penrhyn

Rakahanga

Manihiki

Pukapuka

Nassau

NORTHERN GROUP

Suwarrow

COOK ISLANDS

Palmerston Atoll

Aitutaki

Manuae

Mitiaro

Takutea

Atiu

SOUTHERN GROUP

Mauke

Rarotonga

Mangaia

250 km

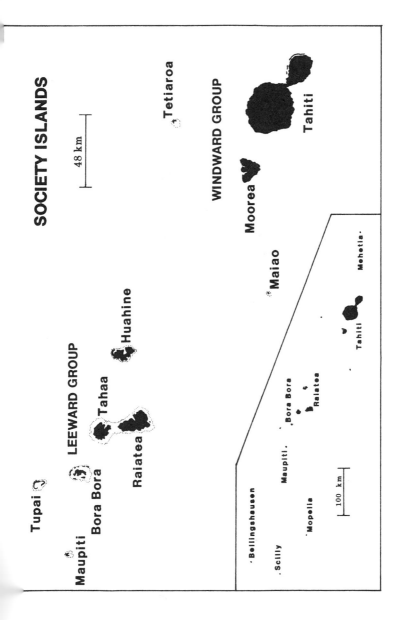

SOCIETY ISLANDS

48 km

Tupai

Maupiti

Bora Bora

LEEWARD GROUP

Tahaa

Huahine

Raiatea

Tetiaroa

Maiao

WINDWARD GROUP

Moorea

Tahiti

Scilly

Bellingshausen

Mopelia

Maupiti

Bora Bora

Raiatea

Tahiti

Mehetia

100 km

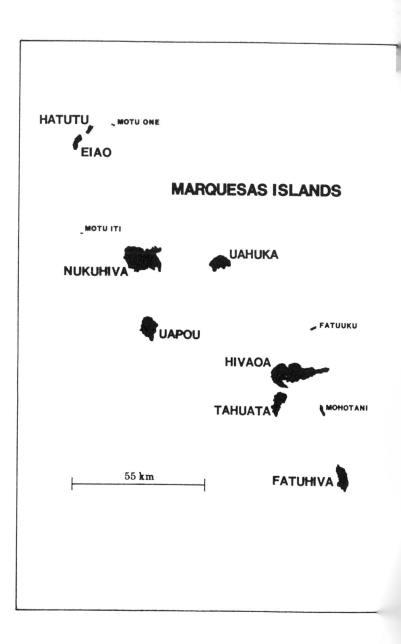

HATUTU

MOTU ONE

EIAO

MARQUESAS ISLANDS

MOTU ITI

NUKUHIVA

UAHUKA

UAPOU

FATUUKU

HIVAOA

TAHUATA

MOHOTANI

55 km

FATUHIVA

GLOSSARY

albinism. Total lack of pigmentation. True albino birds appear entirely white, with pink or orange eyes, bills, and feet. Opposite of melanism. *See* partial albinism.

allopatric. Inhabiting different geographical areas. Used only for closely related taxa.

aquatic. Closely associated with water. Aquatic birds include seabirds, waterfowl, and shorebirds.

arboreal. Living in trees.

breeding plumage. The plumage worn during the nesting period.

brood parasite. A bird that deposits its eggs in the nests of other species, and leaves the care of its young to the foster parents.

buff. A pale yellowish brown or tan. The color of "manila" folders.

buffy. Tinted with buff.

call, or call note. A vocalization, usually short, that serves some function (contact, alarm, etc.) other than territory defense or display.

canopy. The closed upper part of a forest. Shades the understory.

cere. A raised, soft area at the base of the upper mandible of members of the Falconiformes, Psittaciformes, and Columbiformes.

chestnut. A dark reddish brown, darker and less orange than rufous.

chick. A downy hatchling that is able to run about. Precocial as opposed to altricial (helpless at hatching), nidifugous rather than nidicolous (confined to the nest).

circumpolar. Distributed around the pole in the Arctic or Antarctic.

colonial. Nesting in large numbers in a small area, with very small individual territories. Characteristic of many seabirds, swallows, and swifts.

conspecific. Belonging to the same biological species.

cosmopolitan. Distributed worldwide.

coverts. Feathers that cover the bases of other feathers. Usually named for the feathers they cover, as in secondary coverts, which cover the bases of the secondaries.

dimorphic. Of two forms. Used most often for those species whose males and females differ in size or color, i.e. are sexually dimorphic.

distal. Away from the body; terminal. Opposite of proximal.

diurnal. Active by day.

echolocation. The use of high-pitched sound echoes for navigation in the dark, somewhat like radar or sonar. Used by bats and some cave swiftlets.

eclipse plumage. The nonbreeding plumage of male ducks. Usually resembles the female plumage and is of short duration.

endangered. Imminently threatened with extinction. See Table 6.

endemic. Occurring naturally in a locality or region and found nowhere else.

established. Successfully introduced, i.e. artificially transported to an area and breeding there in the wild with a stable or expanding population for at least a decade.

exotic. Foreign; introduced; not indigenous. Not used here in the sense of "strange" or "bizarre."

extinct. Having no living individuals. Used here for taxa that are extirpated throughout their ranges. Thus the Maui Creeper is extirpated on Lanai, but is not extinct.

extirpated. No longer present in a given area, but not extinct. *See* extinct.

feral. Wild; escaped from domesticity and established. Used to refer to introduced species such as pigeons, chickens, and ducks that originated from domestic stock rather than from wild ancestors.

finch. A passerine bird with a thick, conical bill adapted to feeding on seeds and hard fruits. A descriptive, not taxonomic, term applied to members of several avian families.

fledgling. A young bird that has just left the nest; usually still attended by its parents.

flight feathers. The primaries, secondaries, and rectrices.

form. A type, kind, or variety; also a species- or subspecies-level taxon. A purposely vague term used where more specific designations would be misleading.

frugivorous. Fruit-eating.

gallinaceous. Chickenlike. Used mainly for members of the Phasianidae.

game bird. A species hunted for sport. Usually restricted to gallinaceous birds, pigeons, and doves, but also applies to waterfowl and some shorebirds.

genus (pl. genera). A grouping of species believed to be descended from a recent common ancestor. The genus name is the capitalized first word in the scientific name.

gular pouch. An expandable or inflatable pouch in the throat, characteristic of the Pelecaniformes.

high breeding. A transient period during the nesting season of egrets and herons during which the soft-part colors change or intensify.

holarctic. Pertaining to the temperate and arctic parts of the Northern Hemisphere; palearctic (Eurasia) and nearctic (N. America) combined.

immature. Not adult. Used for young birds whose exact age is not readily apparent.

indigenous. Native or natural to an area. Applies to resident species as well as to migratory visitors, and includes endemics.

insectivorous. Feeding on insects and other arthropods.

introduced. Brought to an area and released, usually deliberately.

juvenile. A young bird in its first year and wearing its first feather coat after the fledgling stage.

kipuka. A remnant of ancient primary forest surrounded by younger lava flows.

local. Confined to small circumscribed localities within the larger general range.

mantle. In seabirds, the upper surface of the outstretched wings plus the center of the back. Some publications use this term for the back only.

marine. Of the sea or of saltwater habitats.

melanism. An increase in dark pigments (melanins). Opposite of albinism.

monotypic. Having no taxonomic subdivisions.

montane. Pertaining to mountains.

morph. A variety, kind, or color phase of a species, usually not related to geographical distribution (i.e. not a subspecies).

neotropical. Pertaining to the region from the Tropic of Cancer southward in the Western Hemisphere (South and Middle America and the West Indies).

nestling. A hatchling helpless in the nest and attended by parents. Altricial rather than precocial. *See* chick.

nocturnal. Active at night.

nuptial. Pertaining to the breeding cycle or season.

omnivorous. Feeding on a variety of animal and vegetable matter.

palearctic. Pertaining to the temperate and arctic parts of Eurasia and northern Africa.

pantropical. Distributed around the world in the tropics.

partial albinism. The condition in which some (but not all) of the feathers that are usually pigmented lack coloring and look white. Such feathers may be confined to one part of the body or scattered asymmetrically through the plumage.

passerine. A member of the Order Passeriformes, characterized by perching feet (three toes in front, one to the rear) and complex vocal abilities. A songbird or perching bird.

pelagic. Living in the open sea, usually out of sight of land.

phase. A regularly occurring color variant.

polymorphic. Having several different morphs or phases.

polytypic. Divided into two or more subspecies.

primaries. The flight feathers of the outer wing, attached to the bones of the "hand" or carpometacarpus.

primary forest. Fully developed climax forest of indigenous composition, often virgin.

proximal. Toward or near the body. Opposite of distal.

race. A subspecies (informal).

rain forest. Primary forest characterized by heavy annual rainfall, tall trees, and well-defined strata: canopy, subcanopy, understory, etc.

raptor. A bird of prey that captures live animals. Includes most hawks, falcons, and owls.

rectrices (sing. retrix). The feathers of the tail.

rictal bristles. Bristlelike feathers at the base of the bill; sometimes called whiskers. Characteristically large in birds that hawk insects from the air.

rufous. A reddish brown or rust color. Between chestnut and orange in hue.

scold. A call, usually raspy and loud, usually directed at non-conspecific intruders such as humans, feral cats, or avian predators.

seabird. A bird associated with salt water but not necessarily pelagic. Includes loons, grebes, albatrosses, shearwaters, petrels, storm-petrels, tropicbirds, boobies, pelicans, cormorants, frigatebirds, phalaropes, jaegers, gulls, terns, and alcids.

seamount. An undersea mountain.

secondaries. The flight feathers of the inner wing; attached to the ulna.

second-growth. Vegetation that has replaced primary forest. Often includes exotic plant species or semidomestic ones mixed with indigenous flora.

shaft streak. A contrasting color in the shaft of a feather only, not extending onto the web.

shorebird. In American usage, a short-legged wading bird of the Order Charadriiformes. Equivalent to "wader" in British usage.

soft parts. The unfeathered external parts of a bird, i.e. eyes, bill, feet, eyelids, wattles, and bare patches of skin.

song. A vocalization, often complex, used to proclaim territory, establish or maintain a pair-bond, or for other functions related to breeding.

songbird. A passerine.

species (pl. species). A group of actually or potentially freely interbreeding populations reproductively isolated from other such groups.

speculum. An iridescent rectangular patch on the upper surface of the secondaries of many ducks.

squeak up. To attract by means of a "squeak lure" made by loudly kissing the back of the hand or by "pshing" (an extended *spshspsh* sound) in imitation of natural scolds or distress calls.

stint. In British usage, a small sandpiper of the genus *Calidris*.

straggler. A wandering individual that turns up in a totally unexpected locality; an accidental. Usually restricted to birds that have been found only once in the area in question.

subadult plumage. The last distinctive plumage before the full adult stage.

subspecies. A recognizable population that occupies a discreet portion of the overall range of a species. Interbreeds freely with other conspecific subspecies where they come into contact, or believed likely to do so with allopatric subspecies should contact be naturally established.

taxon (pl. taxa). A unit of scientific classification. Can be used at any level.

terrestrial. Living on or near the ground, but not necessarily flightless.

transequatorial. Crossing the equator.

trill. A vocalization in which a short stereotyped unit is reiterated rapidly.

tube-nose. A member of the Order Procellariiformes, which have nostrils emerging through tubes on the top of the bill.

underbrush. The lowest stratum of the forest above the ground.

understory. The part of a forest under the canopy.

vent. The area surounding the cloaca, often including the undertail coverts.

wader. A bird that feeds by wading in shallow water. In American usage, usually restricted to long-legged birds such as herons and ibises. In British usage, a synonym for shorebird.

warble. A vocalization comprising an extended series of modulated whistles, with pitch varying up and down.

waterfowl. Swimming birds such as ducks, geese, and swans. Also sometimes used for gallinules and coots.

wattle. A dangling ornamental growth of bare skin on the head or neck of some birds (e.g. Wild Turkey, Wattled Honeyeater). Also a kind of shrubby tree from Australia.

web. The skin stretched between the toes of swimming birds. Also refers to the broad surface of a feather as distinguished from the shaft.

wetland. Any temporary or permanent freshwater habitat.

whisper song. A quiet vocalization usually audible only from a short distance and uttered from concealment. Function not well understood.

whistle. A clear, single-noted vocalization that is not highly modulated or broken into choppy segments, but which may slur up or down.

wing bar. A band of contrasting color on the wing, usually formed by the tips of the coverts.

wing lining. The undersurface of the wing except for the primaries and secondaries.

BIBLIOGRAPHY

WE have grouped the following references into seven categories for easier use. The first lists international checklists and other general references that discuss birds of Hawaii and the tropical Pacific. The second is a listing of guides to birds of surrounding areas in which may be found illustrations and more complete accounts of those species that are only discussed briefly here. They also cover species that have not been recorded in the tropical Pacific, but that might occur in the future. Several of these guides are cited repeatedly in our text. The third lists general references on seabirds, including those of the tropical Pacific. The next three groupings are regional listings of references on birds of the Hawaiian Islands, Micronesia, and Polynesia and Fiji. Finally, we give a list of periodicals that frequently publish articles in English that are of interest to birders in Hawaii and the tropical Pacific. We include the names and addresses of the publishers of these journals. All of these lists are intended to be thorough but not exhaustive. Not included in this bibliography are those references that discuss only one or two species, and general monographs that cover specific taxonomic groups on a worldwide basis; those sources of information are cited under their respective species or group accounts in the text.

INTERNATIONAL

American Ornithologists' Union. 1983. *Check-list of North American birds.* 6th ed. Washington, D.C.: American Ornithologists' Union.

American Ornithologists' Union. 1985. Thirty-fifth supplement to the American Ornithologists' Union *Check-list of North American birds. Auk* 102:680-86.

Clements, J. F. 1981. *Birds of the world: A checklist.* New York: Facts On File.

Greenway, J. C., Jr. 1967. *Extinct and vanishing birds of the world.* New York: Dover Publ.

Howard, R., and A. Moore. 1980. *A complete checklist of the birds of the world.* Oxford: Oxford Univ. Press.

King, W. B., ed. 1981. *Endangered birds of the world: The ICBP bird red data book.* Washington, D.C.: Smithsonian Inst. Press.

Rogers, C. H. 1975. *Encyclopedia of cage and aviary birds.* New York: Macmillan Publ. Co.

U.S. Fish and Wildlife Service, Office of Endangered Species. 1984. *Endangered and threatened wildlife and plants*. (Repr. from Federal Register 50 CFR 17.11 and 17.12.) Washington, D.C.: U.S. Government Printing Office.

Walters, M. 1980. *The complete birds of the world*. Newton Abbott: David & Charles.

BIRDS OF SURROUNDING AREAS

Beehler, B. M., T. K. Pratt, and D. A. Zimmerman, 1986. *Birds of New Guinea*. Princeton: Princeton University Press.

Delacour, J. 1966. *Guide des oiseaux de la Nouvelle-Calédonie et de ses dépendances*. Neuchatel: Editions Delachaux & Niestle.

De Schauensee, R. M. 1984. *The birds of China*. Washington, D.C.: Smithsonian Inst. Press.

duPont, J. E. 1971. *Philippine birds*. Delaware Mus. Nat. Hist., Monogr. Ser. 2.

Falla, R. A., R. B. Sibson, and E. G. Turbott. 1979. *The new guide to the birds of New Zealand*. Auckland: Collins.

Farrand, J., ed. 1983. *The Audubon Society master guide to birding*. 3 vols. New York: Alfred A. Knopf.

Flint, V. E., R. L. Boehme, Y. V. Kostin, and A. A. Kusnetsov. 1984. *A field guide to birds of the USSR*. Princeton: Princeton Univ. Press.

Hadden, D. 1981. *Birds of the North Solomons*. Wau Ecology Inst. Handbook no. 8, Wau, Papua New Guinea.

Hannecart, F., and Y. Letocart. 1980 and 1983. *Oiseaux de Nlle. Calédonie et des Loyautes/New Caledonian birds*. Vols. 1 and 2. Noumea: Les Editions Cardinalis.

King, B. F., and E. C. Dickinson. 1975. *A field guide to the birds of South-East Asia*. Boston: Houghton Mifflin Co.

Mayr, E. 1978. *Birds of the Southwest Pacific*. Rutland, Vt., and Tokyo: Charles E. Tuttle Co.

National Geographic Society (NGS). 1983. *Field guide to the birds of North America*. Washington, D.C.: National Geographic Soc.

Peterson, R. T. 1961. *A field guide to western birds*. Boston: Houghton Mifflin Co.

Pizzey, G. 1980. *A field guide to the birds of Australia*. Princeton: Princeton Univ. Press.

Robbins, C. S., B. Bruun, and H. S. Zim. 1983. *Birds of North America*. New York: Golden Press.

Roberson, D. 1980. *Rare birds of the West Coast*. Pacific Grove, Calif.: Woodcock Publ.

Simpson, K., and N. Day. 1984. *The birds of Australia: A book of identification*. Dover, N.H.: Tanager Books.

Slater, P., ed. 1970. *A field guide to Australian birds: Non-passerines*. Wynnewood, Penn.: Livingston Publ. Co.

Slater, P. 1975. *A field guide to Australian birds: Passerines*. Wynnewood, Penn.: Livingston Publ. Co.

Smythies, B. E. 1981. *The birds of Borneo*. 3d ed. Rev. by Earl of Cranbrook. The Sabah Society with the Malayan Nature Society, Malaysia.

Udvardy, M.D.F. 1977. *The Audubon Society field guide to North American birds: Western region*. New York: Alfred A. Knopf.

Watson, G. E. 1975. *Birds of the Antarctic and Sub-Antarctic*. Washington, D.C.: American Geophysical Union.

Wild Bird Society of Japan (WBSJ). 1982. *A field guide to the birds of Japan*. Tokyo: WBSJ.

SEABIRDS

Dixon, K. L., and W. C. Starrett. 1952. Offshore observations of tropical sea birds in the western Pacific. *Auk* 69:266-72.

Gould, P. J. 1983. Seabirds between Alaska and Hawaii. *Condor* 85:286-91.

Gould, P. J., and W. B. King. 1967. Records of four species of *Pterodroma* from the central Pacific Ocean. *Auk* 84:591-94.

Haley, D. 1984. *Seabirds of eastern North Pacific and arctic waters*. Seattle: Pacific Search Press.

Harper, P. C., and F. C. Kinsky. 1978. *Southern albatrosses and petrels: An identification guide*. Wellington: Price Milburn and Co.

Harrison, P. 1983. *Seabirds: An identification guide*. Boston: Houghton Mifflin Co.

Jenkins, J.A.F. 1973. Seabird observations around the Kingdom of Tonga. *Notornis* 20:113-19.

Jenkins, J.A.F. 1980. Seabird records from Tonga—an account based on the literature and recent observations. *Notornis* 27:205-234.

Jenkins, J.A.F. 1982. Seabird records from Tonga—further notes from the literature. *Notornis* 29:233-36.

King, J. E., and R. L. Pyle. 1957. Observations on sea birds in the tropical Pacific. *Condor* 59:27-39.

King, W. B. 1967. *Seabirds of the tropical Pacific Ocean*. Washington, D.C.: Smithsonian Inst.

King, W. B., ed. 1974. Pelagic studies of seabirds in the central and eastern Pacific Ocean. *Smithsonian Contr. to Zool.*, no. 158.

Löfgren, L. 1984. *Ocean birds*. New York: Alfred A. Knopf.

Lovegrove, T. G. 1978. Seabird observations between New Zealand and Fiji. *Notornis* 25:291-98.

Serventy, D. L., V. Serventy, and J. Warham. 1971. *The handbook of Australian sea-birds*. Sydney: A. H. & A. W. Reed.

Tuck, G. 1980. *A guide to seabirds on the ocean routes*. London: Collins.

Tuck, G., and H. Heinzel. 1978. *A field guide to the seabirds of Britain and the world*. London: Collins.

THE HAWAIIAN ISLANDS

Amerson, A. B., Jr. 1971. The natural history of French Frigate Shoals, Northwestern Hawaiian Islands. *Atoll Res. Bull.* 150:1-383.

Amerson, A. B., Jr., R. B. Clapp, and W. O. Wirtz II. 1974. The natural history of Pearl and Hermes Reef, Northwestern Hawaiian Islands. *Atoll Res. Bull.* 174:1-306.

Amerson, A. B., Jr., and P. C. Shelton. 1976. The natural history of Johnston Atoll, central Pacific Ocean. *Atoll Res. Bull.* 192:1-479.

Bailey, A. M. 1956. *Birds of Midway and Laysan Islands*. Mus. Pictorial no. 12, Denver Mus. Nat. Hist.

Berger, A.J. 1981. *Hawaiian Birdlife*. Honolulu: Univ. of Hawaii Press.

Byrd, G. V., and C. F. Zeillemaker. 1981. Seabirds of Kilauea Point, Kauai Island, Hawaii. *'Elepaio* 41:67-70.

Carlquist, S. 1970. *Hawaii: A natural history*. Garden City, N.Y.: Nat. Hist. Press.

Clapp, R. B. 1972. The natural history of Gardner Pinnacles, Northwestern Hawaiian Islands. *Atoll Res. Bull.* 163:1-25.

Clapp, R. B., and E. Kridler. 1977. The natural history of Necker Island, Northwestern Hawaiian Islands. *Atoll Res. Bull.* 206:1-102.

Clapp, R. B., E. Kridler, and R. R. Fleet. 1977. The natural history of Nihoa Island, Northwestern Hawaiian Islands. *Atoll Res. Bull.* 207:1-147.

Clapp, R. B., and W. O. Wirtz II. 1975. The natural history of Lisianski Island, Northwestern Hawaiian Islands. *Atoll Res. Bull.* 186:1-196.

Clapp, R. B., and P. W. Woodward. 1968. New records of birds from the Hawaiian Leeward Islands. *Proc. U.S. Nat. Mus.* 124:1-39.

Conant, S. 1983a. Observations of migrant and vagrant birds of Nihoa Island. *'Elepaio* 44:23-25.

Conant, S. 1983b. Kaho'olawe birds—including first Warbling Silverbill record. *'Elepaio* 44:63-65.

Conant, S., and M. S. Kjargaard. 1984. Annotated Checklist of birds of Haleakala National Park, Maui, Hawaii. *Western Birds* 15:97-110.

Ely, C. A., and R. B. Clapp. 1973. The natural history of Laysan Island, Northwestern Hawaiian Islands. *Atoll Res. Bull.* 171:1-361.

Fisher, H. I. 1951. The avifauna of Niihau Island, Hawaiian Archipelago. *Condor* 53:31-42.

Grant, G. S. 1982. Wildlife on Midway Atoll during the winter and spring of 1980-1981. *'Elepaio* 43:1-4.

Grant, G. S., and T. N. Pettit. 1981. Birds on Midway and Kure Atolls during the winter of 1979-1980. *'Elepaio* 41:81-85.

Hirai, L. T. 1978. Native birds of Lanai, Hawaii. *Western Birds* 9:71-77.

Lewin, V. 1971. Exotic game birds of the Puu Waa Waa Ranch, Hawaii. *J. Wildlife Management* 34:141-55.

Munro, G. C. 1960. *Birds of Hawaii.* Rutland, Vt. and Tokyo: Charles E. Tuttle Co.

Olson, S. L., and H. F. James. 1982. Prodromus of the fossil avifauna of the Hawaiian Islands. *Smithsonian Contr. to Zool.,* no. 365.

Paton, P.W.C., and J. M. Scott. 1985. Water birds of Hawaii island. *'Elepaio* 45: 69-76.

Pratt, H. D. 1979. *A systematic analysis of the endemic avifauna of the Hawaiian Islands.* Ann Arbor: Univ. Microfilms. CDM-79-21977.

Pyle, P. 1984. Observations of migrant and vagrant birds from Kure and Midway atolls, 1982-1983. *'Elepaio* 44:107-111.

Pyle, R. L. 1983. Checklist of the birds of Hawaii. *'Elepaio* 44:47-58.

Rauzon, M. J. 1978. Field observations from Kure Atoll, 1977. *'Elepaio* 39:13-14.

Scott, J. M., S. Mountainspring, F. L. Ramsey, and C. B. Kepler. N.d. Forest bird communities of the Hawaiian Islands: Their dynamics, ecology, and conservation. *Stud. in Avian Biol.* In press.

Scott, J. M., R. L. Pyle, and C. F. Zeillemaker. 1978. Similar species of migratory waterbirds in Hawaii. *'Elepaio* 39:1-5.

Scott, J. M., J. L. Sincock, and A. J. Berger. 1980. Records of nests, eggs, nestlings, and cavity nesting of endemic passerine birds in Hawaii. *'Elepaio* 40-163-68.

Shallenberger, R. J., ed. 1984. *Hawaii's birds.* Honolulu: Hawaii Audubon Soc.

van Riper, C. III, 1982. Censuses and breeding observations of the birds on Kohala Mountain, Hawaii. *Wilson Bull.* 94:463-76.

Warner, R. E. 1968. The role of introduced diseases in the extinction of the endemic Hawaiian avifauna. *Condor* 70-101-120.

Woodward, P. G. 1972. The natural history of Kure Atoll, Northwestern Hawaiian Islands. *Atoll Res. Bull.* 164: 1-318.

MICRONESIA

Amerson, A. B., Jr. 1969. Ornithology of the Marshall and Gilbert Islands. *Atoll Res. Bull.* 127:1-348.

Anderson, D. A. 1981. Observations of birds at Ujelang and other northern Marshall Islands atolls. *Micronesica* 17:198-212.

Baker, R. H. 1951. The avifauna of Micronesia, its origin, evolution, and distribution. *Univ. Kansas Publ. Mus. Nat. Hist.* 3:1-359.

Brandt, J. H. 1962. Nests and eggs of the birds of the Truk Islands. *Condor* 64:416-37.

Bryan, E. H., Jr. 1972. *Life in the Marshall Islands.* Honolulu: Pacific Scientific Information Center, B. P. Bishop Mus.

Casey, E. 1966. The birds of Wake Island. *'Elepaio* 43:69-70.

Engbring, J. 1983. Avifauna of the Southwest Islands of Palau. *Atoll Res. Bull.* 267:1-22.

Engbring, J., and R. P. Owen. 1981. New bird records for Micronesia. *Micronesica* 17:186-92.

Engbring, J., and H. D. Pratt. 1985. Endangered birds in Micronesia: Their history, status, and future prospects. *Bird Conservation* 2:71-105.

Fisher, H. I. 1950. The birds of Yap, Western Caroline Islands. *Pacific Science* 4:55-62.

Fosberg, F. R. 1966. Northern Marshall Islands land biota: Birds. *Atoll Res. Bull.* 114:1-35.

Hailman, J. 1979. Notes on the birds of Eniwetok Atoll, Marshall Islands. *'Elepaio* 40-:87-90.

Hayes, F. 1985. New bird records for the Eastern Caroline Islands. *'Elepaio.* 45:123-25.

Jenkins, J. M. 1981. Seasonality and relative abundance of Guam shorebirds. *Micronesica* 17:181-84.

Jenkins, J. M. 1983. The native forest birds of Guam. *Orn. Monogr.* 31.

Maben, A. F., and G. J. Wiles. 1981. Nine new bird records for Guam and Rota. *Micronesica* 17:192-95.

Marshall, J. T., Jr. 1949. The endemic avifauna of Saipan, Tinian, Guam, and Palau. *Condor* 51:200-221.

Marshall, M., and F. R. Fosberg. 1975. The natural history of Namoluk Atoll, Eastern Caroline Islands. *Atoll Res. Bull.* 189:1-65.

Owen, R. P. 1977a. A checklist of the birds of Micronesia. *Micronesica* 13:65-81.

Owen, R. P. 1977b. New bird records for Micronesia and major island groups in Micronesia. *Micronesica* 13:57-63.

Pearson, A. J. 1962. Field notes on the birds of Ocean Island and Nauru during 1961. *Ibis* 104:421-24.

Pratt, H. D., and P. L. Bruner. 1981. Noteworthy records of non-breeding birds in Micronesia. *Micronesica* 17:195-98.

Pratt, H. D., P. L. Bruner, and D. G. Berrett. 1977. Ornithological observations on Yap, Western Caroline Islands. *Micronesica* 13:49-56.

Pratt, H. D., P. L. Bruner, and D. G. Berrett. 1979. America's unknown avifauna: The birds of the Mariana Islands. *Am. Birds* 33:227-35.

Pratt, H. D., J. Engbring, P. L. Bruner, and D. G. Berrett. 1980. Notes on the taxonomy, natural history, and status of the resident birds of Palau. *Condor* 82:117-31.

Pyle, P., and J. Engbring. 1985. Checklist of the birds of Micronesia. *'Elepaio*. 46:57-68.

Pyle, P., and J. Engbring. N.d. New bird records and migrant observations from Micronesia, 1982-1984. *'Elepaio*. In press.

Ralph, C. J., and H. F. Sakai. 1979. Forest bird and fruit bat populations and their conservation in Micronesia: Notes on a survey. *'Elepaio* 40:20-26.

Ripley, S. D. 1951. Migrants and introduced species in the Palau Archipelago. *Condor* 53:299-300.

Schipper, W. L. 1985. Observations of birds in Kwajalein Atoll, Marshall Islands, 1978-1983. *'Elepaio*. 46:27-32.

Williams. J. M., and P. C. Grout. 1985. Migrants on Guam, fall 1983. *'Elepaio*. 46:41-44.

Yocom, C. F. 1964. Waterfowl wintering in the Marshall Islands, southwest Pacific Ocean. *Auk* 81:441-42.

POLYNESIA AND FIJI

Amerson, A. B., Jr., W. A. Whistler, and T. D. Schwaner, 1982. *Wildlife and wildlife habitat of American Samoa*. 2 vols. Washington, D.C. U.S. Dept. of the Interior, USFWS.

Bourne, W.R.P., and A.C.F. David. 1983. Henderson Island, central South Pacific, and its birds. *Notornis* 30:233-52.

Bruner, P. L. 1972. *Field guide to the birds of French Polynesia*. Honolulu: Pacific Scientific Information Center, Bernice P. Bishop Mus.

Child, P. 1981. Birdlife of Aitutaki, Cook Islands. *Notornis* 28:29-34.

Child, P. 1982a. Additions to the avifauna of Kiribati and Tuvalu. *Notornis* 29:31-36.

Child, P. 1982b. Additions to the bird life of Niue. *Notornis* 29:158-161.

Clunie, F. 1972. *Fijian birds of prey*. Fiji Mus. Educational Ser. 3.

Clunie, F. 1984. *Birds of the Fiji bush*. Suva: Fiji Mus.

duPont, J. E. 1976. *South Pacific birds*. Delaware Mus. Nat. Hist., Monogr. Ser. 3.

Gorman, M. 1979. The avifauna of the exotic pinewoods of Viti Levu, Fiji Islands. *BBOC* 99:9-12.

Holyoak, D. T. 1973 Notes on the birds of Rangiroa, Tuamotu Archipelago, and the surrounding ocean. *BBOC* 93:26-32.

Holyoak, D. T. 1974. Les oiseaux des îles de la Société. *L'Oiseau et RFO* 44:1-27, 158-84.

Holyoak, D. T. 1975. Les oiseaux des îles Marquises. *L'Oiseau et RFO* 45:207-233, 341-66.

Holyoak, D. T. 1979. Notes on the birds of Viti Levu and Taveuni, Fiji. *Emu* 79:7-18.

Holyoak, D. T. 1981. *Guide to Cook Islands birds*. D. T. Holyoak.

Holyoak, D. T., and J.-C. Thibault. 1977. Habitats, morphologie et inter-actions écologiques des oiseaux insectivores de Polynésie orientale. *L'Oiseau et RFO* 47:115-47.

Kinsky, F. C., and J. C. Yaldwin. 1981. *The bird fauna of Niue Island, southwest Pacific, with special notes on the White-tailed Tropic Bird and Golden Plover*. National Mus. New Zealand, Misc. Ser. 2.

Mercer, R. 1970. *A field guide to Fiji birds*. Suva: Fiji Times.

Miles, J.A.R. 1982. Notes on some waders at Vatuwaqa, Suva, Fiji. *Notornis* 29:230-33.

Murphy, R. C., R. J. Niedrach, and A. M. Bailey. 1954. *Canton Island*. Mus. Pictorial no. 10, Denver Mus. Nat. Hist.

Muse, C., and S. Muse. 1982. *The birds and birdlore of Samoa*. Walla Walla, Wash.: Pioneer Press.

Pernetta, J. C., and D. Watling. 1979. The introduced and native terrestrial vertebrates of Fiji. *Pacific Science* 32:223-44.

Petitot, C., and F. Petitot. 1975. Observations ornithologiques dans l'atoll de Manihi (Archipel des Tuamotu) et dans l'île de Tubuai (Australes). *L'Oiseau et RFO* 45:83-88.

Reed, S. 1980. The birds of Savai'i, Western Samoa. *Notornis* 27:151-59.

Rehder, H. A., and J. E. Randall. 1975. Ducie Atoll: Its history, physiography, and biota. *Atoll Res. Bull.* 183:1-55.

Skinner, N. J. 1983. The occurrence of waders at Suva Point, Fiji. *Notornis* 30:227-32.

Thibault, B., and J.-C. Thibault. 1973. Liste préliminaire des oiseaux de Polynésie orientale. *L'Oiseau et RFO* 43:55-74.

Thibault, B., and J.-C. Thibault. 1975. Liste des oiseaux de Polynésie orientale (nouvelles acquisitions faunistiques). *L'Oiseau et RFO* 45:89-92.

Thibault, J.-C. 1974. Les périodes de reproduction des oiseaux de mer dans l'archipel de la Société (Polynésie Française). *Alauda* 42:437-450.

Thibault, J.-C. 1976. L'avifaune de Tetiaroa (Archipel de la Société, Po-
lynésie Française). *L'Oiseau et RFO* 46:29-45.
Thibault, J.-C., and C. Rives. 1975. *Birds of Tahiti*. Papeete: Editions du
Pacifique.
Watling, D. 1982. *Birds of Fiji, Tonga, and Samoa*. Wellington: Millwood
Press.
Williams, G. R. 1960. The birds of the Pitcairn Islands, central South Pa-
cific Ocean. *Ibis* 102:58-70.
Wodzicki, K., and M. Laird. 1970. Birds and birdlore in the Tokelau Is-
lands. *Notornis* 17:247-76.

JOURNALS

American Birds	National Audubon Society P. O. Box 22832 New York, N.Y. 10022
Atoll Research Bulletin	The Smithsonian Institution Washington, D.C. 20560
The Auk	The American Ornithologists' Union National Museum of Natural History Smithsonian Institution Washington, D.C. 20560
Birding	American Birding Association, Inc. Box 4335 Austin, Texas 78765
The Condor	Cooper Ornithological Society Department of Zoology University of California Los Angeles, California 90025
'Elepaio	Hawaii Audubon Society P. O. Box 22832 Honolulu, Hawaii 96822
The Emu	Royal Australasian Ornithologists' Union 21 Gladstone Street Moonee Ponds, Victoria 3039, Australia
The Ibis	British Ornithologists' Union c/o The Zoological Society of London Regent's Park, London NW1 4RY, U.K.

Micronesica	University of Guam UOG Station Mangilao, Guam 96913
Notornis	Ornithologial Society of New Zealand P. O. Box 35337 Browns Bay, Auckland 10, New Zealand
Western Birds	Western Field Ornithologists 17 Camino Lanada Orinda, California 94563
The Wilson Bulletin	Wilson Ornithological Society Museum of Zoology University of Michigan Ann Arbor, Michigan 48104

INDEX

This index may be used as a master checklist. Check boxes are provided, one per species, opposite the entry for the main English name. Other vernacular names are cross-referenced to the main entry for the species, with a page number given only when the main name is not found under the same group heading. Hyphenated group names (e.g. fruit-dove, reed-warbler) in which the second word is capitalized in a species proper name are usually indexed under the second, more general substantive name (e.g. dove, warbler). Entries in checklists and tables are not indexed. Scientific names are indexed by genera only; species epithets are not listed independently. Plate numbers are indicated by the symbol P. Italicized page numbers refer to black-and-white illustrations, which are indexed only when separated from the species account.

PLATES

PLATE 1. Albatrosses and Frigatebirds

GREAT FRIGATEBIRD *Fregata minor*   **p. 84**
Ad. male all dark. Ad. female has white breast and throat. Juv. variable, with less rusty on pale head and breast than Lesser Frigatebird.

LESSER FRIGATEBIRD *Fregata ariel*   **p. 84**
Ad. male has white side patches, ad. female has black throat. Juv. has rusty head and breast, black breast band on younger birds. Older juv. (not shown) lacks breast band, has paler head and breast with white extending onto axillaries.

BLACK-FOOTED ALBATROSS *Diomedea nigripes*   **p. 49**
Uniformly brownish gray with pale face and tail coverts. Some individuals (old birds?) much paler on body.

LAYSAN ALBATROSS *Diomedea immutabilis*   **p. 49**
White body, dark mantle, tail, and ear patch. Underwing variable, with irregular black and white markings.

SHORT-TAILED ALBATROSS *Diomedea albatrus*   **p. 48**
Very large, with heavy pink bill. Ad. white with dark brown wings and tail, center of mantle white. Juv. all dark. Subad. retains dark nape, has blotchy mantle. Many intermediates seen.

1

juv.

ad. ♂

juv.

ad. ♀

**GREAT
FRIGATEBIRD**

displaying
♂

ad. ♀

subad.

**LESSER
FRIGATEBIRD**

ad. ♂

**SHORT-
TAILED
ALBATROSS**

juv.

ad.
♀

Short-t.
ad.

juv.

CK-FOOTED
.BATROSS

Laysan
from
below

**LAYSAN
ALBATROSS**

PLATE 2. Dark-bodied Shearwaters and Petrels

HERALD PETREL *Pterodroma heraldica* **p. 67**
Dark morph has dark primary shafts above, underwing as in lighter morphs. Intermediate morph shows blotchy feathering on underbelly, pale patches in primaries and underwing coverts from below. For pale morph see Plate 4.

KERMADEC PETREL *Pterodroma neglecta* **p. 68**
Dark morph has pale primary shafts above, variable white at base of bill, underwing as in lighter morphs. Intermediate birds have pale gray-brown underparts, white face. White patches in primaries from below somewhat more sharply defined than in Herald Petrel. For pale morph see Plate 4.

MURPHY'S PETREL *Pterodroma ultima* **p. 70**
All-dark underwing, wedge-shaped tail, pale throat.

CHRISTMAS SHEARWATER *Puffinus nativitatis* **p. 55**
Medium-sized, uniformly dark brown. Darkest underwing of all dark-bodied shearwaters.

BULWER'S PETREL *Bulweria bulwerii* **p. 58**
Size of storm-petrel. Very dark with pale bands on upperwings. Tail long, wedge-shaped.

FLESH-FOOTED SHEARWATER *Puffinus carneipes* **p. 53**
Dark chocolate brown with pale bill and feet. Dark underwing may look slightly silvery.

SOOTY SHEARWATER *Puffinus griseus* **p. 54**
All sooty brown, grayer below, with silvery wing linings.

SHORT-TAILED SHEARWATER *Puffinus tenuirostris* **p. 55**
Very similar to Sooty but with gray wing linings (variable; some very pale). May be slightly grayer below.

WEDGE-TAILED SHEARWATER (dark morph) **p. 53**
Puffinus pacificus
Paler throat and breast than other dark-bodied shearwaters. Pale feet, dark underwing. For light morph see Plate 4.

2

HERALD PETREL

KERMADEC PETREL

dark morph

MURPHY'S PETREL

rk ph

intermed. morph

intermed. morph

RISTMAS ARWATER

Brown Noddy for comparison

BULWER'S PETREL

FLESH-FOOTED EARWATER

SOOTY SHEARWATER

SHORT-TAILED SHEARWATER

dark morph

WEDGE-TAILED SHEAR-WATER

PLATE 3. Shearwaters and Petrels (Dark Above, White Below)

HAWAIIAN (DARK-RUMPED) PETREL *Pterodroma phaeopygia*   **p. 68**
Uniformly dark upperparts, petrel bill, bold black wrist patches on underwings. Wings held straighter than those of Juan Fernandez Petrel.

LITTLE SHEARWATER *Puffinus assimilis*   **p. 57**
Very small. White extends above eye. Undertail coverts and undersides of
primaries white.

AUDUBON'S SHEARWATER *Puffinus lherminieri*   **p. 57**
Undertail coverts black, primaries all black below.

NEWELL'S (TOWNSEND'S) SHEARWATER   **p. 56**
Puffinus newelli (= auricularis newelli)
White extends onto sides of rump above. Undertail coverts white.

TAHITI PETREL *Pseudobulweria rostrata*   **p. 59**
Dark upperparts and breast, white belly. Breast/belly border sharp, throat
dark.

PHOENIX PETREL *Pterodroma alba*   **p. 66**
Very similar to Tahiti Petrel but throat usually pale (very hard to see) and
breast/belly border irregular.

JUAN FERNANDEZ PETREL *Pterodroma externa*   **p. 69**
Paler on upper back than Hawaiian Petrel, wrist patches on underwing very
small. Compare White-naped (White-necked) Petrel (Plate 4).

LITTLE
SHEARWATER

AUDUBON'S
SHEARWATER

WAIIAN
(-RUMPED)
.TREL

NEWELL'S
(TOWNSEND'S)
SHEARWATER

JUAN
FERNANDEZ
PETREL

PHOENIX
PETREL

3

PLATE 4. Shearwaters and Large Petrels

BULLER'S SHEARWATER *Puffinus bulleri*　　　　　　　　**p. 54**
All white underwing and underparts, black cap, dark M across mantle.

WEDGE-TAILED SHEARWATER (pale morph) *Puffinus pacificus*　**p. 53**
Pattern cloudy, not clean-cut. Bill pale gray.

HERALD PETREL (pale morph) *Pterodroma heraldica*　　　**p. 67**
Grayer than Kermadec. All-dark upperparts, white undersides of primaries.

KERMADEC PETREL (pale morph) *Pterodroma neglecta*　　**p. 68**
Browner than Herald. White primary shafts above. Pale underwing heavily mottled.

WHITE-NAPED (WHITE-NECKED) PETREL　　　　　　　**p. 63**
Pterodroma cervicalis
White hindneck, black cap, bold underwing pattern (compare Juan Fernandez Petrel, Plate 3).

PINK-FOOTED SHEARWATER *Puffinus creatopus*　　　　**p. 52**
Cloudy, not clean-cut, pattern. Pale bill and feet. Less white on underwing than smaller Wedge-tailed.

STREAKED SHEARWATER *Calonectris leucomelas*　　　　**p. 52**
Dark-tipped long yellow bill, streaks on head and neck.

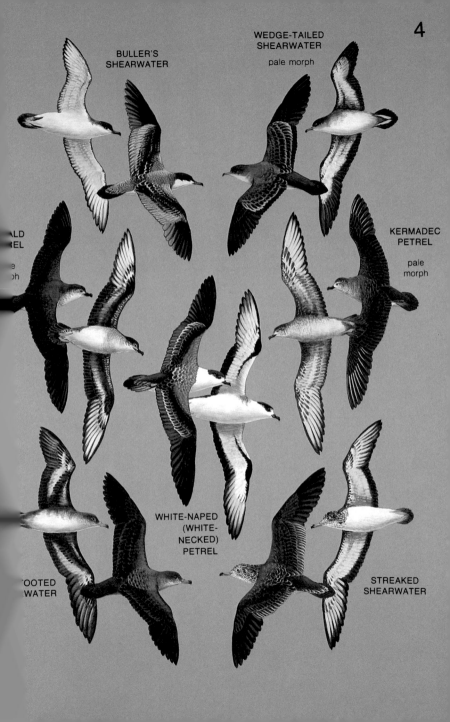

BULLER'S SHEARWATER

WEDGE-TAILED SHEARWATER

pale morph

4

...ALD ...REL

...e ...ph

KERMADEC PETREL

pale morph

WHITE-NAPED (WHITE-NECKED) PETREL

...OOTED ...WATER

STREAKED SHEARWATER

PLATE 5. Smaller Gadfly-Petrels

COLLARED PETREL *Pterodroma brevipes* **p. 65**
Dark collar visible from below (pale morph) or dark gray breast and belly (dark phase). Dark cap contrasts with gray back. Tail all dark.

BLACK-WINGED PETREL *Pterodroma nigripennis* **p. 63**
Dark collar visible from below, no contrasting dark cap. Outer tail feathers pale at base.

MOTTLED PETREL *Pterodroma inexpectata* **p. 64**
Dark gray belly patch, bold diagonal bar on underwing.

COOK'S PETREL *Pterodroma cookii* **p. 66**
Nearly unmarked white underwing, no contrasting dark cap. Tail dark in center, pale on edges (variable).

STEJNEGER'S PETREL *Pterodroma longirostris* **p. 65**
Similar to Cook's Petrel, but with dark cap, no white in sides of tail.

BONIN PETREL *Pterodroma hypoleuca* **p. 64**
Bold black wrist patches and diagonal bars on underwing, contrasting dark cap.

5

COLLARED
PETREL

dark
morph

BLACK-WINGED
PETREL

MOTTLED
PETREL

COOK'S
PETREL

BONIN
PETREL

STEJNEGER'S
PETREL

PLATE 6. Storm-Petrels

WILSON'S STORM-PETREL *Oceanites oceanicus*　　　　　**p. 71**
Rounded tail, clean-cut white rump. Rounded wings held straight out, without prominent bend. Legs long, extending beyond tail. May dangle legs on surface.

LEACH'S STORM-PETREL *Oceanodroma leucorhoa*　　　　**p. 74**
Tail forked, white rump narrow, variably divided down center. Wings have prominent bend at wrist.

BAND-RUMPED STORM-PETREL *Oceanodroma castro*　　　**p. 74**
Shallowly forked tail, clean-cut white rump. Buff bars on upperwings less prominent than in Leach's.

WHITE-FACED STORM-PETREL *Pelagodroma marina*　　　**p. 71**
Gray back, prominent eye stripe. Compare phalaropes.

POLYNESIAN STORM-PETREL *Nesofregetta fuliginosa*　　　**p. 73**
Large, with forked tail, rounded wings, distinctive flight (see text). Varies from all dark in Samoa to dark with white rump, belly, and throat in se. Polynesia.

MATSUDAIRA'S STORM-PETREL *Oceanodroma matsudairae*　　**p. 76**
Very similar to Tristram's, but brownish rather than bluish gray. Lacks pale rump patch. Pale shafts at base of primaries above variable, often hard to see.

TRISTRAM'S (SOOTY) STORM-PETREL　　　　　　　　**p. 75**
Oceanodroma tristrami
Deeply forked long tail, buffy rump and wing bars. Head and body with bluish gray sheen.

WHITE-BELLIED STORM-PETREL *Fregetta grallaria*　　　　**p. 72**
Rounded tail, white rump and underparts. Pale edges to back feathers wear away, so some individuals lack them.

BLACK-BELLIED STORM-PETREL *Fregetta tropica*　　　　**p. 72**
Very similar to White-bellied from above. Dark center of belly may be very narrow. No pale feather edges above.

6

WILSON'S
STORM-PETREL

LEACH'S
STORM-PETREL

WHITE-
FACED
STORM-
PETREL

BAND-
RUMPED
STORM-
PETREL

MATSUDAIRA'S
STORM-PETREL

pale
extreme

LYNESIAN
RM-PETREL

intermed.

dark
extreme

TRISTRAM'S
(SOOTY)
STORM-
PETREL

WHITE-BELLIED
STORM-PETREL

BLACK-BELLIED
STORM-PETREL

PLATE 7. Tropicbirds, Boobies, and Cormorant

RED-TAILED TROPICBIRD *Phaethon rubricauda* **p. 77**
Bulkier, broader-winged than White-tailed, with no black on upperwings.
Red tail spike hard to see at distance. Juv. has little black in outer primaries.

WHITE-TAILED TROPICBIRD *Phaethon lepturus* **p. 76**
Delicate, slender, with black bars on upperwings. Long tail conspicuous.
Some individuals pale peach or rosy color.

RED-FOOTED BOOBY *Sula sula* **p. 80**
All ads. have pink-based blue bill and red feet. Three morphs in tropical Pacific: white with black flight feathers (predominates in n. Pacific); brown with
pale head, white rump and tail (predominates in se. Pacific); and a rare all-
brown morph. Juv. of all types dusty brown with dark bill.

BROWN BOOBY *Sula leucogaster* **p. 80**
Dark brown with clean-cut white (ad.) or pale brown (juv.) belly. Bill pale.

MASKED BOOBY *Sula dactylatra* **p. 79**
White with black mask, tail, and flight feathers (more prominent on perched
bird than in white morph Red-footed). Juv. lacks clean-cut look of other
white-bellied boobies.

LITTLE PIED CORMORANT *Phalacrocorax melanoleucos* **p. 82**
Palau only. Black above, white below. Note long tail.

7

juv.

white form
ad.

ad.

**WHITE-TAILED
TROPICBIRD**

juv.

**RED-TAILED
TROPICBIRD**

rosy
form
ad.

juv.

brown
morph
ad.

white
morph
ad.

**RED-FOOTED
BOOBY**

white-tailed
brown
morph
ad.

**BROWN
BOOBY**

juv.

ad.

juv.

**MASKED
BOOBY**

ad.

**LITTLE
PIED
CORMORANT**

ad.

PLATE 8. Long-legged Wading Birds

WHITE-FACED IBIS *Plegadis chihi*   **p. 92**
Downcurved bill, dark plumage. Iris red.

PACIFIC REEF-HERON *Egretta sacra*   **p. 88**
Short-legged, horizontal posture. Dark morph the only slate gray heron in
most of tropical Pacific. White morph chunkier, less graceful than other white
herons or egrets, with paler legs than most.

CATTLE EGRET *Bubulcus ibis*   **p. 89**
Small, short-necked. Breeding birds show buffy plumes, orange bill and
legs.

LITTLE EGRET *Egretta garzetta*   **p. 87**
Small, with black bill and legs, gray-green lores. Toes with yellow soles or all
yellow.

SNOWY EGRET *Egretta thula*   **p. 88**
Small with black bill and legs, bright yellow lores. Toes (and sometimes back
of legs) always bright yellow.

INTERMEDIATE EGRET *Egretta intermedia*   **p. 87**
Size of reef-heron, but more slender and graceful, with black legs.

RUFOUS NIGHT-HERON *Nycticorax caledonicus*   **p. 91**
Rufous neck, black cap (ad.). Juv. streaky with yellow iris, dark base of lower
mandible.

BLACK-CROWNED NIGHT-HERON *Nycticorax nycticorax*   **p. 90**
Adult has distinctive pattern of gray, black, and white. Juv. streaky, with orange iris, yellow base of lower mandible. Subad. like ad. but browner, without head plume.

LITTLE (GREEN-BACKED) HERON *Butorides striatus*   **p. 89**
Very small, chunky, with black cap. Neck chestnut in Hawaii visitors, gray in
Micronesian migrants, intermediate in Polynesian residents. See text.

YELLOW BITTERN *Ixobrychus sinensis*   **p. 85**
Very small, buff, brown, and black. Bold buff patches in wings. Imm.
streaked.

8

WHITE-FACED
IBIS

nonbr

PACIFIC
REEF-HERON

pied
morph

dark
morph

white
morph

TTLE
RET

br.

nonbr.

LITTLE
EGRET

INTER-
MEDIATE
EGRET

SNOWY
EGRET

juv.

juv.

Hawaii

ad.

ad.

RUFOUS
NIGHT-
HERON

ad.

Polynesia

Micronesia

imm.

LITTLE
(GREEN-
BACKED)
HERON

im,n.

YELLOW
BITTERN

ad.

PLATE 9. Ducks I

LAYSAN DUCK *Anas laysanensis*   **p. 99**
Laysan only. Like small, very dark female Mallard with variable amount of white feathering on head.

HAWAIIAN DUCK *Anas wyvilliana*   **p. 99**
Hawaiian Is. only. Smaller, darker than Mallard. Second-year male shows faint Mallard drake pattern, ad. darker, without black posterior.

GRAY DUCK *Anas superciliosa*   **p. 99**
Mottled gray-brown, with bold stripes on head. Bill gray.

MALLARD *Anas platyrhynchos*   **p. 98**
Male unmistakable. Female larger and paler than Hawaiian or Laysan Duck, lacks head stripes of Gray Duck. "Mariana Mallard," now extinct, intermediate between Mallard and Gray Duck.

NORTHERN SHOVELER *Anas clypeata*   **p. 102**
Male has dark green head, white breast, rusty sides, bold blue wing patches. Fall male (not shown) may show blurry white crescent in front of eye. Female mottled sandy brown. Note broad bill, dabbling feeding behavior.

NORTHERN PINTAIL *Anas acuta*   **p. 100**
Both sexes have sharp-pointed tails. Male shows distinctive white point on side of neck.

EURASIAN WIGEON *Anas penelope*   **p. 102**
Black-tipped pale blue bill. Male has rusty head, gray sides. Female has rusty breast, buffy (or sometimes gray) head.

AMERICAN WIGEON *Anas americana*   **p. 103**
Bill as in Eurasian Wigeon. Male has white forehead and crown, pinkish brown sides. Female has pinkish sides, gray-streaked head.

BLUE-WINGED TEAL *Anas discors*   **p. 101**
Pale blue forewing (both sexes). Male has white crescent in front of eye.

GREEN-WINGED TEAL *Anas crecca*   **p. 97**
Small, with green speculum (both sexes). Male has rusty head with green postocular streak.

CINNAMON TEAL *Anas cyanoptera*   **p. 101**
Wing patches as in Blue-winged Teal. Cinnamon drake distinctive, female (not shown) very similar to Blue-winged female (see text).

GARGANEY *Anas querquedula*   **p. 100**
Gray forewing patches (both sexes). Male has bold white streak on chocolate head. Female's face pattern bolder than that of Green-winged Teal.

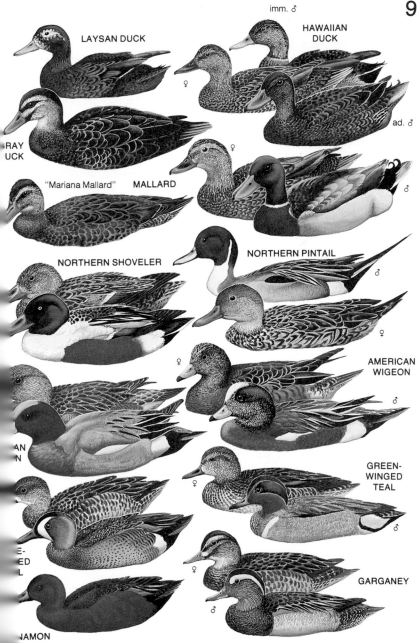

9

LAYSAN DUCK

imm. ♂

HAWAIIAN DUCK

♀

ad. ♂

GRAY DUCK

♂

"Mariana Mallard"   MALLARD

♀

♂

NORTHERN SHOVELER

NORTHERN PINTAIL

♂

♀

♀

AMERICAN WIGEON

EUROPEAN WIGEON

♂

GREEN-WINGED TEAL

♀

♂

BLUE-WINGED TEAL

GARGANEY

♀

CINNAMON TEAL

♂

PLATE 10. Ducks II

BUFFLEHEAD *Bucephala albeola* **p. 106**
Very small. Bold black and white pattern (male) or dusty brown with white ear patch (female).

RUDDY DUCK *Oxyura jamaicensis* **p. 107**
Very small, tail often cocked up. Males in all plumages have bold white cheek patch. Females' cheeks crossed by dark bar.

GREATER SCAUP *Aythya marila* **p. 105**
Whiter on back than Lesser Scaup, with rounder green-glossed head (male). See text for female (not shown).

LESSER SCAUP *Aythya affinis* **p. 105**
Male dark fore and aft, light in between. Head angular with purple gloss. Female dark brown with bold white spot at base of bill.

TUFTED DUCK *Aythya fuligula* **p. 104**
Male looks all black with white sides. Female dark brown, rounder-headed than Ring-necked Duck, with little (if any) white at base of bill.

RING-NECKED DUCK *Aythya collaris* **p. 104**
White subterminal ring on bill (both sexes). Male all dark with gray flanks, white vertical bar at side of breast. Female shows white eye-ring, white at base of bill.

GADWALL *Anas strepera* **p. 102**
White square in speculum (both sexes). Male gray with black posterior.

REDHEAD *Aythya americana* **p. 104**
Bill pale blue with black tip, head rounded. Male grayer above than Canvasback.

CANVASBACK *Aythya valisineria* **p. 103**
Both sexes show distinctive profile. Male white-backed, female whiter on sides than Redhead.

RED-BREASTED MERGANSER *Mergus serrator* **p. 107**
Females only (so far) in tropical Pacific. Shaggy crest, red bill.

HOODED MERGANSER *Lophodytes cucullatus* **p. 106**
Fanlike buffy crest. Bold ad. male plumage rare in tropical Pacific.

10

BUFFLEHEAD

spring ♂

RUDDY
DUCK

GREATER
SCAUP

fall ♂

LESSER
SCAUP

RING-NECKED
DUCK

TUFTED
DUCK

GADWALL

HEAD

CANVASBACK

-BREASTED
MERGANSER

HOODED
MERGANSER

PLATE 11. Birds of Prey

FIJI GOSHAWK *Accipiter rufitorques* **p. 112**
Long-legged, long-tailed profile. Ad. gray above, dull pink below. Imm. brown, streaked below. Fiji only.

COMMON BARN-OWL *Tyto alba* **p. 214**
Very pale with heart-shaped face. Females in Hawaii honey-colored below.

SHORT-EARED OWL *Asio flammeus* **p. 215**
Round-headed, neckless profile. Sandy, streaked and blotched with brown.

HAWAIIAN HAWK *Buteo solitarius* **p. 112**
All dark, or dark above, streaked below. Light-phase imm. pale buff below with dark streak through eye. Ad. has yellow cere and feet, imm. pale blue-green. Hawaii only.

PEREGRINE FALCON *Falco peregrinus* **p. 113**
Fiji subspecies shown. Nearly black above, streaked below, females tinged rusty and larger than males. See also Figure 21.

SWAMP HARRIER *Circus approximans* **p. 109**
Long-winged, long-tailed. Variably colored. Paler individuals have buffy rump and base of tail, streaks below. Darker (younger?) birds nearly uniform chocolate brown.

FIJI GOSHAWK imm.

ad.

Hawaii ♀

11

COMMON BARN-OWL

SHORT-EARED OWL

dark phase

light phase ad.

light phase imm.

HAWAIIAN HAWK

ad. ♀

imm.

PEREGRINE FALCON

ad. ♂

pale form

dark form

SWAMP HARRIER

PLATE 12. Francolins, Quails, and Sandgrouse

BROWN QUAIL *Coturnix australis* **p. 119**
Fiji only. Small, brown, barred below.

ERCKEL'S FRANCOLIN *Francolinus erckelii* **p. 118**
Hawaiian Is. Large, with chestnut cap, streaked breast.

BLACK FRANCOLIN *Francolinus francolinus* **p. 117**
Hawaiian Is., Guam. Male mostly black with white cheeks and chestnut collar. Female mottled sandy brown with chestnut nape. Legs red-orange.

GRAY FRANCOLIN *Francolinus pondicerianus* **p. 117**
Hawaiian Is. Dusty tan with orange throat.

CHUKAR *Alectoris chukar* **p. 118**
Hawaiian Is. Red bill, black collar, bold black bars on flanks.

CALIFORNIA QUAIL *Callipepla californica* **p. 123**
Hawaiian Is. Gray with prominent head plume, scaly belly.

GAMBEL'S QUAIL *Callipepla gambelii* **p. 123**
Like California Quail but with bold black bar across belly (both sexes). Kahoolawe, Lanai.

BLUE-BREASTED QUAIL *Coturnix chinensis* **p. 120**
Guam only. Tiny. Male shows harlequin face pattern.

JAPANESE QUAIL *Coturnix japonica* **p. 119**
Hawaiian Is. Small, mottled sandy brown.

CHESTNUT-BELLIED SANDGROUSE *Pterocles exustus* **p. 188**
Hawaii only. Long, pointed tail, dark belly, pale wing patches. In flocks.

12

BROWN QUAIL

BLACK FRANCOLIN ♂

♀

ERCKEL'S FRANCOLIN

GRAY FRANCOLIN

CALIFORNIA QUAIL

♂ ♀

CHUKAR

GAMBEL'S QUAIL ♂

♂ ♀

BLUE-BREASTED QUAIL

♀

JAPANESE QUAIL ♀

CHESTNUT-BELLIED SANDGROUSE

♂

♂

PLATE 13. Larger Wildfowl

COMMON PEAFOWL *Pavo cristatus* **p. 122**
Unmistakable. Very local on Oahu, Maui, Hawaii.

WILD TURKEY *Meleagris gallopavo* **p. 122**
Large, with bare wattled head, fan-shaped tail. Hawaii, Maui.

RED JUNGLEFOWL *Gallus gallus* **p. 120**
Like domestic chicken but smaller than most.

KALIJ PHEASANT *Lophura leucomelana* **p. 120**
High-arched tail, backward-pointing crest. Hawaii only.

COMMON (RING-NECKED) PHEASANT *Phasianus colchicus* **p. 121**
Long, pointed, barred tail, red facial skin (male). Green form (Hawaii only)
male lacks neck ring. Hawaiian Is., Guam.

13

COMMON PEAFOWL

♀

♂

WILD TURKEY

♀ RED JUNGLEFOWL

♂

♀ KALIJ PHEASANT

♂

green form ♂

COMMON (RING-NECKED) PHEASANT

ring-necked form ♂

♀

PLATE 14. Megapodes, Gallinules, Coots, and Goose

NIUAFO'OU MEGAPODE *Megapodius pritchardii*   **p. 116**
Gray with short crest, yellow bill. Niuafo'ou (Tonga) only.

MICRONESIAN MEGAPODE *Megapodius laperouse*   **p. 115**
Almost black with gray crest, yellow bill and legs. Palau, Marianas.

HAWAIIAN GOOSE *Nesochen sandvicensis*   **p. 97**
Black face, buff neck with dark furrows. Smaller than migratory geese. Hawaii, Maui only.

COMMON MOORHEN *Gallinula chloropus*   **p. 128**
Dark gray with red bill, white streaks along flanks. Hawaiian Is., Palau, Marianas.

PURPLE SWAMPHEN *Porphyrio porphyrio*   **p. 129**
Large, purple-blue with red bill and legs, white undertail.

HAWAIIAN COOT *Fulica alai*   **p. 130**
Slate gray with bill and large bulbous frontal shield white. About 15% have red frontal shields and dark marks near bill tip. Hawaiian Is. only.

EURASIAN COOT *Fulica atra*   **p. 130**
Like Hawaiian Coot but with point of black feathers indenting base of bill and shield. No white under tail.

AMERICAN COOT *Fulica americana*   **p. 130**
Like Hawaiian Coot but with much smaller maroon frontal shield.

14

NIUAFO'OU MEGAPODE

HAWAIIAN GOOSE

[MIC]RONESIAN [ME]GAPODE

[C]OMMON [M]OORHEN

PURPLE SWAMPHEN

HAWAIIAN COOT

[E]urasian

red morph

Hawaiian   white morph

American

[C]OOTS

PLATE 15. Rails

BANDED RAIL *Rallus philippensis*　　　　　**p. 124**
　White eyebrow, reddish brown nape, barred body.

WAKE RAIL *Rallus wakensis*　　　　　**p. 125**
　Extinct. Wake I. only.

GUAM RAIL *Rallus owstoni*　　　　　**p. 124**
　Brown above, barred below. Flightless. Guam only.

BANDED CRAKE *Rallina eurizonoides*　　　　　**p. 125**
　Rufous head and breast, barred underparts. Palau only.

BAR-WINGED RAIL *Rallus poecilopterus*　　　　　**p. 125**
　Large, dark with yellow bill. Nearly extinct, Viti Levu (Fiji) only.

WHITE-BROWED CRAKE *Porzana cinerea*　　　　　**p. 126**
　Small with bold black and white stripes on side of head, red eye.

SPOTLESS CRAKE *Porzana tabuensis*　　　　　**p. 126**
　Small. Plain slaty gray with red eyes.

HAWAIIAN RAIL *Porzana sandwichensis*　　　　　**p. 127**
　Extinct. Tiny, rusty brown. Hawaiian Is. only

HENDERSON ISLAND CRAKE *Porzana atra*　　　　　**p. 127**
　Black with red legs. Flightless. Henderson I. only.

KOSRAE CRAKE *Porzana monasa*　　　　　**p. 127**
　Extinct. Kosrae only.

LAYSAN RAIL *Porzana palmeri*　　　　　**p. 127**
　Extinct. Laysan, Midway only.

15

BANDED RAIL

WAKE RAIL

GUAM RAIL

BANDED CRAKE

BAR-WINGED RAIL

WHITE-BROWED CRAKE

SPOTLESS CRAKE

HAWAIIAN RAIL

KOSRAE CRAKE

LAYSAN RAIL

HENDERSON ISLAND CRAKE

PLATE 16. Shorebirds I: Plovers, Pratincole, and Turnstone

LITTLE RINGED PLOVER *Charadrius dubius* **p. 136**
No wing stripe. Breeding birds have all-dark bill, distinctive head pattern.

SEMIPALMATED PLOVER *Charadrius semipalmatus* **p. 136**
White wing stripe. Darker than other small plovers. Breeding birds have yellow-based bill. Compare Common Ringed Plover in Figure 24.

SNOWY PLOVER *Charadrius alexandrinus* **p. 135**
White wing stripe, black center of tail, broken neck ring. Breeding birds have rusty cap.

GREAT SAND-PLOVER *Charadrius leschenaultii* **p. 134**
Winter birds gray and white, with relatively long bill. Breeders have rusty head and breast band, bold black face pattern.

MONGOLIAN PLOVER *Charadrius mongolus* **p. 134**
Winter birds very similar to Great Sand-Plover (see text) but with smaller bill. Breeders have rusty breast, black ear patch.

DOUBLE-BANDED DOTTEREL *Charadrius bicinctus* **p. 134**
Nonbreeders buffy brown above with indistinct breast band. Breeding plumage has one black, one rusty band below.

GRAY (BLACK-BELLIED) PLOVER *Pluvialis squatarola* **p. 131**
Large bill, thick-headed profile. Paler throughout than Lesser Golden-Plover, with less black below in breeding plumage.

LESSER GOLDEN-PLOVER *Pluvialis dominica* **p. 132**
Nonbreeders golden-buff with black mottling. Breeders have black underparts.

ORIENTAL PRATINCOLE *Glareola maldivarum* **p. 166**
Buffy brown with deeply forked black tail, white rump, and chestnut wing linings. Ternlike in flight.

RUDDY TURNSTONE *Arenaria interpres* **p. 152**
Blotchy dark pattern on breast, orange legs. Breeding plumage rusty above, more clean-cut on face and breast.

SEMIPALMATED
PLOVER

br.

br.

br.

SNOWY
PLOVER

LITTLE
RINGED
PLOVER

nonbr.

nonbr.

nonbr.

br.

MONGOLIAN
PLOVER

GREAT
_AND-PLOVER

br.

nonbr.

nonbr.

nonbr.

br.

GRAY
(BLACK-BELLIED)
PLOVER

br.

nonbr.

DOUBLE-
BANDED
DOTTEREL

ORIENTAL
PRATINCOLE

br.

nonbr.

LESSER
_LDEN-PLOVER

nonbr.

br.

RUDDY
TURNSTONE

16

PLATE 17. Shorebirds II: Stilt, Curlews, Godwits, and Large Sandpipers

BLACK-NECKED STILT *Himantopus mexicanus* **p. 139**
Black and white with coral red legs. Hawaiian Is. only.

LESSER YELLOWLEGS *Tringa flavipes* **p. 141**
Bill about length of head, no bars on flanks in breeding plumage.

GREATER YELLOWLEGS *Tringa melanoleuca* **p. 141**
Bill longer than head, flanks barred in breeding plumage.

WOOD SANDPIPER *Tringa glareola* **p. 142**
Small, with dull yellow or greenish legs, short bill, horizontal posture.

COMMON GREENSHANK *Tringa nebularia* **p. 140**
Slightly upturned bill, greenish gray legs. Larger than yellowlegs.

COMMON REDSHANK *Tringa totanus* **p. 142**
Red legs, brown plumage, bold white wing stripe.

FAR EASTERN CURLEW *Numenius madagascariensis* **p. 150**
Large. Long downcurved bill, no stripes on crown. Rump brown.

WHIMBREL *Numenius phaeopus* **p. 148**
Short downcurved bill, gray-brown plumage with bold crown stripes.

BRISTLE-THIGHED CURLEW *Numenius tahitiensis* **p. 149**
Like Whimbrel but with buffy neck, pale orange-brown rump and tail.

COMMON SNIPE *Gallinago gallinago* **p. 163**
Chunky, long-billed, with prominent stripes on back. In Micronesia, Swinhoe's Snipe more likely, looks nearly identical perched.

MARSH SANDPIPER *Tringa stagnatilis* **p. 141**
Slender, delicate, with needlelike bill, dark legs.

BLACK-TAILED GODWIT *Limosa limosa* **p. 150**
Nearly straight bill, black tail, white wing stripe. Winter birds smaller and grayer than Bar-tailed.

BAR-TAILED GODWIT *Limosa lapponica* **p. 152**
Slightly upturned bill, barred tail.

17

BLACK-
NECKED
STILT

nonbr.

br.

LESSER
YELLOWLEGS

nonbr.

GREATER
YELLOWLEGS

br.

WOOD
SANDPIPER

COMMON
GREENSHANK

WHIMBREL

FAR EASTERN
CURLEW

COMMON
REDSHANK

COMMON
SNIPE

BRISTLE-
THIGHED
CURLEW

nonbr

br.

MARSH
SANDPIPER

br.

br.

nonbr.

nonbr.

BAR-TAILED
GODWIT

LACK-
AILED
ODWIT

PLATE 18. Shorebirds III: Stints and Smaller Sandpipers

NOTE: The birds on this plate are notoriously difficult to identify. Only the most obvious distinguishing marks are noted below. Always refer to the main text when attempting to identify these species. The juvenile plumage will be seen mainly in the latter half of the year.

LEAST SANDPIPER *Calidris minutilla*   **p. 157**
Yellow legs, short pointed bill. All plumages brownish with dark breast.

RUFOUS-NECKED STINT *Calidris ruficollis*   **p. 156**
Short, thick bill, black legs. Winter (nonbr.) birds have pure white center of breast.

LONG-TOED STINT *Calidris subminuta*   **p. 157**
Yellow legs with noticeably long toes. Upright posture. Eyebrow prominent.

WESTERN SANDPIPER *Calidris mauri*   **p. 155**
Long bill drooped at tip, black legs.

DUNLIN *Calidris alpina*   **p. 159**
Larger than stints. Bill long, slightly drooped. Rump dark.

PECTORAL SANDPIPER *Calidris melanotos*   **p. 158**
Yellow-based bill, yellow legs. Sharp lower border to breast streaks. Size variable.

CURLEW SANDPIPER *Calidris ferruginea*   **p. 160**
Similar in winter to Dunlin, but with longer legs, more curved bill, white rump.

SHARP-TAILED SANDPIPER *Calidris acuminata*   **p. 159**
Like Pectoral but without sharp breast/belly demarcation. Cap rusty.

TUAMOTU SANDPIPER *Prosobonia cancellatus*   **p. 147**
Tuamotu Arch. only. Short, thin bill. Plumage varies from dark brown, heavily barred below to streaked above, pale buff below.

SANDERLING *Calidris alba*   **p. 153**
Larger than stints. Nonbreeding birds very pale with black shoulders.

18

EAST
DPIPER

RUFOUS-NECKED
STINT

LONG-TOED
STINT

br.

juv.

nonbr.

br.

juv.

nonbr.

nonbr.

VESTERN
ANDPIPER

br.

DUNLIN

nonbr.

br.

PECTORAL
SANDPIPER

molting

nonbr.

ARP-TAILED
ANDPIPER

CURLEW
SANDPIPER

uv.

pale
form

nonbr.

br.

dark
form

nonbr.

TUAMOTU
SANDPIPER

SANDERLING

PLATE 19. Shorebirds IV: Various Medium-sized Species

WANDERING TATTLER *Heteroscelus incanus* **p. 143**
Plain gray above with dull yellow legs. Breeding birds heavily barred below, including undertail coverts.

SIBERIAN (GRAY-TAILED) TATTLER *Heteroscelus brevipes* **p. 144**
Winter birds nearly identical to Wandering Tattler (see text). Breeders barred on sides and breast only. Tattlers best distinguished by voice.

LONG-BILLED DOWITCHER *Limnodromus scolopaceus* **p. 162**
Stocky, with very long bill. Nonbreeders mostly plain gray. Breeding birds barred on flanks. Compare Short-billed Dowitcher (not shown) in text.

RUFF *Philomachus pugnax* **p. 161**
Males much larger than females, scaly above in winter. Juv. buffy, especially on breast. Ad. female or Reeve (not shown) like juv. but less buffy above.

TEREK SANDPIPER *Xenus cinereus* **p. 147**
Upturned bill, yellow legs. Nonbreeding plumage (not shown) less boldly marked on scapulars.

BUFF-BREASTED SANDPIPER *Tryngites subruficollis* **p. 160**
Warm buff below, scaly above. Bill short. Wing linings silvery.

WILSON'S PHALAROPE *Phalaropus tricolor* **p. 164**
Plain gray and white with dark eye stripe, needlelike bill (winter). Breeders (not shown) have rufous stripe on side of neck.

RED PHALAROPE *Phalaropus fulicarius* **p. 165**
Short thick bill. Winter plumage with bold head pattern, plain gray back. Breeders have reddish chestnut body, molting birds are blotchy.

RED KNOT *Calidris canutus* **p. 153**
Stocky with medium bill, dark green legs. Nonbreeders gray above, white below, larger than most other *Calidris*. Breeding birds have rufous breast.

19

SIBERIAN
(GRAY-TAILED)
TATTLER

nonbr.

br.

WANDERING
TATTLER

br.

br.

LONG-BILLED
DOWITCHER

juv.

nonbr. ♂

RUFF

nonbr.

juv. ♀

WILSON'S
PHALAROPE

TEREK
SANDPIPER

nonbr.

REASTED
OPIPER

br.

nonbr.

molting

nonbr.

RED KNOT

RED PHALAROPE

PLATE 20. Terns

SOOTY TERN *Sterna fuscata*   **p. 182**
Ad. clean-cut black above, white below. Juv. mostly dark with pale wing linings and belly, buff feather edges above. Upright posture.

COMMON FAIRY-TERN *Gygis alba*   **p. 186**
White with black eye, dark shafts on primaries. Bill thick, blue at base.

LITTLE FAIRY-TERN *Gygis microrhyncha*   **p. 186**
Like Common Fairy-Tern but smaller. Bill thin, straight, all black. No dark shafts on primaries.

BRIDLED TERN *Sterna anaethetus*   **p. 182**
Similar to Spectacled (Gray-backed) Tern in all plumages but ad. browner above. See text.

SPECTACLED (GRAY-BACKED) TERN *Sterna lunata*   **p. 181**
Ad. Grayer above than Sooty Tern, with pale nape and narrower white forehead. Juv. scaly above, white below. Distinctive posture.

BLUE-GRAY NODDY *Procelsterna cerulea*   **p. 185**
Dark morph all blue-gray. Light morph with nearly white head, underparts, and underwing coverts. Light morph imm. has very dark primaries. Legs very long.

BLACK NODDY *Anous minutus*   **p. 184**
Ad. sooty black with contrasting gray tail and white cap. Juv. has dark tail and smaller, more sharply defined cap. Smaller and thinner-billed than Brown Noddy.

BROWN NODDY *Anous stolidus*   **p. 184**
Dark brown with darker primaries and tail, pale cap. Juv. has reduced white on head. See also Plate 2.

GREAT CRESTED TERN *Sterna bergii*   **p. 178**
Large. Bill yellow. Nonbreeding birds blotchy above with less black on head, dull-colored bill. Breeding ad. has solid black cap.

BLACK-NAPED TERN *Sterna sumatrana*   **p. 179**
Nearly all white with narrow black nape, thin black bill. Breeding birds tinged pale pink below, juv. scaly on back.

20

COMMON
FAIRY-TERN

ad.

JV.

OTY
RN

LITTLE
FAIRY-TERN

ad.

BLACK
NODDY

juv.

light
morph ad.

dark
morph
ad.

ad.

BLUE-GRAY
NODDY

juv.

ad.

BROWN
NODDY

CLED
GRAY-
CKED)
TERN

ad.

light morph
imm.

juv.

ad.

dark
morph ad.

ad.

juv.

nonbr. ad.

nonbr.

GREAT
CRESTED
TERN

br. ad.

BLACK-NAPED
TERN

juv.

PLATE 21. Micronesian Land Birds I: Pigeons and Doves

MARIANA FRUIT-DOVE *Ptilinopus roseicapilla*   **p. 198**
Marianas only. Gray head and breast, green upperparts, pale band at tail tip. Juv. (not shown) all green.

PURPLE-CAPPED FRUIT-DOVE *Ptilinopus porphyraceus*   **p. 197**
Pale green head and breast, dark green upperparts, yellow-tipped tail. Juv. (not shown) all green. Different subspecies (Plate 26) in Polynesia.

PALAU FRUIT-DOVE *Ptilinopus pelewensis*   **p. 197**
Palau only. Gray head and breast, green upperparts, orange center of belly. Juv. green with yellow feather edges.

MICRONESIAN PIGEON *Ducula oceanica*   **p. 203**
Very large. Gray head and breast, dark upperparts, chestnut underparts.

PHILIPPINE TURTLE-DOVE *Streptopelia bitorquata*   **p. 191**
Marianas only (introduced). Dusty gray with narrow black collar, white outer tail feathers.

NICOBAR PIGEON *Caloenas nicobarica*   **p. 192**
Palau only. Chunky, black, with short white tail.

WHITE-THROATED GROUND-DOVE *Gallicolumba xanthonura*   **p. 193**
Marianas, Yap. Male with buff-tinged white head and breast, purple back, black underparts. Female all orange-brown.

CAROLINE ISLANDS GROUND-DOVE *Gallicolumba kubaryi*   **p. 193**
Truk, Pohnpei. Ad. has white head and breast with black cap and postocular streak, purple back, black underparts. Juv. dark rusty-brown.

PALAU GROUND-DOVE *Gallicolumba canifrons*   **p. 195**
Gray head and breast, rufous nape and upper back.

MARIANA FRUIT-DOVE

PURPLE-CAPPED FRUIT-DOVE

PALAU FRUIT-DOVE

21

ad.

juv.

PHILIPPINE TURTLE-DOVE

NICOBAR PIGEON

MICRONESIAN PIGEON

♀

♂

WHITE-THROATED GROUND-DOVE

juv.

ad.

CAROLINE IS. GROUND-DOVE

PALAU GROUND-DOVE

PLATE 22. Micronesian Land Birds II: Various Nonpasserines

COLLARED KINGFISHER *Halcyon chloris* **p. 221**
Blue above, white below. Color of crown varies geographically.

MICRONESIAN KINGFISHER *Halcyon cinnamomina* **p. 222**
Blue above with rusty cap. Color of underparts varies with age, sex, and geography. Palau birds smaller, slenderer.

ORIENTAL CUCKOO *Cuculus saturatus* **p. 211**
Gray with long tail, barred underparts. Hepatic phase (not shown) all rufous, heavily barred. Compare Common Cuckoo (Figure 39).

POHNPEI LORY *Trichoglossus rubiginosus* **p. 205**
Plum-colored with orange bill, yellow tail. Pohnpei only.

DOLLARBIRD *Eurystomus orientalis* **p. 227**
Big-headed; blue-green with red bill, "silver dollars" in wings.

ECLECTUS PARROT *Eclectus roratus* **p. 208**
Introduced Palau. Males green with red underwing, females red with blue collar.

GREATER SULPHUR-CRESTED COCKATOO *Cacatua galerita* **p. 208**
Introduced Palau. Huge, white with erectile yellow crest.

PALAU OWL *Pyrrhoglaux podargina* **p. 215**
Round-headed. Barred rusty brown. Palau only.

JUNGLE NIGHTJAR *Caprimulgus indicus* **p. 216**
Horizontal perching posture. "Dead leaf" pattern with white spots in primaries. Palau only.

22

Palau

Rota

Saipan

COLLARED KINGFISHER

Pohnpei ad.

Palau

Guam ♀

MICRONESIAN KINGFISHER

Pohnpei juv.

Guam ♂

ORIENTAL CUCKOO

POHNPEI LORY

DOLLARBIRD

♂   ♀

ECLECTUS PARROT

GREATER SULPHUR-CRESTED COCKATOO

JUNGLE NIGHTJAR

PALAU OWL

PLATE 23. Micronesian Land Birds III: Widespread Species and Mariana Endemics

MARIANA CROW *Corvus kubaryi* **p. 232**
Very large. All black with dark eyes. Guam, Rota only.

MICRONESIAN STARLING *Aplonis opaca* **p. 274**
Ad. all glossy black with yellow eyes. Imm. streaked below. Tail short.

BLACK DRONGO *Dicrurus macrocercus* **p. 230**
All black with long forked tail. Introduced Guam, Rota.

BRIDLED WHITE-EYE *Zosterops conspicillatus* **p. 283**
Tiny, green with white eye-ring. Variable island to island. Marianas only.

GUAM FLYCATCHER *Myiagra freycineti* **p. 247**
Dark above, light below. Amount of buff on breast variable. Females duller. Guam only.

MICRONESIAN HONEYEATER *Myzomela rubratra* **p. 277**
Red and black (male) or red and brown (female) with curved bill.

ISLAND (GRAY) SWIFTLET *Aerodramus vanikorensis* **p. 218**
Dark gray with long stiff-looking wings. Never perches on wires or branches. Some show pale rump.

BARN SWALLOW *Hirundo rustica* **p. 228**
Deeply forked tail (shorter on many winter birds), dark upperparts, pale underparts.

TINIAN MONARCH *Monarcha takatsukasae* **p. 242**
Buffy brown with white rump and wing bars. Tinian only.

GOLDEN WHITE-EYE *Cleptornis marchei* **p. 286**
Golden yellow with orange bill and legs. Saipan, Agiguan only.

RUFOUS FANTAIL *Rhipidura rufifrons* **p. 249**
White-tipped fanlike tail, rufous rump and forehead. Amount of black in throat varies from island to island. Marianas, Yap.

NIGHTINGALE REED-WARBLER *Acrocephalus luscinia* **p. 253**
Drab above, yellow below with pale eyebrow, very long bill. Marianas only.

23

MICRONESIAN
STARLING

imm.

MARIANA
CROW

ipan/Tinian

ad.

BLACK
DRONGO

Guam

MICRONESIAN
HONEYEATER

♀

BRIDLED
HITE-EYE

Rota

♂

♂

♀

GUAM
FLYCATCHER

dark-
umped

AND
RAY)
FTLET

GOLDEN
WHITE-EYE

TINIAN
MONARCH

le-
ped

Guam

Saipan

RUFOUS
FANTAIL

mm.

ad.

BARN
SWALLOW

NIGHTINGALE
REED-WARBLER

PLATE 24. Micronesian Land Birds IV: Small Land Birds of Palau and Yap

OLIVE WHITE-EYE *Rukia oleaginea* **p. 287**
Dark olive with white eye-ring, orange legs. Yap only.

PLAIN WHITE-EYE *Zosterops hypolais* **p. 284**
Tiny, nondescript. Iris white. In flocks. Yap only.

YAP MONARCH *Monarcha godeffroyi* **p. 242**
Ad. black and white, juv. brown. Yap only.

CICADABIRD *Coracina tenuirostris* **p. 233**
Male dark slate, female brown barred below. Yap birds much larger than Palau ones, with females less heavily barred and rustier.

PALAU FANTAIL *Rhipidura lepida* **p. 248**
Bright rufous with long tail. Palau only.

MORNINGBIRD *Colluricincla tenebrosa* **p. 238**
Big-headed profile. Dull sooty brown (some darker than shown). Palau only.

MANGROVE FLYCATCHER *Myiagra erythrops* **p. 246**
Slaty above with rusty forehead and breast. Females duller. Palau only.

DUSKY WHITE-EYE *Zosterops finschii* **p. 285**
Dull gray-brown, no eye-ring. Palau only.

CAROLINE ISLANDS WHITE-EYE *Zosterops semperi* **p. 284**
Green and yellow with white eye-ring. Palau (also Truk, Pohnpei). See also Plate 25.

GIANT WHITE-EYE *Megazosterops palauensis* **p. 288**
Plain olive-yellow with dark legs, thick bill, streaked auriculars. Palau only.

PALAU BUSH-WARBLER *Cettia annae* **p. 251**
Like Giant White-eye but slimmer, with orange legs, thin bill, prominent eyebrow and eye stripe. Palau only.

See also Plate 23 (Micronesian Starling, Micronesian Honeyeater, Island [Gray] Swiftlet, Barn Swallow, Rufous Fantail), Plate 25 (Blue-faced Parrotfinch), and Figure 46 (White-breasted Woodswallow).

OLIVE
WHITE-EYE

PLAIN WHITE-EYE

YAP
MONARCH

juv.

ad. ♀

ad. ♂

p ♀

DA-
D

♀

♂

PALAU FANTAIL

NGBIRD

♀

♂

DUSKY
WHITE-EYE

MANGROVE
FLYCATCHER

CAROLINE IS.
WHITE-EYE

GIANT
HITE-EYE

PALAU
BUSH-WARBLER

24

PLATE 25. Micronesian Land Birds V: Small Land Birds of the Eastern Carolines

CICADABIRD *Coracina tenuirostris*   **p. 233**
Male slate gray (see also Plate 24). Pohnpei female rufous with gray top and sides of head. Juv. like female scalloped with white. Pohnpei only (this form).

POHNPEI MOUNTAIN STARLING *Aplonis pelzelni*   **p. 272**
Pohnpei only, possibly extinct. Dull brownish black with dark eyes. Smaller than Micronesian Starling.

MICRONESIAN STARLING *Aplonis opaca*   **p. 274**
Heads only shown for comparison (see also Plate 23). Pohnpei juv. may be all dark below with dark eyes, but has thicker bill than Pohnpei Mountain Starling.

BLUE-FACED PARROTFINCH *Erythrura trichroa*   **p. 316**
Dark green with red rump and tail. Tiny. Pohnpei, Truk, Palau.

TRUK MONARCH *Metabolus rugensis*   **p. 242**
Large. Males white with variable amounts of glossy black. Ad. female slate gray. Imm. rusty buff. Highly variable, with many intermediate individuals. Truk only.

CAROLINE ISLANDS REED-WARBLER *Acrocephalus syrinx*   **p. 254**
Brown above, yellowish below, with prominent eyebrow.

POHNPEI FANTAIL *Rhipidura kubaryi*   **p. 249**
Slaty gray with white "whiskers." Long fan-shaped tail. Pohnpei only.

GRAY WHITE-EYE *Zosterops cinereus*   **p. 286**
Plain gray with narrow white eye-ring. Pohnpei birds browner above.

CAROLINE ISLANDS WHITE-EYE *Zosterops semperi*   **p. 284**
Green and yellow with white eye-ring. See also Plate 24.

GREAT TRUK WHITE-EYE *Rukia ruki*   **p. 287**
Dark olive brown with white "teardrop," orange legs. Tol Group (Truk) only.

LONG-BILLED WHITE-EYE *Rukia longirostra*   **p. 287**
Drab olive-brown with narrow eye-ring, long bill. Pohnpei only.

OCEANIC FLYCATCHER *Myiagra oceanica*   **p. 247**
Glossy blue-black above, white below with rusty breast. Females duller. Truk only.

POHNPEI FLYCATCHER *Myiagra pluto*   **p. 247**
Both sexes all dark, females with reddish tinge to throat. Pohnpei only.

HUNSTEIN'S MANNIKIN *Lonchura hunsteini*   **p. 318**
Tiny, in flocks. Black with gray nape, rusty-yellow tail. Juv. orange-brown with dark brown head. Introduced Pohnpei.

See also Plate 23 (Micronesian Honeyeater, Island [Gray] Swiftlet, Barn Swallow).

25

CICADA-BIRD

juv.

♀

♂

MICRONESIAN STARLING

ad.

juv.

POHNPEI MOUNTAIN STARLING

BLUE-FACED PARROTFINCH

TRUK MONARCH

♂

♀

juv.

CAROLINE IS. REED-WARBLER

?HNPEI ?NTAIL

GREAT TRUK WHITE-EYE

Kosrae

Pohnpei

GRAY WHITE-EYE

?ROLINE IS. ?HITE-EYE

LONG-BILLED WHITE-EYE

juv.

♀

♂

♀

♂

ad.

OCEANIC FLYCATCHER

POHNPEI FLYCATCHER

HUNSTEIN'S MANNIKIN

PLATE 26. Polynesian Land Birds I: Pigeons and Doves of Central Polynesia

TOOTH-BILLED PIGEON *Didunculus strigirostris*   **p. 195**
Ad. chestnut above, black below with hooked, brightly colored bill. Imm. heavily barred reddish brown throughout. W. Samoa only.

WHITE-THROATED PIGEON *Columba vitiensis*   **p. 190**
All dark with white throat and red bill.

PEALE'S PIGEON *Ducula latrans*   **p. 203**
Gray head and breast, dark upperparts, buff under tail. No knob on bill. Fiji only.

PACIFIC PIGEON *Ducula pacifica*   **p. 202**
Gray head and breast, dark upperparts, chestnut undertail. Large knob at base of bill. Juv. (not shown) lacks knob.

PURPLE-CAPPED FRUIT-DOVE *Ptilinopus porphyraceus*   **p. 197**
Green with pale gray-green head, breast, and tail band. Yellow-orange undertail. Differs slightly from Micronesian forms (Plate 21).

MANY-COLORED FRUIT-DOVE *Ptilinopus perousii*   **p. 196**
Male pale yellow-green with crimson cap, undertail coverts, and bar across back. Female like Purple-capped Fruit-Dove but lacks tail band, and in Samoa has crimson undertail.

ORANGE DOVE *Ptilinopus victor*   **p. 202**
Male orange with green head, female mostly green. Vanua Levu, Taveuni, and nearby islands only.

GOLDEN DOVE *Ptilinopus luteovirens*   **p. 201**
Male vivid green-gold, female green. Viti Levu and nearby islands only.

WHISTLING DOVE *Ptilinopus layardi*   **p. 201**
Male green with yellow head, female mostly green. Kadavu Group only.

SHY GROUND-DOVE *Gallicolumba stairii*   **p. 194**
Dark with purple back, brown breast shield with white borders.

26

TOOTH-BILLED
PIGEON

mm.   ad.

PURPLE-CAPPED
FRUIT-DOVE

MANY-
COLORED
FRUIT-DOVE

Samoa

Fiji

-THROATED
GEON

♀   ♂

ORANGE DOVE

GOLDEN DOVE

♀   ♂

WHISTLING
DOVE

♀   ♂

EALE'S
PIGEON

PACIFIC
PIGEON

SHY
GROUND-DOVE

PLATE 27. Polynesian Land Birds II: Pigeons and Doves of Southeastern Polynesia

POLYNESIAN PIGEON *Ducula aurorae*   **p. 204**
Large, dark-bodied with gray head, neck, and breast. Juv. all dark. Knob at base of bill. Tahiti, Makatea only. In Cook Is. see Pacific Pigeon (Plate 26).

NUKUHIVA PIGEON *Ducula galeata*   **p. 204**
Huge with peculiar expanded flat cere over bill. Dark with chestnut undertail, pale eyes. Nukuhiva (Marquesas) only.

RAPA FRUIT-DOVE *Ptilinopus huttoni*   **p. 201**
Large for a fruit-dove. Mostly green with rose cap and undertail coverts. Rapa (Tubuai Is.) only.

WHITE-CAPPED FRUIT-DOVE *Ptilinopus dupetithouarsii*   **p. 200**
Two-toned green with white cap, pale tail band. Females duller. Juv. has pale green cap. Marquesas only.

RED-MUSTACHED FRUIT-DOVE *Ptilinopus mercierii*   **p. 200**
Green, gray, and yellow with red cap and mustache. Marquesas only; probably extinct.

COOK ISLANDS FRUIT-DOVE *Ptilinopus rarotongensis*   **p. 198**
Green and gray with magenta cap. Tail band almost white. Rarotonga, Atiu only.

MAKATEA FRUIT-DOVE *Ptilinopus chalcurus*   **p. 200**
Green with dark purple cap, yellow bill. Makatea (Tuamotu Arch.) only.

ATOLL FRUIT-DOVE *Ptilinopus coralensis*   **p. 199**
Pale coppery green with white tail tip and pale lavender cap. Tuamotu Arch. only.

GRAY-GREEN FRUIT-DOVE *Ptilinopus purpuratus*   **p. 199**
Gray and green with yellow underparts. Leeward Is. birds brighter throughout, with more prominent tail band. Society Is. only.

HENDERSON ISLAND FRUIT-DOVE *Ptilinopus insularis*   **p. 199**
Blue-gray and bronze-green with crimson cap. Henderson I. only.

MARQUESAS GROUND-DOVE *Gallicolumba rubescens*   **p. 194**
Purple above, black below with pale (male) or dark (female) gray head and breast. Amount of white in wings and tail highly variable for both sexes; extremes shown. Fatuhuku, Hatutu (Marquesas) only.

POLYNESIAN GROUND-DOVE *Gallicolumba erythroptera*   **p. 193**
Male purple, black, and white. Female has gray head, rusty breast, and pale eyebrow. Now only in se. Tuamotu Arch.

NOTE: Flying birds not to scale.

27

NUKUHIVA PIGEON

POLYNESIAN PIGEON

juv.

ad.

RAPA FRUIT-DOVE

juv.

WHITE-CAPPED FRUIT-DOVE

ad. ♂

COOK IS. FRUIT-DOVE

RED-MUSTACHED FRUIT-DOVE

AKATEA FRUIT-DOVE

Leeward Is.

ATOLL FRUIT-DOVE

HENDERSON I. FRUIT-DOVE

GRAY-GREEN FRUIT-DOVE

Tahiti/Moorea

MARQUESAS GROUND-DOVE

♀

♂

♀

♂

POLYNESIAN GROUND-DOVE

LONG-TAILED CUCKOO *Eudynamis taitensis*　　　　　　**p. 213**
Long and lanky. Barred brown above, streaked below.

FAN-TAILED CUCKOO *Cacomantis pyrrhophanus*　　　　**p. 213**
Ad. (typical) gray above, rufous below, with boldly barred black and white tail. Imm. barred below. Molt irregular, many blotchy intermediates seen. Dark morph all sooty. Fiji only.

MASKED SHINING-PARROT *Prosopeia personata*　　　　**p. 209**
Big green parrot with yellow and orange belly, black mask. Viti Levu only.

RED SHINING-PARROT *Prosopeia tabuensis*　　　　　　**p. 209**
Long-tailed red parrot with green back and blue on wings, tail, and nape. Varies from island to island in brightness of red and amount of blue. Fiji, Tonga.

BLUE-CROWNED LORIKEET *Vini australis*　　　　　　**p. 206**
Small green parrot with blue crown, red throat and belly.

RED-THROATED LORIKEET *Charmosyna amabilis*　　　　**p. 206**
Small green parrot with red throat, yellow-tipped tail. Viti Levu, Taveuni.

COLLARED LORY *Phigys solitarius*　　　　　　　　　**p. 205**
Small, chunky, short-tailed parrot. Red and green with purple cap, yellow bill. Fiji only.

SACRED KINGFISHER *Halcyon sancta*　　　　　　　　**p. 223**
Blue above, pale underparts and eyebrow tinged rusty. Imm. barred on side of breast. Fiji, Futuna.

FLAT-BILLED KINGFISHER *Halcyon recurvirostris*　　　**p. 223**
Small, blue above, rusty below, with pale spot in front of eye. W. Samoa only.

COLLARED KINGFISHER *Halcyon chloris*　　　　　　　**p. 221**
Blue above, pure white below. Eyebrow may be rusty tinged. Tonga birds bigger, with more blue in crown. Smaller than Micronesian forms (Plate 22), which lack rusty tinge altogether.

28

LONG-TAILED CUCKOO

FAN-TAILED CUCKOO

imm.

dark morph

ad.

MASKED SHINING-PARROT

Kadavu

RED SHINING-PARROT

BLUE-CROWNED LORIKEET

Taveuni

COLLARED LORY

RED-THROATED LORIKEET

SACRED KINGFISHER

imm.

ad.

FLAT-BILLED KINGFISHER

Tonga

Samoa

COLLARED KINGFISHER

PLATE 29. Polynesian Land Birds IV: Parrots and Kingfishers of Southeastern Polynesia

RAIATEA PARAKEET *Cyanoramphus ulietanus* **p. 210**
Extinct. Raiatea only.

BLACK-FRONTED PARAKEET *Cyanoramphus zealandicus* **p. 210**
Extinct. Tahiti only.

STEPHEN'S LORIKEET *Vini stepheni* **p. 207**
Red and green with yellow bill and tail. Henderson I. only.

KUHL'S LORIKEET *Vini kuhlii* **p. 206**
Red and green with purple nape. Rimatara (Tubuai Is.); introduced Line Is.

BLUE LORIKEET *Vini peruviana* **p. 207**
Dark blue with white bib and red bill.

ULTRAMARINE LORIKEET *Vini ultramarina* **p. 207**
Dark blue, light blue, and white with red-orange bill. Marquesas only.

CHATTERING KINGFISHER *Halcyon tuta* **p. 224**
Blue and white with variable black eye stripe and blue crown. Some populations tinged buff on collar and breast. Society Is., Cook Is.

MARQUESAS KINGFISHER *Halcyon godeffroyi* **p. 225**
Similar to Chattering Kingfisher but crown entirely white. Marquesas only.

MANGAIA KINGFISHER *Halcyon ruficollaris* **p. 224**
Similar to Chattering Kingfisher, but with rusty collar, breast, and eyebrow. Mangaia (Cook Is.) only.

TUAMOTU KINGFISHER *Halcyon gambieri* **p. 225**
Similar to Mangaia Kingfisher but with much smaller blue cap. Niau only.

TAHITI KINGFISHER *Halcyon venerata* **p. 225**
Dark above, white below. Tahiti birds have rusty (male) or brown (female) breast band. Moorea birds lack breast band but imm. has streaked throat.

29

BLACK-FRONTED
PARAKEET

STEPHEN'S
LORIKEET

KUHL'S
LORIKEET

RAIATEA
PARAKEET

BLUE
PARAKEET

ULTRAMARINE
LORIKEET

Atiu

CHATTERING
KINGFISHER

Society Is.

Mauke

MARQUESAS
KINGFISHER

MANGAIA
KINGFISHER

TUAMOTU
KINGFISHER

Moorea

Tahiti

♂

imm.

ad.

TAHITI
KINGFISHER

PLATE 30. Polynesian Land Birds V: Smaller Insectivorous Birds

WHITE-RUMPED SWIFTLET *Aerodramus spodiopygius* **p. 219**
All dark with pale rump.

TAHITI SWIFTLET *Aerodramus leucophaeus* **p. 218**

MARQUESAS SWIFTLET *Aerodramus ocistus* (not shown) **p. 219**

ATIU SWIFTLET *Aerodramus sawtelli* (not shown) **p. 218**
Three species virtually identical in appearance, all dark gray with forked tail.

PACIFIC SWALLOW *Hirundo tahitica* **p. 229**
Tail deeply forked. Glossy blue above with chestnut throat. Fiji birds paler below, Tahiti birds darker.

VANIKORO FLYCATCHER *Myiagra vanikorensis* **p. 245**
Male glossy blue-black above, rufous below. Female blue-gray above, diffuse orange-buff below. Fiji.

BLUE-CRESTED FLYCATCHER *Myiagra azureocapilla* **p. 245**
Orange bill (ad.). Male has pale blue crest, chestnut throat (variable in shade). Some subspecies have white-tipped tails. Females have sharply divided two-toned underparts. Fiji only.

SAMOAN FLYCATCHER *Myiagra albiventris* **p. 246**
Glossy blue-black above with rufous throat and breast, white belly. Females paler, less glossy. W. Samoa only.

SILKTAIL *Lamprolia victoriae* **p. 248**
Black with white rump and center of tail, metallic spangles on head and breast. Taveuni, Vanua Levu only.

VERSICOLOR FLYCATCHER *Mayrornis versicolor* **p. 241**
Gray above, cinnamon-buff below. Ogea Levu (Fiji) only.

SLATY FLYCATCHER *Mayrornis lessoni* **p. 241**
Gray with white eyebrow and tail tip. Fiji only.

SAMOAN FANTAIL *Rhipidura nebulosa* **p. 250**
Dark gray with white streaks and/or spots behind eye. Savaii birds have white throats and bellies. W. Samoa only.

STREAKED FANTAIL *Rhipidura spilodera* **p. 250**
Dark brown with prominent eyebrow and streaked underparts.

KADAVU FANTAIL *Rhipidura personata* **p. 250**
Like Streaked Fantail but without streaks. Dark band across breast. Kadavu only.

LONG-LEGGED WARBLER *Trichocichla rufa* **p. 258**
Rusty brown with pale eyebrow. Viti Levu, Vanua Levu only.

FIJI BUSH-WARBLER *Cettia ruficapilla* **p. 253**
Small, thin-billed, with rusty cap and pale eyebrow (Kadavu birds lack the eyebrow). Fiji only.

30

VANIKORO
FLYCATCHER

♀

♂

PACIFIC
SWALLOW

Fiji

Tahiti

WHITE-RUMPED
SWIFTLET

TAHITI
SWIFTLET

-CRESTED
CATCHER

♀

Taveuni ♂

Viti Levu ♂

SAMOAN
FLYCATCHER

♀

♂

SILKTAIL

RSICOLOR
CATCHER

SLATY
YCATCHER

Savaii

SAMOAN FANTAIL

Upolu

Taveuni

STREAKED
FANTAIL

NG-LEGGED
WARBLER

FIJI
BUSH-WARBLER

KADAVU
FANTAIL

PLATE 31. Polynesian Land Birds VI: Trillers, Thrushes, and Wood-swallow

POLYNESIAN TRILLER *Lalage maculosa*   **p. 234**
Highly variable from island to island. Dark cap, pale eyebrow. Some sub-species barred below, some tinged with buff on neck and breast, some clean-cut black and white.

SAMOAN TRILLER *Lalage sharpei*   **p. 234**
Drab brown with orange bill, white eyes, and barred underparts. W. Samoa only.

WHITE-BREASTED WOODSWALLOW *Artamus leucorhynchus*   **p. 270**
Dark gray with white underparts and rump, bluish bill. Fiji. See also Figure 46.

ISLAND THRUSH *Turdus poliocephalus*   **p. 264**
Highly variable from island to island. All subspecies have yellow bill, legs, and eye-ring. All juvs. spotted below (only Kadavu form shown).

31

POLYNESIAN TRILLER

Samoa

Viti Levu

Vanua Levu/
Taveuni

Kadavu

Rotuma

WHITE-
BREASTED
WOODSWALLOW

Ovalau

SAMOAN
TRILLER

Viti Levu

Kadavu juv.

Vanua Levu

ISLAND
THRUSH

Kadavu ad.

Samoa

Gau

Taveuni

PLATE 32. Polynesian Land Birds VII: Whistlers, White-eyes, and Other Small Birds

ROTUMA HONEYEATER *Myzomela chermesina* **p. 277**
Male mostly black with red throat and breast. Female dark olive with red tinge in throat. Rotuma (Fiji) only.

CARDINAL HONEYEATER *Myzomela cardinalis* **p. 277**
Male red and black, female grayish olive with red rump. Juv. male like red-headed female. Samoa.

ORANGE-BREASTED HONEYEATER *Myzomela jugularis* **p. 278**
Black and yellow with red nape and rump. Female (not shown) duller. Fiji only.

SCARLET ROBIN *Petroica multicolor* **p. 237**
Tiny. Black and white with red breast. Female less brightly colored. W. Samoa. Fiji.

LAYARD'S WHITE-EYE *Zosterops explorator* **p. 285**
Chunky, short-tailed. Yellow-green (no gray) with complete white eye-ring. Fiji only.

SILVEREYE *Zosterops lateralis* **p. 285**
Longer-tailed than Layard's White-eye. Yellow-headed with gray back, broken eye-ring. Fiji, Society Is., Tubuai Is.

SAMOAN WHITE-EYE *Zosterops samoensis* **p. 284**
Drab yellow-green with prominent white eye-ring. Savaii only.

RED-HEADED PARROTFINCH *Erythrura cyaneovirens* **p. 316**
Thick black bill. Ad. male blue-green with red head and rump. Female paler, with no red on head. Imm. males gain red on head gradually. W. Samoa, Fiji.

PINK-BILLED PARROTFINCH *Erythrura kleinschmidti* **p. 317**
Huge pink bill, green body, red rump. Viti Levu only.

SAMOAN WHISTLER *Pachycephala flavifrons* **p. 238**
Dark gray above, yellow below. Males have three morphs. Females paler above and on throat. W. Samoa only.

TONGAN WHISTLER *Pachycephala jacquinoti* **p. 238**
Male yellow and olive with black hood. Female has grayish drab head. Vava'u (Tonga) only.

GOLDEN WHISTLER *Pachycephala pectoralis* **p. 237**
Geographic variation complex (see text). All males green above, yellow below, with black cap. Many have black collar. Females of two main types as shown, with some intermediate. Fiji.

32

ROTUMA
NEYEATER

♀

♂

CARDINAL
HONEYEATER

ad. ♀

juv.

ad. ♂

ORANGE-
BREASTED
HONEYEATER

SCARLET
ROBIN

♀

♂

YARD'S
HITE-EYE

ILVEREYE

♀

imm. ♂

ad. ♂

RED-HEADED
PARROTFINCH

AMOAN
ISTLER

SAMOAN
WHITE-EYE

♀

PINK-BILLED
PARROTFINCH

hs

♂

TONGAN
WHISTLER

juv.

ad.

v.

Kadavu

Koro

Ovalau

ad.

w. Viti Levu

GOLDEN
WHISTLER

PLATE 33. Polynesian Land Birds VIII: Shrikebills, Starlings, and Larger Honeyeaters

BLACK-FACED SHRIKEBILL *Clytorhynchus nigrogularis* **p. 240**
Bill thick, slightly upturned. Ad. male has distinctive black face, white ear patch. Juv. male has gray ear patch, spots on throat. Female like Fiji Shrikebill but browner on breast. Fiji.

FIJI SHRIKEBILL *Clytorhynchus vitiensis* **p. 239**
Nondescript drab brown and gray. Thinner bill than Black-faced. Fiji, Tonga, Tau (A. Samoa).

RAROTONGA STARLING *Aplonis cinerascens* **p. 273**
Gray with white undertail. Rarotonga only.

SAMOAN STARLING *Aplonis atrifusca* **p. 272**
Large, slender, with straight thick bill. Looks all black. Samoa only.

POLYNESIAN STARLING *Aplonis tabuensis* **p. 273**
Chunky, round-headed, and short-tailed. Wide geographic variation, forms shown are representative. Most have yellow eyes.

GIANT FOREST HONEYEATER *Gymnomyza viridis* **p. 279**
Uniform olive green with curved bill (color varies geographically). Fiji only.

MAO *Gymnomyza samoensis* **p. 279**
Large, dark, with curved bill. Compare Samoan Starling. Samoa only.

WATTLED HONEYEATER *Foulehaio carunculata* **p. 278**
Olive with curved bill. Note geographic variation (see text).

KADAVU HONEYEATER *Xanthotis provocator* **p. 279**
Streaked olive gray with yellow cheeks, curved bill. Kadavu (Fiji) only.

33

BLACK-FACED
SHRIKEBILL

♂

♀

ad. ♂

FIJI
SHRIKEBILL

SAMOAN
STARLING

RAROTONGA
STARLING

tuila

Manua

NESIAN
RLING

Fiji

TLED
YEATER

Fiji

Samoa

GIANT
FOREST
HONEYEATER

Taveuni

Viti Levu

MAO

KADAVU
HONEYEATER

PLATE 34. Polynesian Land Birds IX: Reed-Warblers and Monarchs

COOK ISLANDS REED-WARBLER *Acrocephalus kerearako*   **p. 257**
Second bird from top left only. Plain dull olive and yellow with pale eyebrow.
Mangaia, Mitiaro only.

PITCAIRN REED-WARBLER *Acrocephalus vaughani*   **p. 257**
Drab brown and yellow with pale eyebrow. Imm. yellower than ad. All ads.
exhibit asymmetrical white feathers, amount varies island to island. Some on
Henderson I. (uppermost bird) nearly white throughout.

TAHITI REED-WARBLER *Acrocephalus caffra*   **p. 255**
Large, long-billed. Olive above, yellow below (typical). Dark morph all chocolate brown. Tahiti, Moorea only.

MARQUESAS REED-WARBLER *Acrocephalus mendanae*   **p. 256**
Like Tahiti Reed-warbler, but with shorter bill, yellower plumage. Marquesas
only.

BOKIKOKIKO *Acrocephalus aequinoctialis*   **p. 255**
Drab gray. Only passerine on Line Is. (Kiribati).

TUAMOTU REED-WARBLER *Acrocephalus atypha*   **p. 256**
Small, rusty brown with pale eyebrow and underparts. Tuamotus only.

TAHITI MONARCH *Pomarea nigra*   **p. 243**
Ad. all black with blue bill, imm. rufous-buff. Tahiti only.

FATUHIVA MONARCH *Pomarea whitneyi*   **p. 245**
Ad. glossy purple-black. Imm. brown above, buff below with pale lores and
eyebrow. Fatuhiva (Marquesas) only.

MARQUESAS MONARCH *Pomarea mendozae*   **p. 244**
Ad. male all glossy black. Imm. buffy brown with white eye-ring. Females
vary from island to island in amount of white and presence of buff in plumage.

IPHIS MONARCH *Pomarea iphis*   **p. 244**
Ad. males black and white, Eiao birds mottled on belly and back. Females
and imms. brown above, white below, Eiao birds streaked on throat and
breast.

RAROTONGA MONARCH *Pomarea dimidiata*   **p. 243**
Ad. male gray and white, ad. female and imm. bright rufous. Rarotonga only.

34

PITCAIRN
REED-WARBLER

Henderson I.

TAHITI
REED-
WARBLER

dark
morph

MARQUESAS
REED-WARBLER

COOK IS.
REED-WARBLER

Rimatara

BOKIKOKIKO

Pitcairn
ad.

PITCAIRN
REED-WARBLER

Pitcairn imm.

TAHITI
MONARCH

imm

TUAMOTU
REED-
WARBLER

imm.

ad.

NUKUHIVA
MONARCH

imm.

ad. ♂

Mohotani ♀

MARQUESAS
MONARCH

Uapou ♀

Uahuka

♂

Nukuhiva ♀

IPHIS
MONARCH

♀

Eiao

♂

♀

♂

RAROTONGA
MONARCH

PLATE 35. Hawaiian Native Birds I: Thrushes, Warbler, and Elepaio

ELEPAIO *Chasiempis sandwichensis* **p. 240**
Wide geographic variation (see text) but all ads. have characteristic tail-up posture, white wing bars, rump, and tail tip. Juv. dull brown above, white or rufous below.

KAMAO *Myadestes myadestinus* **p. 261**
Short, wide bill, mottled breast, brown forehead, dark legs. Juv. like juv. Omao. Kauai only.

PUAIOHI *Myadestes palmeri* **p. 263**
Brown above, gray below, with pink legs. Sides of head paler than in Kamao, bill longer, thinner. Juv. dark brown, heavily scalloped below. Kauai only.

OLOMAO *Myadestes lanaiensis* **p. 262**
Dull brown and gray, with paler belly than Omao. Juv. like Omao. Molokai only.

OMAO *Myadestes obscurus* **p. 262**
Olive-brown above, gray below and on forehead. Juv. heavily scalloped below with dark brown. Hawaii only.

MILLERBIRD *Acrocephalus familiaris* **p. 255**
Small, thin-billed, gray-brown above, white below. Nihoa only.

35

Kona ♂

Mauna Kea ♂

Hawaii
juv.

ELEPAIO

Volcano ♂

Kauai juv.

Kauai ad.

Volcano ♀

PUAIOHI

juv.

ad.

OMAO

OMAO

juv.

ad.

ad.

MAO

MILLERBIRD

PLATE 36. Hawaiian Native Birds II: Crow and Honeyeaters

HAWAIIAN CROW *Corvus hawaiiensis* **p. 231**
Very large, sooty brown (nearly black) with paler flight feathers. Kona only.

KIOEA *Chaetoptila angustipluma* **p. 281**
Extinct. Large, heavily streaked. Hawaii only.

HAWAII OO *Moho nobilis* **p. 281**
Extinct. Black with curved bill, long twisted tail, yellow patches. Hawaii only.

BISHOP'S OO *Moho bishopi* **p. 281**
Black with curved bill, long graduated tail. Yellow ear tufts, undertail coverts, and axillary plumes. Maui only (formerly Molokai).

OAHU OO *Moho apicalis* **p. 280**
Extinct. Black with yellow flanks, white-tipped tail. Oahu only.

KAUAI OO *Moho braccatus* **p. 280**
Black with short tail, white eye and bend of wing, yellow thighs. Kauai only.

36

HAWAIIAN
CROW

KIOEA

HAWAII
OO

NOP'S
O

OAHU OO

KAUAI
OO

PLATE 37. Hawaiian Native Birds III: Drepanidine Finches

LAYSAN FINCH *Telespyza cantans*　　　　　　　　**p. 296**
　Large hooked bill. Males yellow-headed. Only surviving passerine on Laysan.

NIHOA FINCH *Telespyza ultima*　　　　　　　　**p. 296**
　Similar to Laysan Finch but smaller, with no hook on bill. Male grayer on back, female and imm. more heavily streaked with dark brown. Nihoa only.

PALILA *Loxioides bailleui*　　　　　　　　**p. 297**
　Yellow head, gray back, dark face. Females less bright. Mauna Kea only.

OU *Psittirostra psittacea*　　　　　　　　**p. 297**
　Green with hooked pink bill. Male has yellow head. Kauai, Hawaii only.

GREATER KOA-FINCH *Rhodacanthis palmeri*　　　　　　　　**p. 298**
　Extinct. Very large with heavy gray bill. Olive-brown, male with orange head. Kona only.

LESSER KOA-FINCH *Rhodacanthis flaviceps*　　　　　　　　**p. 298**
　Extinct. Like Greater Koa-finch but smaller, male with yellow head. Kona only.

KONA GROSBEAK *Chloridops kona*　　　　　　　　**p. 298**
　Extinct. Dark olive green with huge pinkish-yellow bill. Kona only.

37

LAYSAN
FINCH
♀
♂

NIHOA
FINCH
♀
♂

PALILA
♀
♂

OU
♀
♂

GREATER
KOA-FINCH
♀
♂

LESSER
KOA-FINCH
♀
♂

KONA
GROSBEAK

ULA-AI-HAWANE *Ciridops anna* **p. 309**
Extinct. Red, gray, and black with finchlike bill. Imm. green and brown. Hawaii only.

IIWI *Vestiaria coccinea* **p. 309**
Ad. scarlet with black wings and tail and long, curved, yellow-pink bill. Imm. buffy with black spots, bill dark at first.

HAWAII MAMO *Drepanis pacifica* **p. 310**
Extinct. Black and yellow with long curved bill. Hawaii only.

BLACK MAMO *Drepanis funerea* **p. 310**
Extinct. All black with long curved bill. Molokai only.

APAPANE *Himatione sanguinea* **p. 311**
Ad. crimson with white undertail coverts. Juv. dull brown. Laysan form now extinct.

AKOHEKOHE (CRESTED HONEYCREEPER) *Palmeria dolei* **p. 310**
Dark body plumage. Ad. has red-orange nape, bushy crest. Imm. nondescript with relatively short fan-shaped tail (not graduated as in Bishop's Oo). Maui only.

KAKAWAHIE (MOLOKAI CREEPER) *Paroreomyza flammea* **p. 306**
Straight thin bill. Male scarlet, female brown and white, variably tinged orange in throat. Imm. duller. Molokai only.

AKEPA *Loxops coccineus* **p. 307**
Short finchlike bill yellow or gray. Males orange-red to mustard yellow. Females and juv. drab green.

AKEKEE (KAUAI AKEPA) *Loxops caeruleirostris* **p. 308**
Bill blue, finchlike, surrounded by black feathers. Tail notched. Male brighter yellow than female. Kauai only.

38

ULA-AI-HAWANE

imm.

ad.

IIWI

imm.

ad.

BLACK
MAMO

HAWAII
MAMO

Laysan ad.

APAPANE

imm.

main
islands
ad.

imm.

d.

HEKOHE
CRESTED
EYCREEPER)

♀

♀

KAKAWAHIE
(MOLOKAI
CREEPER)

♂

♀

yellow
Maui ♂

EPA

Hawaii
mm. ♂

Hawaii
ad. ♂

AKEKEE
(KAUAI AKEPA)

♂

PLATE 39. Hawaiian Native Birds V: Yellow, Green, and Brown Honeycreepers

POO-ULI *Melamprosops phaeosoma* **p. 311**
Brown with black face, buff side of neck. Thick bill. Maui only.

MAUI PARROTBILL *Pseudonestor xanthophrys* **p. 299**
Huge bill, bold yellow eyebrow. Female (not shown) has smaller bill. Maui only.

AKIALOA *Hemignathus obscurus* **p. 302**
Probably extinct. Yellow and green with very long thin bill. Females more drab, with shorter bills. Hawaii form smaller with relatively shorter, more curved bill. Possibly survives only on Kauai.

ANIANIAU *Hemignathus parvus* **p. 301**
Mainly bright (male) or dull (female) yellow. Bill almost straight. Kauai only.

NUKUPUU *Hemignathus lucidus* **p. 303**
Upper mandible much longer than lower. Male yellow, female dull green. Kauai, Maui.

AKIAPOLAAU *Hemignathus munroi* **p. 303**
Like Nukupuu, but lower mandible stout and straight. Hawaii only.

OAHU CREEPER *Paroreomyza maculata* **p. 306**
Bill straight. Male yellow and green, female olive and white. Both sexes have broad pale forehead and eyebrow, females have prominent wing bars. Oahu only.

MAUI CREEPER *Paroreomyza montana* **p. 305**
Bill straight. Plumage similar to that of Common Amakihi, but male brighter yellow. Imm. paler than ad. Maui only.

HAWAII CREEPER *Oreomystis mana* **p. 304**
Bill slightly downcurved, short, uniformly pale. Ad. drab olive with black mask, white throat. Imm. has white eyebrow, no mask. Hawaii only.

AKIKIKI (KAUAI CREEPER) *Oreomystis bairdi* **p. 304**
Gray and white with dull pink bill. Imm. has white "spectacles." Kauai only.

COMMON AMAKIHI *Hemignathus virens* **p. 299**
Yellow-green to gray-green with short curved bill. Ad. male yellower than female or imm. Oahu birds lack pale forehead and eyebrow (compare Oahu Creeper).

KAUAI AMAKIHI *Hemignathus stejnegeri* **p. 300**
Similar to Common Amakihi, but bill much larger. Kauai only.

GREATER AMAKIHI *Hemignathus sagittirostris* **p. 301**
Extinct. Like Common Amakihi but with long straight bill. Hawaii only.

39

POO-ULI

AKIALOA

Kauai ♀

Hawaii ♂

MAUI PARROTBILL

Kauai ♂

ANIANIAU

♀

♂

NUKUPUU

♀

♂

Oahu ♀

Oahu ♂

POLAAU

♀

OAHU CREEPER

♀

♂

COMMON AMAKIHI

Hawaii ♀

Hawaii ♂

n.

HAWAII CREEPER

♀

imm.

ad.

MAUI CREEPER

KAUAI AMAKIHI

♂

AKIKIKI (KAUAI CREEPER)

ad.

imm.

GREATER AMAKIHI

PLATE 40. Introduced Birds I: Cardinals, Tanager, Bulbuls, and Doves

NORTHERN CARDINAL *Cardinalis cardinalis*　　　　　　　**p. 289**
Both sexes crested. Male all red with black face. Female yellow-brown with red tinges, red bill. Widespread in Hawaiian Is.

RED-CRESTED CARDINAL *Paroaria coronata*　　　　　　　**p. 290**
Ads. (both sexes) with red head and crest, gray back, gray bill. Juv. has brown crest. Dry habitats in Hawaiian Is.

YELLOW-BILLED CARDINAL *Paroaria capitata*　　　　　　**p. 290**
No crest. Red head, black throat and back, orange bill. Juv. has yellow-brown head and throat. Kohala-Kona coast (Hawaii) only.

CRIMSON-BACKED TANAGER *Ramphocelus dimidiatus*　　　**p. 289**
Velvety red, brighter posteriorly. Silvery lower mandible (male). Female duller overall. Tahiti only.

RED-WHISKERED BULBUL *Pycnonotus jocosus*　　　　　　**p. 235**
Sharp-pointed crest, white underparts, dark rump. Juv. browner, without red "whiskers." Oahu only.

RED-VENTED BULBUL *Pycnonotus cafer*　　　　　　　　**p. 235**
Short crest, dark underparts, pale rump (best seen in flight). Hawaiian Is. (possibly spreading from Oahu), Fiji, Tonga, Samoa, and Tahiti.

SPOTTED DOVE *Streptopelia chinensis*　　　　　　　　　**p. 190**
Large, pinkish below, with collar of white spots. Hawaiian Is., Fiji.

ZEBRA DOVE *Geopelia striata*　　　　　　　　　　　　**p. 191**
Small, gray-brown with pale blue face, narrow "zebra" stripes. Hawaiian Is., Tahiti.

40

CRIMSON-BACKED
TANAGER

♀

♂

SOUTHERN
CARDINAL

♀

YELLOW-BILLED
CARDINAL

juv.

ad.

juv.

RED-VENTED
BULBUL

RED-WHISKERED
CARDINAL

juv.

ad.

RED-WHISKERED
BULBUL

SPOTTED
DOVE

ZEBRA
DOVE

WHITE-RUMPED
SHAMA FOR
COMPARISON

RED-VENTED
BULBUL

RED-WHISKERED
BULBUL

AUSTRALIAN MAGPIE *Gymnorhina tibicen*   **p. 232**
Two forms introduced, many intermediates in population. Both forms large, black and white with pale bills. Juv. tinged with dusty brown. Taveuni (Fiji) only.

JUNGLE MYNA *Acridotheres fuscus*   **p. 276**
Dark gray with white wing patches, yellow eye. No bare skin on face. Fiji, Samoa.

COMMON MYNA *Acridotheres tristis*   **p. 275**
Black head, brown body, white wing patches. Yellow bare skin around eye. Hawaiian Is., Fiji, Cook Is., Society Is., Hivaoa (Marquesas).

HILL MYNA *Gracula religiosa*   **p. 327**
See Appendix A. Glossy purplish black with red-orange bill and prominent head wattles. Hawaiian Is. only.

EUROPEAN STARLING *Sturnus vulgaris*   **p. 274**
Sharp-pointed yellow bill. Glossy black with pale feather tips that gradually wear away. Juv. dusty brown with dark bill. Fiji (s. Lau Arch.) and Tonga only.

NORTHERN MOCKINGBIRD *Mimus polyglottos*   **p. 267**
Gray with bold white wing patches. Juv. streaked below. Dry habitats in Hawaiian Is. only.

WHITE-RUMPED SHAMA *Copsychus malabaricus*   **p. 260**
Ads. (both sexes) show prominent white rump, long, white-sided tail. Juv. spotted below, has shorter tail. Kauai and Oahu only. For flight pattern, see Plate 40.

GREATER NECKLACED LAUGHING-THRUSH   **p. 265**
Garrulax pectoralis
Large, brown above, white below with black "necklace." Tail feathers tipped buff. Kauai only.

MELODIOUS LAUGHING-THRUSH *Garrulax canorus*   **p. 265**
Rusty brown with white "spectacles," yellow bill. Hawaiian Is. only.

GRAY-SIDED LAUGHING-THRUSH *Garrulax caerulatus*   **p. 265**
Brown with gray sides, white throat and breast, and black lores. Oahu only.

intermed. ♀

juv.

black-backed ♂

♂

JUNGLE MYNA

HILL MYNA

COMMON MYNA

ad.

EUROPEAN STARLING

juv.

ad.

NORTHERN MOCKINGBIRD

♂

GREATER NECKLACED LAUGHING-THRUSH

juv.

MELODIOUS LAUGHING-THRUSH

GRAY-SIDED LAUGHING-THRUSH

PLATE 42. Introduced Birds III: Finches and Other Small Passerines

HOUSE FINCH *Carpodacus mexicanus* **p. 293**
Streaked, especially on flanks. Females drab brown, males vary from red to orange-yellow on breast and rump. Hawaiian Is. only.

HOUSE SPARROW *Passer domesticus* **p. 312**
Male has black throat, gray cap, bold white wing bar. Female nondescript dusty brown. Hawaiian Is. only.

EURASIAN TREE SPARROW *Passer montanus* **p. 312**
Sexes alike. Brown cap, black throat, black spot on white cheeks. Mariana Is., Yap, Kwajalein only.

YELLOW-FRONTED CANARY *Serinus mozambicus* **p. 294**
Bright yellow underparts, eyebrow, and malar streak. Gray crown, green back. Oahu and Hawaii only.

JAPANESE WHITE-EYE *Zosterops japonicus* **p. 282**
Bright green above with yellow throat, black lores, white eye-ring. Hawaiian Is. only.

JAPANESE BUSH-WARBLER *Cettia diphone* **p. 252**
Nondescript except for pale eyebrow. Not easily seen. Central Hawaiian Is. only.

RED-BILLED LEIOTHRIX *Leiothrix lutea* **p. 266**
Yellow throat, red bill, forked tail. Hawaiian Is. only.

YELLOW-FACED GRASSQUIT *Tiaris olivacea* **p. 291**
Dull green above (both sexes). Male has black head and breast with prominent yellow eyebrow and throat. Female has yellow throat, black spots on breast. Oahu only.

WESTERN MEADOWLARK *Sturnella neglecta* **p. 292**
Streaky brown above with yellow breast marked by black V. Outer tail feathers white. Kauai only.

EURASIAN SKYLARK *Alauda arvensis* **p. 228**
Streaky brown with shallowly forked tail, white outer tail feathers. Hawaiian Is. (except Kauai) only.

COMMON CANARY *Serinus canaria* **p. 294**
Pale yellow with pink bill and legs. Midway only.

SAFFRON FINCH *Sicalis flaveola* **p. 291**
Male bright golden yellow with orange crown. Female streaky with yellow band across breast. Hawaii and Oahu (status uncertain) only.

HOUSE FINCH

HOUSE SPARROW

EURASIAN TREE SPARROW

YELLOW-FRONTED CANARY

JAPANESE WHITE-EYE

YELLOW-FACED GRASSQUIT

JAPANESE BUSH-WARBLER

RED-BILLED LEIOTHRIX

COMMON CANARY

EASTERN MEADOWLARK

EURASIAN SKYLARK

SAFFRON FINCH

PLATE 43. Introduced Birds IV: Estrildid Finches

BLACK-RUMPED WAXBILL *Estrilda troglodytes* **p. 328**
See Appendix A. Red eyebrow, black rump, pale undertail coverts, square-tipped tail.

COMMON WAXBILL *Estrilda astrild* **p. 315**
Red eyebrow and bill, black undertail coverts, narrowly barred flanks, graduated tail. Oahu, Tahiti only.

RED AVADAVAT *Amandava amandava* **p. 315**
Male red with white spots, black undertail coverts. Female dull yellow-brown with red bill and rump. Oahu, Fiji only.

ORANGE-CHEEKED WAXBILL *Estrilda melpoda* **p. 314**
Brown and gray with orange cheeks, red bill and rump. Oahu and Hawaii only.

WARBLING SILVERBILL *Lonchura malabarica* **p. 317**
Sandy brown with black rump and tail, metallic gray bill. Hawaiian Is. only.

LAVENDER WAXBILL *Estrilda caerulescens* **p. 314**
Blue-gray with crimson rump and tail. Hawaii and possibly Oahu only.

RED-CHEEKED CORDONBLEU *Uraeginthus bengalus* **p. 313**
Pale blue and dusty brown. Male has crimson cheek patch. Hawaii and possibly Oahu only.

JAVA SPARROW *Padda oryzivora* **p. 319**
Gray with prominent white cheeks outlined in black, pink bill. Juv. less boldly marked. Hawaiian Is., Fiji only.

RED-BROWED FIRETAIL *Emblema temporalis* **p. 315**
Green and gray with red bill, eyebrow, and rump. Society Is., Marquesas Is. only.

CHESTNUT-BREASTED MANNIKIN *Lonchura castaneothorax* **p. 319**
Ad. reddish brown with dark brown face and undertail coverts, tan breast. Juv. nondescript buffy brown with black bill. Society Is. only.

CHESTNUT MANNIKIN *Lonchura malacca* **p. 318**
Ad. reddish brown with black head, silvery bill. Juv. dull brown with reddish tail and pale bill. Kauai, Oahu, Palau, Guam only.

NUTMEG MANNIKIN *Lonchura punctulata* **p. 317**
Ad. dark brown with greenish rump and tail, dark face, scalloped breast. Juv. plain dull brown with black bill. Hawaiian Is., Yap only.

43

BLACK-RUMPED WAXBILL

RED AVADAVAT

♀

♂

COMMON WAXBILL

juv.

ad.

ORANGE-CHEEKED WAXBILL

LAVENDER WAXBILL

WARBLING SILVERBILL

♀

-EKED RDONBLEU

RED-BROWED FIRETAIL

JAVA SPARROW

juv.

ad.

juv.

ad.

STNUT-BREASTED MANNIKIN

ad.

juv.

ad.

CHESTNUT MANNIKIN

NUTMEG MANNIKIN

A Ohia-lehua *Metrosideros collina*

B Koa *Acacia koa*

C Mamane *Sophora chrysophylla*

D Naio *Myoporum sandwicense*

PLATE 44. Plants Important to Birds and Birders I: Hawaiian Native Trees

A Scaevola (Naupaka) *Scaevola taccada*

B Beach Heliotrope *Messerschmidtia argentea*

C Haole Koa (Tangan-tangan) *Leucaena latisiliqua*

D Kiawe (Algoroba) *Prosopis pallida*

E Fig *Ficus* sp.

F Pandanus *Pandanus odoratissimus*

PLATE 45. Plants Important to Birds and Birders II: Various Pacific Plants

Library of Congress Cataloging-in-Publication Data

Pratt, H. Douglas, 1944-
    A field guide to the birds of Hawaii and the tropical Pacific.

    Bibliography: p.
    Includes index.
    1. Birds—Hawaii—Identification.   2. Birds—
Oceania—Identification.   I. Bruner, Phillip L.
II. Berrett, Delwyn G., 1935-   .   III. Title.
IV. Title: Birds of Hawaii and the tropical Pacific.
QL684.H3P73 1986   598.29969   86-4993
ISBN 0-691-08402-5
ISBN 0-691-02399-9 (pbk.)

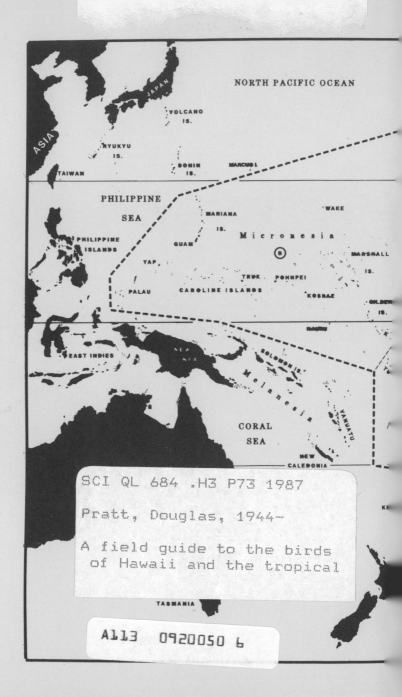

NORTH PACIFIC OCEAN

JAPAN

VOLCANO IS.

ASIA

RYUKYU IS.

TAIWAN

BONIN IS.

MARCUS I.

PHILIPPINE SEA

MARIANA IS.

WAKE

Micronesia

PHILIPPINE ISLANDS

GUAM

YAP

MARSHALL IS.

TRUK   POHNPEI

PALAU   CAROLINE ISLANDS

KOSRAE

GILBERT IS.

NAURU

EAST INDIES

NEW GUINEA

SOLOMON IS.

Melanesia

VANUATU

CORAL SEA

NEW CALEDONIA

TASMANIA